THE
Thermidorians

& THE
Directory

THE
THERMIDORIANS

Two Phases

RANDOM HOUSE

& THE DIRECTORY

of the French Revolution

by GEORGES LEFEBVRE

Translated from the French by ROBERT BALDICK

NEW YORK

CONTENTS

Contents

THE DIRECTORY

FOREWORD

Albert Mathiez died on February 25, 1932, in his chair at the Sorbonne, where in spite of growing ill health he had insisted on giving his lecture at the usual time. He was only fifty-eight; his activity was greater than ever and his premature death deprived us of masterly works which he had been maturing for a long time. There is not one of his countless readers who is not aware of the irreparable loss suffered by French history.

Of all his undertakings, the one dearest to his heart was undoubtedly that history of the French Revolution of which he had already published three volumes. After taking it up to the ninth of Thermidor, he was getting ready to continue it. His book on the Thermidorian reaction, likewise published by Monsieur Jacques Max Leclerc, a work which sheds new light on many aspects of the history of that period, shows how carefully he had prepared, as always, for his next task. But he did not have time to begin the volume for which we were all waiting.

Like Monsieur Jacques Max Leclerc, the editor of the Collection Armand Colin felt that it would be regrettable to leave his work unfinished, and he invited me to continue it. When I accepted this invitation I did so with a full awareness of the difficulty of the task, and I beg my readers to believe that if I undertook this task it was not in any spirit of presumption. Nor was it with the intention of abdicating my personal opinions in order to present nothing but a pastiche. In agreement with the publisher and the editor of the Collection, I simply felt that in continuing the work of Albert Mathiez we should be paying his memory an homage which would have pleased him.

GEORGES LEFEBVRE

NOTE: *This edition has been revised and corrected by Albert Soboul.*

THE

THERMIDORIANS

CHAPTER ONE

After the Ninth of Thermidor

On the ninth of Thermidor, France had been under a revolutionary regime, namely the dictatorship of the Committee of Public Safety, for about a year. The main question of the day was whether this regime would outlast Robespierre.

Brought into existence by the extreme danger in which the Revolution had found itself in 1793, the revolutionary government had restored to the executive the strength it had lacked since 1789: it had given it stability, the Committees of Public Safety and of General Security having been re-elected without any changes since September 1793;

it had restored centralization, all official appointments being made by the Committees or by their representatives on mission; and it had broken all resistance by means of the "coercive force" of the revolutionary courts, in other words by means of the Terror. Making full use of its authority, the Committee of Public Safety, for the first time in modern history, had organized a general mobilization of the national community, by proclaiming the *levée en masse* and obtaining control of the greater part of the economy, thanks to requisitioning and the *maximum*. Its efforts had been crowned with success: it had recaptured Lyons and Toulon; the Vendée insurrection was in its death-throes; the invasion had been repelled and the Republican armies had returned to the attack—since the victory of Fleurus they had been engaged in reconquering Belgium. However, the European Coalition remained in existence, and it was impossible even to envisage a time when a general peace might be concluded. Was this then a suitable moment to relax the grip of the revolutionary defense-system?

The Convention had no intention whatever of capitulating to the counterrevolution, but it felt a secret repugnance for the revolutionary government as it had functioned so far. Although—having suspended the application of the 1793 Constitution, and consequently the elections, until the end of hostilities—it had associated the Convention with its dictatorship, it was nonetheless not of parliamentary origin: the Montagnard minority had imposed it on the Assembly with outside help from the Jacobins gathered together in the popular clubs, and on the *sans-culottes*. To avoid being swept away by an insurrection, the Convention had been obliged to sacrifice the Girondins, accept the authority of the Committee of Public Safety, renounce any sort of opposition, and hand over the Hébertists and the Dantonists. Now that the Committee of Public Safety, in splitting up, had called it in to arbitrate, and it had seized power again by outlawing the Robespierrists, its first thought could only be to defend its authority jealously, not only against the Jacobins of the clubs and the *sans-culottes* of the street, but also against such of its own members as it might appoint to govern in its name. For the moment the principle of dictatorship recommended itself; it was essential to complete the rout of the Robespierrists and suppress any fresh attempt at popular insurrection; besides, no assembly tends to consider its own powers excessive. But it was unthinkable that the Committee of Public Safety should be allowed to retain its stability and omnipotence, and with them the very essence of revolutionary government disappeared willy-nilly.

Even if events had worked out otherwise, that government would henceforth have been incapable of exacting obedience. It had succeeded in doing so only by imposing the Terror, which was bound to come to an end after the ninth of Thermidor. If the Terror had confined itself, as it should have, to punishing rebels and traitors, its swift and bloody repressive measures would still have aroused feelings of pity; as it turned out, during the last months of 1793, certain representatives on mission—Carrier at Nantes, Collot d'Herbois and Fouché at Lyons, Barras and Fréron at Toulon—in the fiery atmosphere of civil war, had allowed themselves to indulge in mass executions that were not always legal even under revolutionary law. The Committee of Public Safety had recalled them, but after regaining control of the repression, it had itself unleashed the great Terror in Paris, by the law of 22 Prairial, and had allowed Joseph Lebon and the Orange Commission to act with increasing severity. What is more, the Law of Suspects had enabled the revolutionary committees in a great many communes to take action, as against enemies of the Revolution, against a host of people whose birth, wealth or opinions marked them out for attack; religious conflicts, the process of dechristianization which the Committee had tried in vain to halt, and economic measures which only police surveillance could enforce, had extended the scope of repressive action even further; in short, the Jacobins had committed the supreme folly of attacking or alarming nearly everybody. Finally, the Terror had turned against the Republicans themselves: the *ultras* like the *citras*, the *enragés* and Hébertists like the Girondins and Dantonists, had all suffered from it; it was Babeuf who would soon be accusing the Committee of Public Safety of having turned it into a method of depopulating France. Once Robespierre had fallen, a tremendous movement of public opinion immediately turned against the Terror. The Convention could not forgive the latter for having decimated it, and Robespierre's colleagues themselves, by using it to blacken his memory, were the first to encourage a reaction. In reality the Terror did not really cease on the ninth of Thermidor any more than did the dictatorship; it was too much in the interests of the new rulers to turn it against their enemies, but it promptly ceased to sanction the essential measures of national defense—the *levée en masse*, requisitioning, the *maximum*—without which revolutionary government was just an empty phrase.

"Down with the terrorists!" immediately became the rallying cry of the Thermidorians, and countless voices repeated it, but not solely out of horror for bloodshed: it

6

made it possible to conceal a movement of social reaction which lends the period its chief interest. In the opinion of the Jacobins and the *sans-culottes,* the need to defend the nation was not the sole justification for the revolutionary government; in rising to impose it on the Convention, the common people had also obeyed their own needs and their desire to modify the organization of society in order to profit, in their turn, from the Revolution. They suffered from unemployment, poverty, and the high prices created by inflation: the revolutionary government had at least provided them with bread at a reasonable price; it had given them work manufacturing armaments and had employed countless men on the surveillance committees and section committees as warders, keepers of the seals, and permanent National Guards; in Paris, "poor" citizens who attended both the decadal meetings of their section were paid forty sols each time. As the peasants clamored for land, either in order to become landowners or to round off their property, the national estates had been divided into small lots before being put up for sale, and certain facilities had been granted to impoverished citizens who wished to buy; a promise had been made to the "defenders of the country" that land to the value of a billion would be set aside for them; and then the decrees of Ventôse had announced that the property of "suspects" would be distributed free to indigent patriots. A free medical service had been instituted, national assistance guaranteed to old people without means and widows with dependent children, allowances granted to soldiers' relatives, and the right to compensation recognized for victims of war damage. In short, in exchange for the sacrifices which the revolutionary government imposed on the members of the national community, it had recognized their right to

7

life and had tried to turn this into a reality. *Sans-culottes*
and Jacobins were not communists: artisans, shopkeepers,
peasants, they were often property owners or, at any rate,
asked for nothing better than to become property owners;
the Montagnards, who came from the upper middle class,
were even more hostile to socialism. But, apart from the
fact that circumstances forced them to rely on the common
people, they all had a sense of national solidarity and, like
Rousseau, felt that political democracy was incompatible
with an excessive inequality of wealth; in their eyes the
"rich man" was suspect of disloyalty to the State, and was
in fact often a counterrevolutionary or, at the very least,
hostile to the Republic. Needing money, and needing it
right away, the revolutionary government obtained it by
forced loans and revolutionary taxes; it consolidated the
authority of the National Debt by inscribing it in the Great
Book and then reviewed life annuities; apart from the fact
that the "enemies of the Revolution" were barred from
holding Treasury scrip and were thus expropriated, the legal
formalities, which often could not be observed in such circumstances, ruined a great many rentiers; moreover, divi-
dends were held back and finally not paid at all. At the
same time, new laws of succession insured the dissemina-
tion of inheritances, and the nationalization of a great part
of the economy deprived the capitalist bourgeoisie of its
usual profits: the armament contractors were eliminated,
the bankers and merchants brought under control, the great
financiers submitted to requisitioning. With their wealth
thus threatened, the "notables" were also profoundly humiliated at losing the monopoly of public offices which
the Constituent Assembly seemed to have promised them,
and at finding themselves governed by members of the

lower middle class who had hitherto been their tenants and their tradesmen, or even by illiterate journeymen.

Consequently the attacks made on the terrorist were not directed simply at the "drinker of blood," nor even at the man who had dared to impose on everyone certain obligations which were considered unbearable (above all personal military service), but at the man who had undertaken to curb social individualism and to bar the way to a nascent capitalism; on this point the lower middle class, for the most part, joined in the chorus of blame, for while they distrusted the upper middle class, they had no desire to deprive themselves of the possibility of entering that class by fundamentally opposing it. Seen in this light, from the economic and social point of view, the Thermidorian reaction acquires an importance and an interest which are not usually recognized. Ostensibly it was a chaos of murderous political struggles in which the mutilated parties engaged only their dregs and which culminated in the crushing of the Jacobin minority, which, like the Thermidorians, is depicted as a rabble stained with crimes. In reality it eliminated democracy from the political and social life of France for nearly a century, renewed the link with the Revolution of 1789, and, with economic liberty and the electoral property qualification, began to establish that supremacy of the middle class which the Constituent Assembly had organized and which, at the end of the eighteenth century, seemed to be the supreme achievement of French history.

9

CHAPTER TWO

The Dismemberment of the Revolutionary Government

The committee members who had taken the initiative on the ninth of Thermidor in order to save their necks had imagined that at the same time they were consolidating their authority; terrorists that they were, particularly Billaud-Varenne and Collot d'Herbois, they had no intention of changing their methods in the slightest. Speaking on their behalf on 10 Thermidor, Barère declared that the previous day had been merely "a slight commotion which left the government untouched," and on the eleventh he presented three candidates to replace the three "conspirators" Robespierre, Couthon and Saint-Just; from July to Septem-

ber, 1793, that was how, by a process of co-optation, the
Committee of Public Safety of the Year II had gradually
taken shape, the Convention confining itself to ratifying its
choices. As Thibaudeau has put it, "the Committee of
Public Safety was rid of Robespierre. The Convention was
not rid of the Committee of Public Safety." But Barère's
proposal led to a memorable debate which left the Convention with none of its illusions.

Merlin de Thionville gave the signal for attack with
other Dantonists, Legendre and Thuriot, and with the
turncoat terrorists, Bourdon de l'Oise and Tallien, who
blamed the Committees for the policy with which they
themselves had been associated for so long. It was doubtless too early to break with Robespierre's colleagues, but
not to force them to share their power. "We have overthrown the triumvirs," exclaimed Tallien, "we do not want
to replace them with decemvirs." This was how the Assembly felt too, and it made haste to regain power; besides,
Barère himself had said: "The Convention is everything."
It was decreed that a quarter of each Committee be replaced every month, and that retiring members be re-eligible only after an interval of one month. The stability of
the government was in danger. For the moment, Barère,
Billaud and Collot remained at their posts, but as it was
decided to replace Jeanbon Saint-André, on the pretext that
he was on mission, and also Hérault de Séchelles, who had
been guillotined with Danton, half the Committee of Public Safety was renewed. On 13 Thermidor (July 31), Eschassériaux, one of Barère's candidates, was elected, together
with the Dantonists Thuriot and Bréard, Treilhard who
had voted for a stay of execution, Laloy whose brother and
brother-in-law were reputed to be Royalists, and finally

Tallien. David, Lavicomterie and Jagot were excluded from the Committee of General Security as Robespierrists, and Merlin de Thionville was brought in, with Legendre, Bourdon's friend Goupilleau de Fontenay, and Dumont whose brother was a suspect. The personnel of the committees was thus modified to a significant extent.

It remained to be seen whether the Committee of Public Safety would retain at least the dominant position which had preserved the unity of the government. As early as the eleventh, Cambon had demanded that it be deprived of that position. During the whole of Year II, only one executive body had escaped from the authority of the Committee of Public Safety. This was the Treasury, which took its orders only from the Finance Committee, controlled by none other than Cambon himself; he proposed that the exception be made general, and that each of the twelve executive commissions which had taken the place of the ministries be put under the control of one of the Convention's twelve committees. On the thirteenth, Barère rushed into the breach and inveighed against the "moral federalism" which certain persons wished to institute; the Committee of Public Safety ought to retain the whip hand over the twelve executive commissions, and the Committee of General Security over the police; the other committees, as before, would have nothing to do but plan legislation. The Assembly hesitated, vaguely aware that it was dangerous to weaken the Executive by dividing it. But the fear of falling under the yoke once more won the day, and after lengthy debates the decree of 7 Fructidor (August 24) consecrated Cambon's proposal. Henceforth the Convention had sixteen committees, twelve of which were each in control of one of the executive commissions, with the right to issue decrees and dismiss officials. The Committee of Public Safety was left with nothing but war and foreign affairs; the Committee of General Security was confirmed in its control over the police; if both Committees retained the right to requisition troops, it was only through the mediation of the Military Committee. The Finance Committee retained its independence. The Legislative Committee was given responsibility for internal administration and justice; its importance was growing and it figured henceforth among what were generally called the "Three Committees." In short, the centralization of the government had disappeared.

On the other hand, with regard to the provinces, the Convention wanted to strengthen its central authority. On 1 Fructidor (August 18), speaking of the reform of the surveillance committees, Goupilleau de Fontenay declared: "We have started from the principle that the lawmakers entrusted with the task of leading the Revolution to its objective should themselves choose the elements intended to contribute to that aim." The central government therefore went on purging local administrations and completing them without having recourse to elections. As before the ninth of Thermidor, the Convention and its Committees sent representatives on mission, invested with more or less extensive powers, to the departments and to the armies; the Montagnards were recalled and generally replaced with moderates: this was the only innovation. Besides, the same mistrust was shown to them as by the Robespierrist Committees. On 26 Fructidor (September 12), Merlin de Douai criticized their independence and their tendency to legislate by means of decrees which were more often than not self-contradictory: "The legislation of the Republic has federalized itself in the strangest way." They were instructed to send their decrees to the Committees, which could annul them. Already all the representatives sent into the departments had been recalled on the twelfth (August 29); the missions had been restricted to six months for the armies and three for the interior, with a ban on any fresh mission before an interval of three months. In reality, the situation changed scarcely at all. Distance, the slowness of communications, and urgency made it necessary to give great latitude to the representatives on mission; like their predecessors, each had his own personal policy according to his temperament, his ideas and his prejudices; ignorant of local conditions or overburdened with work, they allowed themselves to be guided by local political leaders: the only difference was that usually the Jacobins, who until then had more often than not advised the members of the Convention, henceforth saw them listening only to their enemies. It was therefore in vain that the Thermidorian majority showed its intention of strengthening the system of centralization for its own advantage; it had actually weakened it by destroying the unity of the government.

The public did not care about these problems. It was overjoyed at seeing the repression on the wane; in the Convention itself, the organization of the government caused very little excitement, whereas the slightest reference to the Terror provoked an uproar. On 11 Thermidor, Barère had insisted on maintaining the Terror as "the order of the day": "There can be no indulgence except for involuntary errors; but the aristocrats' intrigues are offenses and their errors are crimes." In reality, the "coercive force," one of the essential elements of the revolutionary government, disappeared at the same time as the others. The revolutionary court had ceased to function, its president, Dumas, and several of the jurymen having been guillotined; Fouquier-Tinville and Herman, who had directed the commission of civil cases, were in prison; and the two commissions entrusted with the task of sorting out suspects—the only commissions set up under the decrees of Ventôse—having been deprived of their presidents who had likewise been arrested, suspended their activities and never resumed them. The terrorists wanted this crisis to come to an end; while admitting the need to purge the revolutionary court, Barère had called for "great respect" to be shown to that "salutary institution"; Goupilleau de Fontenay said the same of the revolutionary Committees. But there seems to be no doubt that, in order to carry the Plain with them, they had promised it to modify the law; besides, they threw the responsibility for the Great Terror onto Robespierre and the law of 22 Prairial. This latter law was hated by the Convention because, so it was thought, it allowed the Committees to send deputies before the revolutionary court without consulting the Assembly. It was repealed on 14 Thermidor (August 1). On the twenty-third (August 10), when Merlin de Douai reorganized the revolutionary court, whose president was Dobsen, the man of the thirty-first of May, Bourdon obtained an assurance that in the case of every convicted person the jury would examine the question of motive, and thanks to this decisive clause the court lost no time in releasing a great many convicted prisoners, on the pretext that they had not intended to help the counterrevolution.

In the meantime, all executions having been suspended, attention had been turned to the prisons. From the Hébertists to the Dantonists, there was not a single Repub-

lican clique which did not have some of its members behind bars. Having regained some of their former influence,
the deputies' first thought was to use it on behalf of their
friends; Tallien, who complained about this on 22 Thermidor (August 9), himself moved heaven and earth to obtain the release of his mistress, Thérèse Cabarrus, the
former Marquise de Fontenay. Bentabole and Rovère,
who married respectively Madame de Chabot and the
Marquise d'Agoult, probably had no lack of clients either.
As early as the tenth, Barère had promised that the Committees would examine the case of "patriots" in detention,
and commissioners were sent to the prisons for this purpose. "There is not a single man in prison today," said
Tallien, "who does not claim to be an ardent patriot and
who has not been an enemy of Robespierre's." Between
18 Thermidor and 23 Thermidor, 478 people were released.

However inclined it was towards indulgence, the Convention found right away that its hands were not entirely
free. Once again, pressure was exerted on it from outside;
in the past, the Terror had been imposed on it; now it was
required to abolish it, pending a demand for a terror in reverse. To begin with, public opinion seemed unanimous.
The Jacobin Club, which Billaud and Legendre had gone
together to reopen on 11 Thermidor, called for the release of a great many of its former members. Similarly the
Sections protested at their meetings on 15 Thermidor (August 2), the first they had held since Robespierre's death.
In Fructidor some provincial delegations, from Nîmes
and Lyons, made their appearance. On 18 Thermidor (August 15), the Convention had satisfied a fundamental requirement by ordering the release of those suspects against
whom no charge had been brought and by decreeing that

henceforth the accusations made against prisoners should be communicated to them. On the twenty-ninth, the decree of 21 Messidor which had restored the farm workers to freedom was extended to communes with over 1,200 inhabitants, and liberal use was made of it with the aid of forged certificates.

Calling for the release of suspects amounted to saying that the surveillance committees had arrested them unjustly; consequently a simultaneous attack was launched on these committees. At their meetings on 15 Thermidor, certain Sections had decided to examine their operations; on the twenty-fifth (August 12) the Panthéon Section declared that its revolutionary committee had lost its confidence and the Montreuil Section denounced its own to the Convention. Cambon joined the attackers for economic reasons, since the members of these committees were paid five livres a day; during the course of the autumn he would go on to support the accusations promptly leveled at their integrity, maintaining that they had fraudulently converted some of the silver from the churches and some of the revolutionary taxes. Already, on 7 Fructidor (August 24), the Convention had given way. On a motion put forward by Goupilleau de Fontenay, it agreed that the surveillance committees were too numerous to be supervised themselves, and left only one in each district; its members were to resign every three months and would not be re-eligible until the expiration of a similar period; they were to be able to read and write, could issue a warrant for arrest only on a majority vote, and had to send the relevant file to Paris within twenty-four hours. The forty-eight Sections in the capital were grouped into twelve arrondissements (this was the origin of this territorial subdivision which lasted until 1860) and each four Sections were left with only one committee, which was of course nominated by the Committee of General Security; at the beginning, shopkeepers and artisans continued to predominate on these committees, but it was not long before "respectable folk" were in the majority.

It was in the provinces above all that the decree of 7 Fructidor caused a sensation, for it dealt a mortal blow to Jacobin supremacy. Changing all the local administrations was an extremely lengthy task; besides, in many departments the new representatives on mission did not arrive until the autumn. On the other hand the decree of 7 Fructidor affected the surveillance committees right away: most of them disappeared, while the others were reconstituted and ceased to act outside their residences. Now it was they who had put the Law of Suspects into application and had become the chief purveyors to the revolutionary courts. There were few places where anybody had dared to lay hands on them, as at Nîmes where the district had had Mayor Courbis and fifteen of his friends arrested on 20 Thermidor (August 7). Consequently the Terror had often continued after the ninth of Thermidor. On the thirteenth (July 31) the Convention had suspended the Popular Commission at Orange, but on the same day, at Brest, the revolutionary court sent General Moreau's father to the guillotine. In the Ardèche, on the eighteenth (August 5), five priests and three nuns were executed. At Château-Gontier, the Huchedé Commission began its operations on 9 Thermidor (July 27) and continued them during August. Admittedly the pressure of public opinion increased the number of acquittals; all the same, there were very few releases before Fructidor: at Dreux the first were on August

20, at Verdun in September, at Brest in October. It was after the decree of 7 Fructidor that the Terror really vanished.

Nevertheless, thanks to the slowness of the purge, the Jacobins remained influential for a long time on administrative bodies. Where the Terror had been particularly violent, the reaction was often immediate, for example at Bourg where Boisset had been sent at once, at Avignon where Rovère had sent his friend Goupilleau de Montaigu, and at Marseilles where Auguis and Serre started operations. But in the Seine-Inférieure, the municipality of Rouen was purged only on 6 Vendémiaire, Year III (September 27, 1794) and the department only on 5 Frimaire (November 25); the Hérault, the Ardennes and the Mayenne were affected only in Brumaire, the Haute-Saône, the Ardèche, the Ariège and the district of Dinan in Frimaire, and the Manche in Nivôse; the municipality of Reims remained intact until 7 Germinal (March 27, 1795), that of Vire until 23 Floréal (May 12), and the same was true, with all the more reason, of the little communes. What is more, many representatives, such as Berlier in the Nord and Perrin in the Bas-Languedoc, tried to curb the reaction; at Nîmes, Perrin picked moderate Montagnards from the middle class, for example Bonicel, Guizot's maternal grandfather, and actually formed the surveillance committee out of artisans and laborers. The technique was to distinguish between the agitators and the Republicans they had led astray. It even happened that, in the Meurthe, Michaud restored to office the *sans-culottes* who had been imprisoned as Hébertists before the ninth of Thermidor.

The fact remains that once the institutions of Year II

had been condemned, the terrorist leaders and particularly the members of the former surveillance committees could not help being called to account. In Paris, a great many Jacobins who had been compromised in the events of the ninth of Thermidor had been imprisoned. On 15 Thermidor (August 2), Lebon had been placed under arrest; the day before, the terrorists of Sedan had suffered the same fate. Several representatives on mission imitated the Convention: Boisset, at Bourg, had the terrorists of 24 Thermidor (August 11) arrested; at Saint-Étienne, Reverchon imprisoned Pignon, the prosecutor of the criminal court; on 17 Fructidor (September 3), Goupilleau incarcerated the members of the Orange Commission; at Nîmes, the district had taken the initiative; at Bordeaux, Ysabeau actually set up a commission with instructions to review the revolutionary judgments.

In Fructidor, several provincial delegations started denouncing at the bar of the Convention certain former representatives on mission—Mallarmé on the seventh and Maignet on the eighth—with the support of Guffroy, Rovère and Fréron, who were prompted by a fanatical hatred of their personal enemies. Henceforth the noose promptly tightened around the terrorists on the government committees. In striking down Robespierre, writes Thibaudeau, "they had passed sentence on themselves. They would have liked to make him their scapegoat, so as to be able to blame all the past on him. But it was not a question of secret acts with which they could easily load his memory without fear of contradiction. The facts were public and patent." Billaud, Collot and Barère were the targets at this time. The journalists began to give voice. On 20 Thermidor (August 7), in *La Correspondance politique*, Dusaulx, addressing Fréron, cried: "Remember that you have ghosts to avenge!" How could Danton be avenged without Billaud being attacked? There was nothing left to protect the initiators of the ninth of Thermidor but the fragile alliance which had united them on that day with the turncoat terrorists—now in their turn ready to sacrifice them in order to save themselves—and with the moderates who hated them. Their friends finally broke that alliance by trying to take the initiative once more.

They had good reason to feel alarmed. There were plenty of indications that, now the Terror had come to an end, the government was no longer obeyed. The refractory conscripts or deserters no longer made any attempt at concealment; the peasants began to hold back their grain; the *maximum* was openly flouted; some émigrés had returned— at the news of the ninth of Thermidor, Doulcet de Pontécoulant had left Switzerland; and here and there, churches were reopened by force. In the provinces the Jacobins raised the alarm, but as their friends had no remedy to propose but a return to the Terror, they came up against insurmountable repugnance among the public. On 23 Thermidor (August 10), Granet, protesting at the release of the suspects, succeeded in getting the names of those who were released and of their guarantors published. Merlin de Thionville, Legendre and Tallien saw this as an attack on themselves. On the twenty-sixth, namely the very day that Tallien's mistress was released, they launched a violent attack on the decree of the twenty-third. Meeting a lively show of resistance, Tallien cunningly obtained the passing of a decree that the names of the denouncers should also

be published. It was the terrorists' turn to tremble: this
was civil war, they cried. Tallien agreed and frankly explained the purpose of his maneuver, which was crowned
with success, for Amar proposed and obtained the repeal
of both decrees. On 2 Fructidor (August 19), the debate
took a wider turn. Louchet, the very man who had issued
the official charge against Robespierre, described the progress of the reaction, called for the reincarceration of the
suspects, and declared that it was essential to "keep the
Terror as the order of the day." A great shout of "Justice!
Justice!" interrupted him. Tallien revealed himself openly
as a right-wing orator: "The Terror is the work of tyranny.
. . . I recognize no more castes in the Republic, only good
and bad citizens." On the eleventh (August 28), he added
that henceforth it was justice which would be the order of
the day. He had thus sounded the rallying cries which
would cover all reactionaries including even the Royalists.
Two days before, Fréron had added that of the freedom of
the Press, which, he said, did not exist unless it was absolute. Passions promptly rose to boiling point. As disasters
followed one after another—on 3 Fructidor (August 20),
the great saltpeter factory at L'Abbaye was destroyed by
fire, and on the fourteenth the powder factory at Grenelle
blew up—the terrorists saw the hand of the suspects in
these events. Their enemies replied in the newspapers,
and on the ninth (August 26), Méhée de la Touche published a pamphlet against them which soon became famous: *La Queue de Robespierre.*

Three days later, on 12 Fructidor, Lecointre took it
upon himself to accuse Barère, Billaud and Collot, in the
Convention itself, of having participated in "the tyranny,"

as well as Vadier, Amar, Voulland and David, of the Committee of General Security. Challenged to produce his evidence, he had to admit that he had none. Tallien abandoned him and, on a motion put by Cambon, the Assembly condemned the slanderous accusation. But it still had its effect: on the fifteenth (September 1), Barère, Billaud and Collot resigned from the Committee of Public Safety. It had taken little more than a month for the men of Year II, once they had abandoned Robespierre, to lose the "levers of power." In the Convention, the Mountain, which was given the derisive nickname of the Crest, reduced by daily defections, and led by second-rate men such as Duhem, Goujon and Fayau, lost all influence; Barère, Collot and Billaud had to give up speaking.

In spite of its successes, the Right did not take power. Along with Barère, Billaud and Collot, the turncoat terrorists who directed it—Fouché, Barras and Fréron—were removed from the Committees. Tallien himself, compromised by Lecointre, left the Committee of Public Safety. Rovère wrote to his friend Goupilleau that Tallien and Fréron could no longer count on more than 150 deputies. The majority in the Convention consequently lay in the Center, in the so-called Plain, reinforced by converts from the Mountain and by turncoat terrorists like Bourdon, who were opposed to an extreme reaction. In this majority, Merlin de Douai and Cambacérès occupied an eminent place; moreover, the new members of the committees were all chosen from among the regicides. It is in these men of the Center, represented for us by Thibaudeau, that the spirit of the Thermidorian Convention and indeed of the Convention as a whole is really incarnate. Their loyalty to the Revolution and to the Republic was never in doubt for a moment: on 3 Brumaire, Year III (October 24, 1794), they excluded the deputy Chabot because the primary assembly of Montluçon, which had elected him on August 26, 1792, had given its representatives a mandate to uphold the monarchy; on 25 Brumaire (November 15), they would maintain and codify the laws passed against the émigrés; exiled priests would remain liable to the death penalty if they returned to France. With regard to the constitutional priests, these Thermidorian Republicans were scarcely less hostile than the *sans-culottes*, and on the second *jour sans-culottide* (September 18, 1794), on a motion put forward by Cambon —as usual on the lookout for economies—they suppressed the religious estimates.

But they belonged to the middle class; they wanted to give the businessman his freedom back and reduce the poor man once more to a subordinate position. They were deputies and, jealous of their authority, they feared the dictatorship of the mob more than anything else. Consequently they wanted to avoid at all costs falling once more under the yoke of the Jacobins, who were terrorists and partisans of a social democracy. Realizing however that if they divided, the Republicans risked losing everything, their policy was to grant a tacit amnesty to the men of Year II, with the exception of those who might be convicted of illegalities or of common-law crimes, in order to reconcile all the "patriots of 1789" for the defense of the Revolution.

This was the program which Berlier, among others, put forward from the start in the Nord, in order to hold back the reaction; the committees, for their part, would try during the autumn, by means of their calculated slowness, to prevent the outlawing of the terrorist leaders.

But, as in 1793, the decisive step was not taken by the Conventional majority: the decision came from outside. And as the enemies of the Jacobins had been able to gain control of the mob, it was they who dictated it.

CHAPTER THREE

Jacobin Activity

Encouraged by Lecointre's reverse, the Mountain made an effort to regain the initiative. At the Jacobin Club, Lecointre, Tallien and Fréron, attacked by Carrier, were expelled on 17 Fructidor (September 3). On the twenty-first, Duhem obtained a decision to examine the means of carrying out "the prompt export of the sworn enemies of the Republic," in other words the deportation of the suspects, although several members had argued that this was a hopeless demand and that it was unwise to affront public opinion in this way. At the same time a few provincial clubs which had remained loyal to their mother-society admonished the Convention. The most violent petition was that of the Jacobins of Dijon: it called for the application of the Law of Suspects, the exclusion of nobles and priests from all public offices, and reconsideration of the decree on the question of motive; and it declared that until peace was concluded absolute freedom of the press was inadmissible. Up to 10 Vendémiaire, Year III (October 1, 1794), the Correspondence Committee of the Convention almost daily analyzed similar documents, mainly from the southeast (Lyons, Marseilles, Aix, Toulon, Manosque, Grenoble) and from the Languedoc (Toulouse, Montpellier, Cette), but also from Rennes, Poitiers, Auxerre, and little towns such as Aigueperse, Creuilly and Richelieu. On the third *jour sans-culottide* (September 19), the mother-society addressed a circular to all the affiliated clubs, obviously in the hope of widening the scope of the movement.

It was undoubtedly in order to rally the *sans-culottes* that some Montagnards suddenly began to display a remarkable enthusiasm for social reform. On 22 Fructidor (September 8), Duquesnoy complained that, in the Pas-de-Calais, national property had been monopolized by the rich, and Fayau proposed a return to the law of June 3, 1793, which had granted one acre to citizens who owned no land, in return for a yearly rental and without requiring them to attend the auction sale; he also demanded that the share which had been promised to the defenders of the country should be handed over to them immediately. Barère went further: he spoke of fixing a *maximum* for landed property, and asked that shops and workshops be made over to the workers.

It is just possible that these proposals had a slight echo

in Paris. The terrorists had made an effort, and not without success, to regain control of the Section meetings. As only a small number of citizens normally attended these meetings, it was not difficult for a few determined men—Jacobins or counterrevolutionaries—to get their motions passed, especially at the end of the meeting, when most of those present had gone home to bed. Be that as it may, at the meetings held on 20 and 30 Fructidor (September 6 and 16), at least eight Sections gave their support to the petition from the Dijon club. Two symbolic events made a considerable impression on public opinion and seemed to indicate a return to the Terror: on 26 Fructidor (September 12), the new revolutionary court condemned a wigmaker to death for making royalist remarks, and on the same day the Convention agreed to the transfer of Marat's body to the Panthéon, where it was taken on the fifth *jour sans-culottide* (September 21).

In matters of substance, the Thermidorian majority nonetheless showed a firm determination not to follow the terrorists. The releases continued: between 23 Thermidor and 16 Vendémiaire, 3,615 releases were ordered, which incidentally still left 4,678 people imprisoned in Paris. On 10 Vendémiaire, Year III (October 1, 1794), the Committee of General Security was authorized to decide on the sentences of detention until the conclusion of peace pronunced by the revolutionary courts. On the other hand, when on 25 Fructidor (September 11) the Jacobins, who had been violently denounced the day before by Merlin de Thionville, presented an address in favor of the patriots in prison, it was buried by being referred to the Committees. Legal action against the terrorists was begun. On 7 Fructidor, Ruelle had asked in vain that the new members of the revolutionary committees be forbidden to have their predecessors arrested: on 12 Vendémiaire (October 3), Bourdon announced among other arrests that the former committee of the Bonnet Rouge Section had been incarcerated for having falsified its minute-book. On the seventh (September 28), Cambacérès had pushed through an important decree to accelerate the purge of the administrative bodies. The social measures proposed by the Mountain had been set aside on 27 Fructidor (September 13) with the help of Cambon, who defended the pledging of the *assignat*.

On the fourth *jour sans-culottide* (September 20), Lindet read out, on behalf of the Committees, a long report on the state of the Republic which may be regarded as the program of the majority. He promised protection for the popular societies and for the members of the former revolutionary committees, in other words a political amnesty, which incidentally did not rule out prosecution for common-law offenses or violation of the law. But he repudiated, if not revolutionary repression, at least its excessive extension and above all the mass outlawing of nobles and priests: "Restore freedom to all those citizens who have been useful and can be useful." Finally, he proposed restoring to the business world the right to export under certain conditions, and, without naming Jacobins and *sans-culottes*, he categorically threatened those who dreamed of "the transfer of wealth." Lindet had been the head of the nationalized economy in Year II; without condemning it as a means of revolutionary defense, he visibly reduced its scope, and above all openly abandoned its social tendencies. There can be no doubt that he was in agreement with Carnot, and his speech revealed that those of the men of Year II who still figured on the Committees had rallied to the opinions of the majority in the Center. Later on, Lindet maintained that at the meetings of the Committees he had gone much further in the direction of reaction: he claimed to have proposed reviewing the Law of Suspects, releasing all the "Federalists," in other words the Girondins or self-styled Girondins, and forbidding the clubs to affiliate with one another or to admit civil servants. At the tribune, in any case, he had remained much more conciliatory towards the Left. The latter kept silent, and Lindet's conclusions were unanimously approved; possibly the Mountain realized that, considering how things stood, the wisest course was not to create difficulties for the government, in order to avoid pushing it towards the Right.

But in the Sections less caution was displayed. At the meetings held on 10 Vendémiaire, Year III (October 1, 1794), the reactionaries began standing up to the terrorists again, and three meetings, including that at the Muséum which had hitherto allowed itself to be guided by the Hébertists, passed motions against the Dijon club's address. All the same, several Sections opposed the reading of Lindet's report and at least six expressed support for the Jacobins. Nothing could have been better calculated to upset the majority, for, not believing as yet in the Royalist peril, it was obsessed by the fear of an insurrection by the Sections and a new thirty-first of May. Several incidents stimulated its fear, and the Right did everything to exploit them. During the night of 23-24 Fructidor, Tallien, on returning home, was wounded by an intruder who remained unidentified; his friends attributed the attack to the "Knights of the Guillotine." On the fifth *jour sans-*

culottide, Treilhard read out the letters from Serre and
Auguis, who were on mission in the Bouches-du-Rhône,
on the disturbances in Marseilles. The purges and the release of the suspects had inflamed the passions of the terrorists. One of them, appointed to the post of schoolmaster
at Chabeuil in the Drôme, had taken it into his head to
write to the national agent in that commune that the patriots were only waiting for a signal to eliminate "by
means of a second and third of September all the impure
elements left in Marseilles." The letter had been forwarded
to the representatives who had its author arrested on 26
Fructidor (September 12); two days later, while he was
being moved to Aix, a band of terrorists released him; on
the twenty-seventh, Serre and Auguis had been greeted
with jeers at a meeting of the popular society. The Convention declared Reynier an outlaw and Merlin de Thionville took the opportunity to inveigh once more against the
Jacobin Club, "that den of brigands." But that was not the
end of the affair. Jeanbon had promptly sent reinforcements to Marseilles and, in return, summoned a battalion
from the Corrèze which was garrisoned at Avignon, where
it had gone over to the reaction; in the absence of Goupilleau, who was then at Carpentras, this battalion refused
to obey the summons and started fighting the workers
who supported the revlutionary committee and the club.
Hurrying back to Avignon, Goupilleau sent the soldiers
away but also disarmed the patriots, reorganized the committee and closed the popular society. In Marseilles, the
disturbances started again on 5 Vendémiaire, Year III
(September 26). Serre and Auguis were besieged in their
house and roughly handled by the rioters, who demanded
the release of the imprisoned patriots; that very evening

the representatives appointed a military commission which ordered five executions. A considerable number of terrorists were arrested and sent to Aix and to Paris; the club was purged and Carles, its president, committed suicide. The line adopted by the turncoat Montagnards who had appointed themselves the spokesmen of the Right was to depict these disturbances as the consequence of a single plot laid in Paris by the Jacobins, whose provincial societies were mere tools in their hands. On 26 Fructidor (September 12), Dumont, infuriated by the addresses praising the terrorists, had cried: "The blow comes from here: we must parry it." In Lyons, Charlier and Pocholle had followed Goupilleau's example, and from Toulon Jeanbon had advised the Committees to close the clubs. On 10 Vendémiaire (October 1), the Right succeeded for the first time in having a Jacobin address disapproved. The Committees, who also felt a certain anxiety, had, on the fourth *jour sans-culottide* (September 20), made a considerable concession to the Right, with a decree expelling from Paris all those who had not been living there on 1 Messidor, and consequently all the departmental delegates.

In these circumstances, the sectional agitation of 10 Vendémiaire produced a violent reaction. On the twelfth (October 3), the counterrevolutionaries of the Lepeletier Section complained that two days earlier the terrorists had succeeded in dominating their meeting, and they obtained the arrest of the victualer Chrétien, a former juryman in the revolutionary court, as well as of Clémence and Marchand, leading Jacobins whom the Committee of General Security had recently released. Then, after the William Tell Section had urged the Convention to "reassure Paris," Legendre took the opportunity to renew Lecointre's attack on Collot, Billaud and Barère: "I declare this to the Convention: I regard them as conspirators." Reacting vigorously, the accused asserted that the members of the Committee of Year II were jointly responsible, having always deliberated together. Carnot, Lindet and Prieur de la Côte-d'Or, who still formed part of the government, courageously testified that they were telling the truth: "I was present at all the Committee's deliberations; it is untrue that I was banished to my office, as has been stated," said Carnot, who, in Prairial, would maintain the contrary. "All the Committee's decisions were taken unanimously, apart from the police decrees which were signed only by Robespierre, Saint-Just and Couthon." (This last statement, incidentally, was false). The discussion took on an even wider scope when Cambon, attacked in his turn for not having opposed the thrity-first of May as a member of the first Committee of Public Safety, revealed the divisions which had existed in the Committee on the eve of that day, invoked the protest which he and Bréard had recorded in a secret register, and placed the responsibility on Danton. Judging by this, it was fairly certain that if the reaction triumphed, the thirty-first of May would not fail to be repudiated.

The majority had not yet reached that stage; it was still reluctant to begin its own trial, and Thibaudeau has left us a record of its hesitations. On Legendre's accusation, it went back to its agenda and left the question of the thirty-first of May in abeyance. All the same, on 15 Vendémiaire (October 6), it finally succeeded in establishing itself in the government; by the normal process of change, Carnot, Lindet and Prieur de la Côte-d'Or left the Committee of Public Safety, while Amar, Dubarran and Bernard de

Saintes left the Committee of General Security; the last men of Year II had gone. Neither the Committees nor the majority, however, abandoned their middle-of-the-road policy. Carnot and Lindet continued, in fact, to co-operate with the government. On 12 Vendémiaire, when Fréron called for an inquiry into the government officials' attitude to the ninth of Thermidor and an inspection of the registers of the revolutionary committees, Bourdon demanded that the prerogatives of the Committee of General Security should be respected. Nor did the majority take any radical measures with regard to the popular societies. On 25 Vendémiaire (October 16) it confined itself to forbidding them to affiliate or to organize collective petitions, and to taking steps to insure that lists of their members should be published. It would appear that it had come to an agreement on this issue with the Left, for the *rapporteur* of the decree was Delmas, who had presided over the Club in Fructidor; Billaud and Collot remained silent. Once again, therefore, the Montagnard Deputies revealed themselves ready to cut their losses; once again, the Jacobins complained of their inertia, though they made no attempt to resist.

Could they have done so, and were the Convention's fears justified? In his *Souvenirs thermidoriens*, Duval maintains that, but for the *jeunesse dorée*, the Assembly would inevitably have succumbed "under the blows of the Jacobins and the two horrible *faubourgs* . . . in other words at least three-quarters of the population, the aforementioned three-quarters consisting of pickpockets and thieves." It would follow that not only the laborers and workers, but also the artisans and shopkeepers, were still on the side of the Jacobins—an interesting admission to note. But apart from the fact that Duval never missed an opportunity to exaggerate the merits of the young bourgeoisie to which he had the honor to belong, it is clear that the Jacobins no longer had the means to organize a *journée,* nor would they ever have again.

It should be noted first of all that, as popular agitators, they were not alone and never had been; it might even be said that, among the *sans-culottes,* the *enragés* and Hébertists had exerted far greater influence because, being advocates of direct government, they persistently attacked the deputies, and because from the social point of view they were far bolder. Having been persecuted by the revolutionary government, they turned against it after the ninth of Thermidor, in contrast to the Jacobins, who called for its continuation; they called for the free election of local administrative bodies, and, in order to give ample play to their propaganda, joined with Fréron in defending freedom of the press. As early as 7 Fructidor (August 24), Chasles came forward as their spokesman in the Convention, when he proposed elections for the new revolutionary committees. Soon Legray, whom the ninth of Thermidor had rescued from prison, turned the Museum Section into a stronghold of the party and, on 10 Fructidor, persuaded it to demand in addition the election of a municipal council. Passed on to the other Sections, this address divided the Republicans of the Left: it was adopted, at least, by the Montreuil Section, whereas fourteen other Sections rejected it, and did so under the influence of the Jacobins, for on 22 Fructidor the Mutius Scaevola Section condemned it as "a Moderantist system." The Hébertists also turned their attention to the popular societies, which had revived to some extent after the fall of Robespierre;

the one that met in the hall of the electoral body, that is to say at the bishopric where the *journée* of the thirty-first of May had been organized, fell under their influence; on 20 Fructidor (September 6) it voted a petition at the instigation of Varlet, who had been one of the leaders of the *enragés,* and of the engraver Bodson. Two days later a decree restored the hall to the Hôtel-Dieu, and soon afterwards Varlet and Bodson were arrested; but Legray joined the club to the Museum Section and on 10 Vendémiaire (October 1) club and Section together drafted a new address demanding an elected municipal council. Finally Babeuf came on the scene. Prosecuted during the Terror for having, as administrator of the district of Montdidier, signed a record of allocations of national property which turned out to be fraudulent, imprisoned, and then released not long before the ninth of Thermidor, he laid the blame for all his misfortunes on Robespierre and fought fanatically against the revolutionary government and the terrorists. On 17 Fructidor (September 3) was published the first issue of his *Journal de la liberté de la presse,* in which he supported Fréron; on 14 Vendémiaire (October 5) this became the famous *Tribun du peuple.* Yet it is impossible to doubt the sincerity of these agitators, or to state for certain that there was deliberate collusion with the leaders of the reaction. Babeuf was penniless, and it was the printer Guffroy who published his paper: the turncoat terrorist used him in order to attack their common enemies, the Jacobins. But soon the *Tribun du peuple* would break with Fréron, and in Brumaire Guffroy would withdraw his support from Babeuf, who would be imprisoned. As for Legray, if one passage in the Museum address of 10 Vendémiaire called for free trade, something to which

both *enragés* and Hébertists had always been radically opposed, that is not enough to prove that he was in collusion
with the reaction: the petition was also directed against
requisitioning, which was blamed for causing the disappearance of provisions from the markets and for bringing
about the general shortage of food. Besides, Babeuf immediately protested. In point of fact, the Hébertists turned,
as did Babeuf himself, against the leaders of the reaction
when they understood their maneuver. In Brumaire, when
the reaction won the day, they in their turn fell victims to
it. Legray was arrested; the Museum Section, having changed
hands, served notice on the club.

There is no reason, moreover, to attribute a very great
influence to these men. Their diversion helped to bewilder
the *sans-culottes*; but they were bewildered already, having
seen the Montagnards outlawing one another since the
previous winter and the Committees of Year II singling out
for attack the *enragés* and the Hébertists, for whom the
common people had shown a special predilection. The Jacobins no longer had any orators or journalists capable of
rousing the mob to enthusiasm, and in order to stir the
mob it was not enough to call for the imprisonment of the
suspects. To begin with, the mob no longer had the impression, as in 1793, that the Revolution was in mortal
danger; the Republican armies were victorious and the
Vendée was in its death throes. Then too, it had supported
the Montagnards only on condition that the *maximum* be
put into effect; but the *maximum* was now being abandoned,
and it was in vain that the *sans-culottes* complained that it
had been violated. The Jacobins scarcely ever mentioned it,
either in the Convention or at their club, and seemed resigned to its failure. Moreover, it had divided the *sans-*

culottes themselves, who were not a class party and included, as well as the proletariat, artisans and shopkeepers who were eager to see the peasants' provisions taxed and requisitioned, but most unwilling to suffer the same fate; the workers themselves had opposed the fixing of wages, and not without reason, for since the Committee of Public Safety had reserved the entire benefit of the *maximum* for the State, the civilian population had scarcely profited from it except as regards the price of bread. For want of time and money, the Montagnards had been unable to obtain any great advantages for the poor, especially the poor in the towns, by their social policy; the decrees of Ventôse had not been applied and the proposals put forward by Duquesnoy and Fayau concerned only the peasants; the Treasury being empty, the laws on education and public assistance remained more or less a dead letter. Disillusionment was profound, and at the approach of winter, the scarcity and rising cost of food constituted the sole preoccupation of most people. However, poverty was not yet so widespread as to stir the common people to action: the cold weather had not yet arrived; the Committee of Public Safety was provisioning Paris to the best of its ability; the *maximum* was still in operation and the *assignat* had not yet lost all its value; the armaments workshops had not closed down either, so that unemployment was not too serious. Finally, it should not be forgotten that since 1793 a considerable number of *sans-culottes* had left Paris for the army, and that after the ninth of Thermidor a good many popular agitators had been guillotined or imprisoned; thus the personnel of the *journées* had been considerably reduced.

Besides, even supposing that the common people had been ready to rise, the Jacobins no longer possessed the same means of mobilizing them as on the tenth of August or the thirty-first of May. As democrats, they had tried to reconcile their dictatorship with universal suffrage by imposing their views on the people's representatives by intermittent demonstrations or by the implicit threat of repeating them. In order to organize these demonstrations, they had not thought of enrolling the *sans-culottes* in the cadres of a party, and had contented themselves with the cadres which democracy offered them, taking control of the Sections, the National Guard and finally the Commune. Once in power, they had identified themselves with the State, to the extent of reducing the *sans-culottes* themselves to passive obedience, executing or imprisoning the *enragés* and the Hébertists who tried to turn the same pressure methods against them, and depriving the people of the right to choose its administrators. The Committee of Year II had itself appointed the Robespierrist Commune and the general staff of the National Guard; for the committees of the Sections themselves, it had only allowed candidates to be presented to it. In losing control of the Government after the ninth of Thermidor, the Jacobins had therefore lost everything, for the popular societies—which moreover had never included more than a small number of *sans-culottes*—were in no way organized to resort to force.

The Convention had only to continue along the same lines as the Committee of Public Safety of Year II to complete the disorganization of the Jacobin insurrectionary cadres. It had taken good care not to reconstitute the Commune. Since the ninth of Thermidor, the Committees had been administering the capital themselves: at first they confined themselves to nominating a few police officials; on 14 Fructidor (August 31), the Convention created two mu-

nicipal commissions, one for the police, the other for taxation, while one official for each section was delegated to
the Registrar General's office; as for the new revolutionary
committees, they were chosen by the Committee of General
Security; finally, since 8 Germinal (that is, long before the
ninth of Thermidor), the Committee of Public Safety had
been in charge of provisioning. Thus Paris had lost the
right to administer itself, a right which indeed it has never
recovered. As for the Sections, on 4 Fructidor (August 21),
the indemnity of 40 sols granted to those citizens who attended their meetings was suppressed, on the thoroughly
justified assumption that as a result fewer *sans-culottes*
would attend; moreover these meetings were confined to
the tenth day of each decade. As early as 19 Thermidor
(August 6), the command of the National Guard had been
suppressed as well as the permanent general staff, whose
duties were henceforth assigned in rotation to the commanders of the Sections. Finally, on 1 Fructidor (August
18), the Committee of Public Safety had canceled its newspaper subscriptions, a measure which was aimed exclusively
at the Jacobin papers and which damaged them severely.

In 1792 and 1793, the *journées* had triumphed, thanks
to the connivance of the municipal authorities, and of an
executive which was either disarmed or sympathetic. Already in Ventôse, Year II, the Hébertists had on the contrary failed in the face of the Committee of Public Safety's
determined attitude. The situation had now altered to such
an extent that it was against the Jacobins that the new
journées were organized, under the leadership of the Thermidorians of the Right and with the resigned tolerance of
the majority.

CHAPTER FOUR

The Outlawing of the Jacobins

The method employed by the reaction to fight the Jacobins was to unite their enemies: Republican bourgeois, Constitutional Monarchists and supporters of the *ancien régime*. Up to 1793, they had fought against one another as much as against the *sans-culottes*, and it was this which had enabled the latter to seize power; the lesson had been learned. Not that they were now agreed on what form of government to adopt; that was impossible. But having suffered together from the Terror, and being threatened by both political and social democracy, they had only one idea for the moment: to take their revenge on the Jacobins and to reduce the *sans-culottes* to a state of submission.

They accepted as their leaders the turncoat terrorists Tallien, Fréron and Merlin de Thionville, who had a great many things to expiate and who wanted to start a new career. A group of publicists whose personal interest demanded a return to freedom of the press gave valuable help; they included Dussaulx of the *Correspondence politique*; the Bertin brothers, who owned the *Débats*; Michel, of the *Quotidienne*; Isidore Langlois, of the *Messager du soir*; Richer de Sérizy of the *Accusateur public*; Martainville and Fiévée. The most notable of these men was probably Charles de Lacretelle or Lacretelle the Younger, who has left us some delightful *Souvenirs*, and who ran the *Républicain français* from Pluviôse, Year III, onwards. Most of these men later graced the Royalist press up to and into the period of the Restoration, but as yet they were careful to conceal their true opinions—with the exception of Sérizy, who soon started playing the part of *enfant terrible*. They worked in close collaboration, meeting to dine together and decide on the themes of their campaigns. They were hand in glove with Fréron, who was a friend of Dussaulx and who himself, on 25 Fructidor (September 11), revived his *Orateur du peuple*. For his part, Tallien, with Méhée as his secretary, created the *Ami du Citoyen* on 1 Brumaire (October 22). It was alleged that they even had accomplices among their adversaries: Ange Pitou, who contributed to Chasles's *Ami du peuple* and to the *Annales patriotiques*, was accused by Babeuf of being an *agent provocateur*. They promptly took over the field, for the Jacobins had been deprived of their government subsidies and, as Duhem remarked, did not have Thérèse Cabarrus' riches at their disposal. From Fructidor onwards, the gazettes were supplemented by countless pamphlets. In this Thermidorian press, principles occupied an unimportant place: the method used was to insult the Jacobins and to intimidate their leaders by means of continuous denunciations. They were called "drinkers of blood," "sectarians," "dominators," "thieves" who had robbed the rich for their own profit, and "anarchists" who had given lowly citizens posts which belonged by right to "decent people," in other words to the notables. The attacks on Cambon, the "executioner of the rentiers" and the "Robespierre of landed property," and on Lindet, the director of the nationalized economy hateful to all French businessmen, underlined the social character of the movement, as did the enthusiastic support of society people, whose salons were opening their doors again, and that of the singers, actors, dancers, songwriters and musicians whom the spartan regime of Year II had deprived of a remunerative public. In the Convention, the Montagnards were not alone in protesting at the blackmail and calumny practiced by this press, and on several occasions there was talk of a repressive law—but this never came to anything.

Without the slightest doubt, it was the excesses and abuses of certain terrorists that helped the leaders of the reaction most of all. Their chief targets were the revolutionary committees; the proceedings for embezzlement and falsification of records brought against the committee of the Bonnet Rouge Section, six members of which were sentenced to imprisonment on 7 Brumaire, Year II (October 28, 1794), encouraged their campaign, and on 8 Floréal (April 27, 1795) the dramatist Ducancel attained a tremendous success with a play entitled *L'intérieur des com-*

ités révolutionnaires, which put the finishing touches to the Thermidorian legend of the terrorist institution. But the biggest windfall was the trial of the 132 citizens of Nantes, which gave rise to two further trials that completed the defeat of the Jacobins. These citizens of Nantes had been arrested pell-mell after the defeat of Entrammes, when there was a rumor of a plot to hand the city over to the Vendée rebels; they had been sent before the revolutionary court and this journey, in the middle of winter and in appalling conditions aggravated at will by a hostile escort, had proved fatal to a good many of them. In Paris they had found defenders, notably Réal, and had been lucky enough not to be brought to trial before the ninth of Thermidor; on the fifth of that month, moreover, the representative Bô had had the committee which had charged them arrested and likewise sent to Paris. The trial of the ninety-four survivors began on 22 Fructidor (September 8). The leader of the accused, Phélippes *alias* Tronjolly, former president of the criminal court of Loire-Inférieure, had the members of the committee subpoenaed as witnesses and accused them of the drownings and executions without trial which had occurred; they admitted the facts and threw the responsibility on Carrier. Tronjolly and his companions were triumphantly acquitted on the twenty-ninth.

The press immediately seized on the facts revealed in court; on 29 Fructidor there appeared the pamphlet *Les jacobins démasqués,* on 7 Vendémiaire (September 28) Méhée's leaflet on the drownings, and on the twenty-sixth (October 17) Martinville's pamphlet *Les jacobins hors la loi,* while Babeuf also published one entitled *Du système de dépopulation ou la vie et les crimes de Carrier.*

44

In the Convention, on 8 Vendémiaire, the "infernal columns" were indicted, and Duroy, a Montagnard, obtained a decree ordering the arrest of General Turreau and two of their other commanders. From then on, Carrier hardly dared appear again at the Asssembly. Apparently neither the Convention nor the Committees were eager to pursue the matter, for a fresh incident was required to force them to do so. On 22 Vendémiaire (October 13), the Convention was confronted with the documents which stated that Sergeant-Major Lefèvre had had forty-one Vendée prisoners, nearly all women and children, put on board ship at Bourgneuf, on 5 Ventôse, Year II, with orders for the captain to throw them into the sea—orders which were duly carried out. A decree was passed ordering him to be arrested, together with those who had obeyed his instructions. Dumont took advantage of the Assembly's emotion to express surprise that nearly a month had passed without the Nantes committee being brought to trial for the actions which it had admitted, and the Convention agreed without discussion to send the case before the revolutionary court. A second trial accordingly opened at which Carrier, called as a witness, promptly took on the appearance of an accused man. Consequently, on 29 Vendémiaire, Dumont proposed submitting his case to the Committees; this was tantamount to giving them back the right to indict deputies, and Tallien protested. It was agreed that the procedure should be regulated by a law which was passed on 8 Brumaire (October 29). Any charge made against a representative of the people had to be referred to the Committees, but they would confine themselves to hearing the accused and forming an opinion without giving their reasons; if they were in favor of prosecution, a commission of twenty-one members would carry out an inquiry, and on the basis of its report the Convention would authorize or refuse a trial after hearing the deputy concerned in public session. That very evening, lots were drawn for the commission to investigate the case of Carrier.

As this commission did not present its report until 21 Brumaire (November 11), the agitation had plenty of time to grow. The Jacobins were in a difficult position. Robespierre had recalled Carrier and had intended to prosecute him in order to separate his cause from that of the Revolution, while Carrier had tried to cover himself by helping to bring about Robespierre's downfall; the result was that his trial, as was pointed out to the Jacobins, was serving as a weapon against "all the men of the Revolution." They did not dare to defend him openly and confined themselves to protesting at the intrigues against the accused. The charge against the Nantes committee was in fact being printed, posted, and distributed, and the police received countless notifications that there would be an insurrection if Carrier was acquitted by his colleagues or escaped his judges. However, by dint of repeating—rightly, as it happened—that they were the real targets, certain Jacobins lost their tempers and started uttering threats in their turn. It was Billaud, doubtless exasperated at being criticized for his reserve, who on 13 Brumaire made the most rash pronouncement:

> The lion is not dead when it dozes, and on its awakening it exterminates all its enemies. The trench is open; the patriots are going to bestir themselves again and urge the people to awaken.

This was more than enough for the Jacobin plot to save Carrier to become an article of faith for the reaction; it was

an excellent excuse for extorting the indictment from the
Convention and for simultaneously launching an attack on
the hated club.

The leaders of the reaction had been preparing for this
for a long time. Since 1793 the *sans-culottes* had been
masters of the street, and in spite of the divisions in their
ranks they were still a force to be reckoned with there.
The Thermidorian press frequently denounced the "swash-
bucklers" and the "revolutionaries with big sticks" who attacked its hawkers, dominated the section meetings, and,
with their womenfolk, filled the galleries of the Convention. However, immediately after the ninth of Thermidor,
their adversaries had been able to gauge their own strength
by gathering outside the gates of the prisons and by be-
sieging the Committee of General Security to demand the
release of the suspects. When the final break occurred between the Jacobins and the turncoat terrorists, the latter,
who knew rioting technique from experience, undertook
to organize a shock force to oppose their enemies, and they
recruited it from the middle-class youth. This was not entirely an innovation, since at the end of 1792 it had already
demonstrated in groups against the Montagnards; this
time it had much greater success. According to Duval, who
was then a notary's clerk, all the clerks attached to the
courts of justice and most of the shop assistants and bank
clerks answered the call. These young men undoubtedly
shared the opinions of their class; they also derived a
pleasure from demonstrating which befitted their age. But
often they had a more direct interest in what they were
doing: many of them were absentees, for whom the downfall of the revolutionary government meant security. Carrier, in fact, had denounced them as early as 18 Fructidor

(September 4), and on the twenty-fifth a police report stated that in a raid on the boulevards five of the thirty people arrested had been found to be absentees. What is more, Duval prided himself on the fact.

> They pretended not to notice [he wrote of his leaders] that we were all or nearly all absentee conscripts; they considered that we would be more useful to the commonweal in the streets of Paris than in the Army of the Sambre and Meuse, the Rhine and Moselle or the East Pyrenees, and anyone who had proposed sending us to patrol the frontiers would have had a poor reception, believe me.

It was in vain that the matter was raised several times in the Convention. On 14 Ventôse (March 4, 1795) an article in the *Moniteur* would praise the "young men" in terms much the same as Duval's: "While some were carrying freedom to our neighbors, the others were restoring it to France." Moreover, the best way of evading military service was to go into public service and thus obtain a good position at the same time. As fast as the Jacobins were expelled from the administrative services, the "young men" took their place. Once again, the Montagnards complained in vain. The same article in the *Moniteur* answered them:

> It has been suggested that the government should dismiss from all the posts to which it has been obliged to appoint them, the young men who have taken the place of the stupid, ferocious advocates of the Terror.

It may have been Fréron who had had the idea of using them; in any case they were known as "Fréron's *jeunesse dorée*." But they also regarded Tallien, Merlin de Thionville and Goupilleau de Fontenay as their leaders. The singer Elleviou, the actor Quesnel of the Théâtre français, the dancer Trenitz, the musician Souriguères, and the journalists Martainville and Langlois were their lieutenants, according to Duval. Lacretelle also claims to have been one of their leaders. The latter soon hired a number of thugs, formerly reputed to be *sans-culottes*, such as the Marquis de Saint-Huruge and the "patriot" Gonchon, who undertook the violent operations. The "young men" could be recognized by the square collars of their coats and by their long lovelocks; they were armed with bludgeons and shouted: "Down with the Jacobins! Long live the Convention!" Every evening, they would meet at the Palais Égalité, where they had their headquarters at the Café de Chartres. The leaders would come here to give their orders, which circulated from group to group. According to Duval, a system of communication had been organized which, in the event of an alert, made it possible promptly to call together associates scattered all over the city. If he is to be believed, the leaders of the reaction had gone even further:

> Acting on a proposal made by Fréron and Barras, the regenerated Committees of Public Safety and of General Security had given us some auxiliary leaders who brought us together two or three times a week, on the waterside terrace at the Tuileries, in the Luxembourg Garden, on the Champs-Élysées and in other places, and trained us so zealously that there was scarcely one of us who was not capable of using a rifle and eager to do so. . . . Some officers devoted to the Thermidorian party taught us how to drill.

In point of fact, in Prairial the *jeunesse dorée* was sent into action against the Faubourg Antoine. Its failure was pitiful; its troops could not hold their ground when the workers and artisans left their work to come down into the street *en masse*, but as the workers did not do this until the spring, the "young men" had things their own way for a long time, the connivance of their employers allowing them to leave their work to gather together at will. Even so the tacit approval of the Convention was necessary; it could not bring itself to refuse this approval, having very few troops at its disposal. The National Guard, which in any case was disorganized and practically unarmed, was partially suspect, while the police itself does not appear to have been very reliable: until Frimaire its reports were hostile to the "young men," whom they described as fops, and the attack of 19 Brumaire on the Jacobins was considered in these reports as "a plot hatched up by the aristocracy."

The surveillance committees, on the other hand, usually played into the hands of the *jeunesse dorée*. The police report of 20 Brumaire on Saint-Huruge is typical: "He proves to all those citizens who do not think like him that they are wrong by giving them a thrashing and taking them straight away to the guardhouse, *where he locks them up with impunity*." Obviously the Committee of General Security and the surveillance committees which were simply its tools regarded Fréron's gangs as their auxiliaries. Thus they were able to play their not inconsiderable part, seizing control of the streets from the Jacobins and forcing the hand of the hesitant majority in the Convention.

It was about the middle of Fructidor that their activity began to be manifested. On the twelfth, the day of Lecointre's first attack on the terrorists, they demonstrated in a threatening fashion around the Convention and on the boulevards, shouting that they "would know how to force the Convention to settle this business." On the second *jour sans-culottide* (September 18), Garnier de Saintes denounced them from the tribune. The next day, a deputation called to pay its respects to the wounded Tallien and a serious clash occurred for the first time at the Palais Égalité, between Jacobins and fops; henceforth such clashes took place continually. In Vendémiaire, the *jeunesse dorée* also intervened in the Section meetings, which, as of the twentieth (October 11), escaped from the control of the *sans-culottes* and for the most part signified their adhesion to the Convention. On the twenty-third, an embarrassed explanation from the Dijon club was read out, and the Assembly declared that it regarded it as a retraction of the famous petition; those Sections which had supported the petition thereupon began to repudiate it—on the thirtieth (October 21), for example, the Fontaine de Grenelle, which had hitherto been dominated by Raisson, a former member of the Supplies Commission and the last president of the Jacobins. But it was the discussion of the report on the Carrier case which provided the opportunity for decisive action.

On 15 Brumaire (November 5) uproar had broken out in the Convention, where Billaud's rash outburst at the Jacobin Club had been denounced. The number of defections increased, and on the sixteenth Lequinio solemnly declared that he was leaving the Club. On the nineteenth, Saint-Huruge led the first attack on the Club; the windows were smashed with stones, the men beaten up, the women whipped. The next day, when Duhem and Duroy protested, Reubell retorted by proposing that the meetings of the Club should be suspended. On the twenty-first (November 11), Romme read out the report on Carrier; it concluded in favor of an indictment, though not without revealing certain reservations; as Carrier had to be heard, the issue appeared to be in doubt. In the evening, there was a tremendous crowd at the Palais Égalité, according to Duval

> because of the widespread rumor that the Jacobins were preparing to go, that very evening, to launch an armed attack on the Convention and to slit the throats of those of its members who wanted to undo the reign of the Terror.

Fréron and Tallien appeared between nine and ten. "Let us warn them while there is still time," cried the former. "Let us go and surprise the wild beast in its den. . . . Good young men, let us be on our way!" Marching along the rue Honoré, they reached the Jacobin Club and laid siege to it; the members who were holding a meeting made a sortie and the two sides came to blows. While the police were putting down the riot, the Committees passed a decree closing the Club, which the Convention ratified the next day. The more obstinate Jacobins went with Tissot, Goujon's brother-in-law, to join the popular society of the Quinze-Vingts in the Faubourg Antoine or what remained of the Cordeliers and the Club de l'Évêché, in the Salle du Muséum in the rue de Thionville (formerly the rue Dauphine), then later at a dancing school in the rue des Boucheries-Germain. But the faithful rarely turned up, and then the Committees had Tissot and Raisson arrested. At the beginning of Frimaire, the discomfiture of the Jacobins was complete; one after another, the Sections came to offer their congratulations to the Convention and inveigh against the terrorists.

Meanwhile the Assembly was hearing Carrier's declarations: he denied responsibility for the drownings and justified the firing-squad executions by the decree ordering rebels taken with weapons in their hands to be put to death

upon mere identification. He was confronted with his decrees of 27 and 29 Frimaire, Year II, which stipulated that
they be executed without trial, but he retorted that identification was not a trial and that it was for the judicial authority to which he had belonged to carry it out. Moreover
he challenged the very text of the decrees, of which the brief
contained only copies. The Convention decided to send
for the originals—which, incidentally, corresponded to the
copies—but refused to wait for them, and on 3 Frimaire
(November 23), referred Carrier to the revolutionary court.
He was sentenced to death and executed on the twenty-
sixth (December 16) along with two members of the
Nantes committee. Twenty-seven others were found guilty,
but released in consideration of the clause regarding motive,
and three were acquitted. This verdict raised a storm of
protest: on 28 Frimaire, Legendre had the twenty-seven
retained in custody in order to be indicted before the criminal court of Loire-Inférieure, and the revolutionary court
suppressed.

"The ladies of the aristocracy are beside themselves
with joy," wrote Dyzès on 23 Brumaire (November 13).
"I venture to predict that it will be short-lived." He was
completely mistaken. Apart from the fact that the resistance of the majority in the Convention was weakening
under the pressure of the *jeunesse dorée*, it was being under-
mined by the social life which was blossoming again in the
salons of Paris and whose importance has been shown by
Thibaudeau. In the front rank shone Thérèse Cabarrus—
since December 26, 1794, Madame Tallien—whom her
admirers called "Our Lady of Thermidor" aloud, and under their breaths "Our Lady of September," on account of
the part her husband was said to have played in the massa-

cres of 1792. She had left the Chaussée-d'Antin to install herself in the Cours-la-Reine in a house built for an actress, Mademoiselle Raucourt, known as La Chaumière; here she lived on a grand scale and, setting the fashion for the *merveilleuses*, launched the knee-length Greek dress which left the wearer half-naked. The bankers and contractors had quickly gathered together again all the people who could be useful to them; Madame Récamier and Madame Hamelin, among others, would soon be famous. Then again, now that the storm was over, the nobles and bourgeois of the *ancien régime* who had not emigrated took pleasure in reviving the traditions of the eighteenth century. Thibaudeau mentions the salons of Madame de Vaisnes, whose husband, a former State Councillor, had been a friend of Turgot's, and of Le Hoc, a sometime head clerk in the Navy Ministry and consul at Hamburg. There he used to meet philosophers such as Suard and Morellet, politicians such as Boissy d'Anglas and Siméon, officers such as Menou and Truguet, and diplomats such as Maret and Bourgoing. Soon Madame de Staël would hold receptions which, from the political point of view, would eclipse all the others. It was in these salons that the new rich, who had been created by the Revolution and whose numbers would be multiplied by speculation on the *assignat*, began to mix with the old bourgeoisie and the nobles, to form the new bourgeoisie which reigned in the nineteenth century. It was often a very mixed society, which forgathered with equal pleasure at the great lady's mansion and at the houses of the actresses in vogue: La Contat, who kept a tight hand on Legendre, and La Solier of the Opéra, who was Merlin de Thionville's mistress. As after all great ordeals, while some people returned to religion, others plunged into a frenzied life of pleasure. Dancing, in particular, became all the rage. High society amused itself not only in its own homes, but in the public dance halls which were opening everywhere, at the Carmes, for example, where the priests had been massacred in September, or in the former Saint-Sulpice cemetery. The Terror had clearly unhinged a great many minds, and no eccentricity was found too shocking. The relatives of people who had been guillotined held "victims' balls" among themselves, to which the guests came with Titus haircuts, the nape of their necks shaven as if by the executioner, and a red silk thread round their throats. The men did not bare their bodies like the women, but the *incroyables* were already vying with each other in luxury and eccentricity of dress, and in weird distortions of speech.

On politics the influence of the salons was considerable. Every effort was made to attract the deputies to them, by the bankers in order to buy them, and by the reactionaries in order to win them over to the good cause.

To their faces [writes Thibaudeau], they were plied with all sorts of lures, and behind their backs they were laughed at. That was in order. But there were many of them who did not notice. . . . First of all, a few joking remarks would be made in their presence about the Revolution. How could they take offense when it was a pretty woman who was taking the liberty of making them? . . . After they had been trained to accept banter of this sort, they were imperceptibly encouraged to despise the institutions of the Republic. . . . However strong-minded one may be, it is impossible not to be influenced by the society in which one moves. One gives way at first out of politeness; false shame then prevents one from turning back, and one ends up by adopting, in spite of oneself as it were, other people's opin-

ions. That is how the Republican party suffered a great many
defections, some members made concessions and others sold
themselves completely to the Royalist cause.

These remarks apply to every age, and Rousseau could
have quoted them to justify his hostility to representative
government. But they were especially valid at a moment
when the members of the Convention, after having virtue
urged upon them for such a long time, felt a burning desire for relaxation. "I would not be so bold," Thibaudeau
admits, "as to deny that sometimes, without noticing, I
may have been affected by this contagion, but it never
robbed me of my independence." We may as well believe
him. But there were not many who followed his example.

CHAPTER FIVE

The Beginning of the White Terror, the Amnesty for the Vendeans, and the Law on Public Worship

After defeating the Jacobins, the reactionaries could not be satisfied with Carrier's head; they returned to the attack on the leading terrorists. On 14 Frimaire (December 4), Dumont called for the Committees' report on Lebon; the next day, he asked for another on Maignet, who had been denounced by the inhabitants of Bédoin, a village in the Vaucluse which he had had razed to the ground. Legendre took this demand as an excuse to indict the whole Committee of Year II which had covered Maignet, while

Lecointre distributed the documents he had had printed in support of his denunciation of 12 Fructidor. Cambon, who on several occasions had attacked Tallien and "the new Antoinette," was now threatened; and Aigoin, Robespierre's friend and a commissary at the Treasury, having published a pamphlet against the Thermidorians, was dismissed together with one of his colleagues. However, the Committees continued their passive resistance: the reports that had been called for did not appear.

To force their hand, the reactionaries simultaneously launched another campaign, with a view to reinstating in the Convention those deputies who were still in prison for having protested against the second of June—the seventy-three—and also those whom the decrees of July 28 and October 3, 1793, had outlawed, because they had evaded arrest, but who had remained at liberty. If their seats were given back to them, the Right would be considerably strengthened. As early as 22 Vendémiaire (October 13), Pénières had succeeded in getting the Convention to ask the Committees for a report. However, the majority was hesitating yet again, for it was being asked to do nothing less than solemnly repudiate the *journées* of the thirty-first of May and the second of June, and implicitly admit that, in order to save itself, it had unjustly outlawed those whose reinstatement was being demanded. This was what Thuriot boldly pointed out when, on 1 Brumaire (October 22), Pénières returned to the attack. Lindet audaciously defended the thirty-first of May, and Tallien himself seemed hesitant. In the sittings which followed, the Convention confined itself to authorizing the seventy-three individually to return to their homes, where they were to remain under house arrest. But once the Jacobin Club had been closed and Carrier indicted, their friends returned to the attack, and the Committees, hoping to save Robespierre's former colleagues by making concessions to the Right, decided to give way. On the basis of a report by Merlin de Douai, the Girondin objectors were reinstated in the Convention on 18 Frimaire (December 8), as were several deputies who had supposedly resigned, such as Dulaure and Coupé de l'Oise, and Thomas Paine, who had been excluded as a foreigner. Altogether, seventy-eight deputies returned to the Convention, including moderates such as Daunou, but also some ardent reactionaries—Lanjuinais, Bailleul, Vernier and Delamarre—and others who soon came to terms with the Royalists, such as Aubry and Saladin. There remained the question of the outlawed deputies. On 17 Frimaire (December 7), the decrees outlawing them had been suspended; several of them promptly presented petitions, and the committees finally resorted to a compromise: on the twenty-seventh (December 17), they were amnestied but not reinstated. The Committees had thus avoided passing any judgment on the outlawing of the Girondins. But the consequences of the return of the seventy-eight immediately became apparent: they protested violently, demanding the admission of their friends, and Reubell, who was in the chair, after declaring that the decree had been passed, had to dissolve the sitting hurriedly in the midst of an uproar.

Perhaps there had been an agreement between the government and the leaders of the Right to stop prosecuting the terrorists in exchange for these concessions, for the Montagnards and the majority had approved them without discussion. If so, Montagnards and majority were thoroughly duped, for the reactionaries refused to bury the hatchet. On 30 Frimaire (December 20), Clauzel returned to the attack on the members of the former Committee whom Lecointre had denounced, unexpectedly insisting on their connivance with the Hébertists, which enabled him to add the names of Pache and Bouchotte to the list. At least he added that they were the only culprits who remained to be punished and that all the other members of the Convention were "entitled to public gratitude and esteem." But on 6 Nivôse (December 26), he attacked the entire former Committee of Public Safety, and again called for the Committees' report as well as the reorganization of the revolutionary court. Once again the government gave way. On the seventh, Merlin de Douai pronounced in favor of indicting Collot, Billaud, Barère and Vadier; the commission of twenty-one was appointed in the evening. On the eighth, the same Merlin presented the decree on the revolutionary court whose new members were elected on the thirteenth (January 2, 1795). The same day, a dramatic incident showed how far Carnot himself, who had returned to the Committee of Public Safety on 15 Brumaire, had fallen into disfavor. In announcing the recent successes of the Republican armies, he made this remark: "In view of these events, you must forgive the English if they regard our volunteers as dreadful terrorists." There was a furious uproar. "That's a remark worthy of Barère," cried Tallien. "It's a positive carmagnole," added others, while Bentabole described it as "an appalling insult to our soldiers." Carnot made an *amende honorable*: "The phrases of which Bentabole complains could, I admit, present a certain danger"; and he submitted in advance to the threat of proscription: "I recognize that governments must answer for all their actions and for the principles which have motivated them."

However the Committees had not given way all along the line: they had exonerated David, who was released from prison, as well as Voulland and Amar. It was probably in agreement with them that several attempts were made to put an end to all the prosecutions. On 18 Frimaire (December 8, 1794), Cambacérès had proposed a general political amnesty, excepting only the Royalists; Boudin did the same on 26 Nivôse (January 15, 1795). Champigny-Aubin tried to save at least the lives of Barère and his fellow accused by demanding the abolition of the death penalty on 1 Pluviôse (January 20). It was in vain: "We want no amnesty," declared Lecointre. All the same, the Committees were bold enough to clear Maignet, on 17 Nivôse (January 6), and they adjourned indefinitely the report on Lebon; the commission of twenty-one did not hurry either, for two months went by before it pronounced judgment. From time to time the Montagnards counterattacked. On 11 Nivôse (December 31, 1794), Duhem read out some long extracts from a pamphlet by a Feuillant called Lacroix, whom he succeeded in having charged with incitement to the restoration of the monarchy. Again, when Courtois' report on Robespierre's papers was printed, the Left raised a storm of protest on 29 Pluviôse (February 17), denouncing its deliberate omissions; Dumont and Legendre, who had addressed obsequious letters to the "Tyrant," complained of persecution. The *sans-culottes* had not disappeared from the streets or the Sections, and they were still demonstrating in the galleries. The majority, incidentally, took care to prove the purity of its Republican opinions by decreeing a holiday to commemorate "the rightful punishment of the last King of the French."

The reactionaries therefore continued to denounce a Jacobin plot, hatched this time to save the terrorists on the Committee. "You would be easy in your minds," declared Merlin de Thionville on 24 Nivôse (January 13, 1795), "if you did not have three great culprits to try." They did everything to exploit opportune incidents. On the twenty-seventh, a volunteer in the Eighth Paris Battalion who had reported a worker's remarks to the police was mortally wounded by the accused man, who was guillotined a few days later without anyone explaining what the soldier was doing in the capital. On 7 Pluviôse (January 26), the reactionaries brought up the new disturbances in Marseilles, where a riot had obliged the representatives Escudier and Esprit to bring the criminal court and the departmental administration back from Aix, as well as to release several of the people involved in the Vendémiaire affair; their orders were revoked and they were recalled, as was Saliceti, to be replaced by Chambon, Mariette and Cadroy, who would favor the White Terror. The Right countered the holiday of the twenty-first of January by getting another decreed for the anniversary of the ninth of Thermidor. The denunciations continued: Foussedoire, Babeuf, and Fouché, who admitted his connections with the latter, were attacked from the tribune. On 9 Pluviôse (January 28), Duhem, the most stubborn of the adversaries of the Right, was sent to the Abbaye. The petitions from the Sections became more and more violent. The Unity Section declared on 13 Nivôse (January 2) that it had denounced the Septembrists to the Committee of General Security; on 11 Pluviôse (January 30), the Temple Section attacked its

former revolutionary committee—"Strike down those tigers!"—while Lepeletier inveighed against all the terrorists.
"Let them all die," the Social Contract Section had said before, "or rather let them be deported." But, for the second
time, it was to the gangs of the *jeunesse dorée* that the
Right resorted to break the resistance of the moderates.

As of at least 25 Nivôse (January 14, 1795), their ex-
ploits increased in number. They now began attacking the
Jacobin cafés, but the "young men" also made an unexpected and curious attempt to win over the *sans-culottes* of
the suburbs; they sent them delegations to invite them to
fraternize and brought some of them over to their side by
giving them a dinner at Février's at the Palais Égalité. On
the twenty-ninth, the *Messager du soir* announced their
decision to clean up the galleries of the Convention and to
burn publicly, on 2 Pluviôse, a dummy representing a blood-
stained Jacobin, which in fact they did. On 30 Nivôse (January 19), Gaveaux, an artiste at the Théâtre Feydeau, had
sung at the William Tell Section his song, *Le Réveil du
peuple contre les terroristes,* for which Souriguères had
composed the music and which became, for some months,
the reactionaries' marching song—while the *Marseillaise,*
described as the song of the "drinkers of blood," was
banned. Then began the war of the theaters; during the first
days of Pluviôse, the reactionaries forced the Jacobin actors
—Fusil at the Théâtre de la République, Trial at the Opéra
—to make honorable amends; at every performance they
called for *Le Réveil du peuple,* a request which generally
started a general fight, the Jacobin pit replying with jeers
and revolutionary songs. Finally, on 12 Pluviôse (January
31), at Martainville's instigation, they started a hunt for
busts of Marat, beginning at the Salle Feydeau. The Com-

mittees had the busts replaced. On the fourteenth, they were knocked over again, and this time the disorder spread to the streets and the cafés. In the rue Montmartre, a bust was thrown into the gutter. As the *sans-culottes* protested, the fighting became more or less general. The Committees soon yielded, and on the twentieth (February 8), Dumont put a proposal, which was carried without opposition, that interment in the Panthéon and other similar honors should no longer be bestowed until ten years after the death of the person concerned. This measure was retroactively effective: on the twenty-first, the busts of the martyrs of the Revolution, and David's two pictures showing the death of Marat and that of Lepeletier, were removed from the hall of the Convention while the *jeunesse dorée*, massed in the galleries, sang *Le Réveil du peuple*. Not only Marat, but also Bara, Viala and General Dampierre, who had given their lives for their country, were taken out of the Panthéon. At the same time, the Club Lazovski in the Faubourg Marceau was closed, as was the Club des Quinze-Vingts in the Faubourg Antoine. An order was once again given for Babeuf to be arrested, and he evaded imprisonment only for a short time. As a sign of the times, the *Moniteur* had abandoned its usual neutrality for the first time on the seventeenth, publishing a violent article against Marat and reproducing the famous circular of September, 1792. In the Convention, the fear of a Jacobin rising had once again overcome all hesitation. On the twentieth, Mathieu had attacked, not the *jeunesse dorée*, but "the more dangerous activities" of the *sans-culottes* who were standing up to it. "A plot was on the point of being carried out," Bailleul declared on 29 Pluviôse (February 17), "whose object was nothing less than the killing of a hundred mem-

bers of this assembly and the restoration of the scaffolds
which you have destroyed."

The *jeunesse dorée* now considered itself so powerful
that by urging it to keep calm, Fréron abruptly lost his
popularity: it publicly burnt his paper and it was in vain
that he tried to rehabilitate himself by attacking the 1793
Constitution. On 2 Ventôse (February 20), the Royalist
Lacroix was acquitted by the revolutionary court, and the
Sections obtained a decree abolishing the symbolic "mountains" which had been set up almost everywhere. They
submitted more and more petitions demanding the punishment of the four accused deputies, the recall of the outlawed
Girondins, the disarming of the terrorists and their exclusion from public offices; on 14 Ventôse (March 4), the
Montreuil Section explicitly repudiated the thirty-first of
May, which a pamphlet by Isnard had just denounced.
Massacres had begun at Lyons and in the southeast, and
soon the call for killing spread to Paris. On 4 Ventôse,
Rovère, attributing to the terrorists a murder committed
in the Comtat, had exclaimed: "If you do not punish these
men, there is not a single Frenchman who is not entitled
to slit their throats." The next day, an address from the
popular society of Marseilles was read out:

> Representatives, the people of Marseilles have risen against
> the thieves, cutthroats and despots. . . . Order their arrest;
> order it for their own safety, for it is only a step from resist-
> ance to attack, and a step which is easily taken when bloody
> crimes have been committed and indignation is at its height.

In the past, the terrorists had represented exceptional repressive measures as a means of preventing a massacre of
the suspects: the Committees reasoned in the same way,
especially since, with the worsening of the economic crisis,

hardship was bringing the common people back to Jacobinism. On 10 Ventôse (February 28), Boissy d'Anglas reported that crowds were gathering again outside bakers' shops. "It isn't the young men that are to be seen there," declared Bourdon; "it's Robespierre's rabble, the men he used to hire."

As early as the fifth (February 23), Merlin de Douai had obtained a decision that throughout the Republic the civil and military officials who had been dismissed or suspended since the ninth of Thermidor should retire to the communes where they had been living before that date, and remain there under the supervision of the municipal authorities, under the pretext that it was they who were fostering the disturbances. This was the way in which the refractory priests had been removed from their residences in the past. Here it was a Law of Suspects in reverse, and in the south of France, at least, it marked them out for massacre. Immediately afterwards, Merlin de Thionville protested at the slowness of the commission of twenty-one; "Did Brutus delay so long before assassinating Caesar? Why should the French people whom you represent have any need of a court?" But the majority still wanted to act legally. On 12 Ventôse (March 2), Saladin finally presented the report, which concluded in favor of the indictment of Barère, Billaud, Collot and Vadier. This was agreed without discussion after Legendre had obtained a decree ordering their immediate arrest. Vadier, however, remained impossible to find. On the eighteenth, Chénier and Merlin de Douai proposed recalling the outlawed Girondins, and Sieyès, who had just come onto the Committee of Public Safety, made a long speech against the thirty-first of May. The names of La Revellière and Vitet, who

were said to have resigned, were added to those of the outlaws. There was no opposition; a few Montagnards abstained, but only Goujon voted against the proposal, thus
marking himself out for future reprisals. The next day, Dumont obtained the abolition of the holiday of the thirty-
first of May. In the elections of 15 Ventôse (March 5),
Carnot had finally left the Committee of Public Safety,
which Reubell joined at the same time as Sieyès. Nothing
remained but to decide the fate of the four accused; their
hearing began on 2 Germinal (March 22). With his usual
perspicacity, Mallet du Pan, in a letter of February 18, had
summed up the evolution which, since Brumaire, had gradually been pushing the majority towards a reactionary policy:

> The Convention has once again fallen completely under
> the control of public opinion. Its procedure is to use it
> without allowing it to oppose its progress. That is the secret
> of the advantage enjoyed by the moderates and the Federal-
> ists. Thus the Assembly's strength lies outside of itself.

It lay with the gangs of the *jeunesse dorée*, in whose power
the Convention found itself just as it had formerly been in
the power of the *sans-culotte* battalions.

In similar fashion, the economic system of the revolutionary government had been upset, as will be seen later.
On 1 Ventôse (February 19), the permanent status of the
districts had been revoked and the surveillance committees
suppressed in all towns of fewer than 5,000 inhabitants;
postal censorship had been abolished in principle on 19
Frimaire (December 9, 1794) and the secret postal agency
disappeared on 1 Germinal. The releases went on, some of
them of considerable interest, such as those of Kellermann
and Miranda in Nivôse, and of Servan in Pluviôse. The

67

same was true of the amnesty measures: all the decrees against the Lyonese had been revoked on 14 Pluviôse (February 2); and on 30 Ventôse (March 20), the execution of all revolutionary sentences passed after the law of 22 Prairial was suspended. Already, Thibaudeau and Fréron had proposed the repeal of the Law of Suspects, and Réal had started a campaign for the abolition of the revolutionary court. The 1793 constitution was also beginning to be called in question: Fréron had belled the cat in Pluviôse, and on 11 Ventôse (March 1), he revealed the device which would make possible its destruction, by demanding the preparation of certain organic laws which were supposedly intended to complete it. On the twenty-first, Reubell expressed indignation at the current talk of returning to the 1791 Constitution, in other words to the monarchy. By revealing its secret intentions, the Right alienated some of the most ardent supporters of the reaction: Thuriot, Bentabole and Lecointre. The last two protested at the reinstatement of the outlawed Girondins. Henceforth they were called Jacobins, and Legendre insultingly compared Thuriot to Billaud-Varenne.

The progress of the reaction was greatly assisted by the return of the émigrés. Up to Nivôse, it had remained dangerous for them to come back to France. But on the eighteenth (January 7, 1795), pleas began to be made in favor of the departments which had previously been invaded, those where the enemy's retreat, especially in Alsace and the Nord, had led to a large-scale exodus of people frightened by what they had heard of the Terror, compromised by their collaboration with the enemy or—having accepted official posts under a foreign government—knowing that they were outlawed. Then, on the twentieth, Bourdon asked for a distinction to be made, among the émigrés, between the counterrevolutionaries and those who had fled from tyranny. But how was such a distinction to be made? On 22 Nivôse (January 11), Merlin de Douai proposed and had adopted an arbitrary but simple and useful expedient: peasants and workers were authorized to return before 1 Germinal. In actual fact, a great many nobles and bourgeois managed to obtain certificates. At the same time, a large number of émigrés obtained from the purged authorities documents which falsely testified to their continued residence in France. Together with the absentees and deserters, whose numbers were constantly increasing, they joined in the persecution of the Jacobins, all the more fanatically in that they believed that the reactionaries, after their victory, could not fail to restore their estates to them. Already the Convention had made an indirect concession to them by the decree of 13 Ventôse (March 3) concerning émigrés and convicted persons: their chattels had been returned to their wives and children, and the decree of March 28, 1793, which had declared null and void the rights which third parties might establish to real estate, was annulled; on various grounds the relatives of the outlaws were able to recover a large part of their sequestered property, especially in Normandy.

The Thermidorians' policy towards the Vendeans and the Chouans likewise favored a counterrevolution. After Savenay, it might have been possible to disarm part of the rebels, who were exhausted and discouraged, by means of an amnesty, although by all appearances the peace would not have lasted, since it was incompatible with the outlawing of the non-juring priests, and even less compatible with the process of de-Christianization which Robespierre had been unable to halt. In any case, the opposite course to conciliation had been adopted; the representatives on mission and the generals undertook to turn the region into a desert, after ordering the patriots to evacuate it: Turreau's "infernal columns" seized corn and cattle, cut the hedges, burned the villages, and, all too often, manhandled or massacred the inhabitants. Despair, it is said, rallied 25,000 peasants to the armed bands of Charette in the Marais, of Sapinaud in the Bocage, and of Stofflet in the Mauges. The Committee of Public Safety ended up by attenuating these harsh measures; Turreau was relieved of his command, and proclamations offered a free pardon to rebels who laid down their arms, but by the ninth of the Thermidor the result achieved was nil. All the same, the rebel bands, separated from one another and harried by flying columns, were gradually diminishing in number.

Unfortunately for the Republic, it had been faced simultaneously with civil war to the north of the Loire, in Brittany, and in the wooded districts of Anjou, the Maine and Normandy, where the Vendean invasion had spread disorder and disorganized administration. As a matter of fact, there was never any mass rising in these regions which could have put the nation in peril: the Chouans could form only small bands which killed officials, purchasers of national property, and unarmed constitutional priests; robbed public treasuries; stopped stagecoaches; hampered the provisioning of the towns; and at the very most occupied some small unfortified town for a few days. The nucleus of the Chouan forces had been provided by some Vendeans who had escaped from the rout, and who had been joined by vagabonds, absentees and deserters. The leaders were for the most part nobles: Defay, de Geslin, de la Bourdon-

naye, Boishardy and Boisguy; but they also included a few
non-juring priests and a few commoners such as Coquereau,
alias Jean Chouan. The rebellion began in the Morbihan,
in Pluviôse, Year II; its effects were particularly serious
near Craon and Segré, but did not cause the Committee
of Public Safety much anxiety. Defay was captured and
shot, and some of the troops in the west were withdrawn to
go and fight on the frontiers. However, one Royalist, Joseph
de Puisaye—who had been a Constitutionalist at the beginning of the Revolution, had joined the Federalist movement in Normandy in 1793, and had thus been thrust into
the ranks of the Vendeans—had realized that the Chouan
rising could be turned to good account by putting it at the
service of the Coalition. Between May and August, 1794,
he tried to organize it, created a central council and another in the Morbihan, and divided Brittany into six com-
mands; he then gave the reins to Dezoteux, the so-called
Baron de Cormatin, and at the end of August went to England, where Pitt granted him a subsidy. He also undertook
to manufacture fake *assignats* and got the Comte d'Artois
to appoint him commander-in-chief of the royal Catholic
army. The Thermidorian Committees were soon fully informed, for the arrest of one of Puisaye's agents enabled
them to seize some revealing papers in Fructidor, at La
Cour-Porrée near Dinan. But there as elsewhere, the ninth
of Thermidor had done its work: the moderates, busy harry-
ing the Jacobins, allowed the military campaign and the
repression to grow sluggish. The Chouans were able to terrorize the peasants, starve the towns and cut communications.

After putting an end to the revolutionary government
and the Terror, the Thermidorians saw no other way of

pacifying the west than that of intensifying the policy of
conciliation, and they made it a point of honor to prove
that concessions restored peace. Once they had entered on
this course, they went a long way. To begin with, they
tried to separate the rebels from their leaders by offering a
free pardon to the former while maintaining a standing
order to shoot the latter. New generals were sent to the
west; chief among them was Hoche, who had just been
set free and who, in a proclamation issued on September
15, 1794, recalled that he too had suffered from the Terror
and that it had now come to an end. The representatives
interpreted their instructions in the broadest possible sense:
at Fontenay they released the Vendean prisoners; Boursault extended the amnesty to the absentees, gave a sympathetic reception to Le Deist de Botidoux, a former Girondin
who had gone over to the rebels, and announced in November that Boisguy was prepared to lay down his arms in
return for a promise that his life would be spared. Other
representatives, however, were less optimistic; the Vendeans and Chouans did not appear to have been won over,
and if anything the situation was deteriorating.

The Committees were accordingly urged to go further;
the offers made by the generals and the representatives, it
was said, did not inspire confidence; what was necessary
was for the Convention itself to brand a solemn amnesty
which should include the leaders of the rebellion. On the
basis of a report by Carnot, this was done on 12 Frimaire,
Year III (December 2, 1794) on condition that the rebels
lay down their arms within a month. It was pointed out in
vain that there was nothing to prevent the émigrés from
returning to take advantage of these concessions. Nonethe-

less, there had been no suggestion of negotiating with the Royalist leaders to offer them fresh advantages.

This third stage was reached without delay. In the Morbihan, Guezno and Guermeur restored freedom of worship, even for the non-juring clergy, on 24 Nivôse (January 13, 1795). Representatives and generals agreed to negotiations or even took the initiative. Boishardy made certain offers; de Brue and Béjarry came to Nantes and strolled about in public wearing white cockades; Cormatin went to see General Humbert and got into the Conventional Bollet's good graces by declaring that he had suspended hostilities in the Côtes-du-Nord; Bézard had recourse to the good offices of Madame Turpin de Crissé, Ruelle to those of Charette's sister. Encouraged by all this, the Chouans named their terms, without interrupting their activities: "Already four hundred patriots have been massacred," Génissieu wrote from the Sarthe on 15 Nivôse (January 4, 1795); "They are killing almost every night," Legot reported from Avranches on the twenty-sixth; "We are fighting like sheep against tigers," Boursault admitted on 4 Pluviôse (January 23); and six days later, the Chouans captured Guéméné. Nonetheless, four representatives had gone to Paris, and on 27 Nivôse (January 16), Ruelle had informed the Convention that the rebels had given a rapturous reception to the amnesty. On the twenty-third, a letter from Carnot had authorized a suspension of hostilities; Ruelle and his colleagues were authorized to enter into official negotiations, and from 24 to 29 Pluviôse (February 12-17) they held discussions with Charette and other Vendean leaders, in the presence of Cormatin, at the château of La Jaunaye, a few miles from Nantes. The agreement was ratified on the twenty-ninth by three decrees signed by the representatives. They granted an amnesty to all the rebels, returned their property to them or guaranteed an indemnity if it had been sold, even if they had emigrated, and promised financial assistance for the restoration of farm buildings. The Vendeans were dispensed from military service; they were to be enrolled as territorial guards paid by the Republic and were to keep their arms; the Royal bonds they had issued were to be redeemed up to the amount of two million livres; lastly, freedom of worship was granted, even to the non-juring clergy. Stofflet and a few others had seceded, but, practically surrounded, they treated in their turn on 13 Floréal (May 2). In the meantime negotiations had been held with the Chouans at the château of La Prévalaye, near Rennes; an agreement was concluded on the same terms on 1 Floréal (April 20). All in all, the Republic had capitulated; when the civil war began again, it was even alleged that the representatives had secretly promised the restoration of the monarchy. La Sicotière, the historian of Frotté, has shown that this allegation was unfounded.

The peace was an illusion. "We shall never surrender," Cormatin had written to Puisaye. The only result was that both Chouans and Vendeans were able to prepare in perfect security to resume hostilities; they became the undisputed masters of the west and even penetrated into fresh regions, the Calvados, the Eure and the Cotentin. In the Côtes-du-Nord, according to Palasne-Champeaux and Topsent, "as early as the end of Ventôse, the Chouans behaved like conquerors, not like culprits who had been pardoned." Bonaparte would deal with them in a different fashion. Of the Thermidorians' program he would retain the amnesty and freedom of worship, without which there could have been no agreement for a long time; but he would insist on absolute submission, would flood the region with troops, would shoot the leaders without pity, and above all would methodically disarm the peasants: from Laval, on 23 Ventôse (March 13), the Conventional Baudran had declared that this last measure was absolutely essential.

Of all these concessions, freedom of worship was the most important. As religious controversy was causing disturbances everywhere, there seemed to be no reason why the same remedy should not be adopted. It was a great innovation. Admittedly freedom of worship had been solemnly guaranteed on 16 Frimaire, Year II (December 6, 1793), and since the civil constitution of the clergy had been implicitly revoked by the decree of the second *jour sans-culottide* (September 18, 1794) which had suspended payment of the juring clergy, all Catholic priests had, in this respect, been reduced to the same condition. But many Thermidorians were as hostile to ecclesiastics, of whatever sort, as the *sans-culottes*, and therefore they had gone on treating them, until then, as they had before the ninth of Thermidor; constitutional priests had resigned in a great many places since that *journée*; those who had been arrested were released with the suspects, but several received the attentions of the police again when they tried to restore public worship. In the Haute-Garonne and the Tarn, Mallarmé had them placed under supervision in the chief town of each district, even if they had resigned, with the exception of those who had married (14 Vendémiaire, Year III [October 5, 1794]); in the Bas-Languedoc, Perrin had them arrested or sent fifty miles from their homes. Churches also continued to be closed, for example by Pelletier and Besson, on 30 Brumaire (November 20), in the

Doubs and the Haute-Saône, and by Calès in the Côte-d'Or, in Frimaire; the local authorities, even after being purged, did everything they could to prevent them from being opened again, and on 2 Nivôse (December 22), the district of Bernay forbade the celebration of the Mass. The Protestants and the Jews were not spared: the pastors of Montbéliard had to resign under the threat of arrest and the synagogue at Besançon was closed. As for the nonjuring priests, a certain number were guillotined. At the same time, observance of the tenth day of each decade was strictly enforced; the churches remained dedicated to the Supreme Being or even to Reason; the Committee of Public Instruction was asked to prepare a law on the civic religion, and in Nivôse Chénier presented some reports which, it is true, had no effect; the law of 27 Brumaire, Year III (November 17, 1794) did not forbid priests to be schoolteachers, but it maintained the exclusively secular character of education.

However, a good many French people who were loyal to the Revolution longed for the religious ceremonies of old, although the number of believers varied considerably between one region and another. The civic religion, thought up by bourgeois who had studied antiquity at school and frequented Masonic lodges, remained unintelligible to the common people, except perhaps as a symbol of that patriotic and democratic fervor of the *sans-culottes* which the Thermidorians were particularly eager to suppress. When they were told that the Terror was over, the faithful—especially the women—almost immediately made attempts to regain possession of the churches; in opposing these attempts the authorities provoked disturbances, and as the reaction became more marked, they tended to shut their eyes to what was happening. By the end of the year, the constitutional clergy had become active again; thus, in Nivôse, Grégoire's vicars-general restored public worship in Loir-et-Cher. On the first of that month (December 21), Grégoire himself made a brave speech demanding complete freedom of worship. Legendre replied contemptuously:

> I thought that we had gone far enough in the way of revolution not to bother our heads any more about religion. . . . I do not propose that we should fall in a body on the class of former priests. . . . But I cannot forget that it has always been the priests who have been the firmest pillars of the monarchy.

The Convention set aside Grégoire's motion in the midst of loud applause; all the same, his speech was widely published, and many pamphlets supported him, also heaping ridicule on the civic religion or questioning its utility. During the same period, there were reports that non-juring priests were reappearing everywhere and celebrating the Mass in secret: in the Nord, for example, they were known as "the portmanteau priests," because they carried the sacred vessels around with them. The frontier departments witnessed a great incursion of exiled priests and also of foreign ones, especially Belgians. On 18 Nivôse (January 7, 1795), Merlin de Douai classed the exiled priests with the émigrés, and obtained a decree calling on the authorities to prosecute them.

But when the negotiations with the Vendeans and the Chouans had resulted in agreement, the Committees had to change their attitude; it was clearly impossible to refuse to the rest of the French people what had been granted to the rebels. On 3 Ventôse (February 21) Boissy d'Anglas put forward a decree which was passed without discussion.

In his report he had maintained the principle of the sec-
ularity of the State—"religion has been banished from government, and it will not return"—and had shown a fine
contempt for the revealed religions. "I shall not consider
whether men need a religion," he had said; "if so, it has put
a high price on the consolations men have received from
it"; but "reason alone can triumph over error." He ended
up by condemning the scandals of de-Christianization,
and concluded that "religious practices are not offenses
against society"; moreover, clandestine worship was more
dangerous than public worship. The churches were retained
for decadal observance; religious worship in public was
merely authorized in buildings which the priests and the
faithful would have to obtain themselves, and they were forbidden to form associations, to receive either public grants
or private donations, to display any religious emblem outside, to ring bells or even to indicate by any inscription the
function of the building. In addition to the constitutional
clergy, those priests who, not being public servants, had
not had to take the oath of November 27, 1790, but had
agreed to that of August 14, 1792 (the "little oath" of al-
legiance to liberty and equality), were able to benefit by
this decree; the non-juring priests, who were still legally liable to the death-sentence, seemed to be excluded, except
in the west where they could invoke the terms of the peace
agreement.

Grégoire immediately gathered together the constitutional bishops, who on 25 Ventôse (March 15) published
an encyclical on the reorganization of public worship; a
little later, he issued the *Annales de la religion*; clergy all
over the country who had resigned applied for their certificates of priesthood, but those priests who had married were

not reinstated. Some of the constitutional clergy, incidentally, began making honorable amends in order to return to the Roman obedience. Those non-juring priests who, being infirm or over sixty, had not been deported, and those Roman priests who had taken the "little oath," turned the law to great account; two of them, the Abbé Jauffret and the Abbé Sicard, also published a periodical, the *Annales religieuses, politiques et littéraires*. In point of fact, the government did not derive much benefit from its concession; the non-juring clergy went on agitating and clandestine worship prospered more than ever, while the conflicts between Roman priests and constitutional priests waxed hot again. Worse yet, the faithful could not make head or tail of this freedom of worship which forbade them admittance to their churches and the use of bells and processions; in many places they regained possession of the former with the connivance of the municipal authorities and took no notice of the law. The reactionaries, the absentees and deserters, and the returned émigrés were therefore joined by the non-juring priests and also, probably, by some of the constitutional clergy. Mallet du Pan, at least, rallied them all under his banner. "In re-creating Catholics," he wrote on March 17, "the Convention is re-creating Royalists. Whosoever goes to Mass is an enemy of the Republic. There is not a single priest who does not represent loyalty to this regime as a matter of conscience to his flock."

In the course of the winter, the excitement caused by the progress of the counterrevolution once again went beyond the intentions of the Thermidorian majority. As early as Nivôse, in Lyons and the southeast, individual killings began. Then armed bands—the famous Companies of

Jesus, of Jehu and of the Sun—were organized to hunt the terrorists, and, under this name, soon included all those who had declared their support for the Revolution, and notably the purchasers of national property. Some representatives, for fear of the Jacobins and at the same time as they were having the latter disarmed, favored the formation of these bands, as did Cadroy and Chambon in Marseilles, and Isnard at Brignoles. It has been said that the bourgeois did not join these bands, although we are told at the same time that they brought together the relatives of victims of the Terror. In fact, while they seem to have been more mixed in character than they were in Paris, they were also partly recruited from the *jeunesse dorée*. However, in the southeast at least, their role was different: they had no need to exert pressure on the representatives on mission or on the municipal authorities, for obvious reasons; their task was to carry out the mass murder of the terrorists who were arrested. The first massacre took place in Lyons on 14 Pluviôse (February 2); twelve days later in the same city, Fernex, a member of the Popular Commission of Lyons, who had just been found, was likewise killed; and after that, almost every day saw the murder of one or more Jacobins, who were known as *Mathevons*, without regard to their sex. At Nîmes, on 5 Ventôse (February 23), four prisoners were put to death. The White Terror had begun. Harried without respite for the past six months by the representatives, the Jacobins were powerless to resist, except at Toulon, where the workers at the Arsenal formed an imposing mass and could count on the support of the crews of the fleet. When Mariette arrived at Toulon to carry out a fresh purge of the municipal authorities, a riot broke out on 20 Ventôse (March 10), and seven émigrés who had been arrested on landing at Hyères, whom the authorities were accused of intending to release like many others, were massacred in their turn. The position of the Jacobins throughout the region only worsened as a result. In Marseilles, Cadroy seized the opportunity to distribute arms to the Company of the Sun. The Convention had not taken any measures so far to pacify the south of France; all the same, it must be admitted that it would not have given free rein to the White Terror if a fresh crisis had not occurred to bind the majority closely to the Right. But the time had come when the monetary crisis and the scarcity of food were to provoke popular insurrections whose defeat would complete the downfall of the Jacobins.

CHAPTER SIX

The Abolition of the Maximum and the Monetary Disaster

It is the tragic struggle between the parties which, as always, has drawn the attention of most historians to the Thermidorian period. Its importance, however, is eclipsed by the collapse of the *assignat*. By reason of its economic consequences, whose political repercussions were extremely important; by reason of the effect it had on the conduct of the war and on the revolutionary foreign policy; and by reason of the blows it struck at the social structure of the France of old, the monetary disaster was the major event of the period, and it bore heavily on the history of the Directory.

The Thermidorians brought it on by abandoning the *maximum*. The Montagnards had ended up by accepting the latter, because in order to pay for the war they would have been reduced to runaway inflation if they had not been able to halt the rise in prices. To allow that rise to continue was therefore tantamount to ruining the currency. The Thermidorians were condemned to doing this from the moment when, instead of moderating and regularizing the Terror, they stigmatized it and deprived the revolutionary government of the coercive force which sanctioned its authority. A free economy, based on the profit motive and consequently on individual selfishness, can do nothing but let things be, and is in harmony with political freedom; price limitation, on the contrary, since it reduces profit, comes up against the producer's passive resistance and is ineffective unless it is accompanied by requisitioning, which, meeting the same obstacle, soon forces the State to take over control of the national economy. From then on, dictatorship, police supervision and intimidation become indispensable to the State if it is to exact obedience. It was therefore no accident that a free economy had been advocated in the eighteenth century at the same time as civil and political freedom; for the bourgeoisie, the latter was the necessary condition of the former, in other words of capitalist expansion. Dictatorship might, at a pinch, appear to it as a temporary expedient necessary for the maintenance of its own authority, but only on condition that such dictatorship respected economic freedom. The Thermidorians proved this by restoring the latter while turning the Terror against the democrats who advocated State control, and the social character of the reaction was thus revealed for all to see. Moreover, the resistance of the Montagnards, the Jacobins and the *sans-culottes* was perfunctory because they did not oppose the principle of individual property, as understood by western civilization, but on the contrary tried to generalize it; if they limited its application, either in the name of national defense or because of the obligation incumbent on a community to guarantee each citizen the right to life, the fact remains that any *sans-culotte* who possessed some property instinctively tended to shake off the controls which he thought fit to impose on others. On 3 Nivôse, Year III (December 23, 1794), the Montagnard Taillefer would say: "The abolition of the *maximum* has been demanded on all sides; the need for it is known to every citizen."

As far as the civilian population was concerned, the general *maximum* for basic foodstuffs, laid down on September 29, 1793, had never worked properly because the Committee of Public Safety, contenting itself with providing the population with bread, had given up the idea of feeding it by means of requisitioning, except in a few instances from which Paris benefited most of all. As it was impossible to violate the *maximum* publicly without risk, the shops emptied and clandestine trade developed; all the same, as long as the Terror lasted, this trade was held in check and prices rose only slowly: people complained most of all that they could not find anything for their money. After the ninth of Thermidor, the Convention remained silent for a long time; then, on 21 Fructidor (September 7, 1794), it decided to prolong the general *maximum*, like that for grain and fodder, for the duration of Year III. At that time, the *sans-culottes*, as the petitions from the popular societies show, still imagined that the system was going to continue to be improved, and asked in particular for a tax to be imposed on cattle in order to deprive the butchers of the excuse they used in their defense. But already, as fear died down, there was a perceptible rise in prices and clandestine trade started making rapid strides. In Paris, the efforts made by the police were all in vain and not without a certain danger for themselves. "The commercial aristocracy is boldly lifting up its head," said a report on 3 Vendémiaire, Year III (September 24). Speculation in foodstuffs was already in full swing in the taverns at the Marché des Innocents, and another report noted that "the water carriers and market workers do nothing else but engage in this traffic." For their part, the workers—especially the bakers, stevedores and carters—had demanded wage rises. As early as 20 Vendémiaire (October 11), the police resigned themselves to the inevitable: "In the markets, the *maximum* is no longer observed; everything is sold by private contract." The Convention, on 17 Frimaire (December 7), would be told: "It was abolished a long time ago." Back in the middle of September, people had been saying: "We are no better off than we were in Robespierre's day, because we can't find anything and the little there is is far too expensive." Now, on the threshold of winter, the police regarded the growing murmurs of discontent as positively alarming. The Committee of Public Safety continued its distributions of food through the medium of the Parisian Sections, but they were more inadequate than ever; there was a perpetual uproar at the wood and coal docks, and many people could not obtain candles. In the provinces it was worse, for there the authorities could provide nothing but bread.

For grain and fodder, the system in force dated from the decree of September 11, 1793, which had laid down a national *maximum*, fixed, in the case of corn, at fourteen livres a quintal. It had been observed fairly well, because the decree authorized requisitioning, not only for the armies, but also for the markets. However, the former had priority: the government demanded quotas from regions which it chose at discretion, and it was to the task of obtaining these quotas that its agents devoted most of their energies. For the civilian population, on the other hand, decentralization was almost complete. It was the responsibility of the district to order requisitions for each of its markets, and it could levy them only on the villages which were in the habit of sending provisions to the market in question; in the event of shortage, it had to ask the Committee of Public Safety to levy a requisition on another district, often a long way away, and then make arrangements to obtain the corn and transport it. With the market thus theoretically supplied, supervision of the sale of corn and bread was the exclusive responsibility of the municipality; if it received very little, as was the case in the greater part of the south, the Massif Central, and the mountain regions which did not produce enough to be self-sufficient, it suppressed the market, mixed grain of all sorts together, and divided it among the citizens; to those unable to bake their own bread, it gave ration cards and supplied the bakers with a corresponding amount of grain; finally, in some cases, as at Toulouse, it set up a communal bakery. During this time, in the heavily cultivated regions, the towns left complete freedom to the markets and bakeries and ate white bread. But after the end of summer, stocks had dwindled almost everywhere and the organization of the distribution system in the cities had made noticeable progress. As for Paris, the size of its population had earned it an exceptional system: the capital was granted special requisitions, and since November 1793 the use of ration cards had been the rule.

Up to the ninth of Thermidor, the military requisitions had been carried out more or less successfully, although with considerable difficulties and delays. The towns had been provisioned only on a day-to-day basis; the bread was bad and was regarded as expensive—three sous a pound in Paris, and often five in the provinces—but supplies had not often run out, although the workers did not consider themselves satisfied with less than two pounds a day. As for the peasants, requisitioning had been the symbol of the Terror for them, and very often the only manifestation of the Terror they had known, apart from de-Christianization. If they did not comply, the bailiffs were turned loose on them, and then they were arrested as suspects, beginning with the local councilors. As soon as the Terror had stopped, they plucked up courage, started selling secretly at home, displayed growing ill will, and even refused to thresh and deliver. In Vendémiaire, the Commission of Trade and Supplies reported these disturbing symptoms in a circular to all the districts, and on the twenty-fifth (October 16) the Committee of Public Safety published a decree recommending the application of legal sanctions. But the peasants had found some defenders. On 8 Fructidor (August 25), Eschassériaux criticized the obscurity of that very decree, its arbitrary nature, and the denunciations which its application implied: "A law on food supplies should be a regulation that is easy to follow, not a penal code." Since the general *maximum* and that of wages were no longer observed, various petitions pointed out that the peasants would no longer find it worth their while to sow corn. On

19 Brumaire (November 9), a few concessions were made to them: the failure to supply levies no longer entailed the confiscation of the required quota, and the municipal councilors alone remained liable to punishment, which in point of fact was equally illusory; the national *maximum* was replaced by a district *maximum* based on the 1790 price increased by two-thirds, the result having to be not less than sixteen livres a quintal; on the twenty-third, the cost of transport to the market or the warehouse was granted in addition, if the distance exceeded five miles. The result was that the resistance of the peasants increased; they sensed that the Convention was abandoning the system. The towns, on the other hand, finding their supplies dwindling, tightened up their regulations, which shows that those regulations had been adopted only under the pressure of circumstances.

Perhaps the Thermidorians would have left things there if the general *maximum*, violated among private individuals, had not continued to be applied to all the goods which the State required for the maintenance of the armies, the armament workshops and the administration; and if, again, in order to enforce the *maximum* and encourage production, the State had not enormously increased its economic powers to the detriment of private enterprise. It had created armament factories, notably one in Paris for the manufacture of muskets, which consisted incidentally of a large number of scattered workshops, and had itself organized the manufacture of saltpeter and gunpowder; next, it had thought fit to lay its hands on the transport system, had requisitioned the shops, the boats and barges of the inland waterways, and the wagons and cart-horses, and had taken over the postal service as well; it had even begun building boats and making carts. Admittedly the greater part of the economy had nonetheless remained in the hands of private firms, which continued to operate beside the national factories and transport services, but the State had deprived them of all freedom by requisitioning them, or by giving them contracts at prices which it fixed itself. The worst of it all was that the State had taken complete control of external trade. Under the *maximum* system, the merchants could import scarcely anything; the war had increased the number of bans on sending goods out of the country, and any export gave rise to a suspicion of smuggling; the exporter was also suspected of leaving abroad the money which was due to him. The Committee of Public Safety had arrogated to itself the right of pre-emption on all imports and the control of all exports; it had forced the bankers and merchants to surrender to it their foreign bills and credits; at the same time as it had sequestered the property of the belligerents, it had also compelled its own nationals to pay into its coffers the sums which they owed the latter. Nor was that all; the war and the English blockade had aroused a strong nationalist movement in France, which shipowners and merchants had perhaps viewed favorably at first: English goods had been seized and banned, a navigation act had forbidden foreign ships to bring in goods which did not come from their own country, and an embargo had been placed on neutral ships. Once foreign trade had been brought to a standstill in this way, the Committee of Public Safety had realized that a great many products were unobtainable and that it would have to be started up again. After the outlawing of the Hébertists, it had set about this task: for one thing, it had sent a good many agents to Switzerland, Genoa, Hamburg and Copenhagen, which had not joined the Coalition; it had also suspended the navigation act and restored normal facilities to neutral shipping. Again, in Ventôse and Germinal, it had set up in the ports committees composed of merchants, and instructed them to organize the export of wines and brandies and various luxury products, on condition that they surrender to the State the foreign credits they obtained. By the ninth of Thermidor, the results achieved were far from satisfactory. Fairly large purchases had been made, but the prices had had to be haggled over and paid in kind or in currency; as exports had remained insignificant and the requisitioned bills and credits had been exhausted, the Committee began selling abroad the jewels and articles of value found in the furniture repository or in the sequestered properties; in France, it was obliged to transfer its purchases at the price laid down by the *maximum,* in other words at a loss, so that inflation, although kept within limits, continued all the same: the *assignat,* which had returned to fifty per cent of its face value in December, 1793, had fallen back to thirty-one per cent in July, 1794.

In the Thermidorian Committee of Public Safety, Lindet, who had always had supreme control over the national economy, retained his place until 15 Vendémiaire, and after that he was continually called in for consultation; moreover, he joined the Committee of Trade, Agriculture and the Arts, and became its president. The Executive Commission of Trade and Supplies and the huge bureaucracy which depended on it continued their activities, as if nothing had changed, by virtue of the momentum they had acquired. The system therefore went on functioning more or less in the same way until the end of the year. In Vendémiaire, the requisitioning was still going on: the marcs of grapes and the lees of wine were placed at the disposal of the saltpeter manufacturers; an important decree laid down regulations for the use of offal for the manufacture of candles and oil; on the twenty-second (October 13), it was decided to extend the *maximum* to cover oil seeds; admittedly a considerable number of decisions altered the system of price limitation, but many of them had already been promulgated before the ninth of Thermidor. The manufacture of military supplies, particularly of saltpeter, continued into Brumaire; the government placed contracts, accepted tenders, encouraged the activities of the national factories it had set up; the workshops which the districts had been instructed to organize to provide the troops with clothing and equipment were still in full operation; the cobblers remained under contract to supply footwear and efforts were being made to fulfill an order for a million pairs of clogs. The nationalization of transport had not been abandoned, and fresh orders were being placed for the building of wagons and boats.

But the opponents of the system were at work, and they were many and powerful. The craftsmen and the factory owners, vexed to begin with at being placed under State control and paid at the rates laid down by the *maximum*, were even more irritated at seeing the national factories taking work away from them. What is more, Carnot had never been in favor of the latter and preferred private enterprise as being more economical: on 23 Frimaire, Year III (December 13, 1794), Boissy d'Anglas would declare that a bayonet made in the Paris workshops cost fifteen livres, whereas private tenderers offered it at five livres or five livres, ten sols, and in the provinces it could be made for four livres—which did not prevent the workers in the national workshops from demanding an increase in wages. The press grossly exaggerated the number of these workers: on 30 Nivôse, the *Vedette* stated that there were 45,000 of them; in fact there were 5,300, while the private tenderers employed 1,000. Certain facts show that at an early date the government decided to make some concessions in this respect: In Fructidor, the Toulouse foundry was handed over to private enterprise, and in Frimaire, the foundry at Maubeuge; on 5 Vendémiaire (September 26), the cannon foundry at Avignon had been closed down; on 11 Brumaire (November 1), the government even authorized private contracts for the manufacture of clogs, in violation of the *maximum*. Guyton de Morveau and Prieur de la Côte-d'Or succeeded in saving the Meudon factory, which had been violently attacked by Fréron, who suspected the Jacobins of being in control there and of preparing an insurrection, but the Paris workshops ended up by going to the wall. The agitation of the workers—stirred up, so it was said, by the Jacobins—was taken as an excuse; on 28 Brumaire (November 18), the board which controlled the workshops was suppressed, and on the thirtieth, the Convention appointed a commission of inquiry. As early as the twenty-third, the Commission of Arms and Powder agreed that only repairs should be done in Paris, and that since the provincial armament factories were short of work, it would be best to transfer the current orders to them: the Parisian workers could be dispersed among the provincial factories, a proposal which reveals the political motive which finally decided the government. On 16 Frimaire (December 6), the Committee of Public Safety ordained that as of 1 Pluviôse, the Republic would cease to employ workers on a daily basis, and during the following days it ordered as many as possible to be dismissed or sent into the provinces; a decree published on the twenty-third confirmed this ordinance in spite of the demonstrations against it; on 9 Pluviôse, only 1,146 workers were left on the State's payroll, and they were on piecework. In the provinces, as fast as the municipal authorities were purged, they abandoned all interest in the revolutionary enterprises, particularly the manufacture of saltpeter.

On this point, the system had been affected only partially and indirectly; on others, it was attacked openly and undisguisedly by those who, at that time, represented capitalism: the shipowners, the merchants and the financiers. It was they who suffered from the nationalization of external trade, above all of sea trade, which at that time was still the source of the great fortunes; the requisitioning of foreign exchange had put an end to profitable speculations on the *assignat* carried out from the start by the Parisian banks, which were dominated by foreigners, Swiss, Dutch and English financiers, on a fifty-fifty basis with Baring of London, Hope of Amsterdam and Parish of Hamburg. They now had friends in the government and spokesmen in the Convention. On 28 Fructidor (September 14), a speech was made there for the first time attacking the principles of Year II. Edme Petit asked for trade to be set free again, and Bourdon spoke against the unlimited extension of requisitioning. Cambon, whose family had made its fortune in business, spoke in support, even though he was a Montagnard, protesting at the persecution of which trade had been a victim; on 14 Brumaire (November 4), he would say, even more clearly: "It is impossible for the State to be in business." The Trade Commission, he added, should satisfy the needs of the republic, "but must not engage in trade on its own account"; in other words, it should confine itself to placing orders with merchants.

On the fourth *jour sans-culottide* (September 20), fuller details were given: in his major report on the state of the Republic, Lindet, forced to make some sacrifices, admitted that commercial relations with other countries had to be re-established; and the Convention ordered a decree to be prepared which should restore freedom to export luxury products, on condition that essential foodstuffs were imported in return. This decree makes it possible to guess at the argument which had won over the Committee. It was worried about the rise in food prices, and even more about the scarcity threatened by the harvest, which had been spoiled by the disturbances and by a cold, wet summer; it was told that the only solution was to buy from abroad. Victory offered it the means of doing this: the Republican armies were about to reach Holland, and coasting towards Hamburg, the corn market of the Baltic, would become easy again as a result; in November the royal administration of Prussia would offer its corn to France through the medium of a naval engineer on a mission to Hamburg. The government lacked the means to pay for these purchases, but not the merchants, who would obtain credit and contrive to take advantage of the huge capital which they and many other Frenchmen, whether émigrés or not, had transferred abroad. The advocate of the world of trade was probably Perregaux, a Swiss banker who, in spite of his dealings with the syndicate of international speculators, had managed to get the Committee of Year II to accept his services, and who now became the gray eminence of the Thermidorian Committee. He shone in the front rank of the council which a decree of 14 Vendémiaire, Year III

(October 5, 1794), signed by Eschassériaux, instituted to advise the Trade Commission. There were nine other members, most of them provincial merchants and manufacturers. This was setting the fox to keep the geese, and Lindet's proposal was no longer adequate. On 26 Vendémiaire (October 17), the manufacturers were given back the power to import freely, and anything they bought from abroad for the needs of their workshops was exempted from requisitioning; on 6 Frimaire (November 26), the import of food and unprohibited goods became completely free. But, as Cadroy and Expert pointed out from Marseilles, the result would be nil unless goods bought from abroad were exempted from the *maximum*. At the same time, the Committee of Public Safety officially confirmed the abolition of the navigation act and made it up with the neutrals; a decree of 25 Brumaire (November 15), signed by Lindet, ordered them to be respected at sea and opened up the French ports to them again, allowing them to do business by private contract. The only exception made was for contraband of war and enemy goods as long as the other belligerents refused to admit that the neutral flag covered the cargo; even so, it was added that neutral captains should be reimbursed for the freightage of enemy goods which were a lawful prize. Cadroy and Expert concluded that it was unreasonable not to allow the French to import at the same rates as foreigners.

It is a matter for surprise that the fixing of prices, which had brought nationalization in its train, had not been attacked more frequently in the Convention. On 30 Fructidor, Year II (September 16), Villiers had declared that its abolition was the key to any reform, while hastening to add that this was unthinkable; on 14 Brumaire, Year III (November 4), the Convention had asked for a report on "the disadvantages of the *maximum*," without any result but a modification of the *maximum* for grain and fodder. Thibaudeau boasts that he was the first to dare to go to the root of the evil, on 13 Frimaire (December 3), but nothing more was heard about it until 2 Nivôse (December 22), when the decisive debate finally opened. It was as if the opponents of the *maximum*, fearing, in spite of its degeneration, popular reaction and parliamentary opposition, had thought it best, by means of secret propaganda, to obtain the Assembly's unanimous consent beforehand, so as to confront the public suddenly with a *fait accompli*.

In the open, they preferred to attack the officials of the national economy and criticize their numbers, their mistakes and their misdeeds. Control of the economy was theoretically in the hands of the Executive Commission of Trade and Supplies, but other bodies were also concerned, such as the Transport Commission and the Commission of Arms and Powder. Each of these commissions controlled numerous agencies which, in their turn, were subdivided into bureaus. There were thousands of employees and the cost was enormous; in the agency concerned with the clothing, equipment and billeting of the troops, supervision of the workshops alone involved nearly 400 clerks, most of them heads of departments; the "management" of the armament works in Paris cost, by itself, 180,000 livres. In the provinces and also abroad, a host of agents checked accounts, supervised the enforcement of requisitioning, placed contracts, guarded warehouses. In point of fact, they themselves were subject to no supervision whatever; in Paris, nothing was known about their accounts, and in spite of a formidable mass of documents it was impossible to obtain a clear idea of requirements and resources. At a time when the concentration of enterprises was barely beginning and had hardly ever passed the commercial stage, this state of affairs is hard to understand, but it lent itself to criticism, and on this point Cambon's eloquence was inexhaustible; on 8 Brumaire (October 29), he had an order sent to the Trade Commission to produce details of its purchases and requisitions, and of the use of these: it was unable to comply.

There was also much criticism of the abuse of the unlimited requisitions which filled the producers' or the merchants' warehouses with goods which were never collected; it was said too that certain agents of the government trafficked in these goods for their own profit, and there were indeed recorded instances of this. Eschassériaux devoted much of his energy to putting an end to these abuses. On 19 Vendémiaire (October 10), he called on the commissions to draw up a list of their requirements for Year III, confining themselves to absolute essentials, and, finally, he secured the passing of the decree of 19 Brumaire (November 9), which not only nullified the sanctions applied to defaulters, but also forbade unlimited requisitioning and laid down the conditions and period of future operations. In the national warehouses too, piles of goods remained unused: from Marseilles, the representatives reported in Frimaire that 8,000 hides had been immobilized for seven months. The previous month, the Convention had sent representatives to the ports with instructions to inspect the warehouses and dispose of their contents; on 12 Frimaire (December 2), it restored freedom to the trade in the prizes brought in by the privateers. The results were not exactly impressive: in Germinal, for example, there remained at Le Havre 400,000 bottles of champagne, and crates of books, window-glass, batistes, lawns, laces and silks which had been accumulated there with a view to exporting them; and in Thermidor, it was reported that there were still 1,700 barrels of wine at Bordeaux, stocked there for the same purpose.

Now politics came into the matter. The members of the commissions and their agents had been chosen in the time of Robespierre and were slow to be purged. In Brumaire, Tallien denounced them at the tribune and in his paper as terrorists, and on 23 Frimaire (December 13), the Corn Market and Lepeletier Sections attacked them at the bar: "These commissions were created simply to serve the criminal purposes of our oppressors; they are composed only of their creatures and their followers." On the thirteenth (December 3), Garnier de Saintes, after sharply criticizing their administration, had secured the appointment of a commission consisting of one delegate from each of the Convention's committees, to prepare a complete overhaul of the executive; this was the Commission of Sixteen, which, as things turned out, achieved nothing.

Nobody, moreover, had so far proposed abolishing the system created by the men of Year II to obtain directly for the State the resources in kind which it needed; all that was suggested was that the government officials should confine themselves to provisioning the armies—a suggestion which was not absolutely novel, since the Robespierrist Committee, in decentralizing control of the grain intended for the civilian population and in refusing the latter the benefit of requisitioning in respect of other essential goods, had already given a clear indication of its desire to limit its economic activity to the State's requirements. But the financiers were looking further. Up to 1793, in order to provision the armies, the government had not confined itself to abstaining from requisitioning and price-fixing: as a general rule it had not made purchases itself. For want of financial resources it had been in the habit, for centuries past, of entrusting these services to companies which maintained them on credit, but which fleeced the Treasury while their agents swindled the troops. The "commissaries" had always been the kings of finance and built up huge fortunes. It was partly in order to do without them that the revolutionary government had accepted the *maximum* and the nationalization of the economy. And it was in order to re-establish their profitable monopoly that the commissaries lured members of the Convention into their salons and preached commercial liberty and the abolition of the commissions to them.

The combined efforts of the supporters of economic freedom finally won the day. On 19 Frimaire (December 9, 1794), Giraud submitted to the Committee of Trade, Agriculture and the Arts a report which concluded in favor of the abolition of the *maximum*. The decisive defeat of the men of Year II was underlined by the retirement of Lindet, who did not sign the minutes of the meeting and abandoned the presidency, which passed to Giraud; on 11 Nivôse (December 31), Lindet even resigned from the Committee. On 3 Nivôse (December 23, 1794), the report went to the Convention, where it gave rise to a mediocre debate. Giraud was aware of the danger involved: "We must not shut our eyes to it: we may well be horrified at the temporary upheaval which may be caused by the rapid rise in prices which will occur at first." Lecointre, who asked that a *maximum* be retained for grain, showed that he saw disturbances ahead. Pelet above all, without being a supporter of fixed prices, argued strongly against the hurried abolition of the *maximum*, asking how a million soldiers could be kept alive without it. This was tantamount to saying that, at least so far as its principle was concerned, the system of Year II should have been maintained until the end of hostilities. But not a single Montagnard stood up to say so; nor did anybody utter the decisive words: runaway inflation, the *assignat* rendered worthless, the Republic reduced to bankruptcy. Objections were answered with self-contradictory arguments of incredible frivolity or naïveté. Beffroy, one of the most ardent advocates of controls in 1793, said:

> Once the *maximum* has been abolished, you will be able to hand over to private enterprise the supplies for our armies and the transport involved. . . . Then your expenses will be enormously reduced and you will no longer be forced to increase the number of *assignats* in circulation at such a revolting rate.

Réal declared: "The people are wise and will not demand the impossible." And Cochon said: "We are sailing between two reefs: having nothing or paying dear; the latter is better than the former; it is best to choose the lesser of two evils." The Convention was eager to cut down its expenses and to reabsorb the paper money, but it is hard to believe that it deceived itself; the more or less distinterested conviction that freedom would restore prosperity at the same time as profits, in conformity with the dogmas of political economy, and above all hatred for everything that came from the Montagnards—"Abolish an abominable law!" Bréard had cried—persuaded it to throw itself into the abyss. The law of 4 Nivôse, Year III (December 24,

1794) abolished the *maximum* and all controls. The peasants, in particular, became free again to sell at home and to circulate their produce without permit. As a transitional measure, the government confined itself to maintaining the market requisitions for two months and insisting on delivery of those which were in the process of being levied for the armies and for Paris. Finally the Trade Commission retained the right of pre-emption for the armies, on condition that it pay at current rates and take possession within a month.

Many other measures were required in order to put the principle into practice, and, as could have been foreseen, it was external trade which benefited most of all. As early as 2 Nivôse, Johannot had presented the report which served as the basis of the law of the thirteenth (January 2, 1795): it restored complete economic freedom and promised to reduce customs duties to mere nominal levies sufficient to cover the cost of trade statistics, a promise which was fulfilled on 12 Pluviôse (January 31); at the same it raised the sequestration of the property belonging to the other belligerents, a measure which indicated its intention to resume trade with them through the medium of the neutral countries, and which was also extremely profitable for Thérèse Cabarrus' father; on 20 Germinal (April 9), the ban on English goods would be maintained, but those which the merchants had managed to release from sequestration were allowed to be sold, and in point of fact the neutrals would henceforth import them without let or hindrance. On 3 Pluviôse (January 22), the Committee of Public Safety had revoked the requisitioning of foreign bills and securities; on the twenty-third (February 11), it rescinded the decree of 23 Ventôse, Year II, which had permitted the merchants of the great trading centers to export a host of various goods and had exacted payment to the Treasury of securities to a corresponding amount; as early as 2 Nivôse, as was only right and proper, the group to which Perregaux belonged had been dissolved and paid off; on 3 Germinal (March 23), it was confirmed that the circulation of foreign bills was free.

Internal trade benefited to a lesser extent. True, on 29 Pluviôse (February 17), the Committee recalled that the *maximum* for transport had been abolished; on the fifth (January 24), it had tried to revive the coasting trade by a secret decree admitting the neutrals to it, and by authorizing French ships to cover themselves with a false neutrality; it also raised several requisitions such as those of the eighth pig, of cast metal, of the oats required for the provisioning of Paris, and of 110,000 barrels of wine for Guinea; it gradually sold off the contents of the warehouses, which were henceforth useless; the armament factories closed down little by little or were handed back to private enterprise; and on 11 Pluviôse (January 30), it had decided to enter into contracts for the *service des étapes,* in other words for the provisioning of troops on the march. But it could not think of everything: it was only 14 Thermidor (August 1), that it remembered to raise the requisitioning of shipping; and since the need was great, the authorities resorted more than once, not only to pre-emption, but also to requisitioning, to which carters, bargees and workers concerned with charcoal and timber-floating remained theoretically liable; in Ventôse, 141,000 quintals of grain were commandeered for the armies in the west, and in the same month they were authorized to requisition fodder. The peasants were forced to complete the quotas previously laid down for the armies; on 12 Pluviôse (January 31), the Supplies Commission received an order to fix new quotas for Paris and the armies, and the requisitioning of markets was prolonged from month to month until 1 Messidor. What is more, the agents of the Supplies Commission had been instructed to make purchases for Paris on 14 Nivôse (January 3, 1795), and for the armies on 18 Pluviôse (February 6); as they were armed with the right of pre-emption, they disturbed the free operation of trade.

Finally, on the point which the financiers regarded as the most important of all, the Convention had not capitulated. On 17 Nivôse (January 6), acting on a proposal made by the Committee of Trade, Agriculture and the Arts, it had abolished the Commission of Trade and Supplies, but had simultaneously re-established it, calling it the Supplies Commission, in order to make it clear that it was giving up economic government—or as Boissy d'Anglas put it, abandoning the attempt to turn France into "a corporation of monks." It stipulated that the functions of the new body, as stated in a decree of the Committee of Public Safety on 4 Ventôse (February 22), were "not so much to direct the trade of the Republic as to safeguard the supplies which it might require," in other words to keep the armies provisioned; it was to the same end that on 22 Nivôse (January 11), control of the customs was taken away from it and transferred to the Commission of National Revenue. As a result the number of its agencies was reduced from eight to three. But one of these was specifically entrusted with purchases, which meant that the Convention did not intend to follow Beffroy's advice and hand over to the commissaries the responsibility for supplying the armies.

Meanwhile the Trade Council remained in existence;

it was abolished on 4 Ventôse (February 22) only to be re-established under the name of the Trade Bureau, now attached to the Committee of Public Safety and increased to fifteen members, one of whom was naturally Perregaux. The new commission was soon as discredited as its predecessor. It agents were held responsible for the rise in prices; and not without reason, since they paid any price to carry out their orders and competed with one another. On 6 Ventôse (February 24), in answer to complaints from Garnier de Saintes, Cambon put through a decree ordering that they all be recalled and forbidding the Commission to send any more out. But how was it possible to dispense with them? On the contrary: now that it was easy for them to leave the service in abeyance on the pretext that they could not find any sellers, the government had to give them a financial interest in their purchases by restoring their commission which Bouchotte had abolished; on 23 Ventôse (March 13), they received six sous for each quintal of grain, retroactively effective from January 1, 1793; the cost of the service increased by this amount. At the same time, on the pretext of pressing need, they bought without orders, thus exposing themselves to the suspicion of speculating for their own benefit, while representatives and war commissioners also placed contracts: in Messidor, the Committee of Public Safety quashed Beffroy's contracts for the armies of the Alps and Italy, and canceled the permits the representatives had granted to the war commissioners of the armies of the North and the Sambre and Meuse. However, it seems that, as under the *ancien régime*, it was the poverty of the Treasury which forced the government to give in: on 6 Ventôse (February 24), the Supplies Commission was authorized to accept tenders for the transport of fodder for the armies, and on the same day it placed a contract for the supply of the horses and mules needed for military transport, with a company directed by Lanchère, a well-known old commissary who, among other associates, had taken on Cerf Berr, a Strasbourg Jew who enjoyed a similar notoriety; on the third, a decree had forbidden the Transport Commission to make any purchases. This represented an initial success for the financiers, but nearly a whole year was to go by before the contractors had won the game and could pillage the Republic, so great was the reluctance of the Thermidorians themselves to abandon it to them.

However, the disaster was already obvious. On 8 Nivôse (December 28, 1794), a proclamation issued by the Convention had told the French people that the abolition of the *maximum* would be a source of blessings. "I should like it," Bentabole had nonetheless remarked timdly, "to contain a request to tradesmen not to take advantage of this law to crush the poor." As might have been expected, it took only a few days to reveal that prices were rising by leaps and bounds. In Paris, a pound of butter cost three livres at the end of Nivôse; two months later, it had doubled in price. Meat did not cost more than forty sous on 1 Pluviôse (January 20); it cost seven livres, twenty sous on 12 Germinal (April 1). Horrified, the Committee of Public Safety could not think of anything better to do than institute an inquiry into prices, on 20 Pluviôse (February 8)—which constitutes a valuable source of information but nothing more—and re-open the Stock Exchange on 13 Ventôse (March 3), under the pretext of cleaning up the market by making clandestine dealings useless. Speculation in essential foodstuffs increased to a fantastic extent, and Tallien, who needed a great deal of money, is said to have speculated in soap and candles, and also probably in *assignats* and currency. The depreciation of paper money was greater than ever in relation to metallic currency, although dealings in the latter were still forbidden, and above all in relation to the rate of exchange since international trade had been resumed. In frontier regions like the Haut-Rhin, close to Basle and Mülhausen, it was particularly debased. On an average, the violation of the *maximum* had made paper money lose a third of its value from July to December, 1794: it had fallen from thirty-one to twenty per cent. At the beginning of Germinal, it was worth only eight per cent at the most. The rise in prices was out of proportion with the increase in paper money, because the producers were unwilling to sell except in return for metallic currency, and were counting on an indefinite rise in prices and on bankruptcy.

The rise in prices did in fact condemn the Republic to inflation, all the more so in that the taxation system was working badly. In Year II, the French people had not paid many taxes, the *patente* had been abolished in 1793 and the land tax for 1794 was fixed only at the end of the year by the Thermidorians; moreover, the latter also abolished the personal tax; arrears would come in only slowly, and in the form of worthless *assignats*. There was a lot of talk about economizing, and it was partly in order to save money that the manufacture of arms was stopped and the number of government officials reduced. But the rise in food prices made it necessary to increase wages in the course of Nivôse and Pluviôse, and the members of the Convention themselves raised their daily emolument from eighteen to thirty-six livres on 25 Nivôse (January 14), effective retroactively from 1 Vendémiaire, a measure which created a scandal. Already there was no lack of people who could see no solution but the demonetization of the *assignat:* it would not be used except for paying taxes or buying national property, and the country would go back to using metallic currency. They forgot to add that this would produce a deflationary crisis, that it would hinder the revival of trade, the natural consequence, so it was said, of the return to economic freedom, and that as a result it would reduce even further the revenue from taxation. Moreover, how was the war to be financed, since it was obviously impossible to raise any loans? Demonetization was the ardent wish of the speculators, who hoped by monopolizing the *assignats* to lay their hands on what national property there remained, and of the enemies of the Revolution, who were counting on it to complete the discredit of the Convention in the eyes of the public. Cambon, the Montagnards and the Thermidorians who had remained Republicans therefore repudiated it, so that it became the bone of contention between the parties, and could not triumph until the Left had been finally crushed. In Pluviôse, there was talk of trying a loan in the form of a lottery, life annuities and tontines, or even of resorting to a complusory loan. But in his reports of 3 Pluviôse (January 22) and 7 Ventôse (February 25), Cambon laid particular emphasis on the rapid sale of national property and on the speeding-up of payment for it. In Ventôse, it was decided in fact that the purchaser should henceforth pay a quarter of the price within a month and the rest in six years, with the right to a bonus if he discharged his debt before 1 Vendémiaire; previous purchasers were granted the same favor, and measures were taken to speed up the sale of chattels. But the mass of *assignats* which it was hoped to reduce by these measures was increased during this time by continued issues. At the end of 1794, the total number of *assignats* was less than ten billion, of which eight billion are admitted to have been in circulation; between Pluviôse and Prairial, in four months, seven billion were printed and it is believed that the number in circulation rose to 11.5 billion. There was no remedy for the disease.

Everybody therefore tried to get rid of his paper money, and the flight from the *assignat* lowered its value to a far greater extent than the increase in circulation. From November 1794 to May 1795, the latter rose by 42.5 per cent, while the Treasury tables, based on the value of the precious metals, registered a drop in the value of 100 livres in paper money from 24 to 7.5 livres, in other words of sixty-eight per cent; at Basle, the exchange rate varied between twenty-seven and twenty-five livres in November and between nine and seven in May, which shows a more or less comparable fall. The *assignat* was so unpopular that in a department such as the Haut-Rhin it stopped being accepted immediately after the abolition of the *maximum*.

It should be noted, however, that in order to understand the effect of the depreciation on living conditions, it is by the price of foodstuffs and goods that it must be measured, rather than by the value of precious metals and foreign bills. When, in Year V, a depreciation table was drawn up in each department, it seems indeed that it was usually prices which were taken as a basis. It emerges from these figures that, on an average, 100 livres in paper money were worth thirty-two livres in November and eleven livres in May, which represents a fall of sixty-four per cent; it varied a great deal between one department and another,.

and the variation has been estimated at 110 per cent. But this rectification made by the local tables is in fact deceptive in that they have taken into account the market value of property, which had increased much less than the price of food. Mr. Harris, in his study *The Assignats,* estimates that the property index in March–April, 1795, had not risen above 439 in comparison with 1790, whereas the index of the prices noted in the Committee of Public Safety's inquiry stood at 758, and for foodstuffs alone at 819; at that date, the *assignat* index, on the basis of seventeen livres of metallic currency for 100 livres of paper money, stood at 581. Consequently the rise in the prices of basic essentials was far greater than the monetary depreciation would suggest, and from the social point of view, that is what matters.

The rise in prices was accompanied by a growing scarcity of food, because the peasant was reluctant to part with his grain. Yet it was he who had benefited least of all from the law of 4 Nivôse; as usual, he had been sacrificed to the towndwellers; up till 1 Messidor (June 19), he was subjected to market requisitioning; as far as Paris was concerned, twenty-five districts, at the beginning of Nivôse, owed a balance of 281,000 quintals out of the quota called for in Thermidor, Year II; thirteen others had to supply 87,000 quintals every ten days from 1 Nivôse; on the seventh (December 27, 1794), another thirteen districts were called upon to supply over 1,500,000 quintals up till 1 Messidor. In the provinces, all the district authorities lost no time in making similar demands for the benefit of their own markets. But as the peasants were now permitted to sell at home, they were slow to obey, and emptied their granaries either for the agents of the Supplies Commission who bought for the armies, or for the dealers who supplied the well-to-do. As early as 3 Pluviôse (January 22, 1795), the Convention authorized the arrest of recalcitrant peasants, but only on the authority of the representatives on mission, and subject to the allowances which the latter might grant—so that this decree came to nothing. The districts took it upon themselves to send National Guards to install themselves in the villages as bailiffs, in order to extract the indispensable grain from the peasants, and throughout the winter the latter were subject to military distraint. At the beginning of spring, it had to be admitted, even in the most fertile regions, that no further results could be obtained: the harvest had been too poor, and, since the peasants had succeeded in surreptitiously getting rid of their available stocks, they were left with just enough to live on until harvest time. At the beginning of Germinal, 700,000 quintals of the quota promised for the capital were missing; Versailles was no longer receiving any supplies from the Eure; in the district of Bergues, not a single grain came from the country after the end of Ventôse: the local authorities recalled the troops on 10 Germinal (March 30), and the markets of towns like Bergues and Bourbourg, which had always been well stocked in Year II, were henceforth completely deserted. The situation was almost the same at Orléans, at the gateway to the Beauce. As for the south of France, which in normal times was always short of food, its situation had been disastrous as early as the beginning of the winter.

While trying to share resources equitably among the various regions of France, the Committee of Year II had been obliged to buy outside: this represented the Thermidorians' last hope. Their first thought was for the south of

France. As early as 20 Brumaire (November 10, 1794), an agent had been sent to Montpellier to organize, either through trade channels or on the State's account, the export of wine to Genoa in return for grain; on 18 Frimaire (December 8), Toulouse was authorized to export 600,000 livres' worth of goods, and was given an advance to that amount with which to buy an equivalent return in the form of grain; on the twenty-sixth (December 16), Bayonne obtained six million livres for direct purchases; on 11 Nivôse (December 31), Cadroy and Expert were granted six million livres for advances to merchants willing to export, on condition that they imported corn in return, and Cadroy, having failed to obtain their help, set up a supply bureau which, in Ventôse, had already received thirty-five million livres from Paris and was consequently entrusted with the task of supplying the southern departments. The department of the Hérault created a similar body and requisitioned the brandies of the region for its benefit—a measure which, incidentally, it was hurriedly ordered to revoke. After the law of 4 Nivôse, the Committee of Public Safety showed a readiness to generalize the system in order to encourage purchases, without undertaking these itself: on 16 Pluviôse (February 4, 1795), it authorized the Supplies Commission to grant advances to districts which applied for them; in point of fact, the poverty of the Treasury obliged it to refuse these advances, and finally, on 30 Germinal (April 19), a decree decentralized purchases completely, making them the exclusive responsibility of the municipal authorities, which had to raise the necessary funds by freely subscribed loans.

These circumstances helped effectively to re-establish the preponderance of the upper middle class, for it alone was capable of providing the essential funds, especially as these had to be in metallic currency. A golden opportunity was also provided for those members of the upper middle class who, having emigrated, had settled abroad; their help had to be invoked to open credit accounts; the Protestant bourgeoisie thus served as a link between Nîmes and Genoa. But for Paris as for the armies, the State had to resign itself to making purchases itself by sending agents abroad and by making contracts either with French merchants such as Cerf Zacharias, who on 30 Pluviôse (February 18) undertook the feeding of the armies of the Rhine and the Moselle, or with the exporters of Amsterdam, Hamburg and Copenhagen. It also reserved Belgium for itself, and on 18 Floréal (May 7) banned all exports to that country without its permission. But consignments of grain only began arriving in large quantities after Floréal, especially in the north, where the main contracts dated from Prairial. The neutrals and particularly the Americans offered their cargoes spontaneously; in Ventôse, twenty ships docked at Bordeaux; others brought nearly 50,000 quintals to Le Havre in Germinal. In short, the purchases made abroad served essentially to help the country to get through the summer.

There was considerable suffering. At the time of the *maximum*, the French people had had cause to complain of the scarcity of foodstuffs; now they had to endure a serious shortage and even famine, and were faced at the same time with high prices. At Nantes, Madame Hummel, a draper's wife whose account book has been analyzed by M. Gaston Martin, had bought regularly from the baker until Pluviôse: from then on she received no more bread, and had to strain her ingenuity from day to day to find some flour which she had kneaded and baked; she was even reduced to eating biscuits. The plight of the poorer classes is easy to imagine. At Amiens, at the beginning of Germinal, the bread ration had not been more than three quarters of a pound for three months; since the summer of Year II, the municipality of Verdun had given only one pound to the workers and three quarters of a pound to others: at the end of Ventôse, Year III, it reduced this ration by half. At Toulouse, the price of bread had suddenly risen from five sous to eleven, immediately after the law of 4 Nivôse; the same thing happened at Verdun, where it rose at the end of Ventôse to twenty sous. The result was that in the towns controls became increasingly strict; the last municipalities which had succeeded in avoiding them were nearly all obliged to comply with them; Dunkirk, for example, finally resigned itself, on 7 Ventôse (February 25), to the mixing of grains and the distribution of ration cards.

The most unfortunate of all were the day laborers in the country: the towns had stopped giving them anything since their markets had disappeared, the rural municipalities rarely helped them, and they had to go from farm to farm begging the farmers to sell them food at an exorbitant price in order to keep their families alive. In the towns, at least, the authorities usually sold bread below cost price, for fear of riots. Gradually crowds began to gather again in the country, to prevent the departure of the grain or to loot the convoys.

The capital, which was supplied by the government, was in a privileged position. It was provided, not only with bread, but also with meat, wood, coal, candles and soap, at prices which had increased by a third on 22 Nivôse

(January 11), but which remained far below those current elsewhere. Consequently a great many people made for Paris to take advantage of this situation, and soon a housing crisis was added to the prevailing poverty. Even fraud was not uncommon. On 15 Pluviôse (February 3), the Committee of Public Safety had ordered a census and a complete change of ration cards: by the end of Germinal the operation had not been completed. For most foodstuffs, distributions were small and irregular, and taking into account this deficiency which obliged people to buy at current prices, Mr. Harris has calculated that the cost-of-living index must have risen in Paris from 580 in January to 900 in April. At least there was bread until the end of Ventôse, although queues at the bakers had formed again several times at the end of Nivôse and about 10 Ventôse. As early as Pluviôse, transport had ceased to be reliable. At Luzarches, Corbeil, and Soissons, mobs threatened grain deliveries on their way to the capital, and representatives had to be sent on special missions to safeguard them. Finally, on 24 Ventôse (March 14), the supply of bread failed completely, and the following day a decree reduced the ration to one pound, except for manual workers who were allowed a pound and a half. But on the twenty-ninth (March 19), the Committee of Public Safety wrote to the representatives that it had only 2,390 sacks left, from which 1,900 were being deducted for that day: "You will understand that we may well go without bread one day, but that we shall no longer have any control over the consequences. Think and act." On 3 Germinal (March 23), it requisitioned one fifth of all the grain and dried vegetables in the departments set apart for the provisioning of Paris and the armies, then, on the fourth, everything over and above the local consumption for two months within a radius of fifty miles. On the fifth, there were only 115 sacks left in stock; on the seventh, it gave instructions for the ration to be made up at the rate of three ounces of biscuits or six ounces of rice for half a pound of bread; but there was no longer any wood or coal over which to boil the rice.

The common people had made no attempt to save the Montagnards and the Jacobins from being outlawed. Now, exasperated by hardship, they stirred once more.

CHAPTER SEVEN

The Journées *of Germinal and Prairial; the White Terror*

It was customary for the people of Paris, especially since 1789, to display their anger every time there was a shortage of bread—unless the government inspired their respect, which was certainly not the case in 1795. On 27 Ventôse (March 17), delegates from the Faubourg Marceau and the Faubourg Jacques appeared before the Convention and declared: "We have no bread. We are on the verge of regretting all the sacrifices we have made for the Revolution." Greeted with an uproar, they retired shouting: "Bread! Bread!" and rejoined the crowd surrounding the Tuileries. On 1 Germinal (March 21), it was the turn of the Faubourg Antoine. On the seventh (March 27), several Sections held illegal meetings and rioting broke out at the Gravilliers; on the tenth, the section meetings were stormy, and on the eleventh, the Faubourgs once again appeared at the bar. The *journée* of the twelfth of Germinal only put the finishing touch to this gradual mobilization of the masses.

If these disturbances took a threatening turn, it was because the shortage of food coincided with a political crisis, as had happened several times since 1788. The Constitution of 1793 was in serious danger. The Commission of Sixteen set up on 31 Frimaire, after giving its attention to the so-called organic laws, had declared on 25 Ventôse (March 15) that it was abandoning the task, and on 10 Germinal it was decided to entrust it to another commission: as Ballieul and Thibaudeau had openly attacked the Montagnard constitution, the decree seemed ominous. Then again, on 2 Germinal discussion had begun of the indictment of the "Four"—Barère, Billaud, Collot and Vadier. Their former colleagues defended them courageously, especially Lindet and Carnot, who recalled the Convention to a sense of its own dignity by pointing out that it had approved the Committees of Year II: "On all occasions you did what you had to do; you could not have followed a different course without shattering the foundations of the democratic system to which you had sworn loyalty." And all of a sudden, on the eighth, Merlin de Thionville proposed that the trial should be referred to the future legislative body, the election of which was to begin on 10 Floréal (April 29): this was putting into effect that Constitution of 1793 which the reactionaries wanted to have done with, and, to explain this step, it must be assumed that Merlin no longer had any hope of obtaining the indictment of the Four, while in the existing situation in France he was convinced that the elections would insure victory for the Right. But the Committees secured the rejection of the motion and it was agreed to continue with the hearing of the accused. In the meantime, another great trial, that of Fouquier-Tinville, had opened on the eighth, before the revolutionary court.

In spite of the Thermidorians' accusations, there is no reason to believe that the Montagnards fomented a *journée* in order to save the terrorists; as for the members of the Sections, they did not mention the names of the accused, either because their leaders had no sympathy for them, or more probably because the people were not interested in deciding between the warring deputies. But it was a different matter for the Constitution, which was the symbol of democracy; its application had been an essential item of the program of the Hébertists, whom the *sans-culottes* had always regarded as their spokesmen; on the tenth, the Indivisibility Section called for it, and on the eleventh, the Quinze-Vingts demanded an elected municipality. It was on this point that the members of the Sections and the Montagnards may have come together; Léonard Bourdon is said to have stirred up the people at the Gravilliers; Vanheck, who acted as spokesman on 12 Germinal, was the agent of Dobsen, Thuriot's friend. We know little or nothing about the activity of the popular agitators, and it is impossible to state with any certainty that they combined together to stir up the Sections.

The Thermidorians were so sure that a *journée* was going to take place that Dyzès and Choudieu have accused them of having provoked it. The leaders of the *jeunesse dorée* had called on it to go into action once more. On 27 Ventôse, its bands, "in file and four abreast," tried to break up gatherings in the streets; they obtained control of several Sections which, on the eleventh and in the morning of the twelfth, came and harangued the Convention. For their part, the Committees tried to organize resistance. On 1 Germinal (March 21), Sieyès had a police law passed which laid down the death penalty for those who came to the Convention in a concerted movement and uttered seditious cries; arrangements were made for the National Guards of the Sections to be called in, and even the armies, in the event of the "oppressed" national assembly having to move to Châlons. But it would have been preferable to have troops near at hand; the Committees had only some National Guards from the prosperous districts of Paris at their disposal and were taken by surprise before they were called up. According to Duval, the *jeunesse dorée* was summoned, on the eleventh, to assemble the following morning in the courtyard of the Louvre, whence Tallien and Dumont led it to the Tuileries.

On 12 Germinal (April 1), the session of the Convention was interrupted by a crowd which invaded the chamber with cries of "Bread! Bread!" and created a prolonged uproar. Vanheck, at the head of the Cité Section, imposed silence and demanded the application of the Constitution of 1793, measures to deal with the shortage of food, and the release of the imprisoned patriots. The demonstrators finally allowed themselves to be persuaded, by the Montagnards themselves, to march past the bar and evacuate the chamber. In point of fact, it is impossible to talk of an insurrection organized by the Sections; two of them, indeed, in respectful addresses, expressed themselves to the same effect as the Thermidorians. It is therefore obvious that the movement had no leaders worthy of the name, and that the agitators, launching forth into speeches, had been unable to reconstruct the bands which in the past had insured the success of the *journées*. The demonstrators were unarmed; they had repulsed the *jeunesse dorée* easily, but when the National Guards of the western Sections, led by Merlin de Thionville, appeared, they withdrew without offering any resistance. However, the city was seriously disturbed; the Panthéon and Cité Sections declared themselves in permanent session; when Auguis and Pénières went to their headquarters, the former was arrested and wounded and a shot was fired at the latter. On the thirteenth, the agitation continued at the Quinze-Vingts. In the preceding night, the Convention had placed Paris under martial law and given command of the city to Pichegru, who happened to be there at the time, detailing Merlin de Thionville and Barras to assist him.

This pitiful scuffle immediately gave the Right the upper hand. The "Four" were finished with on the spot, during the night of the twelfth: in violation of the law of 12 Brumaire, they were deported without trial to Guiana and were promptly sent off on their way to the Île d'Oléron, with the exception of Vadier who had still not been arrested. Then it was decided to decimate the Left: eight of its members, including Amar, Duhem, and Choudieu, were arrested and sent to Ham. On the fourteenth, Cambon was expelled from the Finance Committee, and on the sixteenth a warrant was issued for his arrest (he managed to escape to Lausanne) and that of eight others, including not only Levasseur and Maignet, but also two leading Thermidorians, Lecointre and Thuriot, who had recently defended the thirty-first of May. Then, on 21 Germinal (April 10), a decree which the reactionaries had been demanding for a long time ordered the terrorists to be disarmed throughout the Republic—a new Law of Suspects which gave an extraordinary extension to that of 5 Ventôse. On 17 Floréal (May 6), the trial of Fouquier-Tinville came to an end, and he was executed the following day with Herman and fourteen jurors of the former revolutionary court. That same day, Lebon was brought before a commission of twenty-one. Denunciations of the former representatives on mission began again. "The assembly is in honor bound," declared Durand-Maillane, "to have these complaints examined."

The Right also succeeded in getting the condemnation of the thirty-first of May followed through to its logical conclusion. On 22 Germinal (April 11) those citizens who had been outlawed after that *journée* were quite simply reinstated in their civic rights, even Précy, the Royalist leader of the Lyons insurrection; the decree of March 27, 1793, which had outlawed the enemies of the Republic, was similarly revoked; those outlaws who, having gone into hiding, had been placed on the list of émigrés were to have their names struck off that list without further ado. It was obvious that a host of émigrés who had never had anything in common with the Girondins would thus be able to return freely to France. The Convention also considered the question of the restitution of the property of convicted persons; on 1 Floréal (April 20), it authorized all those who asserted joint rights on the property of émigrés, notably their wives and children, to recover their share; their parents were given permission to divide their property in anticipated succession and to buy back that part of their inheritance which reverted to the State at the estimated price, unless a third party bid at least a quarter more. The Republic even granted them a preference legacy of twenty thousand livres and abandoned all claims upon any inheritance which did not exceed that value. Finally, it renounced, for the future, all inheritances which might fall open in favor of the émigrés.

The constitutional question was meanwhile becoming more urgent every day. On 27 Germinal (April 16), the departmental authorities recovered the powers of which the law of 14 Frimaire had deprived them and the attorney-general-syndics were reinstated. Two days later, Cambacérès finally produced the Committees' report on the drawing-up of the organic laws, and in place of the commission of seven set up on 10 Germinal, had a commission of eleven appointed to this end. So far the validity of the Constitution of 1793 had not been disputed; Sieyès himself, dismissing the Convention's vote as worthless, had declared that he bowed to the plebiscite. It was a different matter now: on 25 Floréal (May 14) the Republic Section denounced "the decemviral Constitution, dictated by fear and accepted under the influence of fear"; in the midst of an uproar, Larivière expressed formal approval. On the eleventh (April 30), Lanjuinais had declared that the institution of two chambers was indispensable.

Meanwhile, barely a month after the twelfth of Germinal, the Thermidorians of the Center were beginning to grow alarmed at the progress made by the reaction.. Reports were coming in from all sides that the émigrés and the non-juring clergy were returning in large numbers; in Floréal, the massacres at Lyons and Aix upset them. On the twelfth (May 1), Chénier, on behalf of the Committees, had a decree passed that émigrés and non-juring priests would be prosecuted if they did not leave France again before the end of the month, as would those who incited the restoration of the monarchy, a clause chiefly aimed at the journalists; a penalty of six months' imprisonment was laid down for anyone who offended against the law on religious worship, after a violent attack by La Revellière on clerical plots. On the sixth (April 25), the Convention had already decided to give a decision itself on the striking off of émigrés, and on the twenty-sixth (May 15), the return of the inhabitants of Toulon, taken away in 1793 by the English and the Spaniards, was bitterly denounced. But there was lively resistance. Tallien defended the freedom of the Press, inveighing against Chénier whom he blamed for his brother's death, and opposed any fresh interference in the religious question; Thibaudeau even suggested that it was advisable to hand back the churches. On the other hand, the Committees went on protecting by their inertia the representatives who had been denounced. The gap between the Center and the Right had therefore opened up again. A complete split might have occurred before long if the Republican Thermidorians had been able to persuade themselves that order was going to be maintained. But a fresh *journée* occurred to patch up the coalition.

The financial situation was deteriorating from day to day. The fall of Cambon had marked a turning point in the history of the *assignat*, and demonetization, openly advocated in the press and at the tribune, was meeting with less and less opposition. On 26 Germinal (April 15), Johannot's report declared in favor of it, and on 6 Floréal (April 25), by revoking the decree of April 11, 1793, which had forbidden dealings in metallic currency and the practice of

two prices, the Convention appeared to give official sanction
to the collapse of the paper money. But it remained to be
seen how it was to be liquidated and what was to take its
place. On the first point, Johannot was in favor of exchanging the *assignats* for promissory notes bearing interest and
redeemable in the form of national property; on the second
point, Dubois-Crancé proposed a tax in kind: Bourdon declared this to be impracticable, especially in the midst of a
food shortage, and suggested softening it, at least, by authorizing the payment in *assignats* of the value of the
grain demanded, calculated according to the 1790 prices.
This idea was going to be adopted before long, but for the
State to get something out of it, there had to be a decree
that the *assignat* would no longer be accepted except at
the current rate of exchange. The same Bourdon revealed,
with two other projects, that speculation was lying in wait
and had agents in the Convention. He attacked the demonetization of the *assignats* bearing the royal head, which
had been decided on in July 1793, and proposed that those
which had not been able to be exchanged within the prescribed period should be accepted in payment for the property of émigrés: apart from the fact that this would increase
the mass of paper money in circulation, it was pointed out
that the speculators had bought these *assignats* cheap in
the expectation of a concession of this sort. A little later,
Bourdon also proposed that henceforth national property
should be sold without auction to the first applicant and on
a simple valuation: this measure, adopted the following
year by the Directory, would permit the pillaging of the
Republic's inheritance. The Convention came to no decision. A fresh report from Vernier, on 23 Floréal (May 12),
which incidentally contained nothing new, was debated,

but the first of Prairial arrived before anything had been done. Inflation therefore continued, as did the rise in prices.

As for food, it became increasingly scarce as the spring wore on. Disturbances multiplied all over France. In Paris particular attention was paid to those which broke out on 14 and 15 Germinal, at Amiens and Rouen, to shouts of "Long live the King!" and "Bread and a king!" At Vernon, Évreux, Dreux, Montdidier, Chantilly, Crépy and La Chapelle, rioters stopped convoys on their way to the capital. At the beginning of May, a fairly large quantity of grain, bought by the government in Belgium and Holland, arrived at Dunkirk, Ostend and Le Havre, while from Marseilles came news of the unloading of 300,000 quintals. To safeguard the transport to Paris of the grain from the north, Barras was given full powers, and subsequently Rouyer and Féraud were appointed to assist him; he came to an arrangement with Lanchère, who supplied him with 6,000 horses, and he obtained the services of 3,500 troopers to escort the convoys. But this assistance was not enough to provide the Parisians with the promised ration. "We are reduced to two ounces of bread, and sometimes to nothing," a correspondent wrote to Goupilleau de Montaigu on 21 Floréal (May 10). As a result, agitation had started again among the Sections. On 10 Floréal (April 29) the Montreuil Section declared itself in permanent session and called upon the others to follow its example in order to discuss the food problem. The Convention lost no time in annulling the seditious decree, but the following evening rioting broke out in the rue de Sèvres, where women brought the grain wagons to a halt. On the thirtieth (May 19), the Mutius Scaevola Section came in a body to ask for bread, and the police reported that in the Invalides Section the workers were planning to join those of the Faubourg Antoine. It was rumored that the demonetization of the royal *assignats* was going to apply to notes of less than five livres, which were chiefly in the hands of the lower classes; this set the seal on their exasperation.

A pamphlet, published in the evening of 30 Floréal (May 19, 1795) and entitled *Insurrection of the People to obtain bread and reconquer their rights*, gave the signal for the movement. This pamphlet, which was known as *The Plan of Insurrection*, provided the popular agitators with definite objectives, the first of which was expressed in a single word: *Bread!* Its political aims were expounded at greater length: the putting into practice of the Constitution of 1793, the election of a legislative assembly which should take the place of the Convention, the release of the imprisoned patriots. The people were asked to march in a body to the Convention on 1 Prairial. There can be no doubt about the preparation of the insurrection by the *sans-culotte* leaders. As early as 29 Germinal (April 18), Rovère had reported a plot to the Convention. Several plans for an insurrection seem to have been prepared, particularly by the incarcerated patriots in the prisons themselves. Brutus Magnier, former president of the Military Commission at Rennes, and a prisoner at Le Plessis in Paris, had written at the end of Pluviôse an *Opinion on the insurrection required to save the country*, which outlines the same program as the *Plan* of 30 Floréal.

As for the deputies of the Left, their attitude on the first of Prairial showed that they looked favorably on the movement, yet they did nothing to organize or direct it. Lacking leaders, it spent itself, like that of the twelfth of Germinal, in violent but chaotic demonstrations.

Once again, it had been foreseen, and Thibaudeau had done his best to put some life into the Executive. On 7 Floréal (April 26), he had proposed abolishing the Committee of General Security and concentrating all power in the hands of the Committee of Public Safety, which should be in direct control of the police, the military, and even the Treasury. This was more than Robespierre had asked for, and the reactionaries set up a loud protest. On the fifteenth (May 4), Daunou presented another project which did not appease them. Cambacérès intervened as a mediator: the Committee of General Security was retained, but the Parisian military force was entrusted to it; the Committee of Public Safety, increased to sixteen members, divided into four sections, was authorized to issue decrees over the whole range of its jurisdiction and to sanction expenditure in conjunction with the Finance Committee. There is nothing to suggest that the executive was any stronger as a result. When La Revellière joined the Committee of Public Safety on 15 Fructidor (September 1), the latter, he said, had fallen

> into complete dissolution . . . ; each of its members busied himself only with his own affairs and those of his friends or supporters; each part of the administration was exclusively entrusted to one of them. He directed it as he pleased. . . . As there was no co-ordination on the Committee itself, the administrative commissions for their part acted on their own, in isolation, as they wished and as best they could.

At moments of crisis, in Prairial and Vendémiaire, the best that could be done was to create, as in Germinal, a provisional executive of a few representatives supposedly placed in control of the military force. At least the Committees increased the latter. On 28 Germinal (April 17), the National Guard was reorganized, and the Committees re-established the grenadiers, the light infantry and the cavalry, admission to which involved expenses limiting it to the rich; however, by the end of Floréal, this decree had been implemented only in the western districts, and there to a very limited extent. Numerous detachments which were protecting the food convoys could be drawn at need from the environs of Paris. On 30 Floréal, moreover, two divisions of gendarmes arrived from the Army of the Rhine. However, the Thermidorian reaction was not popular with the troops, and the staffs themselves did not seem to be entirely reliable; on 5 Floréal (April 24), the Convention had given full powers to the Military Committee and, in point of fact, to Aubry, to purge the latter, but this operation had not yet been completed.

On 1 Prairial (May 20), the tocsin rang and the alarm was sounded in the Sections in the east and center of Paris; the assembly rooms and guardhouses were broken into and the weapons removed. Then the demonstrators, wearing on their hats or pinned on their jackets the seditious inscription: "Bread and the Constitution of '93," marched on the Tuileries. About two o'clock, they invaded the palace by way of the Pavillon de Marsan, on the rue Honoré side, and entered the Convention hall. They were cleared out, but at about half-past three they broke open the doors and burst into the hall in a body; in the midst of the uproar, Féraud, who had attracted the invaders' attention by the resistance he had put up against them, was knocked down and murdered; his head was then carried around on a pike. Mingling with the deputies, the *sans-culottes* shouted at the tops of their voices; some of them made proposals at the tribune but could not manage to make themselves heard.

The President, Vernier, and Boissy d'Anglas, who took his place for a while, did not dissolve the meeting, and the din went on until seven o'clock. There were not many rebels and they were nearly all unarmed. According to Duval, the *jeunesse dorée*, summoned from its homes, had assembled in the garden about two o'clock. "It was left there, I do not know why," he remarks. In a short time, Raffet, the commanding officer of the Butte-des-Moulins Section, was able to bring up part of the National Guard of the western districts. The Committees were in session and had not been threatened; they were able to communicate without much difficulty with the Convention office. Yet nothing was done to expel the rioters. "This is a mystery," writes Dyzès. It is hard to avoid the suspicion that the Convention was waiting for the Montagnards to compromise themselves before it took action.

About seven o'clock, Vernier asked the deputies to gather together on the lower benches in order to deliberate, and the mob made way for them. Then at last a few Montagnards went so far as to put forward the definite motions: Romme and Duroy, the permanence of the Sections and the election of their committees, the release of the imprisoned patriots and of the deputies arrested since 12 Germinal; Goujon, the appointment of an extraordinary Food Council; Soubrany, the abolition of the Committee of General Security, which should be replaced by a commission consisting of Duquesnoy, Duroy, Bourbotte and Prieur de la Marne. It was after eleven o'clock at night and Soubrany was still speaking, when Raffet and Legendre burst in through opposite doors, at the head of detachments of the National Guard. The demonstrators promptly fled without anyone standing in their way. Immediately after-

wards, a storm of denunciations broke out. The arrest of the
six deputies who had just compromised themselves, as well
as that of six others, was decreed. They were sent off immediately to the Château du Taureau at Morlaix.

It was a quiet night, but at eight o'clock the tocsin rang
again. The Convention had just outlawed the rioters arrested the previous day when it learned that the rebels had
occupied the Hôtel de Ville. In the afternoon, the military
force went there and found nobody in the building, but
soon it was pushed back to the Palais Égalité by the Faubourg Antoine, which was joined by other Sections. The
gunners and the gendarmes deserted. However, instead of
routing the Thermidorian National Guards, the rebels
halted and ten members of the Convention came to parley
with them: at eight o'clock it was announced that the two
sides had "fraternized." Some petitioners were allowed to
appear at the bar, where they once again called for bread
and the Constitution of 1793. Vernier embraced Saint-
Geniez, their orator. The *sans-culottes* had let their last
chance slip through their fingers.

On the third, the Convention placed Aubry and two
other deputies at the head of the military force, over which
Menon assumed command. Reinforcements came pouring
in; however, in the afternoon, the mob released Féraud's
murderer as he was being taken to the scaffold. During the
night, the government obtained control of most of the Sections and had the Faubourg surrounded. In the morning
of the fourth, the *jeunesse dorée*, burning to distinguish itself, advanced into the Faubourg Antoine, where it was cut
off; no harm was done to it, and eventually it was able to
beat a rather inglorious retreat. Threatened with bombard-
ment, and destitute of arms, ammunition, and bread, the

Faubourg allowed itself to be occupied toward evening. Already, the Assembly had given orders for the shooting without trial, not only of those who were taken carrying arms, but also of those who were wearing emblems other than the cockade; it entrusted the repression to a military commission, and instructed the Sections to meet on the fifth in order to initiate the disarming or the arrest of the terrorists. "Decent people" once again invaded the general assemblies and the anti-terrorist repression grew in scope.

These *journées* were decisive. For the first time since 1789, the government had put down a popular insurrection by force of arms, and thus broken the mainspring of the Revolution; for the first time the Army had answered its appeal and broken the tacit pact which, since the fourteenth of July, had bound it to the common people of the *journées*. The gap would go on widening; the common people would not budge again until 1830, and the Army would gradually take control of the Republic for the benefit of its generals. The National Guard was once again reorganized on the twenty-eighth (June 16): workers were debarred from it unless they demanded to be enrolled; the majors were henceforth elected by the officers and sergeants. The gendarmerie of the courts and the two divisions of gendarmes actually in Paris had been disbanded as early as the sixth. On 9 Messidor (June 27), a Parisian police legion was formed, the prototype of the Municipal Guard; on 24 Thermidor (August 11), a police administration of three members was set up, which Bonaparte was to replace by the Prefect of Police. Stern repressive measures, which decimated and intimidated the *sans-culottes*, were taken. The Military Commission pronounced some thirty death sentences, two-thirds of them on gendarmes. In the mean-

time, the Sections decided on their own authority to disarm
or arrest the terrorists and Jacobins. The Convention continued to purge itself. On 5 Prairial, the deportation of Billaud, Collot and Barère was revoked and they were committed to the criminal court of the Charente-Inférieure.
Luckily for them, Billaud and Collot were already on their
way to Guiana, and as for Barère, the Committees saved his
life by forgetting him at Oléron. The same day, Pache, Au-
doin, Bouchotte and others were handed over to the criminal court of Eure-et-Loir. On the sixth, Pautrizel was arrested; on the eighth, at the news of a revolt at Toulon, a
decree was issued for the arrest of Escudier, Ricord and
Saliceti, accused of complicity, and of three others including Panis and Laignelot who had done so much for the
reaction; not satisfied with this, Clauzel committed to the
Military Commission the Montagnards who had compromised themselves on the first of Prairial, in spite of the
protests of Lesage and Fréron themselves, who invoked the
law of 21 Brumaire. Brought back from Morlaix, they were
sentenced on the twenty-ninth (June 17), six of them to
death and one—Peyssard—to deportation. As they were
leaving the courtroom, the condemned men stabbed themselves, the weapon passing from hand to hand. Romme,
Goujon and Duquesnoy fell dead; Duroy, Soubrany and
Bourbotte were taken, bleeding, to the scaffold. These
were the "martyrs of Prairial" whose memory remained
green among democratic Republicans for a long time.

Meanwhile, on 9 Prairial (May 28), Larivière had demanded the expulsion of the members of the former Committees. Lindet, Jeanbon, David, Élie, Lacoste, Dubarran
and Lavicomterie were arrested, as well as Bernard de
Saintes. In spite of Larivière, Carnot was saved by a deputy

who cried: "He organized victory." The name of Louis du
Bas-Rhin was also set aside, and there was no more talk of
Prieur de la Côte-d'Or. The other representatives who had
been denounced were attacked in their turn by Durand-
Maillane on the thirteenth (June 1); nine were arrested, including Sergent, Dartigoeyte, Javogues, Mallarmé and Bau-
dot. Ruhl and Maure, who were also threatened, committed
suicide. A little later, on 22 Messidor (July 10), Lebon was
finally sent before the criminal court of the Somme.

As usual, the Right accompanied its acts of repression by
measures calculated to gratify its friends. On 12 Prairial
(May 31), the revolutionary court had been abolished; on
the 20th (June 8), the Convention gave up striking off
émigrés itself; the next day, it restored the unsold property
of convicted persons, with a few exceptions, and quashed
all sentences for federalism; on the twenty-second, those
who had been listed as émigrés after the thirty-first of May
were struck off in a body; on 18 Thermidor (August 5),
certificates of citizenship were abolished. The priesthood
also came in for its share. On 11 Prairial (May 30), Lanjuinais had the churches placed at the disposal of the faithful if they asked for them; they nonetheless remained the
temples of decadal worship and, what is more, the Roman
priests had to share the use of them with the constitutional
clergy; in order to be admitted to them, all had to make an
act of submission to the laws of the Republic before the
municipal authorities. The restoration of religious worship
immediately gained speed, but religious pacification was not
complete; in theory, religious demonstrations were still
forbidden outside the churches, as was the use of bells; the
simultaneum provoked continual conflicts; on the question
of submission, the Roman priests split up, as in 1792 in

connection with the "little oath," into *soumissionnaires*, who followed Ennery's example, and *non-soumissionnaires* who continued clandestine worship. The deportation of non-juring clergy was not revoked, but on 19 Fructidor (September 5), their unsold property was returned to their heirs.

As for the *assignat*, the crushing of the *sans-culottes* necessarily led to its condemnation. True, under the pretext of saving it, it was decided on 12 Prairial (May 31) to sell national property without auction, as Bourdon had proposed; the districts were promptly besieged by prospective buyers, since the first applicant had priority; as early as the twenty-seventh (June 15), the Convention, realizing that everything was going to be bought cheap, in return for worthless *assignats*, re-established bidding, except for Parisian real estate—an exception which seems significant. At that point it abandoned the *assignat* to its fate; on 3 Messidor (June 21), it established a "scale of depreciation": the issue was retrospectively divided into blocks of five hundred million, and each of these involved an increase of one quarter on all debts. Then efforts were made to create new resources. On 26 Messidor (July 14), a loan of a million livres was floated, the subscription for which went on until the end of 1795; on 2 Thermidor (July 20), half the land tax was demanded in grain or in *assignats* at the current food prices; on the fourth, the *patente* was re-established, and on the seventh, the *mobilière*. As none of this produced any funds for the moment, inflation continued in spite of everything; about four billion livres were now being issued every month; in Messidor, the *assignat* dropped to five per cent, and in Thermidor to three per cent.

In the provinces, the *journées* of Germinal and Prairial

had given a strong impetus to the White Terror. Most towns now had their *jeunesse dorée*, whom the authorities allowed to act very much as they pleased. At Le Havre, Hardy told the Convention on 6 Thermidor (July 24): "A youngster of seventy is at their head, and they include men of eighty, sixty and fifty; these people call themselves the youth of Le Havre and presume to give orders to the authorities, who are in fear and trembling before these new terrorists." No patriot was spared: Hardy, who had seen thirteen of his relatives outlawed, was nonetheless called a terrorist and a Jacobin. At Bordeaux, in Messidor, when an agitator was arrested in the theater, the "young men" were called in to release him. At Nantes, green cravats, black collars, and hair put up "in victim style" were, as in Paris, their identification marks. They laid down the law at Toulouse, under the direction of the former members of the Parlement. At Avignon, they had formed "a defensive league which met at a given signal"; the department of Vaucluse changed it into a paid departmental force. At Marseilles, the National Guard was partly composed of young men called to the colors under the first levy. Everywhere as in Paris, therefore, the reactionaries had leagued together to obtain control of the streets. However, the White Terror, like that of Year II, raged to a very unequal extent, according to the region. In the southeast, where the massacres had begun during the winter, it was appalling. Elsewhere, excesses of this sort were avoided and the reactionaries confined themselves to the police measures and the legal action which the Convention had authorized, even at Brest, Arras and Cambrai where there had been a great many executions but where the reaction was rarely bloody.

The authorities had had no need to do anything but turn

the terrorists' own Law of Suspects against them. During the winter, a certain number had been arrested, but quite often they had been released; under the law of 14 Frimaire, government officials affected by the purge could have been imprisoned, but generally this was not done; however, the decree of 5 Ventôse placed them under surveillance. The first really general police measure was the disarming, ordered on 21 Germinal, of all who had "co-operated in the horrors committed under the tyranny which preceded the ninth of Thermidor." This involved placing the persons involved under surveillance. But as a general rule, even in Paris, no great haste was shown in carrying out this measure; it was the *journées* of Prairial which gave the signal. They aroused a wave of feeling in the provinces, where people thought that the country was on the eve of falling once more under the dictatorship of the *sans-culottes*. The authorities accordingly started zealously disarming them. Sometimes the municipality called a public meeting, where the terrorists were denounced and private hates were given full scope; if by some chance the popular society was still Jacobin in character, the opportunity was taken to suppress it, as at Lille on 17 Prairial (June 5); often the people who were disarmed were imprisoned into the bargain. Numbers varied considerably, but were never large, except in Paris and the southeast.

Legal action was taken chiefly against the representatives' commissioners, district administrators, mayors and national agents, and members of the revolutionary courts and surveillance committees. Here again, the process of exclusion created in 1793 was turned against the terrorists. The representatives opened inquiries and arranged denunciations, either through administrative channels like Boisset in the

Ain and Saône-et-Loire, or through the Public Prosecutor, like Boursault in the Mayenne; afterwards they would commit the accused to the revolutionary court, or more often to the criminal court of the department, which conducted trials in the revolutionary manner—in other words, without a jury. In either case, the rules of criminal procedure laid down by the decree of September 16, 1791, remained a dead letter and the jury of indictment was not consulted. However, until the summer, there do not seem to have been many convictions. A few people are known to have been condemned to irons in the Manche, the Doubs and the Hérault. It is true that the judicial archives have yet to be submitted to a methodical analysis.

On 17 Germinal (April 6), the jurisdiction of the revolutionary court was reduced to the crimes of emigration, treason, support for the monarchy and forgery of *assignats*; all the other trials connected with the Revolution were referred to the ordinary criminal courts, so that the normal process was restored. The terrorists took advantage of the decree. In the Mayenne, the judicial inquiry into the case of the Huchedé Commission, which had been carried out for months by the Public Prosecutor, had to be begun all over again. True, on 20 Floréal (May 9), the Convention did new violence to the law by authorizing administrative bodies themselves to denounce terrorists to the police; it repeated the offense several times by outlawing its own members without trial and by referring to the criminal courts, by decree, the terrorists of the Ardennes, the revolutionary court of Brest and the Jacobins of the Mayenne. Since, at this time, the Convention was sending on mission reinstated Girondins who put professed Federalists and Royalists into positions of power, the number of trials rose steadily. In the Aube and the Marne, Albert ordered the municipalities to receive plaints; the municipality of Verdun went to great pains to put on trial the men who had sentenced the Federalist Delayant, and had the minute-book of the surveillance committee read out in public. The "young men" also tried to take the initiative; at Tours, they asked Pocholle to hand over to them the archives of the authorities of Year II. "It is the same everywhere," said somebody at the Convention, while Mailhe, speaking approvingly of the young men of Tours, demanded that the minute-books of the "infamous revolutionary committees" be inspected everywhere.

However, once these noisy denunciations had been recorded, the subsequent process was usually quite regular: the magistrate carried out the preliminary investigation and sent his file to the indictment jury. On examination, the indictment was generally found to be untenable: it was based on unfounded accusations, mere threatening remarks, acts in conformity with the law and with the representatives' decrees. At Reims, the indictment jury dismissed two charges and the trial-jury acquitted the other thirteen accused on 25 Vendémiaire, Year IV (October 17). The slowness of the preliminary investigation enabled many of the accused to benefit from the amnesty without having been tried; this was the case with the revolutionary court of Brest, the revolutionary commission of the Cantal, the terrorists of the Mayenne, and Pache and Bouchotte at Chartres. At Verdun, the efforts of the municipality— opposed by Pons, a member of the Convention and the brother of one of the accused—did not even lead to a prosecution. However, a few terrorists were sentenced to irons or imprisonment. The record office at Coutances is the only one whose files have been adequately examined in this respect: in the districts of Coutances, Valognes, Carentan and Cherbourg, the public prosecutor took action against seven people and administrative or private denunciations resulted in the prosecution of sixteen others; of these twenty-three accused, four were discharged, six were finally not tried, and nine were acquitted; thus only four were sentenced, one to irons and three to imprisonment. It is impossible at the moment to calculate the number of executions, but there do not seem to have been many. The most famous was that of Lebon, at Amiens, on 17 Vendémiaire, Year IV (October 9, 1795). Seven terrorists of the Ardennes had been guillotined on 28 Prairial (June 16). In the Marne, where the Septembrists of 1792 had also been prosecuted, two were put to death on 1 Fructidor (August 18). If matters had been left to the Thermidorian bands, much harsher measures would have been taken; on more than one occasion, they intervened to intimidate the witnesses and the court, or to start a riot in the event of an acquittal. In Thermidor, at Dijon, where a lieutenant of the gendarmerie, a former member of the surveillance committee, had been discharged under the motive clause, the authorities were forced to arrest him again, and Ysabeau got the Convention to commit him to the criminal court of the Haute-Saône with his fellow accused. It should be added that prosecution was somethimes accompanied by a civil action. At Rouen, a member of the surveillance committee, acquitted of the charge of arbitrary arrest, was nonetheless ordered to pay 10,000 livres in damages; at Troyes, the national agent, sued by a citizen whom he had taxed "in the revolutionary manner," was acquitted by the jury, but sentenced by the magistrates to restitution and a fine.

Moreover, these trials give only an inadequate impression of the ordeals inflicted on the terrorists. Everywhere they were subjected to countless annoyances; they were reduced to poverty and their lives were made unbearable; those who were able to do so moved to another part of the country in order to be forgotten.

Yet their sufferings were mild compared with those of their brothers in the southeast. At Bourg, toward the end of Germinal, the district persuaded the representatives on mission at Lyons to commit the terrorists, who had been in custody since Thermidor, to the criminal court of the Jura; on the thirtieth (April 19), as they were being taken out of the town, six of them were murdered. The murderers, who were prosecuted in Year VII, are known to us: they included some artisans and shopkeepers, but also a notary, a bailiff, the clerk of the criminal court, and a former secretary of the department. At Lons-le-Saulnier, the prison was broken into twice, on 6 and 7 Prairial, and three men died. For their part, the Jacobins of the Jura had been sent to Bourg, whence they were brought back on 13 Prairial (June 1): some masked men ambushed the convoy and killed ten of them. The public prosecutor had stirred up feeling with his speeches and none of the authorities had taken any precautions; the mayor later declared that the murderers belonged to the cream of society and were boasting about their exploit in the salons; the inquiry into the affair yielded no results. On the 16th, at Lons-le-Saulnier, two more Jacobins were attacked; one of them survived, only to be sentenced to irons on 19 Vendémiaire, Year IV (October 11).

At Lyons, the mass killings began again on 5 and 15 Floréal (April 24 and May 4). The second was the bloodier

of the two: one of the city's prisons was set on fire and
some of the inmates put to death, about a hundred it is
said. Several of the murderers were masked; others were
tried, acquitted and carried away in triumph; the National
Guard had not lifted a finger to enforce law and order. The
infection spread to the department of the Loire and raged
furiously at Montbrison and Saint-Étienne, where the murders were embellished with tortures; several thousand workers fled into the woods and mountains.

In Provence, the Marseilles Company of the Sun went to
Aix and, on 22 Floréal (May 11), massacred twenty-nine
of the thirty accused in the Vendémiaire affair; on 27
Thermidor (August 14) another fifteen prisoners were
killed. Toulon remained the last fortress of the Jacobins; a
fresh insurrection provided an opportunity to subjugate it.
On 27 Floréal (May 16), the municipality having decided
to raise the price of bread as soon as the squadron had put
to sea, the *sans-culottes* tried to prevent its departure and
took up arms; one of the representatives in the town succeeded in getting the ships to put to sea, and the others fled.
Having gained control of the town, the rebels marched
on Marseilles; General Pactod routed them on 4 Prairial
(May 23). These events, which were seen as an extension
of the disturbances in Paris, filled the reactionaries with a
bloodthirsty fury. At Marseilles, Chambon gave the Company of the Sun a free rein. On the 17th (June 5) it forced
its way into the Fort Saint-Jean; the prisoners put up a
spirited resistance, but eighty-eight of them died. At Taras-
con, in the Château du Roi René, forty-seven Jacobins died
in the nights of 5-6 Prairial (May 24-25) and 2-3 Messidor (June 20-21). If we are to believe Fréron, the members of high society installed themselves comfortably on

the banks of the Rhône to watch the bodies being thrown from the towers into the river. Lambesc and Salon witnessed more murders; at Nîmes, Courbis and two of his companions were killed on 16 Prairial (June 4). Other prisoners were killed on the highway, thirteen during their transfer from Orange to Pont-Saint-Esprit on 8 Prairial (May 27). Individual attacks on Jacobins who remained at liberty continued throughout the summer. "Throats are being slit everywhere," Goupilleau wrote from Montaigu on 13 Prairial (June 1); people went patriot-shooting instead of partidge-shooting.

As for the *sans-culottes* of Toulon, the forces of the law had taken them in hand. On 8 Prairial (May 27), the Convention had set up a military commission for this purpose and committed the representative Charbonnier to trial as instigator of the rebellion. The Commission, to which Chambon had added a jury, showed a tendency to indulgence; consequently on 20 Messidor (July 8), Royer transferred it to Marseilles, where Isnard was absolutely pitiless. The jury was suspended and sentences were passed without delay: fifty-two to death and fourteen to other penalties. Nonetheless 152 of the accused had been acquitted and about a hundred benefited by the amnesty as did Charbonnier. The southeast also witnessed some trials before the civil courts; the best known was that of seven members of the Orange Commission who were executed at Avignon on 8 Messidor (June 26); at Marseilles, the terrorist Izoard was guillotined on 3 Vendémiaire, Year IV (September 25). In this region, the trials were nothing but farces. At Avignon, the preliminary investigation was carried out in public; the witnesses for the defense were not allowed to give evidence, and at the trial the defense counsel threw up their briefs.

At an early date, the White Terror began to worry the Thermidorians of the Center because they realized that it was aimed indiscriminately at all supporters of the Revolution. As early as 11 Prairial (May 30), Clauzel brought the operations of the Parisian Sections to a stop; in Messidor, Doulcet de Pontécoulant, an outlawed Girondin, called for "stern, prompt measures"; on the sixth (June 24), the Lyons authorities were suspended, the National Guard disarmed, and the military commandant charged with treason; that was enough to bring the Company of Jesus to its senses. But these measures were not extended to Provence, and there disorder continued. True, Mollevaut, another outlawed Girondin, had got an exceptional law passed on 30 Prairial (June 18), in the name of the Committees; this made murder a capital offense, abolished the intervention of the indictment jury, and insisted on a trial within twenty-four hours, without appeal. But in doing so he nearly played into the hands of the reactionaries. The Committee of General Security and the provincial authorities had begun releasing the imprisoned terrorists (of whom there were said to be 30,000) and the Sections were protesting. Taking up the defense of the law, the Right proposed the re-establishment of the indictment jury, but its project also ordered the prosecution, not only of the murderers of the south of France, but also of the Septembrists and the authors of "thefts, despotic acts, judicial murders and abuses of authority." The frightened Committees recoiled; Cambacérès restored unanimity by setting aside the new decree and getting Mollevaut's decree revoked. Everything accordingly went on as before; the White Terror continued, but the Committee of General Security was also able to release those terrorists who were not accused of any offense in common law, in spite of the Sections who had begun claiming the right to pronounce judgment on them.

If the reaction alarmed those Thermidorians who were still Republicans, it was because the Royalists were openly turning it to their account. Nearly all the papers now favored them. The *Moniteur* was one of the rare exceptions: "The most insane hopes are being expressed on all sides," Trovère wrote in it on 17 Prairial (June 5). "It seems that there is nothing left for the Convention to do but proclaim the restoration of the Monarchy." In the provinces, the trees of liberty were cut down and the tricolor cockade trampled underfoot. At Le Havre, the secretary of one Section had declared: "We want a king . . . to achieve that aim, we must make sure of England." Brought to trial, he had been acquitted, to the cheers of an armed crowd of "young men." At Bordeaux, Bresson wrote on 27 Messidor (July 15): "There is a party of avowed Royalists who are undoubtedly in communication with the other Royalists of the other large communes of the Republic." In Provence, Goupilleau was astounded at the progress they had made: "I am regarded as one of the biggest terrorists in the Republic; . . . to please those gentlemen, I would have to accept a post as major-domo to the Pope." There were rumors to the effect that a good many deputies were prepared to come to terms with them. Those mentioned included Boissy d'Anglas, who had given Lacretelle a post in an office; Aubry, who was hunting out Republican officers; Larivière, Cadroy and Chambon. In their letters, Louis

XVIII, Grenville and Mallet du Pan mentioned Tallien, Merlin de Thionville and Cambacérès.

But these members of the Convention could not give themselves up bound hand and foot; the Royalists were unable to agree on the concessions to be made to them. Some of them were Constitutionalists who would have been satisfied with a return to the Constitution of 1791, in a revised form; they would have governed on behalf of Louis XVII, who would have been released from the Temple and provided with a regency council. Outside, they had no lack of supporters: Archbishops Cicé and Boisgelin, Mallet du Pan and Calonne himself. But the boy died at a date difficult to establish, and Monsieur, the Comte de Provence— then installed at Verona with his loyal supporters d'Avaray and Saint-Priest—was not prepared to negotiate with the regicides. Having taken the name of Louis XVIII, he published on June 24 a manifesto in which he promised to punish them and to re-establish the three orders, the *parlements*, and the predominance of the Church. The Comte d'Artois, who had gone from Hamm in Westphalia to England, was no more conciliatory. In the entourage of the Princes, there was talk of hanging the members of the Constituent Assembly, shooting the purchasers of national property, and returning purely and simply to the *ancien régime*. At Verona, d'Antraigues, who was in the pay of the English, was reputed to be one of the most fanatical Royalists. The more moderate among them would not agree to anything more than a pardon for the Constitutional Monarchists. But, protested Mallet du Pan:

> If, under the sword of the omnipotent Republicans, they worked at their risk and peril to obtain recognition for the

King, would they not consider themselves entitled to gratitude rather than pardon?

They were left with no option but to come to an agreement with the Republican Thermidorians to obtain a temporarily tolerable constitution.

> The death of the young King Louis XVII [wrote Mallet du
> Pan on 21 June] is the most disastrous of events at this mo-
> ment. It has dismayed and discouraged the Monarchists, in-
> sured the triumph of the Republicans, and guaranteed the
> success of the new gibberish which they are going to decree
> in the name of a constitution.

In his opinion, there was only one mistake which the
Absolute Monarchists could make, and that was to resort
once more to insurrection combined with invasion and treason.

> There can be no hope of a spontaneous insurrection in Paris
> or anywhere else in favor of the Monarchy. . . . Civil war
> is a pipe-dream of the same sort. . . . The expedient of a
> foreign war is just as threadbare: there is nothing to com-
> pare with the contempt felt in France for the arms and poli-
> cies of the Allies, unless it be the no less general hatred
> which they have inspired.

Yet such was the plan of the Absolutists. The Toulouse
Royalists, wrote the representative Bousquet,

> say that the Convention has helped them to achieve a bet-
> ter state of affairs, but that nonetheless it will be destroyed
> before long, that not one of its members will escape them,
> that they have enough people in Paris to cut all their throats,
> and that it will then be a simple matter for them to cleanse
> the earth of that mob of patriots who are all terrorists.

In Lozère, in the Haute-Loire and the Ardèche, and in
Franche-Comté, the Royalists were trying to rebuild their

insurrectional groups and were convinced that they could start a rebellion at the first news of invasion. From Switzerland, Imbert-Colomès was organizing a plot in Lyons. In Paris there existed a "Royal agency" which was financed by the English and included among its members the Abbé Brottier, the Chevalier des Pommelles, the former Lieutenant-Commander Duverne de Praile, the former Councilor of State La Villeheurnois, and Sourdat, a sometime police lieutenant at Troyes. On May 23, Montgaillard called on Pichegru, the general in command of the Army of the Rhine, on behalf of the Prince de Condé, who was encamped in the region of Baden, and returned on June 14 to offer him money and the rank of lieutenant-general. The Comte d'Artois had an agency too, in Jersey, where an attack on Saint-Malo was being planned. Finally, at the beginning of Prairial, the Chouans had taken up arms again to support the expedition which the English had at last announced as imminent. It was a bad time to choose, for the Coalition had never been in such a bad way. The Absolutists were rushing into an adventure which, as Mallet du Pan had foreseen, would turn to the advantage of the Revolution.

CHAPTER EIGHT

The Thermidorians
and the Coalition;
the Quiberon Disaster

After destroying the organization which had insured victory, the Thermidorians, at grips with the whole of Europe, were nonetheless saved by two lucky chances: they gathered the fruits of that same victory, and they saw the Coalition, which had been tottering for a long time, finally collapse.

At the time of Robespierre's death, Belgium had been reconquered; victorious at Fleurus on 8 Messidor, Year II (June 26, 1794), the Army of the Sambre and Meuse had entered Brussels, where Pichegru, after occupying Flanders, joined it with the Army of the North. From

Brussels, Jourdan had marched on Liège and Pichegru on Antwerp: the two cities were reached on the same day, 9 Thermidor (July 27). However, the enemy's armies had not been destroyed: Clerfayt retired behind the Roer and the Duke of York into Holland; in the rear the French had to recapture Valenciennes, Condé, Le Quesnoy, and Landrecies. They also had to take control of the conquered territory; on 16 Thermidor (August 3), the Committee of Public Safety forbade any attempt to "municipalize" it and to repeat the experiment of 1792. It was placed under military government and exploited to the utmost; nonetheless, military operations were delayed for a while.

This delay was a brief one because the fortresses in the north capitulated much more quickly than had been expected, possibly as the result of a decree which had stipulated that no quarter be given to their garrisons if they put up a prolonged resistance. In September, the armies moved off again. The Army of the Sambre and Meuse forced the passage of the Ourthe, then that of the Roer at Aldenhoven, on 11 Vendémiaire, Year II (October 2, 1794), and pushed Clerfayt back beyond the Rhine, while the Armies of the Moselle and the Rhine were invading the Palatinate. Soon the French reappeared before Mainz and attacked Mannheim, which surrendered on 4 Nivôse (December 24); in the rear, they laid siege to Luxembourg, which held out for a long time.

In the meantime the Army of the North was making its way to the Meuse and was subjugating the Dutch fortresses, notably Maestricht. Pichegru showed no great eagerness to press on, but at the end of December, the harsh winter opened the way for him: the rivers froze and the Republicans crossed the Meuse, the Waal, and the Lek in succession. As early as December 2, the Duke of York had set off for Hanover; the Prince of Orange set sail for England, and Holland was occupied almost without firing a shot; off the island of Texel, his fleet, trapped by ice, was seized by the hussars. The Dutchmen who had fled their country after the failure of the revolution of 1787 accompanied the Army of the North, and Daendels proclaimed the Batavian Republic. In the Alps, Carnot had abandoned the invasion plan proposed by Bonaparte and supported by Robespierre, and was on the defensive; near the Pyrenees, on the other hand, Dugommier had defeated the Spaniards at the Montagne Noire on 27 Brumaire (November 17); he was killed, but his army nonetheless descended into Catalonia, where it took Figueras and Rosas. In August, 1794, Moncey, for his part, had captured Fuenterrabia and San Sebastian. These victories, and above all the conquest of the Netherlands, were of prime importance to the Republic; the liberation of French territory and the moral effect in France and Europe were not the only advantages: the blockade, which in any case had never been complete, was finally broken as soon as France had the resources of the Netherlands and the left bank of the Rhine at her disposal and, by means of coasting vessels, could resume direct contact with Hamburg and the Scandinavians; in the conquered regions, the evacuation agencies, set up in Floréal, Year II, collected grain, cattle, cloth and metal, either for the use of the armies or for sending to France. Finally, Tuscany, Spain, and the Princes of Southern Germany henceforth showed themselves prepared to negotiate.

This was not the first sign of weakness revealed by the Coalition: Prussia was also showing a tendency to abandon

it, and this was much more important. Her hesitations
dated back a long time. When they had joined the war
against France, the Germans had been agreed that they
were to recoup themselves, and not simply at their enemy's expense: Austria had her eye on Bavaria, while Prussia had designs on Poland. Defeated at Valmy, Frederick
William II had declared that he would only continue fighting if he could collect his rewards immediately, and since
Catherine II, delighted at the opportunity to divide the
Germans, had concurred in his views, Russia and Prussia
had carried out the second partition of Poland on January
23, 1793. Thugut, the new Austrian Chancellor, had had to
resign himself. The Prussians nonetheless fought very half-
heartedly in the west, and in 1794, when the Poles rose in revolt, their King went and laid siege to Warsaw. However,
things turned out badly; he was forced to raise the siege on
September 6, 1794, and it was Suvoroff who recaptured the
city; the Austrians took the opportunity to make it up with
Catherine II, who allowed them to occupy Cracow and
Sandomir. As a result the Prussians went back across the
Rhine, and after Pitt had taken this as an excuse to cut off
their subsidies, the King decided in November to send
some agents to Basle to get in touch with Barthélemy,
who represented the French Republic in Switzerland: he
wanted to come to terms with France in order to take all
his troops to Poland and force his rivals to admit him to
the third partition which was being prepared. Sweden also
served him as an intermediary: Baron de Staël set off to negotiate with the Thermidorians, and in December, Madame
de Staël published her *Réflexions sur la paix.* Prussia's defection created a tremendous sensation. "The legalized
victory of the Revolution," wrote Mallet du Pan, "will be a

license for insurrection addressed to all the peoples of the world."

Frederick William II was well aware of this and had yielded only reluctantly to the arguments of his generals and his minister Haugwitz. He also foresaw that the regicides would demand the Rhine frontier, and was afraid that, in giving way to them, he would compromise Prussia's reputation in the eyes of all the Germans. Hardenberg, his other adviser, played on his reluctance, as did the English; he finally stuck to the decision he had made, after Russia and Austria had settled the final partition of Poland, on January 3, 1795—without consulting him, and reduced his share to the minimum. What is more, in exchange for his Rhenish possessions, Prussia was entitled to hope for some compensations in Germany; since on December 22 the Reichstag had declared itself in favor of peace, it was not impossible that the Princes should turn to her, if Austria continued the war, to form within the Holy Roman Empire a sort of confederacy designed to protect their neutrality under her direction. These were attractive prospects.

The Republic, for her part, also needed peace. Carnot had already said as much before the ninth of Thermidor, and the need had become much more pressing for the Thermidorians, who lacked both money and authority. Besides, the nation's wishes were not in doubt. "The most ardent and the most general feeling," noted Mallet du Pan, "is a desire to achieve some sort of end to the Revolution and to have done with the war." However, certain difficulties could be foreseen. The Committee of Year II could have negotiated for peace if it had thought fit, because it dominated the Convention and because it could not be suspected of coming to terms with the Royalists. The

Thermidorian Committee was in a very different position. When, on 22 Pluviôse (February 10), Cambacérès
presented the treaty concluded the day before with the
Duke of Tuscany, the Assembly showed an unexpected
chilliness: having failed to consult it, the Committee
seemed guilty of usurpation in its eyes, and it ratified the
treaty only reluctantly. It was even worse on 13 Ventôse
(March 3), when the Committee asked for authority to in-
sert secret articles in future agreements. How could the
Convention give its approval to articles when it did not
know what those articles were? The Committee was obliged to explain that peace with Prussia depended on this condition. On the twenty-seventh, the required authority was
granted, on condition that the secret articles should not
attenuate the others.

The question of the annexations was even more delicate.
At the beginning of 1793, the Convention had allowed itself to be persuaded to give the Republic its "natural frontiers" and, on the basis of hasty plebiscites, to annex
Belgium and the left bank of the Rhine. It is unlikely that
the Committee of Year II considered itself bound by these
decisions. The Thermidorian Committee too realized that
if it insisted on the Rhine as a frontier, it ran the risk of
postponing a general peace indefinitely, and it maintained
a prudent reserve. France, declared Merlin de Douai on 14
Frimaire, Year III (December 4, 1794), "will trace with
her victorious but generous hand the limits within which
it befits her to remain"; and on 11 Pluviôse (January 30,
1795), Boissy d' Anglas added that the Committee was
ready to conclude a peace "consistent with our dignity and
likely to guarantee our safety." The conditions of such a
peace therefore remained to be discussed. But the counter-

revolutionaries immediately started a campaign in favor of peace at any price and the return of all the Republic's conquests; and as early as 24 Brumaire (November 14, 1794), Barère had denounced the advocates of "a patched-up peace." The leaders of the *jeunesse dorée*, needing the Royalists, did not oppose them; on 14 Brumaire, Tallien stated that the only means of halting inflation was a peace which would "make us withdraw within our former limits." Gradually the Royalists and those who humored them became the party of "the former limits." This was enough to make the Thermidorians who had remained Republicans hesitate; besides, in their eyes it was playing the Jacobins' game to suggest abandoning the Republic's conquests, for the nation would not relinquish them without regret, however much it might long for peace; and as for the army, whose support was so essential to the government, there could be no doubt about its feelings on this score. On 8 Nivôse (December 28, 1794), Bourdon spoke out unequivocally: "There are some who want to squander the successes of our armies and waste the blood they have shed by confining you to your former limits. How can you hope to ruin England except by the conquest of the three rivers [the Escaut, the Meuse and the Rhine]?" And on 11 Pluviôse, he stated explicitly what Boissy d'Anglas had deliberately left uncertain: "We shall confine ourselves within the limits which Nature has set, beyond which all peoples shall be our allies." Thus, because of the weakening of the Executive, the basic problem that French diplomacy had to solve became a party issue, and gradually it became possible to measure the warmth of a man's Republican convictions by his attachment to the country's natural frontiers.

Meanwhile the Committee, informed of Prussia's offers, had asked her to send an agent to Paris, and on January 7, 1795, notified her that in signing a peace treaty she would have to agree in advance to the eventual cession of the left bank of the Rhine, in return for compensations to be decided later, but naturally in Germany; without compromising the future by public declarations, it therefore intended to reserve the decision for itself. The King, who would have preferred an armistice, agreed to negotiate, but as Goltz, his ambassador in Basle, had died, he sent Hardenberg to take his place; Hardenberg contrived not to meet Barthélemy until March 19, and raised a new difficulty by insisting that North Germany should be neutralized under a Prussian guarantee. The Committee took umbrage at this. On 15 Ventôse (March 5), Sieyès and Reubell had joined the Committee and had acquired considerable influence on it. Now it so happened that the Alsatian Reubell was an ardent annexationist, and Sieyès, like Dumouriez and Danton, wanted an alliance with Prussia against Austria; Hardenberg's demand ran counter to their plans and the Committee described it as an ultimatum. The Thermidorians of the Right worked themselves up into a fury. La Revellière recounted later how Rovère and Lanjuinais inveighed against Sieyès, "an ambitious character who sacrificed his country to his private opinions, opposed peace with Prussia and, having sold himself to Russia, wanted to sacrifice our northern allies and Turkey"; in order to damage his reputation, it was said that he had been the man who "made" Robespierre, and there was talk of taking diplomacy out of the hands of the Committee of Public Safety. But in the meantime the King decided to give way on the question of the Rhine, and Barthélemy, catching the ball on the bounce, took it upon himself to accept the neutrality of North Germany; the peace treaty was signed during the night of 15-16 Germinal (April 4-5). In any case, the Committee, threatened with an insurrection, had withdrawn its veto.

The agreement with Prussia led to the capitulation of the Dutch, whose envoys, since their arrival on March 10, had doggedly disputed the leonine conditions which Sieyès and Reubell wanted to impose on them, counting on the resistance of Frederick William II. It was in vain that they pleaded that the Batavian Republic, founded by the friends of France, was entitled to special consideration. The Committee sent Sieyès and Reubell to The Hague, armed with an ultimatum which shattered the Dutch resistance. By the treaty of 27 Floréal (May 16), France acquired Dutch Flanders, Venloo and Maestricht, which she could not keep without annexing Belgium, so that another mortgage had to be taken out on the future; she also occupied Vlissingen until the end of hostilities. Holland became her ally and agreed to maintain an occupation corps of 25,000 men; she promised an indemnity of 100 million florins and reimbursement of the *assignats* which the conquerors had distributed throughout the country, to the value of about thirty million florins. The French had taken an advance on the indemnity, which was estimated at ten million florins, by levying a succession of requisitions; the balance was to be paid in currency and in bills which the Committee hoped to discount at banking centers in the vicinity of France. But it was the Directory which benefited most of all by this agreement: in September, out of the twenty million florins which had fallen due, Holland had paid only

11.25 million, of which less than five million were in currency.

The peace with Spain was delayed for a while, because Godoy had cherished some fantastic illusions, proposing the creation of a kingdom for Louis XVII in the south of France and the restoration of the privileges of the Catholic Church; for its part, the Committee wanted to annex Guipuzcoa and the Spanish part of Santo Domingo, recapture Louisiana, win over Spain as an ally and make her attack Portugal, in order to wound England which was in control of that country. Spanish envoys were finally sent to Basle and Bayonne; an offensive launched by Moncey, who occupied Bilbao and advanced as far as the Ebro, made Godoy more conciliatory, while the Committee, preoccupied with the landing of the émigrés at Quiberon, modified its demands. On 4 Thermidor (July 22), Spain got off with the renunciation of its part of Santo Domingo.

The time had come to settle the question of the country's frontiers if a general peace was to be negotiated. Thugut was not in favor of negotiating, for he had just obtained some subsidies from England, but on May 17, an agreement had established the demarcation line which consecrated the neutrality of North Germany; on July 3, the Reichstag accepted Prussia's good offices to negotiate with France, and on August 28, Hesse-Cassel, without waiting any longer, signed a peace treaty. The princes of South Germany, being restrained only by fear of Austria, would have followed her example unhesitatingly if Prussia had promised them her support. In that case, Austria would have been unable to attack France except across the Alps, thanks to an alliance with the King of Sardinia, and her efforts would have been hopeless; all the more reason why she would have agreed to conclude peace if Belgium had been returned to her. But it was impossible to obtain Prussia's support without giving up the Rhine. Hardenberg kept pressing France to do this, arguing that it did not follow that she would gain nothing: it would be agreed that she should adjust her frontier with Belgium, and that she should keep Trier, part of the Palatinate, and Luxembourg which had capitulated on June 8.

In the absence of Reubell and Sieyès, the Committee had hesitated again, even with regard to Belgium. Questioned in Floréal about the Rhine frontier, Merlin de Thionville replied: "You are putting me to a cruel test. Who can have any definite opinion on that terrifying question?" However, he ended up by advising the Committee to confine itself to annexing Speier, Trier and Luxembourg "as far as the Meuse which would become our limit," thus abandoning the greater part of Belgium. On 3 Prairial (May 22), Merlin de Douai wrote to Barthélemy that since the Convention had not expressed an opinion it remained at liberty to give up the Rhine. But Reubell and Sieyès returned on 4 Prairial and, with Treilhard, formed an unshakable block. The Committee did not commit itself in public, but it rejected Hardenberg's suggestions. True, it tried to coax Thugut by offering him Bavaria and by exchanging Madame Royale for the members of the Convention handed over by Dumouriez in 1793, but the proposals it put forward on 8 Messidor (June 26) allowed no room for hope: in return for Bavaria, it wanted Belgium, and also Lombardy for the King of Sardinia; Poland was to be restored for the benefit of a Prussian prince, and Austria was to join a league against Russia and England. It goes without saying that Thugut refused.

This being so, there was nothing to be done but fight Austria to the bitter end: it was necessary to cross the Rhine and march on Vienna. But the Thermidorians could not manage to agree on this point either. On 15 Prairial Merlin de Douai had left the Committee; on 15 Messidor, it was the turn of Reubell and Sieyès, and Aubry's influence immediately began to grow; hoping that some day or other the party of the former limits would carry the day on the Committee, he did all he could to stop the offensive and even proposed breaking up the Army of the Rhine for the benefit of the other armies. Treilhard succeeded only in getting a decision postponed until the generals had been consulted.

These hesitations cannot be explained simply by the instability of the Executive and the ulterior motives of those Thermidorians who were favorable to the Royalists. Aubry also knew that the country could no longer afford to undertake large-scale operations, and cited the complaints of the generals and the representatives about the appalling destitution of the armies. The Thermidorians were no longer in a position to wage war, and this was the most serious consequence of their policies. Under the pretext of economy, but also out of hostility toward the *sans-culotte* workers and toward State enterprise, they had gradually stopped the manufacture of armaments. In Pluviôse, the Parisian workshops which still remained had been closed; the building of national factories, particularly at Tulle, Saint-Denis, and Saint-Cloud, was abandoned in Germinal. Since Brumaire, the manufacture of saltpeter had slowed down; it had been stopped at Troyes in Frimaire and at Aubusson in Pluviôse; finally, on 17 Germinal (April 6), it ceased to be compulsory and was abandoned completely. On 21 Germinal, the Powder Agency had been reorganized and its personnel reduced. Similarly, the workshops set up by the districts to provide the armies with clothes, equipment and bedding were neglected; then, on 12 Ventôse (March 2), orders were given to suspend purchases and dismiss the workers. Only the requisitioning of "decadal" shoes was retained.

Then again, as the quotas were no longer delivered punctually, the armies were deprived of bread and fodder. The purchases made by the Supplies Commission remained inadequate because of the food shortage. On 5 Germinal (March 25), the ration was reduced from twenty-eight to twenty-four ounces, and the soldier who received a pound could consider himself lucky; on 5 Prairial (May 24), sifting was abolished for flour intended for ration bread; three quarters of it was supposed to be corn, but in fact corn gave place to oats and rye.. As for the army's pay, it was issued irregularly, and in *assignats*. Now, the soldier received only bread, and theoretically, half a pound of meat. On 5 Thermidor (July 23), it was finally decided to promise him two of his ten sous a day in metallic currency, and to grant officers eight francs a month. But finding them was a problem.

The Supplies Commission, known as the "Starvation Commission," was held responsible for the armies' destitution as well as for the hunger riots, and the contractors' campaign to obtain the abolition of the agencies made rapid strides. The government gradually handed over to private enterprise the manufacture of armaments and what remained of the national factories; it increased the number of contracts, particularly as far as food supplies were concerned. The most important contract was placed through the instrumentality of the representative Lefebvre de Nantes who, assisted by an Antwerp trader called Werbrouck, had got in touch in Brussels with the big banking and trading firm directed by Walckiers; they promised to supply Paris and the armies of the North and of the Sambre and Meuse for eighteen months, beginning on 1 Messidor.

Once the agreement had been concluded, they came to an understanding with their fellow countrymen, the Simons brothers, former traders and bankers in Paris whence they had fled at the end of 1793 to settle in Hamburg. The Simons brothers sold them 4,000 lasts (200,000 quintals) of grain, making a profit of over one and a half million livres. An operation on such a vast scale, although it kept the form of a contract for specific quantities, was clearly another step towards the return to those contracts of the *ancien régime* which left the task of supplying the armies to private contractors, in return for a fixed price. This was certainly how Lefebvre saw it:

> In accepting the proposed tender, I see first of all the advantage of ridding the government of the agencies and their peculations; I see the Committees relieved of a host of cares which are wasting their valuable time. Looking further afield, it would not be impossible to set up a similar establishment in the south of France.

The government seems to have anticipated this advice, for it had already placed a contract with a certain Fondreton Company to supply grain to the western armies. Similar developments were taking place in the sphere of transport. On 11 Prairial (May 30), the Transport, Post and Parcels Commission was abolished and its place taken by a Post and Parcels Office; the Internal Navigation Agency remained, but land transport was entrusted to the Army Movements Commission, which used the existing matériel and hired horses from the Lanchère Company. It was thus made clear that in future the State intended to undertake responsibility for military transport only. Even so, on 3 Thermidor (July 21) the latter was entrusted, in the case of the Armies of Italy and of the Alps, to the Michel and Roux Company, which took over the Republic's wagons and undertook to supply, on a contractual basis, the necessary equipment and animals: here the wheel had turned full circle.

In point of fact, the system did not become general as yet, the principal reason probably being that the shortage of food and the instability of prices confronted private enterprise with excessive difficulties. Many contracts were in fact canceled and the contractors did no better than the commissions and their agencies. The representatives with the Army of the Rhine and Moselle reported on 22 Ventôse (March 12) that Cerf Zacharias had failed to supply anything; those with the Army of the Western Pyrenees noted on 22 Messidor (July 10) that the Lanchère Company had kept none of its engagements; on 20 Messidor, the Fondreton Company canceled its contract for the western armies. That is why the Supplies Commission and its agencies continued their operations; for example, they resumed their work for the western armies. Moreover, the contractors did not afford the Treasury as much relief as had been thought: Walckiers and Werbrouk had asked for an advance of one third or one quarter on their con-

tract. Finally, extortions had started immediately; on 4
Thermidor (July 22), the Committee of Public Safety expressed indignation at the fact that Cerf Berr, having
been provided with the horses which the Republic had
bought abroad for between 580 and 600 livres in metallic
currency, proposed to pay only 1,500 livres for them in
assignats which were not worth more than fifty.

In Year III, therefore, the troops suffered much greater
hardship than in Year II, and their plight was the same
as that of the civilian population. If the discipline and
civic devotion of the armies did not diminish—and the
representatives admiringly bore witness to this—it was because the number of soldiers who remained loyal fell to an
unprecedented extent: the malcontents deserted *en masse,*
as soon as they could do so safely. In Ventôse, out of a theoretical strength of 1,100,000 men, there already remained
only 454,000 in fact; 119,000 of these were in France,
leaving only 335,000 for operations beyond the frontiers.
During the summer, the scale of desertion increased. In
Messidor, in the Army of the Alps, it was at the rate of
1,000 to 2,000 men every ten days; a battalion of 800 men,
going from Lyons to Grenoble, lost 650 of them. On 10
Thermidor (July 28), Aubry proposed granting an amnesty, but the fugitives incurred no risk by ignoring it.

It should be noted that, in spite of everything, Jourdan
and Moncey were able to render the services required of
them. If the offensive began late and went badly, that
was largely because of Pichegru's treachery. His easy
success in Holland had earned him an unjustified reputation which had turned his head; in that country he had
contracted luxurious and above all intemperate habits, and
his mistress, the wife of Lajolais, his chief of staff, cost

him a great deal of money. The agents of the Prince of Condé—especially Fauche-Borel, a Neufchâtel bookseller enrolled by Montgaillard in agreement with Wickham, the English representative in Switzerland—filled his purse every time they saw him, and he took the money shamelessly. The Royalists asked him to deliver Hüningen into their hands and to declare himself against the Convention; he disappointed them, for he was waiting to see how things were going to turn out in Paris, but he gave no reply to the Committee's demands and made no preparations. Thus he delayed the offensive until September, and when the order was given for it to be launched, his army was not in a position to make an effective contribution. It must be granted that the Committee of Year II would not have given him so much rope.

The Thermidorians were therefore incapable of bringing the war to an end, either by offering a peace without conquests or by forcing Austria to extremities with a merciless offensive. Both abroad and at home, far from directing events, they let things drift. All the same, Thugut, busy watching Prussia and settling the Polish affair, could not cause them any serious anxiety. This was precisely the moment the English chose to stage the landing which would have been so effective in 1793, at the time of the Vendeans' victories. In April 1795, Puisaye had finally won approval for his plans from Windham, Pitt's colleague. However, the British ministers did not commit themselves very far: they provided money and a naval squadron, but not a single man. Puisaye formed an army of émigrés who were equipped, it is true, with British uniforms; he hoped to recruit 12,000 men, but as the number of volunteers fell short of this, he filled the gap with French prisoners who agreed to enlist in order to escape from the hulks into which they were crowded; two divisions were formed in this way under the command of d'Hervilly and Sombreuil. The émigrés expected the south of France to rise in revolt, and Condé to enter Alsace and Franche-Comté, thanks to Pichegru, but they did not wait for this support to become apparent because they cherished illusions about the extent of the revolt which the Chouans and the Vendeans had been asked to foment. At the beginning of May, Puisaye, commander-in-chief of the expedition, had informed the Comte de Sils, his principal confederate in the Morbihan, who summoned the Royalist leaders to a meeting at Grandchamp on 1 Prairial (May 20). Two days later, a Royalist courier was arrested at Ploermel, and his dispatches acquainted the Committee of Public Safety with what was afoot: Cormatin was arrested on the fifth and, the troops having started moving, de Sils was killed on the eighth. Cadoudal took his place, but as Hoche had advanced in force towards the south coast of Brittany, the Chouans were able to carry out only a few operations and the greater part of the population did not budge. As for the Vendean leaders, annoyed that the expedition was not intended for them, they waited for it to arrive before taking up arms. The Convention sent three representatives to the west; on 30 Prairial (June 18), it attached a military commission to each army and pronounced sentence of death on any rebel found bearing arms.

From the captured dispatches Hoche knew approximately where the landing was due to take place; from the conversation of the Royalists in Paris, the Committee knew that it was imminent. Admiral Villaret was ordered to bar the way to the invasion fleet, but Bridport defeated him and forced him to take refuge at Lorient on 5 Messidor (June 23). The same day, an English frigate landed Tinténiac and du Bois-Berthelot, who gathered together a certain number of peasants—14,000, it is said—provided them with red coats, and, at their head, seized control of the coast near the Quiberon peninsula. D'Hervilly's division was then able to land on the ninth (June 27).

A strange conflict had just broken out between its commander and Puisaye, for d'Hervilly had displayed a document appointing him commander-in-chief. Puisaye, it is true, had told Windham that if the landing proved impossible, he would nonetheless go ashore with a few officers to encourage the Chouans, whereupon the English minister had remarked that, while waiting to rejoin their leader, the troops ought to be directed by another general whom Puisaye could appoint his second-in-command. But the letter of appointment delivered to d'Hervilly would appear to have contained no qualification, and seemed to dispossess Puisaye. It is difficult to imagine that Windham would have been guilty of such ineptitude, and some historians, instead of blaming the negligence of his subordinates, have preferred to suggest that among the latter the Absolutists of the Paris agency had found an accomplice to thwart the Constitutionalist Puisaye; in support of this thesis, they cite the Abbé Brottier's letters to d'Hervilly, addressing him as commander-in-chief and putting him on guard against his rival, as well as to the leaders of the Chouans in the Morbihan, warning them not to take up arms except on the orders of the Council of Princes. Whatever the truth of the matter, the dispute paralyzed the command of the expedition. A few days went by before d'Hervilly agreed to take the offensive; during the night of 14-15 Messidor (July 2-3), Fort Penthièvre, which commanded the entrance to the peninsula, was finally captured; the Chouans had already taken Auray and a few villages to make the approaches secure. However, d'Hervilly and his forces went no farther, and it was decided that they should wait for Sombreuil, who, with his division, did not leave England until the twenty-first (July 9).

Hoche thus had time to concentrate his troops. In order to avoid engaging them piecemeal, he had chosen Hennebont as a rallying point. Once he was ready, he recaptured Auray from the Chouans and pushed them back on to the peninsula, where they quarreled with the émigrés who, full of contempt for these peasants, had failed to give them any support. In a single week, Hoche established a solid line of trenches which turned the peninsula into a mousetrap, handed over the command to Lemoine and went off to the rear to speed up the arrival of reinforcements.

Thoroughly alarmed, the Royalists attempted a breakout on 19 Messidor (July 7), but suffered a costly defeat. In order to take the Republicans in the rear, they then sent some detachments of Chouans to Pont-Aven, Pouldu, Carnac and Sarzeau. The first three detachments scattered or failed to achieve anything; the émigrés counted above all on the fourth, which had been placed under the command of Tinténiac and Cadoudal, but after landing on the twenty-third, it made northwards, creating yet another mystery.

From Jersey, an attack was supposed to be launched on Saint-Malo during the night of 21-22 Messidor; as it happened, it was abandoned because the men who were to deliver the city into the émigrés' hands were arrested in time; but Boisguy, in Ile-et-Vilaine, had not budged, waiting, it is thought, for this attack, and it may have been to join him and the expeditionary corps that Tinténiac went north. However, pending the intervention of this new army, the émigrés on Quiberon would have been left to their fate, and it is difficult to believe that this was the mission with which they had entrusted Tinténiac; his attitude, like that of Boisguy, has therefore been attributed to the activities of the Paris agency. In the absence of the planned diversions, the attack made by the émigrés, supported by Sombreuil, ended on 28 Messidor (July 16) in a fresh reverse; d'Hervilly was mortally wounded. As for Tinténiac, he was defeated and killed on the 30th. Cadoudal took over the command and led his men as far as the sea: they scattered at the news of the final disaster.

At the news of the encounter of the twenty-eighth, Hoche had hurriedly returned. Tallien and Blad, sent along on the thirteenth by the Convention, joined him. The decisive attack was fixed for the night of 2-3 Thermidor (July 20-21). The columns on the left and in the center, hampered by a storm, spotted and bombarded, were hesitating when, in the light of dawn, they saw the tricolor flag flying on Fort Penthièvre: a small band of men, keeping to the west coast, had entered the fort, thanks to the defection of the soldiers recruited in the English jails. The émigrés, taken by surprise, were unable to restore the battle and fell back to the tip of the peninsula in appalling confusion. Puisaye had regained the English squadron, and some of the émigrés were able to follow his example. The others laid down their arms with Sombreuil. To begin with, nobody said anything about a formal capitulation, which would have guaranteed that the émigrés' lives would be spared, and Sombreuil himself did not avail himself of this opportunity; but in front of one of the military commissions, some of the prisoners invoked it. Hoche and Blad flatly denied that any such agreement had been concluded, although it is possible that the accused believed that it existed when they saw their leader conversing with Hoche and the representatives, and even that some officers and men made reassuring remarks to them.

The exact number of the prisoners is not known; there were about a thousand émigrés, between three and four thousand Chouans, and three thousand Republicans enrolled in England. Many of them escaped. The rest were tried by twenty military commissions set up by Blad. Tallien, who had returned to Paris, did nothing to recommend clemency and the Convention remained silent. Two thousand nine hundred and eighteen Republicans and twelve hundred Chouans were acquitted. But the decree of 23 Brumaire was applied to the émigrés and 748 were shot. The law was clear, and Blad, in the midst of rebel country, was no more inclined than was the army to spare the Coalition's auxiliaries, captured wearing British uniforms, especially as the Vendean insurrection had begun again and Charette had inaugurated it by wiping out a guard-post in a surprise attack and putting to death hundreds of prisoners afterwards. For a moment he had grounds for hoping that the English were at last going to come to his aid. On September 30, Warren appeared off the coast and captured the island of Yeu, where he landed the Comte d'Artois with a few troops. But the Prince was in no hurry to join the Vendean leaders, who were already hard pressed; he secretly asked the British government to recall the expedition, and finally the island of Yeu was evacuated without any attempt being made to reach the mainland. As for Stofflet, he only resumed operations at the end of January 1796.

The pitiful adventure of the émigrés, ill-conceived and ill-conducted, raised the hatred which England inspired in France to fever-pitch. Moreover, the danger had re-awakened the revolutionary spirit: Hoche's victory finally consolidated the Republic.

CHAPTER NINE

The Constitution of Year III

The émigrés' enterprise had deeply moved public opinion; the Royalists, full of hope, lost no opportunity of exciting it still further. They spread a rumor that distributions of food were going to be suspended in Paris, that there was going to be a new levy of men, and that, as Bailleul reported on 25 Messidor (July 30), "the Committees of Public Safety and of General Security had met to decide whether to re-establish the system of the Terror and that only two voices had been raised in opposition." In their papers, as the Committee of General Security observed on 21 Thermidor (August 8), every page contained "the most revolting satires on the government's activities, cries of sedition, and expressions of hate for the Republic."

The Republicans had no such dark designs, but it was true that the danger they had undergone had reawakened the revolutionary spirit in them. On 26 Messidor, the anniversary of the taking of the Bastille was celebrated by great pomp in the Convention, where the National Institute of Music performed the *Marseillaise*. "It is impossible," said the *Moniteur*, "to describe the effect produced by those unexpected strains which we had forgotten for some time past"; it incidentally expressed regret that the *Réveil du peuple* had not been played too, and this omission was indeed characteristic. In the midst of general enthusiasm, Debry got a decree passed that the *Marseillaise* should be played every day at the changing of the guard.

The Thermidorians did not show an exclusive spirit and appealed to all those who had co-operated in the Revolution. "Republicans, Anglomaniacs of '89, Constitutionalists of '91," cried Doulcet on 13 Messidor (July 1), "the same fate awaits you, the same flag must unite you; march all together to exterminate executioners who have no other desire but that of vengeance." But if the Constitutional Monarchists dreaded the victory of the émigrés, they were reluctant to declare against them. It was the *sans-culottes* who responded to the cry of alarm; it would have been easy for them to protest that in 1793, the moderates, rather than join with them to save the nation and the Republic, had preferred to unleash civil war at the risk of losing both; they forgot their grievances as soon as it was a question of fighting the aristocrats.

At the Palais Égalité and on the boulevards, the workers from the suburbs reappeared and made common cause with the soldiers, now so numerous in Paris, against the fops. "Attacks are being made on the green cravats and the black collars," announced the *Courrier républicain* on 8 Messidor (June 26). Duval has said something of this "war of the black collars":

> After the shouts came oaths; after the oaths came blows. They hit us, they struck us, they threw mud in our faces and at our poor collars; then they set to work with scissors and it was our hair's turn to suffer. They beat up those of us who were on our own and more than one of us was obliged to receive baptism by immersion in the Palais Royal fountain.

After the Convention had paid honor to the *Marseillaise*, a new quarrel arose and spread all over France. A report by Delaunay sums it up as follows: "The hymn to liberty, it is said, accompanied the victims of the bloodthirsty Robespierre to the scaffold, and the Convention wants to revive the Terror. The hymn of the *Réveil du peuple* fills the terrorists with alarm: it alone must be sung." In the evening of the twenty-sixth, the "young men" imposed the latter at the Opéra; on the twenty-eighth, at the Café de Chartres, they loudly declared that "if the Convention decreed a levy, they would rather let their ears be cut off than join the colors"; on the thirtieth, their gangs laid siege to the Committee of General Security to obtain the release of two actors arrested the day before, during the disturbances in the theatres, and gave a thrashing to Sergeant-Major Devaux, who had covered himself with glory at Fleurus. But the time had passed when the government treated them as auxiliaries; Fréron and above all Tallien, who was heaped with insults as the man responsible for the slaughter at Quiberon, had become Republicans again. The police closed the Café de Chartres, made raids on the boulevards, and surrounded the theatres and ballrooms to look for absentees and deserters among the fops. The Committees had a few journalists arrested, and, by restoring subsidies, reconstituted a Republican press. The *Moniteur* was joined in Messidor by Louvet's *Sentinelle*, and Lemaire's *Journal du Bonhomme Richard*; in Fructidor, Réal's gazette became *Le Journal des patriotes de 89*, and Poultier, a former monk and member of the Convention, founded *L'Ami des lois*.

It might therefore have been thought that, in the Convention, the division which had appeared once more, after Prairial, between the Center and the Right, would become wider. Nothing of the sort happened. The Constitutional Monarchists inveighed against Hoche and Tallien in the corridors and salons, but could not think of anything to do for the moment but collaborate in the constitutional task and speed up the elections, from which they hoped for great things. For their part, the Thermidorians of the Center needed the Right to complete their work: they accordingly made concessions. On 8 Messidor (June 26), the Committee of General Security had recalled that citizens were free to dress as they pleased; on the twenty-eighth (July 16), it forbade the singing on the stage of any song which did not form part of the play or opera being performed; at the celebration of the anniversaries of the ninth of Thermidor and the tenth of August, the *Réveil du peuple* was sung at the same time as the *Marseillaise*. The Center was not sorry to exclude from the coming election those deputies who were denounced as terrorists. It was in vain that Dubois-Crancé, who had returned to the Left, demanded that the decree of 21 Brumaire should be respected: on 21 and 22 Thermidor (August 8 and 9), the arrest of ten more Montagnards was decreed, among them Fouché himself. It was more difficult to reach agreement about the imprisoned patriots, a few of whom were released by the Committee of General Security every day, to the fury of the Sections. On 3 Thermidor (July 21), the Committees had proposed a compromise and offered to send them before the indictment juries, except in Paris where their case would be submitted to a commission chosen by the Convention. Bentabole and Berlier obtained a decision, on the sixth, that this commission would have full powers throughout France. But the Right reacted strongly. "The truth must out," declared Bailleul; "this means impunity for the guilty." The Sections spoke up in support. The Committees gave way, and on the nineteenth (August 6), the decree of the sixth was revoked. It was only on 11 Fructidor (August 28) that agreement was reached: all those who had been arrested without a warrant were sent before a police officer who would decide, in conformity with the Penal Code, whether there were grounds for prosecution. In point of fact, the Committee of General Security went on releasing prisoners, and on the second *jour complémentaire* (September 18), the Convention itself appreciably reduced the scope of its decree by deciding that the persons arrested on the orders of its Committees or of the representatives could not be committed for trial except by a decree of the former. In public, the reactionaries accused it of having contrived to save the terrorists, and this accusation played a considerable part on the thirteenth of Vendémiaire. A good many *sans-*

culottes nonetheless found themselves in prison at the time
of the plebiscite and the elections, the decree of 11 Fructidor having been too late to obtain their release.

These discussions had not prevented the Thermidorians
of all shades of opinion from passing the Constitution of
Year III, which was substituted for that of 1793, now
tacitly considered as canceled, like the plebiscite which had
sanctioned it. The commission of eleven, appointed on
29 Germinal (April 18) had worked on it for two months.
It included some sincere Republicans such as Thibaudeau,
La Revellière, Louvet, Berlier, Daunou and Baudin des
Ardennes, and a few deputies whom Thibaudeau regarded
as Monarchists—Boissy d'Anglas, Lanjuinais and Lesage
d'Eure-et-Loir—but who were postponing their hopes until
a later date. Boissy was elected chairman and presented
the project on 5 Messidor (June 23). The debate, in two
readings, took two months, and the final vote was taken on
5 Fructidor (August 22).

In the preparation of this Constitution, two principles
guided both the Thermidorian Republicans and the Constitutional Monarchists: barring the way to democracy and
preventing the advent of a dictatorship of any description.
They returned to the principles of the Constituent Assembly, interpreting them as the latter had done at the
time of the revision of 1791, while retouching its work in
the light of recent experience and referring to the lower
classes in a tone of suspicion and contempt which it had
never used. If they thought fit to formulate a Declaration
of Rights, they were careful to eliminate from it the essential article: "Men are born and remain free and equal
in rights." To those who proposed restoring it, Mailhe
and Lanjuinais replied on 26 Thermidor (August 13) that

it was ambiguous and therefore dangerous: men were no doubt equal in rights, but not in ability or in property either; in adopting this article, the Constituent Assembly had not realized that it was banning in advance the property qualification for suffrage. "Civil equality," Boissy had said, "is all a reasonable man can demand." The following definition was therefore adopted: "Equality consists in the fact that the law is the same for all." This was indeed what the Constituent Assembly had meant to say; thus defined, equality became a sort of attribute of liberty which it confined itself to insuring for everybody. The State had no other function but to guarantee that liberty by maintaining order, which in practice amounted to allowing one group of citizens to subjugate the rest by means of their ability and above all by means of their wealth. This was also the view of the Thermidorians and they consequently struck out the articles in the Declaration of 1793 which had expressed a different idea of the State, that of a social democracy which intervenes to restore, for the benefit of the poor, the equilibrium destroyed by money. The article to the effect that "the aim of society is the common happiness" aroused Lanjuinais' sarcasm; and when the right to work was brought up, Thibault exclaimed: "They will come and ask you for bread again!" In the sphere of politics, universal suffrage disappeared, without finding any defenders other than Paine, Lanthenas and the little-known Souhait. The referendum suffered the same fate; the new regime was purely representative, although the Declaration had stated that "the law is the general will expressed by the majority of the citizens or by the majority of their representatives." The right to insurrection naturally went the same way. Freedom of the press was retained but the Legislature was authorized to suspend it for a period of one year. The right of public meeting was restored, but with all the restrictions which had been imposed on the Jacobin clubs before their suppression. Economic freedom on the other hand was, needless to say, fully consecrated. Finally, it was thought fit to add to the declaration of the citizen's rights a declaration of his duties which was to serve as a catechism for the decadal religion, and which preached, to citizens deprived of the right to vote, obedience to laws that they had not made.

In some respects, the Convention showed itself more democratic than the Constituent Assembly: the Constitution of Year III was submitted to popular ratification, and, as it would have taken time to draw up a list of voting and tax-paying citizens, or *citoyens actifs*, universal suffrage was maintained for the plebiscite as well as for the first election. The electoral qualification was fixed in a more liberal way than in 1791: all Frenchmen over twenty-one years old, and in residence for one year, became *citoyens actifs* if they paid any sort of tax, even a voluntary contribution. In the future, however, the suffrage was to sustain a restriction which was extremely severe for the times: as of Year XII, the *citoyen actif* would have to be able to read and write; it is true that in compensation it was stipulated that he should be engaged in a manual occupation, but this tribute to Rousseau could only be a pure formality. Besides, in Year III, the provisional retention of universal suffrage was not as important as it might appear, because the election of deputies took place in two stages and a solid barrier was raised between the *citoyens actifs* and the electors. The former met in a primary assembly at the seat of a canton to choose the latter from among Frenchmen over twenty-five years old, who were the owners of a property yielding a revenue equal to the value of 200 days of work in places of 6,000 inhabitants or more, and tenants anywhere else of a house with a rent equal to 150 days or of a country property with a farm rent of 200. The electors traveled at their own expense to the electoral assembly to appoint the deputies. The Commission had required the latter to be landowners and had stipulated that, in order to qualify for the Legislature, they should have passed by way of the lower elected positions. The Convention set aside these two articles: no qualification was therefore imposed on the representatives of the people, but simply an age requirement.

In the organization of the public powers, the separation of powers was the guiding principle, since the Commission wanted to avoid a dictatorship, even that of an assembly. As the aristocracy seemed to have been finally eliminated, there was no longer any objection to the two-chamber system: the legislative power was divided between the 250 Ancients, who had to be over forty and either married men or widowers, and the Five Hundred, who had to be at least thirty. What is more, one third of each house had to retire and be replaced every year. The Five Hundred had the initiative and passed resolutions which the Ancients could turn into laws. As a precaution against popular riots, the latter had the right to move the seat of the assemblies and the government outside Paris. As a precaution against the army, a constitutional belt, into which it could not penetrate without permission, surrounded the capital. As for the executive power, the Commission refused to entrust it to a President of the Republic, who might have attempted to gain personal power, and to allow him to be chosen by the people—who, Louvet had said, according to Thibaudeau, would have been perfectly capable of picking a Bourbon. It was conferred on a Directory of five members, appointed by the Ancients from a list of ten candidates nominated by the Five Hundred; one of the five was to retire and be replaced every year. According to Boissy, it was to act as a continuation of the Committee of Public Safety: "It will have the same range of power." In place of the executive commissions, six ministers were subordinated to it whom it chose and dismissed at will, and who were merely its agents. Like the Committee, it had no authority over the Treasury, which was entrusted to six commissioners elected under the same conditions as the Directors; what is more, it was not allowed the initiative in proposing laws, and it was simply permitted to give the councils advice in the form of *messages*. Nor did it have the authority over departmental administration which the revolutionary government had given the Committees and the representatives on mission and which had been retained for the Legislative Committee. The decentralization carried out by the Constituent Assembly was restored, though not without considerable modifications; for reasons of economy, the department no longer had a general council or a directory, but simply a "central administration" of five members chosen by the electoral assembly; the district was abolished because of the part it had played in Year II and in order to reduce the influence of the towns on the country areas. The result was that the district courts likewise disappeared, and only one civil court remained in each department. "Municipal administrations" were set up which were directly subordinate to the departmental administration. However, as it had been impossible to recruit competent and educated personnel in the villages, they were grouped together with the small towns of fewer than 5,000 inhabitants to form a single municipality for each canton, the *citoyens actifs* of each commune appointing an agent and an assistant who, together with the agents and assistants of the other communes, formed the municipal administration in the chief town. Since the agent was the executor in his commune of decisions adopted in an assembly over which its electors could exercise no supervision, and was himself supervised only at a great distance by the departmental administration, he became a sort of potentate who could do as he pleased. The big towns, on the contrary, lost their autonomy; Paris remained under the control of government officials, as she had been since Thermidor; the other big towns were divided into areas whose municipalities were linked only by a central office. Here, therefore, the State saw its power indirectly increased, since it no longer had any reason to fear either the rivalry of the Commune of Paris or the secession of Lyons, Marseilles and Bordeaux. Moreover, the Directory was granted rather more power over the departmental authorities than the Constituent Assembly had conferred on the King. It was authorized to suspend them and change their personnel until the following elections which were annual, and above all, commissioners chosen by the Directory were attached to the central administration of each department and to the municipal administrations. These officials rendered important technical services; they were comparatively stable in comparison with the elected officials, who were liable to be changed frequently, and became the real regional officials, so that they were able to prepare and co-ordinate the work of the assemblies. Legally, they could only demand the enforcement of the law, and, having been chosen in the region, could not always escape from local influence. The departmental commissioner, in fact, was more like the Secretary-General of the Consulate than the Prefect, whose authority he lacked, so that the departmental regime was closer to that of the Constituent Assembly than to that of Year II or of the Consulate. But as the commissioner often exceeded his powers, he nonetheless served in practice as a link between these last two systems.

Taken by itself, outside the context of time and place, it may be that this Constitution of Year III deserves the praise which has often been given it. Destined for a country whose revolution, more social than political in nature, was not complete, a country which had to wage a war that showed no sign of coming to an end, without money, without currency and in the midst of a grave food shortage, it was a sort of wager, since everything about it was arranged so that legislation should be as slow as possible and, above all, so that the Executive should remain weak and lifeless. Yet if Sieyès had had his way, the central power would have been weaker still. The account he gave on 2 Thermidor (July 20) of his ideas on the Constitution was the most interesting episode in the commission's discussions. Against the social idea of the rights of man, which can only acquire reality through the protection of the State and *ipso facto* accept the restriction applied by the State, to the degree implied by its very existence, Sieyès set the natural rights prior to the State and showed that the essential object of the Constitution was on the contrary to limit the latter's power to the strict minimum. In very strong terms, he therefore refused to grant the general will the omnipotence which Rousseau had attributed to it; in other words, he repudiated the sovereignty of the people which was simply a transposition of royal absolutism and, as a result, challenged the representatives' "unlimited powers," which he described as "a political monstrosity." He said:

> When a political association is formed, the members do not pool all the rights which each individual brings to that society, or the power of the entire mass of individuals. They pool, under the name of public or political power, the least they can, and only what is necessary to preserve the rights and duties of each individual. This portion of power is a long way from resembling the exaggerated notions with which some people have been pleased to invest what they call sovereignty: and note well that it is the sovereignty of the people that I am talking about, for if any sovereignty exists, that is it. This word makes such a profound impression on the imagination only because the French mind, still full of monarchical superstition, has made a point of endowing it with all the heritage of pompous attributes and absolute powers that have lent glory to the usurped sovereignties.

In order to prevent the State, regarded as a sort of public enemy, from encroaching on the rights of the individual, Sieyès too resorted to the separation of powers, but in this respect the Thermidorians' work struck him as superficial; in his eyes the division of the legislative power between two chambers was totally insufficient to destroy its omnipotence. He proposed reserving the initiative for the government, considered on this account as a *jurie de proposition*, entrusting a tribunate with the task of examining projects and a legislature with that of passing them, and finally setting up a *jurie constitutionnaire* to which one of the councils, the minority of one of them, or any citizen, could denounce the promulgated law, as well as electoral operations, judgments of the appeal court and acts of the executive and its officials, as being inimical to the Constitution.

This *jurie constitutionnaire* was no doubt simply an imitation of the Supreme Court of the United States. But this was not the sum total of its powers. Every ten years, it would be entitled to take the initiative in revising the law of the land, and the primary assemblies, on presentation of its proposals, could then confer upon the Legislature constituent authority to accept or reject those proposals, but without being able to modify them. Finally, every year, one tenth of its members, drawn by lot, would form a *jurie d'équité* which the courts could ask for judgments, on the plea that it was impossible for them to pass judgment, either because the law was silent, or because to do so would have been "contrary to their conscience." As for the government, once a law had been passed, it became a *jurie d'exécution* and appointed the ministers, each of whom was to be the sole master of his sphere of activity, so that, with the central power broken up in this way, unity of action would be nothing but a myth.

The basic thesis could only appeal to the Thermidorians, and the Commission of Eleven gave its support to Sieyès' proposals; La Revellière defended them before the Convention. Berlier and Eschassériaux also approved the idea of a *jurie constitutionnaire*, but they did not fail to see that the system, if adopted in its entirety, would end up in practice by paralyzing the State and lead to anarchical individualism; Berlier did not agree with the possibility of an appeal by the minority of the representatives, while Eschassériaux rejected the *jurie d'équité*. Louvet and Thibaudeau attacked the *jurie constitutionnaire* itself, and, together with Lesage, maintained that the two-chamber system provided all the safeguards it was reasonable to expect. They carried the Assembly with them and on 25 Thermidor (August 12),

Sieyès' project was unanimously rejected. Deeply hurt, Sieyès adopted, right from the start, an attitude of opposition to the Directory, and in Year VII brought about its downfall. Several elements of his plan were then incorporated in the Constitution of Year VIII, with the lamentable result that they helped Bonaparte in his rise to power; the *jurie constitutionnaire* became that Conservatory Senate which was the tool of despotism and conserved nothing at all. More moderate and realistic in her views, Madame de Staël, in her *Réflexions sur la paix intérieure*, had suggested reinforcing the authority of the Ancients and giving the Executive a limited right of veto.

Once the Constitution had been approved, the Thermidorians tried to rally the Constitutional Monarchists and the Democrats to its support. Thus Réal, on 7 Fructidor (August 24), said: "Patriots of '89, Constitutional Monarchists, Jacobins; moderates, *exagérés*, democrats, Republicans; all of you, in fact, who have made the Revolution or allowed it to be made, open your eyes: nothing remains for you but liberty or death." And Louvet, on the fourth, declared: "Each of the parties that have divided France can recognize in the Constitution all the wisest things it has called for." They had no cause to feel anxious about the plebiscite which was to ratify their work. The Feuillants had collaborated in it; the Absolutists saw in it the advantage of getting rid of the Convention; as for the *sans-culottes*, with social democracy set aside, instinct advised them to keep the future open to it by maintaining at least the form of a Republic. But once the plebiscite was over, the elections would have to follow and the situation would be entirely different. There was no reason to be afraid of the Jacobins: their leaders were in prison and on 5 Fructidor (August 22) those deputies who had been indicted or whose arrest had been decreed were declared ineligible. The danger came from the Royalists, for, if they had accepted the Constitution, it was because they felt certain of obtaining a majority; in that case the Republic would be called in question once more and the Revolution itself threatened sooner or later.

CHAPTER TEN

The Thirteenth
of Vendémiaire, Year IV

That the elections were bound to prove fatal to most of the members of the Convention went without saying. The nation did not want to return to the *ancien régime* and had no interest in Louis XVIII; the enemies of the Convention kept denying that they were Royalists—"Royalism," the Montmartre Section had said on 11 Thermidor (July 29), "is a word the terrorists are always using in order to discourage the Republicans who have defended you"—and they took even greater care not to talk about the tithe, feudal privileges and the property of the clergy. But the French people had suffered a great deal and were suffering more every day; the counterrevolutionaries played on their bitterness at the sacrifices which the Convention had imposed on them, conjured up the specter of the Terror, and promised peace and prosperity. Even if these arguments had failed, no majority could possibly have obtained forgiveness for the prevailing inflation and famine.

There was still practically no course open to the Convention but a massive issue of *assignats*; on 1 Brumaire, the total number in existence would be 22,800,000,000, of which about twenty billion were in circulation. During the course of the summer, the catastrophic consequences of inflation had begun to appear. Since everybody was trying to get rid of the paper money whose value was decreasing from day to day, speculation had reached fever pitch, not only in the vicinity of the Stock Exchange and the Palais Égalité, which was generally known as the Black Forest, but all over Paris, which Mallet du Pan said had become a city of second-hand dealers, and all over France. Prices rose hour by hour and were now ahead of the issue of currency. Since it was impossible to make any plans for the future, the life of business undertakings was threatened: in Fructidor for example, the mines at Littry, in the Calvados, closed down. At Nantes, in Brumaire, Madame Hummel, thoroughly disheartened, would put away her account book, for it had become useless to try to keep household accounts. The social structure of the country was shaken to the foundations, with rentiers, officials and all creditors heading for ruin, while farmers, tenants and debtors liquidated their debts at practically no cost to themselves, and speculators, finding themselves suddenly rich, flaunted scandalous luxury. As for the workers, they were incapable of obtaining wage increases to keep step with the increase in prices which were rising too fast. In Paris, in Thermidor, butter cost eighteen francs a pound and meat eight francs; in Vendémiaire, they cost thirty francs and twenty francs respectively; in the course of that month, the price of a load of wood rose from 500 francs to 800; a pair of shoes cost between 200 and 250 francs. For the great majority of people, these prices were prohibitive. On 12 Thermidor (July 30), Bergoeing had got the Convention to ask the Committees for a plan to "establish uniform food prices based on a proportional scale and reconcilable with the necessary freedom of trade"; but they did not waste their time trying to square this circle, and when, on 3 Brumaire, Year IV (October 25, 1795), Roux proposed returning to the *maximum*, nobody paid any attention.

The peasants no longer brought anything to market, and the towns, which now bought all their food direct from farms or abroad, gradually gave up providing bread for everybody, and looked after nobody but the poor; in other words they simply returned to a system of public assistance, as at Bergues in Messidor, and at Verdun, where in Thermidor the communal bakery was closed down. In other places, the population was divided into classes which were charged different prices for bread; at Dunkirk, in Floréal, three classes were established which paid respectively forty-five, thirty and fifteen sous for a pound loaf, while foreigners were charged ten livres. But these innovations led to constant disturbances: there was a riot at Dunkirk in Thermidor, and at Chartres, on the first *jour complémentaire* (September 17), the representative Tellier, forced by the rioters to fix the price of bread at three sous, committed suicide out of despair. The harvest produced a slight improvement in the situation, but it was not uniformly good, on account of a cold, rainy summer. Consequently the Thermidorian authorities, under the pressure of circumstances, decided to imitate their predecessors and call for a temporary return to controls. The Convention resigned itself to this step. The law of 4 Thermidor (July 22) restored compulsory marketing, except for the benefit of non-harvesters in the country, and limited the individual's purchases for his own consumption until the harvest of Year IV, at the rate of four quintals a head. On 1 Fructidor (August 18), the Committee of Public Safety once again authorized the districts to levy requisitions in order to supply their markets, and once again National Guards were sent out into the country and billeted on recalcitrant farmers. Finally, on 7 Vendémiaire, Year IV (September 29, 1795), a new law on the grain trade laid down, often in fresh detail, the arrangements which had been tried since 1793, with the exception of a fixed price. But the enforcement of the law remained entirely in the hands of the local authorities.

The Parisian population remained in a privileged position, since the government continued to provide it with bread at three sous, while it cost sixteen francs on the open market in Messidor and Thermidor; but it received only a quarter of a pound a head, with a little rice, until the end of Messidor; at the beginning of Thermidor, the ration was generally half a pound, and in Fructidor three-quarters of a pound, which was still very little. As for other foodstuffs, a decree of 27 Thermidor (August 14) granted government officials, rentiers and workers a monthly allowance of four pounds of cod and salt meat, one pound of sugar, one pound of soap and half a pound of oil; for the first time, citizens paying over 150 livres in taxes were excluded, and the others were divided into four classes, the third receiving a quarter less than the fourth, and so on. Even taking into account these allowances, which incidentally it is difficult to estimate with any accuracy, Mr. Harris has calculated that the cost-of-living index, starting at 100 in 1790, nonetheless rose for the Parisian to 2,180 in July, 3,100 in September and 5,340 in November.

The rich themselves found it difficult to obtain food, and a hostess inviting her friends to dinner found herself obliged to ask them to bring their own bread. From Brussels on 14 Prairial (June 2) Lefebvre de Nantes wrote to Merlin de Douai: "I have just posted off a double ration of bread to you." With their thirty-six livres a day, those representatives who did not speculate like Tallien and Fouché were as hard up as the common people; but the latter refused to believe this, and the fops, talking about white bread, used to say: "That's deputy's bread; not everybody can have it." It must be admitted that the members of the Convention obtained a few privileges for themselves; the decree of 27 Thermidor on food allowances granted them twenty-five pounds of cod and salt meat, twelve of sugar, twelve of soap and twenty-five of candles. The most favored were the members of the Committees, and La Revellière has left us an amusing picture of the meetings of the Committee of Public Safety at the end of Year III. Cambacérès, he says, used to arrive about ten o'clock. "The first thing he did was to have a good *pot-au-feu* prepared, and to have some excellent bread and excellent wine put on the table—three things which could scarcely be obtained anywhere else in Paris." His col-

leagues turned up one after another between noon and two
o'clock, and, on being told as usual that there was nothing new,

> visited the *pot-au-feu*, took some broth, and pulled the piece
> of beef out of the stockpot to help themselves to a slice,
> which they ate with some good white bread and washed
> down with an excellent burgundy; then the quivering piece
> of beef would be put back into the stockpot until successive
> cuts had reminded the last comers of the truth of the prov-
> erb, *tarde venientibus ossa*.

It was impossible for these feasts not to be known about
outside, and even more impossible for them not to be
transformed into Rabelaisian banquets to which all the
representatives were invited. Similarly the frauds and speculations of a minority were prejudicial to all, and it was in
vain that the Assembly tried to vindicate the honest deputies by passing a decree, after the thirteenth of Vendémiaire, that every member of the Convention should produce an account of the changes in his fortune since 1789.
The police report on the holiday of the tenth of August,
which was celebrated "in a state of apathy," tells us of
some of the remarks made by members of the public: "The
representatives are celebrating today; the Revolution benefits nobody but them"; and "Public opinion is still very
critical of the representatives who have squandered the
nation's wealth." Some people also said "that they would
rather be under Robespierre's regime; that at that time the
Convention looked after the unfortunate; today, they eat,
drink and enrich themselves at the people's expense."

Conscious of their enormous unpopularity, the Thermidorians, after passing the Constitution, therefore found
themselves faced with the same problem as the Monta-

gnards in 1793. The latter had sidestepped the danger of elections by extending the powers of the Convention until the end of hostilities—an action which, in the midst of civil and foreign war, was easy to justify. As they had repudiated this expedient, the Thermidorians, obliged to institute elections, looked for another device which would at least insure the outgoing members of a majority of seats in the new legislative assembly. The latter was to be renewed one-third at a time to avoid sudden changes in the majority; it was therefore agreed, for the same reason, that the Convention, likewise consisting of 750 members, should bequeath two-thirds of its strength to the new assembly. This was what Baudin explained on behalf of the Commission of Eleven, incidentally without disguising the real motives behind the proposal: "Into what hands is the sacred trust of the Constitution to be placed? . . . In any case we shall be accused of crime or complicity."

But how were the two-thirds going to be chosen? Sieyès, in his project for *jurie constitutionnaire*, had indirectly solved the problem. The jury, renewable one-third at a time by means of co-optation, was to be appointed for the first time by the Convention from among the members of the first three revolutionary assemblies, an arrangement of which the principle at least would be one of the cornerstones of the Constitution of Year VIII. Baudin therefore proposed that the Convention should itself name the outgoing third, but ruled out a ballot on the pretext that it would recall the Jacobin purges. He counted on a sufficient number of resignations; if there were not enough of these, the number would be made up by drawing lots; if the contrary were the case, a jury of nine deputies would choose from among the representatives tendering their resignation those who should be set at liberty. This complicated scheme aroused a certain amount of suspicion, especially as the jury was authorized to consult whatever documents it needed in the archives, and because the plan struck off the active list of deputies, and consequently classified them as outgoing members, those who had been charged or placed under arrest—an obvious attempt to eliminate the deputies of the Left. Tallien and Chénier protested. The next day, 3 Fructidor, Bailleul accordingly proposed that the outgoing members should be selected by ballot; for the Left, the result risked being the same; as for drawing lots, it seems that nobody was in favor of that method, which is understandable. The Right was therefore in a strong position: it wanted the choice of the two-thirds to be left to the electoral assemblies, feeling sure that these would eliminate the Montagnards, as Bailleul bluntly pointed out. The majority of the Thermidorians of the Center, also wanting to get rid of the Montagnards, no longer raised any objections. The decree of 5 Fructidor (August 22) decided that the electoral assemblies would have to select the two-thirds of the future deputies from among those members of the Convention on the active list. As it was quite likely that some of the assemblies would not obey or that their choice would fall upon the same men, a decree of the thirteenth instructed them to draw up a triple list of deputies, and sitpulated that if they failed to elect 500 members (in point of fact 483, for the deputies for Corsica and the colonies were provisionally maintained in their seats), the required number would be made up by co-optation. In the end, therefore, there had been a partial return to this last method and the Fructidor decrees represented a compromise. But the advantage which the Republicans had counted on obtaining from the retention of the two-thirds was considerably reduced in advance.

The Royalists did not fulminate any the less for that, especially the Feuillants, who included a great many former members of the Constituent and Legislative Assemblies who wanted to return to power, and a great many journalists eager to come to power. The conflict which had been threatening for such a long time finally broke out between them and the Republican Thermidorians, now that, with the terrorists out of the way, they were free to fight for supreme authority. The Monarchists attacked Tallien the Septembrist, "Chénier-Cain," and all the members of the Convention, whom they nicknamed the Immortals; while Lezay-Marnésia, asking why the Commission of Eleven had fixed the number of Directors at five, and the number of Ministers at six, had already replied: "because five and six make Eleven." The Republicans replied by calling their adversaries deserters, Chouans, and agents of Pitt. Madame de Staël was appalled. As Sweden was about to conclude with the Republic a treaty of friendship which was signed on September 29, the Swedish Ambassador, the Baron de Staël, had come back to Paris. "Everybody is talking about Madame de Staël's dinner parties," the *Courrier républicain* reported on 17 Fructidor (September 3). Her salon had become the headquarters of statesmen waiting to be called to power; she had set to work to secure the return of Talleyrand and of Montesquiou, whom, so it was said, she wanted to see appointed Directors. Her policy was to unite the Constitutional Monarchists and the Republicans in order to consolidate the Republic of the Notables. The decree of the two-thirds dashed her hopes to the ground.

The next move was up to the primary assemblies, which

were to be held from 20 Fructidor (September 6) to 10 Vendémiaire (October 2). The Royalists turned their attention to these assemblies in the hope of obtaining control over them with the secret help of the clergy. There is nothing to show, however, that at this time the Royalists were grouped together in a party under a central direction, as would be the case in Year V; admittedly on 29 Fructidor (September 15), the Lepeletier Section decided to send an address to all the communes in France, but if there was any consultation between one region of the country and another it must have been a result of personal relations. It was only in Paris and the surrounding area that Royalist propaganda seems to have been put over in a methodical way. At Beauvais, copies of a printed circular were seized; and while it is impossible to take the word of the Republicans, who blamed every riot on the activity of agents sent out by certain Sections in Paris, one conclusive fact must be noted: when the Royalists of Châteauneuf-en-Thimerais rose in revolt, they lost no time in dispatching commissioners to the Lepeletier Section, which sent them to call on all the other Sections.

For their part, the Convention and its Committees also tried to exert a certain influence on the primary assemblies. They believed that they could count on the support of the army. At Nantes, between 28 and 30 Thermidor (August 15 and 17), the troops had come to blows with the "black collars," and had thrown into the water some Chouans they had just captured; and on 11 Fructidor (August 28), a deputation from the camp outside Paris came and promised loyalty to the Convention. As early as the second (August 19), a circular from the Committee of Public Safety had asked the representatives of the armies to speed up the voting, and as fast as the results came in, it published them in the hope of swaying public opinion. Then again, it did not hesitate to resort once more to measures of exclusion. On 1 Fructidor (August 18), a decree deprived those émigrés who had not obtained complete reinstatement, of their civic rights, a measure which barred them from the primary assemblies. On the fifth *jour complémentaire* (September 21), the relatives of émigrés were ordered to abandon all public employment. An article of the Constitution forbade any new exception to the laws against the émigrés and declared their property to be irrevocably transferred to the nation. Hostility to the non-juring and refractory clergy became very fierce again. On 20 Fructidor (September 6), a fortnight's grace was granted to deportees to go into exile once more, but the laws against them were confirmed and those who failed to comply with them were ordered to be arrested. The Constitution deprived of civic rights those who had joined "any foreign corporation" that implied "distinctions of birth" or required "religious vows." The law on the control of religious worship, passed on 7 Vendémiaire, Year IV (September 29, 1795), introduced into the formula of submission imposed on all priests recognition of the sovereignty of the people, and laid down sentences of two years' imprisonment for any priest who attacked the sale of national property, and imprisonment for life in the hulks for any priest who preached the restoration of the Monarchy. On the other hand, on 15 Fructidor (September 1), the right to vote was conceded to the terrorists, and the following day the Convention annulled the judgments and proceedings of the courts that were directed against members of revolutionary bodies and authorities on account of controls and requisitions ordered by representatives on mission. But the primary assemblies did as they pleased: they admitted the émigrés and excluded the terrorists. When the latter complained, the Convention ignored their protests; on 6 Fructidor (August 23), moreover, it had closed the popular clubs.

The Parisian Sections did not stop at that. They maintained that the government was reinforcing the troops at its disposal in Paris and the surrounding region, and pretended to fear an armed action in the event of the plebiscite giving a negative result. On 20 Fructidor (September 6), the Lepeletier Section passed an act of guarantee placing the citizens under the protection of the Sections, and when all the other Sections had given their support, it proposed, the following day, the formation of a central committee. Although the Convention had banned it, the Fontaine de Grenelle Section nonetheless maintained its approval, and declared itself in permanent session; twelve others followed its example. "I have material proof," declared a member of the Convention on 5 Vendémiaire (September 27), "of the formation of the central committee in Paris." Finally, a great many deputations went and harangued the troops, and not without success: in the Parisian region, the army returned a considerable proportion of negative votes on the decree of the two-thirds.

At the end of Fructidor, the plebiscite was sufficiently advanced for the result to be regarded as established. Although voters were required to answer with a yes or no, over 250 primary assemblies had made observations, very rarely in favor of the Constitution of 1793, and rather more often in favor of the Monarchy; eighty had asked that Catholicism be given back its freedom, or even given a dominant position. The Constitution had been accepted by

all the departments, with the exception of the Mont Terrible, which had protested in this way against annexation.
But it was not easy to draw any conclusions from this
vote for, in Vaucluse for example, only the Royalists had
been able to vote and they had given their approval only in
order to get rid of the Convention. The decree of the two-
thirds had been given a much less favorable reception, and
for the same reason. The west, the Parisian region, and all
the Sections apart from the Quinze-Vingts in Paris itself
had rejected it; Provence had shown strong opposition to it;
the Rhône and the Isère had voted against it; the center of
France had been divided, while on the other hand the
north and the east had produced a strong majority in favor,
although the Bas-Rhin and the Doubs had declared themselves against. Altogether, nineteen departments had rejected the decree. Many assemblies had neglected to make
any comment on it, so that the mass of abstentions seemed
enormous. But here again any interpretation remained problematical. The Convention had not stated explicitly that
the plebiscite applied to the decree of the two-thirds, and
in any case had not asked for a separate vote. That is why,
although the considerable number of abstentions with regard to the Constitution is an important fact, it does not,
insofar as the decree is concerned, have the importance
which has often been attributed to it: in the uncertainty
which the Convention had allowed to remain, perhaps
deliberately, about the system of voting, it is possible to
argue that those who had accepted the Constitution did
not consider it necessary to mention the decree. When it
came to the counting of votes, another difficulty arose: at
least 269 assemblies had not given the numerical results of
the ballot, with the result that their opinion was not taken

into account; and this happened to be the case with thirty-three Parisian Sections. Moreover, in the *Moniteur* of 7 Vendémiaire (September 29), Trouvé declared that the omission had covered fraudulent misrepresentation: one Section, he said, had accepted the Constitution almost unanimously, with over a thousand citizens present; on the decree, only 342 had voted, of whom 314 had voted against; however, the official record, omitting these two figures, declared the decree to be unanimously rejected, implying that the same number had voted on it as had voted on the Constitution.

Whatever the truth of the matter, when the Convention had declared, on 1 Vendémiaire, Year IV (September 23, 1795), that the Constitution was accepted by 914,853 votes to 41,892 and the decree of the two-thirds by 167,758 votes to 95,373 (the corrected figures given on the sixth were 1,057,390 to 49,978 and 205,498 to 108,754), eighteen Parisian Sections disputed the result and demanded a re-count, especially in the case of the capital, by the commissioners of the primary assemblies. The agitation spread to the streets, and on the evening of the second, shots were fired at the guard at the Palais Égalité; crowds gathered in several districts. In the night of 3-4 Vendémiaire, the Convention sat until three o'clock, expecting an insurrection. The Bonne Nouvelle Section announced that it had put the terrorists in prison and the Théâtre Français Section that it was going to purge itself of those "monsters." The Convention forbade the jailers to receive them, and forbade the Sections to send out their armed forces; it was not obeyed.

On the ninth (October 1), the news of the rising in the Thymerais brought the revolt to a head. On 27 Fructidor

(September 13), the primary assembly of Châteauneuf had risen in revolt and had seized the public treasury. A crowd formed, raising the *fleurs de lys* flag. Dreux, called to the rescue, sent a contingent. The representatives on mission at Chartres reoccupied that town, from which a detachment led by Bourdon marched on Nonancourt: the rebels were routed, leaving ten of their number dead. The Lepeletier Section immediately called upon all the electors in Paris to assemble on 11 Vendémiaire (October 3) at the Théâtre Français to protest against this massacre, asking: "Are we going to see a recurrence of those days of horror and carnage we have lived through?" But only about a hundred electors, belonging to some fifteen Sections, turned up. The former magistrate Lebois, president of the Théâtre Français, and Lacretelle and Fiévée harangued them until nightfall: when the military arrived during the evening, the hall was empty. All the same, according to the report which Merlin de Douai read out on 14 Vendémiaire, seven Sections which he named and some others as well had raised the flag of revolt during this time. The Convention declared itself in permanent session and set up an extraordinary Commission of Five to organize their defense; Barras was the strong man on this body.

They had not many troops at their disposal: barely 4,000 men in the suburbs who, for the most part, were sent off every day in detachments; 3,000 more, sent for from Saint-Omer, arrived too late. After the *journées* of Prairial, the Sections had handed over their cannons, but they were at the camp at Les Sablons. To obtain reinforcements, the Commission appealed to the officers removed by Aubry, and above all decided to enroll the *sans-culottes*: 1,500 "patriots of '89" formed three battalions. On 12 Vendé-

miaire (October 4) the Convention revoked the decree of
21 Germinal on the disarming of the terrorists, and that of
5 Ventôse which had placed under surveillance the government officials dismissed after Thermidor. Although the
Law of Suspects had been revoked at the same time, this
caused an indescribable sensation and rallied a host of
waverers to the rebels: the terrorists had to be dealt with and
consequently the Convention too, since it was taking them
into its service.

As usual, the Lepeletier Section took the initiative; it had
the news given out to the rolling of a drum and called on the
citizens of Paris to take arms. The *rappel* was beaten; the
shops were closed; a good many Republicans were arrested
and assumed that they were doomed to be killed; in point
of fact, on the thirteenth, about a hundred musket shots
were fired at the Prison de la Force where the prisoners
armed themselves with logs to defend their lives. The Five
ordered Menou, the head of the military force, to occupy
the hall of the Lepeletier Section, in the convent of the
Filles Saint-Thomas, where the Stock Exchange now stands.
Now it happened that Menou sympathized with the rebels:
he had just protested against the decrees of the twelfth
and had refused to place the patriots under his command;
his troops did not set off until half-past nine in the evening;
when they reached the Section, with the representative Laporte, the president, Delalot, offered to send his members
away if they withdrew, and Menou agreed. The Convention stripped him of his command, but it was too late to
send fresh troops: the Sections were on the move and
coming to the help of their colleagues. The leaders set up a
central commission under Richer-Serizy; the Committees
were outlawed, an extraordinary court established, and the

Treasury occupied. The military command was given to Danican, a former Hébertist who had gone over to the reaction, and who had written a letter, published by the *Moniteur* on 5 Fructidor, which called for a purge of the army; sent in disgrace from Rouen to Dieppe, he had resigned and had just arrived in Paris.

The greater part of the capital had escaped from the Convention, which indeed found itself in a state of siege. On 13 Vendémiaire (October 5), at half-past four in the morning, Barras was given the task of organizing resistance, and Generals Bonaparte, Carteaux, Brune, Loison and Dupont were placed at his disposal. Bonaparte was not appointed second in command, as he later related; but he acted as if he had been. Murat was sent to Les Sablons and brought back the cannons that were there. The Louvre and the Tuileries were fortified and the guns positioned so as to cover all the streets leading to the Carrousel; Carteaux occupied the embankment and the approach to the Pont-Neuf. At the end of the morning, Danican, coming from the Left Bank, pushed him back and joined up with the Right Bank where the Sections, under the command of the émigré Lafond, were marching on the Tuileries. There were about twenty thousand of them; having no cannons, they tried to win over the defenders of the Convention by inviting them to fraternize. As Barras had forbidden his forces to open fire first, the danger was undeniable. In the assembly, the Right was trying to intervene. In the evening of the twelfth and about three o'clock on the thirteenth, it suggested at the very least modifying the decree on the re-arming of the terrorists. But all of a sudden musket firing started without anybody knowing exactly where. After some fierce fighting, the Sections were repulsed all along the line;

Danican tried to take the Republicans in the rear by advancing along the Left Bank; caught in a cross fire of grapeshot from a position at the end of the rue de Beaune and from Carteaux's troops on the Right Bank, he had to withdraw. At nightfall, Barras took the offensive and occupied the Palais Égalité. In the rue Honoré, however, the Sections remained in possession of the Church of Saint-Roch until the following day, and it is just a legend that depicts them shot down by gunfire from Bonaparte stationed on the steps of the church. On the fourteenth, columns of troops crossed the city without meeting any resistance; the rebels had retired to their homes and the leaders were in hiding or on the run. There had been between two and three hundred killed on each side.

The repression was very moderate. As early as the fourteenth, there were complaints in the Convention that the Committees were releasing crowds of prisoners. On the fifteenth, three military commissions were set up, but sentence of death was pronounced only on the leaders and the "agitators in writing," in other words the journalists. In point of fact, most of the accused were sentenced in their absence and no attempt was made to find them. Only Lebois and Lafond were executed. As for Menou, he was acquitted. The *journée* of the thirteenth of Vendémiaire nonetheless had the effect of giving the government complete control of the capital. Henceforth the city was placed under military occupation. The National Guard was disarmed, and its cavalry, artillery, crack companies, and general staff abolished; it was subordinated to the commander of the garrison and to the general of the home army, who was Bonaparte. The revolutionary role of Paris was at an end.

At least the danger they had run had revived revolutionary feelings once again in the Thermidorians of the Center and had put them back in the frame of mind they had shown after the fall of Robespierre, when they had called for the reconciliation of all Republicans; thus they finished as they had begun, which is another reason why the *journée* of the thirteenth of Vendémiaire is important. On the twentieth, it was decided to reinstate the officers removed by Aubry, and on 3 Brumaire (October 25), on the other hand, to purge the army of the counterrevolutionary elements that he had introduced into it. As early as 15 Vendémiaire, the patriots of '89 had been disbanded, but now the Convention began to pass, not without a certain hesitation, measures of reparation in favor of the Jacobins: on the twentieth, the indictment of Barère was revoked; on the twenty-second (October 14), sentences and current proceedings against the patriots, for actions which were not punishable under the penal code, were annulled, and orders were given for their release; on the twenty-first, all prosecutions based on arrests carried out under the Law of Suspects were forbidden and sentences pronounced on this account were annulled. It was the fate of the imprisoned deputies which remained longest in doubt; the Convention pardoned them only on 4 Brumaire (October 26), just as it was dissolving its last meeting, by passing a general amnesty for "acts simply connected with the Revolution," the offenses against common law being set apart and the émigrés being excluded together with the deportees, the accused of Vendémiaire and the manufacturers of counterfeit *assignats*. The decree of 5 Fructidor, which declared the arrested Montagnards ineligible, nonetheless remained in force, as forming part of the Constitution.

In the meantime, an offensive had been launched against the reactionaries. On 19 Vendémiaire (October 11), Fréron was sent to the south of France to stamp out the White Terror, and on the twenty-ninth, Chénier referred to the Committees an inquiry into the conduct of Chambon and Cadroy. On the twenty-third, after Delaunay had read out his report on the papers seized at the lawyer Lemaître's house, which proved complicity between the Vendémiaire rebels and the émigrés, Tallien reproached him for not having named the compromised deputies, and got the assembly to go into secret session. He then accused Rovère and Saladin, whose arrest was decreed the next day. On the thirtieth (October 22), Letourneur's report on the operations of the Rhine armies was the occasion for a fresh batch of charges: a decree was issued for the arrest of Aubry and three others, including Miranda, the Venezuelan adventurer formerly known as Lieutenant de Dumouriez, who had been imprisoned during the Terror and rightly suspected, for he had never ceased to be in communication with the English. None of these people in fact came to any harm, and a few days later they all benefited by the amnesty.

Soon after the electoral assemblies had met on 20 Vendémiaire (October 12), it became obvious that the Convention was getting excited to no avail and that in the next Legislature the Right would be more powerful than ever. Only 379 members of the Convention were re-elected, of whom 124 were substitutes, and nearly all of them were moderates or suspected Royalists, including Defermon, Boissy d'Anglas and Lanjuinais, Larivière and Durand-Maillane, Rovère and Saladin, whose arrest had recently been decreed. As for the new Third, the majority was made up of Royalists and Catholics; in Paris, for example, the electors had returned Dambray, the future Chancellor of Louis XVIII; Portalis, who would be Director of Religious Worship after the Concordat; and the banker Lecoulteux de Canteleu, a Feuillant. The turncoat Montagnards who, after making themselves the leaders of the reaction, had been blocking its way since Fructidor—Tallien, Fréron, Legendre, Bourdon and Dubois-Crancé—were beaten and could be sure that the re-elected moderates would leave them to their fate, as did indeed happen with most of them. Now the election was of dubious legality, since the émigrés had been allowed to vote while the Jacobins had been excluded. Consequently several members of the Convention proposed that the results be set aside. On 30 Vendémiaire (October 22), after Daunou, ignoring this proposal, had got the rules of procedure for the installation of the Legislature passed, Bentabole suggested that at least the re-elected members of the Convention should immediately divide into two chambers to elect the Directory, without waiting for the new Third. He was referred to the provisions of the Constitution. Tallien, coming out into the open, promptly declared that "if they did not get rid of the Royalists in the government and the courts, the counter-revolution would be carried out constitutionally within three months' time," and suggested asking the Commission of Five to decide what measures should be taken "to save the country." Merlin de Douai, on their behalf, declined the task, and a special committee of five was appointed, including Tallien. But the former Girondins, Republicans though they were, refused to follow him and return to a revolutionary government by violating the Constitution. On 1 Brumaire (October 23), Thibaudeau denounced the plots which were being hatched for the arrest of the deputies of the Right who had previously been denounced, the annulment of the elections and the postponement of the meeting of the Legislature. He attacked Tallien the Septembrist, the person chiefly responsible for the Royalist reaction, whom an intercepted letter from Louis XVIII laid open to suspicion himself. Tallien gave way under the attack, and, not daring to admit his plans, confined himself to proposing that the Convention should declare itself in permanent session, a proposal to which Thibaudeau replied by demanding that the Commission of Five should report immediately before breaking up. He won the day without any difficulty: on the third, Tallien contented himself with getting the émigrés and also their relatives excluded from public employment under pain of exile. The way therefore remained open for the new constitutional experiment. Although the moderate Republicans had remained within the law, they were not blind to the dangers threatening them, so that they persisted, to a certain extent, in no longer seeing any enemies on the Left—on condition, of course, that the democrats confined themselves to supporting them and made no attempt to compete with them for power. It was under these auspices that the Directory was installed: the election of Carnot was proof of that.

The volte-face of the Republican Thermidorians, consecrated by the *journée* of 13 Vendémiaire, had another far-reaching consequence: it allowed the annexationists to resume the war on the Rhine and to obtain union with Belgium. Aubry had left the Committee on 15 Thermidor (August 2); true, Threilhard followed him, but Sieyès and Reubell came back on the Committee as did Letourneur and Merlin de Douai, whom they won over. Thus the majority of the diplomatic section found itself determined

to extend the frontier to the Rhine; the *Moniteur* published
Roberjot's report on his mission in the occupied regions,
which concluded in favor of union with France, and petitions to this effect were obtained from the Rhenish population. The negotiations with the Germans promptly came to
an end. On July 29, the Emperor, in ratifying the Diet's
conclusum in favor of negotiations, had specified that the
integrity of the empire had to be respected; at Basle,
Hardenberg repeatedly declared that Prussia would not go
beyond the treaty of April 5 if France did not give up her
claim to the Rhine; when, on August 3, Frederick William
was notified of the third partition of Poland, he was therefore obliged, not wishing to make common cause with the
Republicans, to resign himself to accepting it in principle,
while at the same time insisting on a larger share. After
some stormy conferences, he contented himself with what
he was offered, namely the region situated to the south of
East Prussia, including Warsaw. The Committee of Public
Safety continued to throw out feelers toward Austria, but
Thugut refused to take part in discussions without England's support. On September 28, Russia joined the Coalition. Against England, France secured in theory an alliance with Sweden, but to turn theory into fact, she
would have had to be able to send Sweden money. Godoy
showed readiness to accept an agreement of this sort; but
as a commercial treaty was asked for in addition, the whole
project came to nothing.

Determined to keep its conquests, the Committee de-
cided to give categorical orders to the generals, and on 20
Fructidor (September 6), the Army of the Sambre and
Meuse, under Jourdan's command, crossed the Rhine at
Düsseldorf and Neuwied; Clerfayt retreated step by step as

far as the Main. At the end of July, Wurmser had brought
up a new army to the upper Rhine; from there, in September he simply sent Quasdanovitch northward with 12,000
men, to maintain liaison and cover the huge stores at
Heidelberg. Pichegru's role could have been decisive: if he
had emerged from Mannheim, Clerfayt would have been
surrounded, but he was not ready and his troops remained
strung out from Basle to Mainz. Not until 13 Fructidor
(September 16) did he concentrate two weak divisions,
12,000 men in all, leaving Mannheim the next day to advance on Heidelberg. Quasdanovitch was there already and
launched a vigorous attack on September 23; one of the
French divisions merely bombarded his troops, while the
other was put to flight. However, this diversion had been
sufficient to draw Clerfayt away towards the Neckar, so
that Jourdan was able to take the Main line and complete
the blockade of Mainz, while Marceau was laying siege to
Ehrenbreitstein. By working together, Jourdan and Pichegru could still manage to defeat Clerfayt; a specific order
had been necessary to decide Wurmser to go to his help
and he was still a long way away. On September 27, the two
French generals had a meeting and decided to wait for the
Committee's orders, which failed to arrive.

It must be assumed that it was too busy keeping an eye
on the Parisian Sections; all the same, it found time to
prepare the annexation of Belgium. On 8 Vendémiaire
(September 30), Merlin de Douai put the proposal for
annexation to the Convention, setting forth at the same
time the plebiscites of 1793, the economic advantages of
annexation, and the need to make sure of a good strategic
frontier. Harmand de la Meuse and Lesage objected that
Austria would never resign herself to this loss; besides, the

Belgians were too different from the French, in their way
of life and their religious ideas, ever to be assimilated; their
supposed desire for union with France was worthless,
since it had not been freely expressed. Lesage was particularly aggressive, maintaining that the Belgians were
happy under their old Constitution, and that they should
be returned to Austria or given their independence. "It
was typical of the Mountain to obtain votes with the sword
and issue decrees without thinking. . . . How can the
Committee be so blind about such projects? . . . How
can it make itself the agent of brigands?" This Girondin
was forgetting that it was his party which, at the end of
1792, had made annexations the order of the day, and in
linking this question with home affairs, he was stating in
advance that the thirteenth of Vendémiaire would also
determine foreign policy. On the ninth, Merlin de Douai
and Roberjot returned to the attack and Carnot gave them
his support. They carried the proposal. Merlin had also
spoken in favor of the Rhine frontier, but he had postponed any decision until a general peace had been declared.

Soon afterward, military events revealed that peace was
anything but imminent. At the beginning of October,
Wurmser appeared before Mannheim with 55,000 men, and
on the tenth, Clerfayt managed to cross the Main. He
turned Jourdan's flank by violating the demarcation line,
and pushed him back towards the Lann. Pichegru did not
budge. On October 29, he finally received the order to
attack. It was too late. The same day, Clerfayt routed the
division blockading Mainz and liberated the town. Jourdan
had already fallen back on Düsseldorf and was crossing the
Rhine. Going up the valley at the beginning of November,

the Austrians forced Pichegru to retreat behind the Queich, and on the twenty-first they recaptured Mannheim.

In speaking out definitely in favor of the annexations, the Republican Thermidorians had finally broken with the Royalists, but they had been unable either to make peace or to wage war, and on the frontier as at home they bequeathed nothing but dangers and difficulties to the Directory.

CHAPTER ELEVEN

The Achievement
of the Thermidorians

The Convention broke up on 4 Brumaire, Year IV (October 26, 1795), after sitting for over three years and studding its existence with some of the most striking contradictions in the history of parliamentary assemblies. The Thermidorians were guilty of some of these contradictions and their reputation stands very low because there was a certain duplicity in their conduct: they inveighed against the despotic actions of the revolutionary government, but, when dealing with their adversaries, they paid little attention to the law; they denounced the Red Terror, but they organized or tolerated a White Terror; they vilified the intervention of the State in the economy, but they gave a free reign to businessmen greedy for scandalous speculation, and to corrupt deputies. Even historians hostile to the Montagnards admit that there was neither beauty nor grandeur in the reign of their enemies.

However, in favor of the Thermidorians, it can be pleaded that the great majority of them were honest men and that they suffered from a lack of first-class leaders. The spirit of vengeance raging around them could not, humanly speaking, completely fail to affect them, and yet more than once they tried to resist it. They were faced with insurmountable difficulties, at a time when the guillotine and exile had deprived them of leaders. Drifting along usually on the current of events, they nonetheless had definite ideas about the form of government which ought to be set up in France; if they were unable to organize it in its entirety, the Directory and the Consulate would, in many respects, simply continue their work. That is why, removed from the ephemeral tumult of political conflict and replaced in a historical perspective, the period is seen to have been both meaningful and important: going back beyond the attempt at social democracy that the Montagnards were led into by the requirements of the struggle against the Revolutions' enemies, the Thermidorians linked up again with the tradition bequeathed by the Constituent Assembly, which condemned both the *ancien régime* and democracy, to insure the predominance of the bourgeoisie whose rise to power, prepared for by the entire history of France and sanctioned by its capabilities, could alone, in its opinion, insure the prosperity of the national community.

Constitutional Monarchists and Republicans were no

doubt divided as to the title and powers to be conferred on the chief of the Executive; above all, the former wanted him to be hereditary and the latter, elected; this disagreement weighed heavily on the history of the period and that of the nineteenth century. But the Thermidorians, when preparing the Constitution of Year III, were agreed that it was incumbent upon the "notables" to rule and govern, and the cardinal principle of their activity had to be to maintain liberty and equality before the law, so that the ranks of the bourgeoisie should remain open to all who were destined to rise in society as a result of their merit, work, or good fortune. It might also be added that the Constituent Assembly, chiefly preoccupied as it was with overthrowing the *ancien régime*, had shown more verbal generosity towards the lower classes, more confidence in their virtues, and more hope too in a social evolution, which liberty would be sufficient to render fruitful and peaceful. In Year II, the bourgeoisie had seen itself deprived of power: the nationalization of the economy had dried up the main sources of its wealth, and the Montagnards, who had sprung from its own ranks, had put themselves at the head of the *sans-culottes*. It had been frightened, and could not forget it. That is why, with its attention concentrated henceforth on its own defense, it became hard and gloomy in spirit. Its distrust of and contempt for the common people were revived, and were intensified by a rancor sometimes bordering on hate; very little was needed to transform the bourgeoisie into a new aristocracy which would work unscrupulously to keep for itself all the benefits of the Revolution. It was during the Thermidorian period, in a reaction against the spirit of Year II, that there awoke in the upper ranks of the French bourgeoisie that class consciousness which became more and more exclusive, and which ended up by typifying the July Monarchy.

Let us listen to Boissy d'Anglas justifying the property qualification for suffrage:

> We must be governed by the best citizens; the best citizens are those who are most educated and most interested in the keeping of the law. Now, with very few exceptions, you will find such men only among those who possess some property, who are attached to the country that contains it, the laws that protect it, and the peace that maintains it; men who owe to that property and to the affluence it affords the education which has made them fit to discuss, wisely and equitably, the advantages and the drawbacks of the laws that determine the fate of the country. . . . A country governed by landowners is in the social order, whereas one governed by persons other than property owners is in a state of nature.

As for Dupont de Nemours, he rose to metaphysical heights:

> It is obvious that the property owners, without whose consent nobody in the country would have either food or lodging, are that country's leading citizens. They are sovereigns by the grace of God, of Nature, of their work, of their progress, and of the work and progress of their ancestors.

Admittedly, none of this was new, and Dupont, in particular, spoke as the Physiocrats had spoken in the past. In substance, some members of the Third Estate had said the same thing in the Constituent Assembly, but never in this dogmatic tone and never without meeting any contradiction. Madame de Staël, demanding the monopoly of power for the notables, claimed to be uniting in their ranks men of merit and men of wealth; Bonaparte would pride himself on reserving a place for talent. With Dupont de Nemours, the mask dropped, and Boissy was really no less explicit in his intervention in the debate on the foundation of central schools: he obtained a reduction in the number of these schools, explaining that to raise the number would be to incur the danger of increasing "the parasitical and ambitious minority." As far as possible, what we call secondary education was to be reserved for the children of property owners.

The Thermidorians did not have time to give the bourgeoisie, at the same time as a political constitution, the social charter which it would receive in the form of the Civil Code. The bill, tabled on 23 Fructidor, Year II (September 9, 1794)—the second project of its kind—remained in abeyance. But they dealt an initial blow at the laws of succession of Year II, which aimed at systematically splitting up inheritances, by abolishing the retroactive effect on 9 Fructidor, Year III (August 26, 1795). They also passed a mortgage code on 9 Messidor (June 27). The re-establishment of imprisonment for debt was already being called for, by such bodies as the Bonne Nouvelle Section on 24 Thermidor (August 11). The change in morals and above all the emancipation of women also aroused anxiety. Corruption had not increased to anything like the extent that certain historians, and consequently most novelists, suggest, simply because they consider only "society," in other words a few hundred wealthy families. On the contrary it is clear that morals, and above all the concept of what they ought to be, had not developed at all as one would have imagined under the influence of the liberal principles proclaimed in 1789, especially as far as women were concerned. The French people, on the whole, went on living as they had always lived. The Jacobins had often been puritans, and rarely feminists. The *Catéchisme du citoyen* in which Volney in 1793 had laid down the moral obligations of the good Republican was extremely traditionalist, particularly as far as the family was concerned. This discrepancy would soon awaken the rancor of certain women—notably Madame de Staël—and the emancipation of women, at least on the emotional level, would be one of the features of Romanticism. In spite of everything, some women had nonetheless been seen taking an interest in politics and neglecting their homes for the club, the tribune and even the riot. Divorces were quite frequent; nobles and bourgeois had resorted to them when they emigrated, in order to save their property by transferring it to their former wives who remained in France, and in many cases the pretended separation had become real and final. In Paris, at least, the salons of Madame Tallien and Madame Hamelin were anything but schools of virtue for the upper middle class. The Thermidorians ended up by becoming alarmed at this weakening of marital and paternal authority and the damage caused to the "standing" of the bourgeois family by the dissolute conduct of women; at least, on 15 Thermidor (August 2), they suspended the laws of 8 Nivôse and 4 Floréal, Year II, which had made divorce easier.

However, on one essential point—the influence of religious ideas—the Thermidorian Republicans did not act as the precursors of the Consulate. Admittedly it can be maintained that by restoring to a certain point the free practice of religion, they allowed the religious revival which culminated in the Concordat to make its initial progress.

But they made this concession only reluctantly, first in order to pacify the west, and then out of consideration for the Right, whose help they needed. This is not to say that the Constitutional Monarchists were usually believers, but they were more faithful to the Voltairian tradition which called for "a religion for the people." The Thermidorian Republicans, on the contrary, shared the hostility of the *sans-culottes* to dogmatic religions in general and to the Roman Church in particular. It did not occur to them to call on these to reinforce by their teaching the foundations of morality; on the contrary, they rather unexpectedly borrowed from Robespierre, the hated "tyrant," the idea of a civic religion which, in the churches themselves, would be set against the traditional religion, with the hope that it would end up by defeating its rival. Marie-Joseph Chénier made himself the champion of this civic religion, and drew up several reports on the decadal feasts from which it was left to the Directory to draw its conclusions. In the ranks of these Republicans there shone the future "ideologists," who installed themselves in the Institut; several of them were materialists and the most famous, Destutt de Tracy and Cabanis, worked out a philosophy in which it is possible to discern a few features of the later positivism. On 21 Fructidor (September 7), Dupuis presented to the Convention his work on *Les Origines de tous les cultes*, which explained the origin of religions by purely human causes.

It was from the economic point of view that the Thermidorians broke most clearly with the legislation of the Montagnards, which, among other justifications, had invoked the right to life. Like the Constituent Assembly, they freed capitalism from all restrictions by giving up control of the national economy and by restoring freedom, at the very least, to industry, trade and finance, in other words to the urban bourgeoisie. Only the grain trade, by the force of circumstances, remained provisionally under control. For months, the Thermidorians had not dared to touch the Montagnard laws, which laid down rules for the sale of national property favoring the small purchaser; finally, however, they were repealed on 12 Prairial and henceforth national estates were sold without being divided up. The law of June 10, 1793, with respect to the division of common land, began to be attacked, as was the process of arbitration applied to differences between a community and its former manor lord as to the ownership of common land; on 20 Thermidor (August 7), Barailon had the law referred to the Committees, with a view to having it repealed. It was Lozeau who, on 27 Fructidor, Year II (September 13, 1794), best expressed the opinion of the majority on the agrarian policy of the Mountain: it was ridiculous to think of "making most of the people land-owners," since there was not enough cultivated land for this to be done; even if there had been enough land, the idea was no less fantastic, for "since according to this hypothesis, every man was obliged to cultivate his field or his vineyard in order to live, trade, industry and the arts would soon be annihilated"; in other words, a proletariat had to remain in order to provide the bourgeoisie with the labor force that was essential for it.

As for the national assistance scheme which the Constituent Assembly, before the Convention, had promised to organize, the Thermidorians showed their intention of abandoning it once more to the discretion of local authorities, by suspending the sale of the property of hospitals and alms-houses on 9 Fructidor, Year III (August 26). It was only too easy to justify the indifference shown toward national assistance by the shortage of funds. It was a different matter for education, but in this sphere as well, the necessary economies served as a pretext for reaction.

The Thermidorians displayed a proper solicitude for the great scientific establishments which the Montagnards had begun to set up. On 1 Brumaire, Year III (October 22, 1794), they opened the School of Public Services, intended to train engineers for the army, the navy and public works; on 6 Vendémiaire, Year IV (September 28, 1795), it became the Central School of Public Works; presently, it is the École Polytechnique, or Military Academy of Artillery and Engineering. The Conservatoire des Arts et Métiers, or School of Arts and Crafts, was installed on 19 Vendémiaire, Year III (October 10, 1794), at Saint-Martin-des-Champs, and a school of clockmaking created at Besançon in Messidor. On 14 Frimaire, Year III (December 4, 1794), plans had been approved for three schools of medicine, and the Deaf and Dumb Institute was founded on 16 Nivôse (January 5, 1795). The Museum, founded on June 10, 1793, was reorganized and Cuvier joined it in 1795. The decree of 7 Messidor, Year III (June 25, 1795) gave birth to the Bureau des Longitudes or Central Astronomical Office, and classes in astronomy were initiated at the Observatory. The School of Oriental Languages dates from 10 Germinal (March 30). Archeology and the arts also came in for their share: Grégoire's reports and the activities of the temporary Commission of Arts, of which Alexandre Lenoir was the moving spirit, led to the formation of the Museum of French Monuments at the Augustins and at the Louvre, on 15 Fructidor (September

1); archeological classes on inscriptions and medallions were begun at the Bibliothèque Nationale. The preparation of the metric system continued: on 1 Vendémiaire, Year IV (September 23, 1795), use of the meter was made compulsory in Paris and the department of the Seine, as of the beginning of Nivôse; on 28 Thermidor (August 15), the franc had become the monetary unit. Finally, just before breaking up on 3 Brumaire, Year IV (October 25, 1795), the Convention placed at the head of the country's establishments of higher education, in order to provide them with unified guidance, the Institut National, in which, beside a department of literature and fine arts, it also provided for one for the physical and mathematical sciences and one for the moral and political sciences; the latter was a considerable innovation.

This splendid efflorescence was the consecration of the great intellectual movement of the eighteenth century, and particularly of the efforts of the Encyclopedists and of Condorcet. But only the organization of a system of secondary education could provide the world of learning with a public and interest the sons of the bourgeoisie in the liberal professions which were to offer them a lucrative career. For the Republican State, it was of prime importance that this education should not be left to private initiative or even to local authorities, for this would enable the Roman Church gradually to secure a monopoly for itself once more. In the opinion of the scientists and philosophers, it was not enough to put the former colleges under central control; deprived of their property and their old teachers, they were in a wretched state of stagnation. They were unevenly distributed, and the education given in them, despite a few improvements, was out of keeping with modern thought and the new society. It was almost entirely devoted to the humanities; as for the sciences, only mathematics at the very most was given a place; often, too, the French language was not included in the curriculum. On 6 Ventôse, Year III (February 24, 1795), acting on a report by Lakanal, the Convention therefore created the "central schools" at the rate of one to each department. The curriculum of the three years' course was laid down by the decree and henceforth included French, history, the experimental sciences, law, drawing, and, as far as possible, modern languages. However, this national system of education remained decentralized, partly so that the State should not have to pay for it; the departmental administration bore the cost of it and was allowed to appoint the schoolmasters from among the candidates approved by a board of education. From the technical point of view, the curriculum was too ambitious and the organization unsuited to the needs of children coming from primary school. The three years of the course were independent of one another; the pupils picked the classes they wished to attend; there were no preparatory classes to inculcate the rudiments of each subject, nor any provision for boarding. In theory the central schools were more like the modern universities than the modern *lycées*; between them and the primary school there was a gap, as if the State had wanted only the rich to be able to fill it, by means of private tutors; what is more, education in these central schools was not free.

As for the primary school, the State had at first taken responsibility for it by the law of 27 Brumaire, Year III (November 17, 1794). The teachers were to be housed in the nationalized presbyteries and paid by the Republic;

unfortunately, it was found impossible to provide a school for every commune, and for reasons of economy several villages were grouped in a single school district, a measure which made it difficult to keep the law on compulsory attendance, in spite of the fact that schooling was free. The choice of teachers also remained decentralized; the department appointed them after an examination carried out by a board of education.

The enforcement of this law was far from perfect when, on 3 Brumaire, Year IV (October 25, 1795), the Convention replaced it with another law which revealed the regression of democratic ideas. There was no longer any mention of compulsory attendance and the teacher ceased to be paid by the State: he was left only his lodging, and for the rest he had to return to a salary fixed by the municipality and paid by the parents. It was easy to see that, as had already happened with poor relief, primary education would soon sink back into the same state as at the end of the *ancien régime*. Moreover, the recruiting of teachers was presenting insurmountable difficulties. On 19 Vendémiaire, Year III (October 10, 1794), a training college had been opened which functioned from January to May, 1795. The districts sent 1,300 young men to it to attend lectures given by eminent professors; it was intended that, on their return, they should form the staff of training colleges in the departments, but this project was abandoned. As for the decadal religion which was supposed to act as an extension of school, it had not been organized by the time the Directory came to power.

The central and primary schools were entirely secular, and although priests were not forbidden to teach in them, religious teaching was banned; morality, in the eyes of the ideologists, was based on social utility and on reason. But the Thermidorians did not give them a monopoly of education, so that in many places their secular teaching made parents prefer the independent schools, which in actual fact were Catholic ones. This question of freedom of education was not debated until 28 Brumaire, Year III (November 18, 1794); it was not seriously taken up by the Montagnards, but they expressed some anxiety about the teaching which would be given by the masters in the private schools. In their opinion, the latter should have been placed under the supervision of the authorities; they suggested that it would be advisable to check their qualifications and to compel them to follow a definite curriculum and use certain elementary books. The Thermidorians brushed these objections aside, displaying an indifference which is rather surprising in view of their anticlericalism. Their underlying motives are shown by the reception they gave to Duhem's speech: "I am afraid that the public schools might become, with regard to the private schools, what the poor schools used to be with regard to those which demanded fees; I am afraid that they may be attended only by the children of the *sans-culottes* and that the rich will send their children to the other schools." "May I ask," retorted Dubois-Crancé, "if an attempt is being made to prevent a father from educating his son as he wishes?" and Lecomte declared: "The previous speaker is so attached to the egalitarian system which he wants to establish at all costs, that he cannot bear one citizen having more merit than another." These debating courtesies allowed the Thermidorians to refrain from admitting that they wanted to reserve for the bourgeoisie the opportunity to keep their children away from the national school where they would have found themselves sitting beside the children of the poor; class consciousness had won the day over anticlericalism.

While the Thermidorians were thus beginning, by legal methods, a social reaction which was not to come to a stop for a long time, they simultaneously set off, by giving way to inflation, a social upheaval which would bring about a profound change in the structure of the bourgeoisie. During the summer of 1795 it was already visible. The collapse of the *assignat* ruined the rentiers and the government officials. Just as taxpayers and purchasers of national property lost no time in liquidating their debts to the State by means of valueless paper money, so debtors paid off, at almost no cost to themselves, not only the interest but the capital sum of their mortgages. On 25 Messidor (July 13, 1795), the Convention suspended the possibility of repaying the capital sum of mortgages taken out before January 1, 1792, and banned anticipated repayment for all others; but this was only an imperfect remedy. Conversely, it had to forbid sellers, on 14 Fructidor (August 31), to claim back their former property, many courts having acceded to applications for the annulment of contracts and dispossessed the purchasers. Landed property, which at that time formed the principal wealth of the bourgeois who "lived nobly" and even of the others, also suffered considerably. It was real estate that was ill-treated most of all. The decree of 3 Messidor (June 21) stipulated that rents should be paid in *assignats* at par, whereas farm rents should be paid at the rate of six to one; the decree of 2 Thermidor (July 20) was even more advantageous to country landlords in that it granted half of farm rents in kind. It was then that the housing crisis worsened in Paris and the big cities, where the population was rapidly swollen by the return of city dwellers who, in 1793 and 1794, had emigrated or taken refuge in the country, as also by the influx of people who wanted to take advantage of government distributions and the sale of cheap bread; building and repairs came to a stop and the congestion became irremediable during the following winter. However, it would be a mistake to have any illusions about the fate of landed property. The farmers were only obliged to pay half their farm rents and taxes in kind if they had a surplus, and they did not fail to get rid of such surpluses surreptitiously or to plead market requisitions in order to be able to pay in *assignats* only. It is true that in the greater part of France it was the *métayage* system, by which the farmer paid rent in kind, which predominated, and it necessarily made considerable progress, since the landlord, on the expiration of a farming lease, naturally preferred, in the prevailing conditions, a concession with a share in the produce. However, as early as Year II he had been hit by another device. The tenant farmer leased the livestock and farm equipment from him, on condition that the farmer return it when he gave up the lease or reimbursed its value. He did not fail to sell everything and liquidate his debt, at the price of the incoming inventory, in depreciated *assignats*. On 2 Thermidor, Year II (July 20, 1794), the Montagnard Committee of Public Safety had obliged him to pay for the livestock in kind, and on 17 Fructidor (August 31), the Thermidorian Committee extended this rule to the equipment of the estate. These decrees were confirmed by the decree of 15 Germinal, Year III (April 3, 1795), but it is doubtful whether the landlords were able to make use of them in most cases. On 10 Floréal (April 29), a deputy consequently demanded the annulment of all leases, but without success.

Without the slightest doubt, the revolutionary bourgeois were sorely tried by the consequences of inflation, and that must have contributed not a little to thinning their ranks. However, among the commoners who had put their fortune into government stocks or land, in order to live a life of leisure, supporters of the Monarchy and even of the *ancien régime* were probably in a majority. Their ruin was added to that of so many others who, like the privileged classes, had been stripped of their feudal rights or had seen their property confiscated as a result of emigration or convictions. The social revolution, brought about by the revolutionary laws, was therefore completed after Year III by the revolution produced by inflation, and in most cases it weakened the influence of those Frenchmen who were hostile to the Republic and even to the work of the Constituent Assembly.

The bourgeoisie, taken as a whole, could have been deprived by the monetary disaster of a considerable part of its capital and thus hampered in its economic progress. In point of fact, nothing of the sort happened. First of all it must be pointed out that the disaster could not reach the same proportions as in our time, because the personal estate as yet occupied only a modest place; if the landed proprietors were impoverished, they were generally able to retain their property and wait for better days; moreover, many of them made good their losses by buying national property cheap. Even if this had not been the case, their class would not have been diminished as a result. The members of the old bourgeoisie who disappeared gave place to others; even before the Terror, and above all after 1795, war supplies and speculation of all sorts—in *assignats* and currency, in merchandise and national property—pushed into the forefront a host of adventurers of whom a certain number succeeded in consolidating their gains and founding bourgeois families. These *nouveaux riches* were far inferior to those of the eighteenth century as far as moral and intellectual culture was concerned. They had no respect for disinterested research and no understanding of revolutionary idealism; a narrow, limited utilitarianism was their law, and for a long time they retained, from their origins, a fierce, unscrupulous and almost innocent eagerness to take advantage of all the chances offered to them by troubled times and the unlimited liberty which the Thermidorians had restored to the economy. But if boldness and a capacity for enterprise do not necessarily form part of such characters, it must be admitted that they are very often stimulated by these qualities. It was men such as these who, in the eleventh century, with the help of the revival of trade, had been the first bourgeois, and every monetary and economic crisis, every period in which production alters in order to increase, sees the appearance of fresh examples. Without them the bourgeoisie would waste away, for after a few generations the descendants of the *parvenu* stop working and try to join the aristocracy. The *nouveaux riches* of Year III provided the bourgeoisie with a strength and, as it were, a new blood which prevented it from ossifying. It was from their ranks that, under the Directory and Napoleon's rule, there came many of the leading businessmen who, pressing on with the industrial renovation begun on the English model at the end of the *ancien régime*, were the initiators of modern capitalism in France. In this respect, the Thermidorian period was no doubt simply the dawn of a new age; it is none-theless important to recognize that dawn.

Nor was it unimportant for the future of the bourgeoisie that the decomposition of the rural community should speed up under the influence of the revolutionary laws, and inflation contributed to this process as well. Year III was a period of triumph for the big farmers; relieved of the *maximum* and of requisitioning, they sold their produce at high prices, and the country took its revenge on the town; at the same time, they paid taxes, farm rents, and the price of national property in worthless *assignats*. They rapidly rose above the common herd of small-holders, *métayers* and day-laborers, to form a peasant bourgeoisie which, producing in order to sell, joined the capitalist ranks.

Consciously or not, the Thermidorians therefore strengthened the social predominance of the bourgeoisie at the same time that they gave it political authority. But on this last point, by requiring it to govern according to liberal rules and with frequent elections, they compromised its future. They doubtless had the best intentions, and in this respect men like Daunou and Chénier showed themselves to be true sons of the eighteenth century. Unfortunately they were also ahead of their time. The Revolution was essentially of a social order and the dispossessed were to go on fighting for a long time yet, with the support of the foreign aristocracy, before resigning themselves. Charette and Stofflet remained in arms. In the south of France, Job Aimé who, as president of the primary assembly of Valence, had forbidden the electors to recognize the decrees of Fructidor, organized an insurrection with the help of the Marquis de Lestang; they seized Montélimar and Avignon and held out there for a few days. In the spring, the war was going to begin again. To their successors who had to wage it, the Thermidorians left no resources other than an almost worthless *assignat* and broken-down armies. To have any chance of governing constitutionally without putting the Revolution in peril, the rulers of France would have had to conclude a general peace, and, declaring themselves annexationists, the Republicans of Year III had been unable to do this. In the coming elections, the Directory would therefore be confronted with the same problem that had faced the Montagnards and the Thermidorians themselves. The former had boldly solved it by means of the dictatorship of a democratic Convention. It was truly ironical that, having repudiated that dictatorship, the Thermidorians, as soon as their Constitution had been passed, found themselves reduced to adulterating its application by the introduction into the Legislature of a majority of members of the Convention. But embarrassed by this very contradiction, and lacking the necessary boldness, they had not dared to choose those members. The result was a disguised dictatorship, which was ineffective and which yet sufficed to ruin the prestige of the new Constitution. In any case, even if the Thermidorians had entrusted the reins of power to reliable members of the Convention, they would have found themselves faced with the same difficulty at the elections of Year V. What followed is common knowledge: they got out of the difficulty on the eighteenth of Fructidor, by means of a *coup d'état* which, this time openly violating their own Constitution, re-established the revolutionary dictatorship. As it was impossible for them to appeal to the people, they carried out this *coup d'état* with the help of the army, and thus their policy ended up by turning the revolutionary dictatorship into a military one.

BIBLIOGRAPHICAL SUGGESTIONS

On the sources, see: P. CARON, *Manuel pratique pour l'étude de la Révolution* (Paris, 1912, 2nd ed., 1947); C. SCHMIDT, *Les sources de l'histoire de France depuis 1789 aux Archives nationales* (Paris, 1907); and for general bibliography, L. VILLAT, *La Révolution et l'Empire*, vol. I, *Les Assemblées révolutionnaires* (1789-1799), in the Collection Clio (Paris: Les Presses Universitaires, 1936). For the parliamentary debates see the reprint of the *Moniteur* (which is an ordinary newspaper and not an official document), vols. XXI-XXV, and BUCHEZ & ROUX, *Histoire parlementaire de la Révolution française*, vol. XXXVI. The most important laws and decrees will be found in DUVERGIER, *Collection des lois et décrets*, vol. VII-VIII; the decrees of the Committee of Public Safety in the collection of AULARD, vols. XV-XXVI; a selection of police reports and newspaper extracts in A. AULARD, *Paris pendant la réaction thermidorienne et sous le Directoire*, 5 vols., 1898-1902 (A collection of documents relating to the history of Paris during the Revolution).

Memoirs which may be usefully consulted include those of BARRAS, 4 vols. (1895-1896), LAREVELLIÈRE-LEPEAUX (1895), DURAND DE MAILLANE (1825, Collection Berville and Barrière); and above all THIBAUDEAU, 2 vols. (1824, same collection); LACRETELLE, *Dix années d'épreuves pendant la Révolution* (1842); DUVAL, *Souvenirs thermidoriens*, 2 vols. (1844); TISSOT, *Souvenirs de prairial* (Year VIII); FRÉRON, *Mémoire historique sur la réaction royale et sur les massacres du Midi* (1824; Collection

232

Berville & Barrière); H. MEISTER, *Souvenirs d'un voyage à Paris en 1795* (Paris, 1910; Collection de la Société d'histoire contemporaine); *Correspondance inédite du conventionnel Rovère avec Goupilleau de Montaigu en mission dans le midi après la Terreur, 1794-1795* (published by M. Jouve & M. Giraud, 1908).

GENERAL HISTORY

SCIOUT, *Le Directoire* (begins at the ninth of Thermidor), 4 vols. (Paris, 1895-1897, vol. I); G. DEVILLE, *Thermidore et Directoire* (vol. V of *L'Histoire socialiste*, 1904); G. PARISET, vol. II of *L'Histoire de France contemporaine*, published under the direction of E. LAVISSE (Paris, Hachette, 1920); A. AULARD, *Histoire politique de la Révolution française* (Paris: A. Colin, 1901; 5th ed., 1921); A. MATHIEZ, *La réaction thermidorienne* (Paris: A. Colin, 1929); G. LEFEBVRE, *La Révolution française* (vol. XIII of the Collection *Peuples et civilisations*, Paris: P.U.F., 1957).

On the institutions of France, see: J. GODECHOT, *Les institutions de la France sous la Révolution et l'Empire* (in the Collection *Histoire des Institutions*, Paris: P.U.F., 1951); On one particular point, see M. BOULOISEAU, "Les comités de surveillance d'arrondissement de Paris sous la réaction thermidorienne" (*Annales historiques de la Révolution française*, 1933-1936).

On the *journées* of Germinal and Prairial, the bibliography, which for a long time consisted solely of the account of the first Prairial in F. THÉNARD & R. GUYOT, *Le conventionnel Goujon* (Paris, 1908), has been enriched by some comprehensive studies: R. COBB & G. RUDÉ, "Le dernier mouvement populaire de la Révolution à Paris," "Les journées de germinal et prairial an III" (*Revue historique*, October–December, 1955), and above all: E. TARLÉ, *Germinal et Prairial* (Moscow: Foreign Language Publications, 1959); K. D. RONNESSON, *La défaite des sans-culottes, Mouvement populaire et réaction bourgeoise en l'an III* (Oslo & Paris, 1959). See also: G. RUDÉ, *The Crowd in the French Revolution* (Oxford: Clarendon Press, 1959), particularly Chapter X, "Germinal-Prairial"; and A. GALANTE GARRONE, *Gilbert Romme, Storia di un rivoluzionario* (Torino:

Guilio Einaudi, 1959). On the Germinal disturbances in the departments, see particularly: R. Cobb, "Les journées de germinal an III dans la zone de ravitaillement de Paris" (*Annales de Normandie*, October–December, 1955); "Une émeute de la faim dans la banlieue rouennaise, Les journées des 13, 14 et 15 germinal an III à Sotteville-lès-Rouen" (*ibid.*, May, 1956). On the repression which followed the *journées*, see: R. Cobb, "Note sur la répression contre le personnel sans-culotte de 1795 à 1801" (*Annales historiques de la Révolution française*, 1954, p. 23-49).

THE WHITE TERROR

See works of local history and a few special studies such as: P. Vaillandet, *Les débuts de la Terreur blanche en Vaucluse* (*Annales historiques de la Révolution française*, 1928); *Le Procès des juges de la Commission révolutionnaire d'Orange* (*ibid.*, 1929); E. Courcelle, *La Réaction thermidorienne dans le district de Melun* (*ibid.*, 1930); G. Laurent, *J.-B. Armonville* (a member of the Convention from Reims) (*ibid.*, 1924) *L'insurrection du 1er prairial an III et la situation économique de la ville de Reims* (*ibid.*, 1927); S. Blum, *La mission d'Albert dans la Marne en l'an III* (*La Révolution française*, 1903, *vol.* XLV); É. Poupé, *La répression de la révolte terroriste de Toulon* (*Comité des Travaux historiques*, 1924, vol. X). For Lyons, see: E. Herriot, *Lyon n'est plus*, vol. IV, "La Réaction" (Paris, Hachette, 1940); but this exclusively political study stops at the autumn of 1794. See therefore: Renée Fuoc, *La réaction thermidorienne à Lyon* (1795) (Lyons, 1957). The examination of the judicial archives remains to be done, except in the case of those in the registry at Coutances: E. Sarot, *Les tribunaux répressifs de la Manche en matière politique pendant la Révolution*, 4 vols. (Paris: Champion, 1881-1882), vol. IV.

THE VENDÉE, THE CHOUANS, QUIBERON

C.-L. Chassin, *Les pacifications de l'Ouest*, 3 vols. (Paris, 1896-1899); L. Dubreuil, *Histoire des insurrections de l'Ouest*, 2 vols. (Paris: Rieder, 1930); E. Gabory, *La Révolution de la Vendée*, 3 vols. (Paris, 1925-1928), vol. III; T. de Closmadeuc, *Quiberon* (Paris, 1898).

FINANCIAL AND ECONOMIC HISTORY

M. Marion, *Histoire financière de la France depuis 1715* (Paris: Rousseau, 1921), vol. III; J. Morini-Comby, *Les assignats, révolution et inflation* (Paris, 1925); S. E. Harris, *The Assignats* (Cambridge, Mass.: Harvard University Press, 1930); G. Lefebvre, *Documents relatifs à l'histoire des subsistances dans le district de Bergues*, 2 vols. (Lille: Robbe & Marquant; Paris: Leroux, 1913-1921; Publication de la Commission d'histoire économique de la Révolution), Introduction; *Les paysans du Nord pendant la Révolution française* (Lille: Marquant; Paris: Rieder, 1924); J. Stern, *Le mari de Mlle Lange: M. J. Simons* (Paris: Plon, 1933); Gaston Martin, *La vie bourgeoise à Nantes sous la Convention d'après le livre de comptes de Mme Hummel* (*La Révolution française*, 1933); R. Cobb, "Les disettes de l'an II et de l'an III dans le district de Mantes et la vallée de la Basse Seine" (*Mémoires de la Fédération des Sociétés historiques et archéologiques de Paris et de l'Ile-de-France*; Paris, 1954); "Disette et moralité, La crise de l'an III et l'an IV à Rouen" (*Annales de Normandie*, October–December, 1956). On the state of the army, see: H. Bourdeau, *Les armées du Rhin au début du Directoire* (Paris, 1902); F. Vermale, "La désertion dans l'armée des Alpes après le 9 thermidor" (*Annales Révolutionnaires*, 1913, pp. 506-16 and 643-57).

RELIGIOUS HISTORY

A. Aulard, *Histoire politique de la Révolution, op. cit.*; P. de La Gorce, *Histoire religieuse de la Révolution française* (Paris: Plon, 1921), vol. IV; A. Mathiez, *Le régime légal des cultes sous la première séparation*, in *La Révolution et l'Église* (Paris, 1910), and the numerous local studies of religious history. See in particular: Abbé J. Boussoulade, *L'église de Paris du 9 thermidor au Concordat* (Paris, 1950).

EDUCATION

A. Troux, *L'École centrale du Doubs à Besancon* (Paris: Alcan, 1926; with a bibliography on the central schools); for the Convention's institutions, see the bibliography of Pariset, *op. cit.*; on society: E. & J. de Goncourt, *Histoire de la société fran-*

çaise sous la Révolution (Paris, 1854; 3rd ed., 1888); J. Turquan,
La citoyenne Tallien (1898); R. Arnaud, *Le fils de Fréron*
(1909).

CONSTITUTION OF YEAR III

M. Deslandres, *Histoire constitutionnelle de la France de
1789 à 1870*, 2 vols. (Paris: A. Colin, 1932), vol. I; A. Lajusan,
Le plébiscite de l'an III (*La Révolution française*, 1911), vol.
LX; H. Zivy, *Le 13 vendémiaire an IV* (1898; Bibliothèque de
la Faculté des Lettres de Paris); M. Dessal, "La révolte de
Dreux et les origines du 13 vendémiaire" (*Bulletin de la Société
d'Histoire moderne*, January–February, 1957, p. 5); G. Rudé,
"Les sans-culottes parisiennes et les journées de vendémiaire an
IV" (*Annales historiques de la Révolution française*, 1959, pp.
332-46).

On the question of Louis XVII there exists a vast and often
totally uncritical literature. See the bibliography of G. Pariset,
op. cit. As far as recent studies are concerned, in one of the articles gathered together under the title *Énigmes du temps passé*,
vol. I (Paris, 1944), L. Hastier has elucidated the problem of
the registration of the death; in another work, *La double mort de
Louis XVII* (Paris, 1951), the same author concludes that the
little prince died in January, 1794. On this same problem, see:
M. Garçon, *Louis XVII ou la fausse énigme* (Paris, 1952);
L. Hastier, *Nouvelles révélations sur Louis XVII* (Paris, 1954).

FOREIGN POLICY

A. Sorel, *L'Europe et la Révolution française* (Paris, 1892),
vol. IV; H. von Sybel, *Geschichte der Revolutionszeit* (Düsseldorf, 1853-1879), translated into French by Mlle Dosquet, 6
vols. (Paris, 1869-1887); L. Legrand, *La Révolution française en
Hollande* (Paris, 1894); J. B. Manger, *Recherches sur les relations économiques de la France et de la Hollande pendant la
Révolution française* (Paris: Champion, 1923).

THE

DIRECTORY

CHAPTER ONE

Thermidorians and
Directorials

On 4 Brumaire, Year IV (October 26, 1795), the Convention broke up; the Thermidorians abandoned power and, right away, took it back again under cover of the Constitution of Year III. Thermidorians and Directorials were all one: the same men, the same ends, the same means. They had outlawed the Jacobins and announced the return to liberty; but in destroying the organization of Year II, they had also ruined the *assignat*, abandoned the common people to the miseries of inflation, reduced the armies to impotence, and revived the hopes of the counterrevolution. Then they had forced the electors to choose two-

239

thirds of the new deputies from the Convention, broken the insurrection of the thirteenth of Vendémiaire, and revived the exceptional laws against the émigrés and the clergy. The whole history of the Directory lives up to these portents.

In repudiating democracy, the new Constitution gave political power back to the bourgeoisie and to the notables, by property qualification for suffrage, and, with economic liberty, a pre-eminent position to society. True, in order to be a *citoyen actif*, it was enough to pay a direct tax of any kind, but in order to be appointed an elector one had to be the owner or tenant of an estate or a house for which the land-tax, it seems, was thirty or forty francs. It was these electors—about 30,000 at the most—who chose the representatives. This regime the Thermidorians knew to be threatened, on the one hand by the Jacobins and *sans-culottes*, and on the other hand by the counterrevolutionaries.

It was to the former that they had given most thought. A considerable number of measures had been taken with a view to preventing any popular movement. There was no longer a mayor or a commune of Paris; the big towns were divided among several municipalities, and their central office, which was in charge of the police, was appointed by the department, subject to confirmation by the government. In Paris, a military guard surrounded the Directory and the Councils. The latter admitted only a restricted audience and could go into secret session. What is more, the Council of the Ancients, if it thought fit, could move the government outside the capital. The clubs were still authorized, but could no longer be anything but public gatherings, deprived of all means of action; they were forbidden to affiliate with one another, to correspond with one another, or to send deputations and collective petitions. Moreover, the Legislature could authorize domiciliary visits and suspend the freedom of the press for a year with nothing to prevent it from repeating these measures. Better still, the Directory could have individuals suspected of conspiracy arrested without intervention by the law, in other words by *lettre de cachet*, on condition that they be questioned within twenty-four hours and handed over, if there were sufficient grounds, to the appropriate judge; but they had no possibility of appeal.

Finally, once the Constitution had been passed, the Montagnard members of the Convention indicted or arrested during the White Terror were declared ineligible. The amnesty granted on 4 Brumaire for actions "connected with the Revolution" did not benefit them; moreover, its vagueness placed the terrorists at the mercy of the courts and the juries, henceforth composed of their enemies, and also left them exposed to civil law-suits for damages.

In spite of everything, the bourgeoisie did not feel reassured, and if its fear turned into an electoral maneuver against the "terrorists," "exclusives," "anarchists," "brigands," and "drinkers of blood," this fear was nonetheless sincere. What it dreaded was not only arbitrary arrests and summary executions, but also the resurrection of the popular government which had deprived the notables of power, treated the rich with suspicion and helped the poor. In its eyes, political democracy would lead to social democracy, as a prelude to the "agrarian law" and the division of property. The Directory had scarcely been installed before Dauchy would declare to the Five Hundred that "graduated taxation is the real germ of an agrarian law"; a little later Pons de l'Aveyron would say sententiously: "The poor man's interest is his neighbor's wealth"; on 18 Fructidor, la Revellière would prefer to expose himself to the "daggers of the Royalists" rather than appeal to the Faubourg Antoine. "Social" fear dominated the history of the Directory and served as a pretext for the eighteenth of Brumaire just as it later dominated the history of the Second Republic and served as a pretext for the second of December.

However the Thermidorians were just as determined to prevent a Royalist restoration, which, they maintained, would call in question the social achievement of the Revolution. Now the enemies of the Republic were still in arms: Condé's army was encamped opposite Alsace; Charette had taken the field again and was waiting for the Comte d'Artois, who had landed on the island of Yeu; their confederates had carried out the Vendémiaire rebellion and were conspiring everywhere; supported by foreign governments, they would remain formidable until a general peace reduced them to their own strength. Against them too, combat measures remained in force.

The émigrés, whose list remained open, were banished for life and liable to the death penalty on identification if they were caught carrying arms or if they re-entered France. They were deprived of all civic rights and their property was confiscated and sold. Yet in Year III, a good many of them had come back, and got the Thermidorian authorities to strike them off the list temporarily. Then again, when the Federalists who had been outlawed after the thirty-first of May had been rehabilitated, those who had been listed as émigrés had been struck off; this was an open door and the citizens of Toulon who had handed their town over to the English had taken advantage of it. Having accepted the idea that people could have emigrated innocently and out of fear, the Thermidorians had also amnestied the Alsatians, who had followed the Austrians in their retreat, provided that they were artisans or farm workers, and excluding nobles and priests. But after Quiberon, severity had prevailed: the Toulon offenders had been outlawed once more; the Constitution forbade any new exceptions; the émigrés who had been provisionally struck off the list were excluded from public office.

The émigrés were not the only ones to be affected. Those individuals of whom they were the heirs presumptive could not dispose of their property, because the Republic had appropriated in advance the successions which might devolve upon the fugitives during the fifty years after their listing, when, deprived of their civic rights, they were incapable of inheriting and doubly so if they died before their parents. On 12 Floréal, Year III (May 1, 1795), the latter had been instructed to redeem their debt by sharing an anticipated succession with the Republic, thus liquidating their succession before it had been opened. Then the Right, protesting at the responsibility imputed to the émigrés' relatives, made these judicial contradictions a pretext for setting aside all this legislation. After the thirteenth of Vendémiaire, the relatives of émigrés—husband, father and stepfather, son and grandson, uncle and nephew —had nonetheless been affected by it in another way: the law of 3 Brumaire, Year IV (October 25, 1795) excluded them from public office.

Finally, the counterrevolutionaries who had not emigrated also had their share of trouble: the Vendeans, the Chouans, and the Vendémiaire rebels were handed over to military commissions; the same law of 3 Brumaire was applied to all those who, in the primary and electoral assemblies, had put forward or signed seditious motions, and thus to the ostentatious supporters of the Vendémiairists; moreover, the measures which threatened the Jacobins served a double purpose and were aimed equally at the Royalists.

The priests were not spared either. Those who, ordered to take the oath of November 27, 1790, had refused or retracted—the non-juring clergy—had been deported, or, to be more precise, banished; if they had insisted on remaining in France, they were liable to be transported to Guiana; those who returned exposed themselves to the death penalty, simply on identification. Sentence of transportation was also pronounced on all other secular and regular ecclesiastics, even constitutional priests, if they had refused the "little oath" of loyalty to liberty and equality of August 14, 1792, or if they were denounced as agitators by six citizens in their department. Priests who were infirm or over sixty years of age were excepted, but were punished by compulsory retirement. These laws had fallen into abeyance in the course of Year III and the Constitution had made no mention of them; the deportees had returned like the émigrés, and the priests who had gone into hiding had reappeared. But the law of 3 Brumaire had revived this harsh legislation.

The Thermidorians had laid themselves open to cutting sarcasm by retaining this legislative arsenal while raging and fuming at the terrorists, especially since, as always happens, these laws, when not completely ineffective, were unfairly generalized. Not all terrorists were criminals, and not all democrats were terrorists. Similarly, not all émigrés were traitors, and not all non-juring priests counterrevolutionaries. But there was more to it than that: Jacobins and Royalists—at least some of the latter—were, for the Thermidorians, interchangeable allies.

Against the Royalists, the Republicans had formed a solid front, as had been seen on the thirteenth of Vendémiaire. It was only natural that in exchange for their support the Jacobins should ask that at least the amnesty should be faithfully interpreted, that they should be admitted to public office and that their leaders should be returned to them.

Inversely, it was in vain that the Thermidorians affected to treat all Royalists as counterrevolutionaries: they nonetheless found support in their ranks against democracy. The Monarchists were just as divided as the Republicans. The former Feuillants were willing to recall Louis XVIII only if he accepted the Constitution of 1791 in a suitably revised form, whereas the King had publicly declared his support for the Absolutists who wanted to re-establish the *ancien régime*. That is why they had resigned themselves to passing the Constitution of Year III, and, in spite of the decree of the two-thirds and of the thirteenth of Vendémiaire, they were prepared to respect it until such time as the restoration of the monarchy became possible. But it went without saying that in exchange they demanded that the Jacobins be outlawed once more, that all official positions be given to "decent people," and that the exceptional laws be repealed or at least considerably amended.

Thermidorians and Directorials were quite willing to be indulgent towards docile Jacobins, and they never stopped urging the Royalist bourgeoisie to join them in order to

245

consolidate the conservative Republic; but they still refused to give up the exceptional measures. They have been generally praised for their attitude towards the Jacobins, but their distrust of the "decent people" has been severely criticized. Yet it is easy to explain: first of all, by prejudices and interests of a personal nature. The Republican bourgeoisie was usually of low extraction and of modest or too recent fortunes; the Monarchist bourgeoisie, on the other hand, represented inherited wealth; its connections and way of life drew it towards the aristocracy. Then again, the blood of Louis XVI, or at least the tenth of August, separated Republicans and Royalists; what would be the fate of the former if the latter won the day? Moreover, was it likely that they would remain content with a Republic without Republicans? The experiment of Year III was conclusive: they had been given a free rein and the country had found itself on the verge of a restoration. It was not for nothing that the Thermidorians accused the Constitutionalists of complicity with the Absolutists: in control of the Republic, they would have left it defenseless; they found violent action repugnant, but would have allowed it; they did not want an invasion, but would have resigned themselves to it; they had negotiated with foreign countries before the tenth of August and they would take their money. The work of the Revolution remained unfinished, and, if it was to resist all attacks, it needed time. Yet the fact remains that the Thermidorians wanted the Republic to live while excluding those who had founded it; they wanted it to be bourgeois while refusing to give any power to a great part of the bourgeoisie; they wanted it to remain despotic while calling itself liberal.

They could obtain help in sustaining these paradoxes only by the offer of places and the bait of profitable business.

To tell the truth, their opponents, if they had dropped their masks, would not have appealed to the voters and electors. Nobody cared very much about Louis XVIII, and as for returning to the *ancien régime*, there could be no question of that. On the other hand, people's minds were no longer obsessed with the "aristocratic plot," now that the French armies were victorious and the Coalition shattered; as a result, nobody recalled anything of the Jacobin dictatorship except the memory of its demands and its severity. But the Thermidorians were no less unpopular than their rivals. The French people were weary. Having carried out the Revolution to be happy, they wanted to live in peace and longed for the war to come to an end so that they might have fewer taxes to pay, and not have to go and fight. Fundamentally, what they blamed the Jacobins for was their intransigence which, carrying the Revolution to extremes, had imposed too many sacrifices. Had the Thermidorians done much better? Bankruptcy was imminent, famine was rampant, and the war went on.

Nor was this all. This longed-for peace depended, to a certain extent, on an agreement between the Republic and the Catholic Church, whose conflict kept civil war alive and brought discord even into individual families. The civic religion which had been proposed to the people did not appeal to them; the new calendar disturbed their daily life and they preferred to rest one day in seven rather than one day in ten. The Catholic revival was one of the most striking features of the time. Now, the Constitution confirmed the separation of Church and State, and, if it recognized freedom of worship, it was on condition that the rules governing religious worship were observed. The clergy had to promise submission to the law and recognize the French people as their lawful sovereign. Not all of them were *soumissionnaires* and the schism between them had become more complex. Moreover, the people were showing increasing irritation at the ban on all demonstrations outside the churches, such as processions and pilgrimages, inscriptions and crosses, the wearing of ecclesiastical dress, and the ringing of bells. This was not how they understood freedom of worship, and accordingly they broke the law. Most of the time, the local authorities shut their eyes; if they intervened they encountered resistance. There can be no doubt whatever that, although the Thermidorians did not close the churches, they were as eager as the *sansculottes* to de-Christianize France, because they regarded the Revolution and Catholicism as incompatible. The majority of the French people were not of this opinion. Yet those who criticize the Thermidorians on this score usually fail to recall that many of the non-juring clergy upheld the same point of view and put their religion at the service of their politics; some took up arms with the Chouans. The Thermidorians were convinced that, far from disarming them, concessions would make them more dangerous than ever.

Accordingly, if the opposing sides refrained from advocating monarchical or revolutionary government, they had no scruples about attacking the rulers of the day, whom they held responsible for everything that was amiss. It was the Royalists who obtained the readier hearings; they argued that peace was impossible as long as power remained in the hands of the regicides and the persecutors of religion, who had made the sovereigns of Europe irreconcilable by extending France to her so-called natural frontiers and by threatening every throne with propaganda for universal revolution. Consequently it was another paradox on the part of the Thermidorians to return to the electoral system with nothing to offer but bankruptcy and war, especially at a time when, with many of the best patriots in the army, the absentees, the deserters, the rebels and the émigrés who had returned to France would rush to the ballot boxes. It was yet another paradox to have ordered annual elections to replace one-third of the Councils, half the municipalities, and one-fifth of the Directory and the departments; the partial character of the change only slightly reduced the inconvenience of its frequency, especially as re-eligibility was limited. In the midst of war, the government, exposed to continual agitation, would have neither stability nor permanence.

The electoral methods increased the danger. To choose the electors, the *citoyens actifs* met in cantons and voted when their names were called; they therefore had to travel to the seat of the canton and then wait in patience. As the system provided for repeated ballots, the assembly could last for several days, and because of the considerable number of absentees, a determined minority could win out by perseverance. It was the assembly which decided arguments about the admission of *citoyens actifs* and the eligibility of candidates; how could it be prevented from degenerating into a club? A party that did not shrink from violent methods could gain control of it. An appeal to the courts and to the Legislature was permitted, but it had not been possible to make it suspensive. The only course open to malcontents was to secede and go off to deliberate somewhere else; in this way there could be two or more lists of electors in competition. There was nothing to prevent things taking the same turn at the electoral assembly.

These methods benefited the extremist parties. To favor the White Terror, the Royalists had excluded the Republicans; if the Royalists were outlawed once more, the electoral system could benefit the Jacobins. The Thermidorians had provided against the danger by means of the decree of the two-thirds, which had assured them of a majority until the elections of Year V. But would a respite of eighteen months be sufficient to heal wounds and win over the electors? It was unlikely, and if not, only a *coup d'état* would be able to maintain the bourgeois republic; imitating the Jacobin Republic after having denounced it, it would return to a dictatorship—and a dictatorship very different from that of Year II. Since there could be no question of support from the common people, it could only be installed by the army. Then it would be challenged again every year: an annual *coup d'état* would make a stable government impossible. Above all, it would have to do without the Committee of Public Safety, the government's powers being so organized that their division would be inevitable.

The Thermidorian bourgeoisie in fact was not only afraid of democracy and Royalism; it also wanted to guard against the omnipotence of the State, and, to that end, had been careful to achieve a multiplication and balance of powers. The Legislature was divided into two Councils which could only communicate through "*messages*": the Five Hundred, aged at least thirty, and the Ancients, 250 in number, aged at least forty and married men or widowers. The Five Hundred had the initiative: they passed "resolutions" which the Ancients turned into "laws" if they thought fit. The Thermidorians believed that they had done everything to prevent an audacious minority from imposing its will: positions were drawn by lot, the committee was appointed for only a month at a time, and no permanent commission could be set up. The executive was entrusted to a Directory of five members, aged at least forty, and to the ministers appointed by the Directory. The Treasury, the Accounts Department, the judges, and the High Court constituted yet other powers.

All were independent of one another. The Directory could not adjourn the Councils, still less dissolve them; it was entitled to ask them to pass a law, but forbidden to present them with the text; access to the Councils was barred to it except by means of *messages*. Inversely, if the Legislature elected the Directors—the Ancients choosing them from a list of ten drawn up by the Five Hundred—it had no means of exerting pressure on them except by indicting them; it had no contact with the ministers. As for the judges, they were elected. Everything was arranged so that the constituted authorities, acting as checks on one another, were incapable of oppressing the citizens.

But everything was also arranged so that discussion should be slow and execution hampered. Yet, as in 1793 the Republic was engaged in civil and foreign war, and it was just as important for the government to be able to act speedily and energetically. The danger had apparently not escaped the Thermidorians' notice, for they had granted the Directory considerable powers: the right to issue decrees; control of foreign affairs and the ability to conclude treaties, even secret ones; the choice of generals and the conduct of the war; and the control of the police and local administration. The latter had been reorganized in such a way as to condense its authority and strengthen government control. There was no longer a departmental council, but only a central administration of five members. The district had been abolished, as had the general council of the commune; towns of 5,000 inhabitants and more had only municipal offices; the smaller communes retained only an agent and his assistant, the municipality consisting of an assembly of these agents at the seat of the canton. The Directory could quash without appeal the deliberations of the local administrations, dismiss their members and replace them if all their seats fell vacant at the same time, the vacancies otherwise being filled by co-optation. It attached to each administration a commissioner who was subject to dismissal. The departmental commissioner, a permanent official beside temporary, elected officials, in direct correspondence with the government, directing the committees and giving orders to the other commissioners, foreshadowed the Prefect of the future.

However, this was a long way from the centralization of the Jacobins or the Consulate. It was difficult for the central commissioner, by himself, to keep a close watch on the municipalities, of which there were so many, often far apart. The assessment and collection of taxes remained in the hands of the elected administrations. The Directory had no control over the Treasury. In the courts, it was represented only by a commissioner who could take no part in the prosecution, which was left to the gendarmerie officer, the justice of the peace, and the director of the indictment jury. Here, the difference from the system of Year

II was obvious: short of setting up countless military commissions, the Directory lacked "coercive force."

But worst of it was that there was nothing to guarantee co-operation between the Directory and the Councils; rivalry between the Executive and the Legislature is an inherent evil of the representative system. The Directory's powers were considerable and circumstances made it necessary to increase them still further. The Councils often paralyzed it by their inertia, yet never ceased to be jealous of it. The Convention had overthrown the great Committee of Public Safety to escape from its influence. The Directory of Year VII would have its ninth of Thermidor. The nature of things imposed a return to revolutionary dictatorship, but the Constitution of Year III, in the form the Thermidorians had conceived it, forced them to exercise that dictatorship ineffectively.

Could it be changed? Yes, no doubt it could, but a delay of seven years was required for any proposal to come into effect. Another *coup d'état* would be necessary to revise the Constitution of Year III, and it would not survive the operation.

CHAPTER TWO

The Beginning of
the Directory

The electors had observed the decree of the two-thirds, but only 379 members of the Convention had been re-elected, because several had been elected simultaneously in a large number of departments. Provision had been made for this eventuality. They gathered together in the "Electoral Assembly of France" and filled the vacant seats. After the new Third had made its entry, the Councils took their seats, the Ancients in the Tuileries in the hall which the Convention had just left, and the Five Hundred in the Riding School, where the Constituent Assembly, the Legislative

Assembly, and the Convention in its early days had sat. In Year VI, they would move into the former Palais-Bourbon.

Generally speaking, the electors had rejected the Jacobins and chosen the mildest members of the Convention; Royalists like Boissy d'Anglas, Lanjuinais and Henry-Larivière had been elected in over thirty departments. The choices of the Electoral Assembly of France had fallen somewhat further left; the new Third, further right. On the whole, only a few Jacobins had survived; the majority in the Directory was extremely varied; there were some Montagnards, Merlin, Barras, Tallien; a good many members of the Plain in the Convention, Sieyès, Ramel, Letourneur; some Girondins, La Revellière, Louvet, Chénier; and some members of the Constituent and Legislative Assemblies, Creuzé-Latouche and Lecoulteux. A small group hostile to the exceptional laws—Thibaudeau, Doulcet, Cambacérès—formed a link with the Constitutional Monarchists, who included Dupont de Nemours, Mathieu Dumas, Portalis, Tronson-Ducoudray, Pastoret, Dumolard, Vaublanc and Barbé-Marbois. Further right was the extremist opposition, which was also mixed; next to Gibert-Desmolières and Boissy d'Anglas, there were Henry-Larivière, organizers of the White Terror such as Cadroy and Isnard, and Job Aymé, a real Chouan and an auxiliary of the Marquis de Lestang who had recently been shot. These Councils were full of capable, educated men who would figure in large numbers in the personnel of the Consulate, but there were few orators among them; neither Sieyès nor Carnot could speak well; Portalis was known as the "warm water tap" and Dumolard as the "overflow of the Isère."

The choice of the Directors was of major interest, and,

on the morrow of the thirteenth of Vendémiaire, the majority allowed no breach to be made in its numbers. The members of the Convention in the Five Hundred got together to draw up a list of second-rate individuals, except for five regicides whom the Ancients would be obliged to choose; at the sitting, the Right only managed to slip Cambacérès into the second rank. In the Council of the Ancients, protests were made at the maneuver, but the Five were elected. They were La Revellière, Letourneur, Reubell, Sieyès and Barras. Sieyès refused: he had quarreled with Reubell, and, furious at having had his project for a Constitution rejected, was biding his time. Carnot was elected in his place.

La Revellière, the son of a Poitou notary, transplanted to Angers by his marriage, had been elected by that town to the Constituent Assembly and to the Convention. A Girondin, he had been obliged to go into hiding during the Terror, and his brother had been guillotined. He was therefore passionately hostile to the Jacobins, and as conservative as any Constitutional Monarchist; but he differed from them, not only in his indefectible attachment to the Republican form of government, but in his violent anticlericalism and a pronounced liking for propaganda warfare. Honest, disinterested, and living a modest family life, he was unfortunately a mediocrity and lacked prestige, especially as he was slightly deformed.

The Alsatian Reubell, a capable self-assertive man, had more personality. A barrister before the Revolution, he too had sat in the Constituent Assembly and the Convention; he had been a Montagnard and, according to Barras, he once said that he had never blamed Robespierre for anything but being too gentle. To tell the truth, his conduct at

Mainz had aroused the suspicions of the Committee of Public Safety, and this had driven him into opposition. His was the steadiest head in the Directory and he also stood out as the advocate of the natural frontiers, especially that of the Rhine. There were doubts about his probity, but no proof to back them up.

The Vicomte Paul de Barras was, like Mirabeau, a corrupt, dissolute noble who had thrown himself into the Revolution to seek his fortune. As a member of the Convention he had behaved as an extreme terrorist at Marseilles and Toulon and, recalled to Paris, had turned against the Committee of Public Safety. This handsome man, a former officer with an imposing manner, offered a striking contrast with his commoner colleagues, but nobody had any illusions about the "King of the Republic"; it was known that he made money out of everything and surrounded himself with a crowd of dishonest individuals and loose women. All the same, he was probably sincere when he said that the most important thing was to "save the men of the Revolution," or showed a penchant for annexations and propaganda. In any case, since he had saved the Convention in Thermidor and Vendémiaire, it was felt that he was an inevitable choice.

Carnot, as a member of the Committee of Public Safety, had nearly been outlawed with his colleagues, and he was repugnant to La Revellière as also to the Right; Reubell hated the despot in him and Barras the honest man. The majority did not like him either, imagining that he would protect the Jacobins; but it had considered him necessary to the conduct of the war. He had some strange surprises in store for one and all. Letourneur, a former engineering officer like himself, acted as his auxiliary.

Thus the Directory, right from the start, was as divided as the Committee of Public Safety in its last days; on the one hand, Carnot and Letourneur; on the other, La Revellière and Reubell, who moreover were far from being always in agreement; and then Barras, on whom no one could rely, since he could be bought and thought of nothing but himself.

The Directors installed themselves uncomfortably in the Luxembourg, which was completely unfurnished and delapidated, having served as a prison for over a year. Since the Treasury was empty, it took several months before they could cut a figure there. Each of them presided in turn for three months. A certain specialization was established among them: the conduct of the war fell to Carnot, foreign affairs to Reubell and education to La Revellière. They shared the departments among themselves when organizing local administration. The Constitution granted them a secretary, who was Lagarde, a former councilor to the bailliage of Lille and secretary of the department of the Nord. His position was an extremely important one, for it was through him that business was divided up among the ministers and returned to the Directory; the organization that he set up was retained by Bonaparte and became the Secretariat of State.

Six ministers were appointed to begin with: as Minister of the Interior, Bénézech, a capable man whom the Committee of Public Safety had employed, but who, married to an aristocrat, rapidly fell under suspicion on account of his manners and connections; as Minister of Finance, Faipoult, a former nobleman promptly replaced by Ramel-Nogaret, a regicide and brilliant financier who kept the post until Year VII; as Minister of Justice, Merlin de Douai, the

author of the Law of Suspects and now an anti-Jacobin, a
great worker and an eminent jurist, but lacking in character; as Minister of External Relations, Delacroix, another
regicide, who was far from untalented but was little more
than Reubell's clerk; as Minister of War, Aubert-Dubayet,
for whom Carnot soon substituted Petiet, a former war
commissioner and a good administrator; and finally, as
Navy Minister, Admiral Truguet. Before long a seventh
ministry was created, that of the Police, to which Merlin
was appointed, his place as Minister of Justice being taken
by Genissieu, a former member of the Convention.

The organization of the local authorities was much more
difficult. The Directory had to appoint thousands of commissioners in a hurry. A great many electoral assemblies,
for example that of the Seine, had not finished their task in
the ten days allowed by the Constitution, and they were
forbidden to meet in extraordinary session. Without raising many difficulties, the Councils instructed the Directory
to fill the places in the central and municipal administrations which were vacant. As far as the judges were concerned, there was strong resistance, but it eventually
subsided. As the Convention had postponed the election
of the municipalities of the big towns, the Directory was
similarly authorized to nominate them. It was a seemingly
endless task, for there were countless refusals and resignations; moreover, the elections having been favorable to
the Royalists, the number of dismissals increased. Admittedly, co-optation was used; but this was surely a ridiculous
remedy when over half the members of an administration had disappeared. In such cases the Directory arrogated
the choice of the replacements to itself, and it retained
that choice, in spite of protests from the Councils. Thus,

right from the start, its power grew considerably. To a great extent, it appointed the courts and the local administrations, as the Committees of the Convention had done and the Consuls would do. By its decrees, it promptly encroached on the legislative power, without the Councils ever trying to bar its way, although they never stopped complaining. And, in spite of everything, the composition of the courts and the administrations was never stable or satisfactory, partly because the members could not be paid, so that the Directory was never scrupulously obeyed.

Its task was unenviable. It had no financial resources, and although winter would bring hostilities on the frontier to a halt, disturbances were continuing at home. In Paris, which was still under military occupation, the commissions were trying the Vendémiaire rebels, two of whom were executed; Royalist demonstrations nonetheless continued in the streets, at the Café de Valois, and above all in the theaters; there, the Directory banned the *Réveil du peuple* and ordered the *Marseillaise* and other patriotic songs to be sung. The newspapers suppressed in Vendémiaire gradually reappeared; in the spring they had 150,000 subscribers, compared with 4,000 to the Republican papers. The Directory set up a Public Spirit Office to supervise them; it had some official papers of its own—the *Rédacteur* and the *Moniteur*—and subsidized others. In the southeast, where the Marquis de Lestang had been shot after occupying Avignon, the White Terror was still raging; the Directory supported the representatives sent there by the Convention, Fréron in Provence and Reverchon in Lyons. It did not take long to uncover a plot by Bésignan, a veteran of the counterrevolution in that region, and another aimed at delivering Besançon and the Comté into the hands of the Prince de Condé. The latter had been negotiating for a long time with Pichegru, who was in command of the Army of the Rhine and Moselle, but whose disastrous autumn campaign led to his replacement at the end of December. Yet it was the west that was giving most trouble. Charette waited in vain for a landing by the Comte d'Artois, who, at the end of October, had returned to England, but in January, 1796, Stofflet in his turn took up arms again. After Quiberon, Hoche had been put in supreme command, and on his advice the Directory had given him permission to let the laws on the clergy and religious worship fall into abeyance. But, contrary to legend, he pacified the region only by the use of great strength and severity. He surrounded it with lines of fortified posts and forced the peasants to surrender their arms in a series of raids which left them without any resources. Finally Stofflet and Charette were captured and shot, the former at Angers on February 25, 1796, and the latter at Nantes on March 29. After that, "Palluau's Vendée" had to be crushed in the Indre, and another insurrection in the Sancerrois. Then Hoche had to subjugate the Chouan leaders north of the Loire; Cadoudal and Guillemot, "the King of Bignan," in the Morbihan; Boisguy in Ille-et-Vilaine; Frotté in the Bocage Normand; and Scépeaux in the Maine. In June, the war was declared to be over, and the Army of the West was dissolved. But isolated bands continued to carry out murders and robberies.

Threatened in this way by the counterrevolution, the Directory, for some weeks, went on appealing to that union of Republicans which had been the order of the day since Vendémiaire. In its appointments, it gave the Jacobins a large place. It treated the Leftist press sympathetically, subsidizing Poultier's *Ami des Lois* and Duval's *Journal des hommes libres*. A holiday in commemoration of the twenty-first of January was ordained, and an oath of hatred for monarchy was imposed on public servants. Orders were given to enforce the laws against the clergy and the émigrés. Above all, no obstacle had been placed in the way of the re-opening of the clubs. The most important of the clubs, that of the Panthéon, inaugurated on 25 Brumaire, Year IV (November 16, 1795), soon had a thousand members. To begin with, it was deferential in its attitude to the government and showed a readiness to wait and see how it performed. Gracchus Babeuf, who had just resumed publication of his *Tribun du peuple*, in which he immediately declared war on the bourgeoisie, was condemned at first by the whole of the Leftist press.

In the Five Hundred, the Right fulminated most of all over the reinstatement of Jacobins in the local administrations, while the Left obtained the exclusion of the deputies who came within the provisions of the law of 3 Brumaire, notably Job Aymé. The result was often brawling worthy of the Convention. The majority remained fairly solid. In the case of the West Indian settlers who had taken refuge in the United States, and whom the Directory wanted to consider as émigrés, the Right only obtained an adjournment. As for the relatives of the émigrés, it could not prevent a revival of the division of anticipated successions, but succeeded in getting it declared optional.

However, circumstances gradually began to favor them. This was because the Jacobins had not been long in getting out of hand. They had humored the Directory only in the hope of carrying it with them, and they soon became impatient. Gradually they took the offensive under the influence of Darthé, Lebon's collaborator at Arras; of Lebois, the journalist on the *Orateur plébéien*; of Le Peletier, the brother of the murdered member of the Convention; of the Italian refugee Buonarroti; and of two members of the Convention who had been declared ineligible, Amar and Robert Lindet. As early as 14 Frimaire (December 5), a warrant had been issued for the arrest of Babeuf, who henceforth lived in hiding; Lebois was prosecuted; on 1 Pluviôse (January 21), Reubell declared menacingly in a speech: "Let good citizens be reassured." The Jacobin Club and the Leftist newspapers protested violently. The Directory took fright and broke completely with the Jacobins at the idea that they might be going to start an insurrection in the suburbs. For at this moment the *assignat* was in its death-throes, and in the depths of winter the common people were suffering terrible hardship.

CHAPTER THREE

The Monetary Crisis and
the Conspiracy of the Equals

At the time the Directory was installing itself, inflation was entering its final period. The *assignat* of 100 francs was worth from fifteen to sixteen sous, and prices were rising hour by hour. The sale of national estates had to be suspended and a moratorium declared to save creditors from ruin. The Directory could not manage to get enough *assignats* printed during the night for the following day and found itself at the mercy of a strike. In less than four months, the issue had approximately doubled.

Yet the Left persisted in maintaining that the revolutionary currency could be put on its feet again; the Right, on the other hand, declared that bankruptcy was inevitable, with tremendous benefit to its propaganda. Behind the political conflict it was possible to catch a glimpse of the social antagonism: the Left wanted the rich to be compelled to pay a graduated tax which would reduce the amount of the "token"; the Right wanted to spare them this sacrifice and satisfy the bankers. In any case, the special interest of bulls and bears compromised both sides.

Before breaking up, the Convention had passed a war tax which the Right regarded as excessive, and which the Left condemned because it was not graduated. The Directory proposed replacing it with a compulsory loan and agreed to graduation. After the Five Hundred had relaxed the stringency of their directions, the Ancients adopted the resolution on 19 Frimaire, Year IV (December 10, 1795). The loan was demanded from the most heavily taxed quarter of the country's taxpayers, whom the central administration of the department had to divide into sixteen classes according to the registers of taxes. A few weeks was sufficient to show that the desired result would not be obtained: the *assignat* was accepted at one per cent, whereas the market rate was three or four times less; payment had to be made within two months, but the mere drawing up of the registers took longer, and as soon as they appeared, there was such a chorus of recrimination that the Councils passed a rectifying law, so that everything had to be begun all over again. Finally, the hard-pressed Directory diverted part of the loan from its purpose: it distributed among its creditors about ninety million francs in *rescriptions* which enabled them to obtain the yield of the loan from the tax collectors, a measure which put back in circulation the *assignats* that the Directory had taken out. Altogether, it obtained twenty-seven billion francs in paper money and twelve million francs in metallic currency. One can judge the extent of the sacrifice imposed on the bourgeoisie and the resentment that it inspired in that class from the fact that the Puy-de-Dôme, which had paid up 250,000 livres in face value at the time of the compulsory loan of 1793, had to pay two million in real value this time. Yet before the Directory had collected anything, it was obliged to recognize that the effort would be in vain: the *assignat* was no longer worth the paper it was printed on. On 30 Pluviôse (February 19, 1796), the issue came to a stop: the amount in circulation was estimated at thirty-nine billion.

Was it intended to revert in this way to metallic currency? In that case, the *assignats* which the loan had not absorbed had to be called in first of all. Eschassériaux had proposed exchanging them for "mortgage debentures," in other words bonds on national property which could not be paid for with anything else. But in the Ancients, Lebrun and Lecoulteux objected that the monetary and financial problem would remain. The metallic currency which had reappeared was put at no higher than 300 million, whereas at the end of the *ancien régime*, it had been estimated at over two billion; once the *assignat* had been withdrawn, the economy, deprived of currency and consequently of credit, would be mortally stricken. Then again, what would taxes be paid with? And where would the government find the money to finance the spring campaign? These arguments prepared the way for the bankers. One of them, Laffon-Ladébat, proposed in fact that they create an issuing house. As well as the bank notes which would guarantee its capital, it would print others, in return for the cession by the State of 1,200 million francs of national property, half in order to redeem the *assignats*, half in order to supply the Treasury. Perregaux, Fulchiron, and Récamier, who were among the founders of the Bank of France, were prepared to join in this arrangement. What they wanted was a super-bank which they would control and which, rediscounting the bills their clients would bring them, would give their business an unlimited extension. The Directory was in agreement. But the Left resisted. Robert Lindet, on behalf of the Jacobins, conducted a violent campaign in the *Ami des lois* against the subjection into which the Republic was going to be forced. On 3 Ventôse (February 22), in the Five Hundred, the project fell through. If a new paper money was indispensable, the majority wanted to issue it itself and this had to be accepted.

After Defermon had again proposed mortgage debentures which he called *mandats*, the Directory intervened to insist that they should be legal tender, and agreement was reached on the basis of this compromise. The law of 28 Ventôse, Year IV (March 18, 1796) created 2,400 million francs in *mandats territoriaux* which would be accepted in payment of national property, to be handed over to any applicant on request and without auction. Six hundred million were to redeem the *assignats* and the rest was to go to the Treasury. The scheme raised such great hopes that the moratorium was annulled. For it to succeed, there would have had to be an immediate fiscal effort to balance the budget and restore confidence; measures would also have had to be taken to prevent a rise in prices by means of price control, and to prevent the collapse of foreign exchange by the control of imports and the obtaining of external credits. These conditions were excluded or unrealizable. Moreover, the *mandat* was discredited right from the start, because the *assignat* was accepted at the rate of thirty to one, whereas its real value was 400 to one at the very most. The catastrophe was overwhelming. At the beginning of April, the *mandat* of 100 francs was already worth only twenty; in July, it was no longer accepted in the commercial world. This time, thoroughly disillusioned, everybody accepted the need for a return to metallic currency. In Thermidor and Fructidor, the various taxes were declared payable in metallic currency or bills; on 1 Frumaire, Year V (November 21, 1796), the same condition was laid down for national property. Finally, on 16 Pluviôse (February 4, 1797), *assignats* and *mandats* ceased to be legal tender.

Public servants, rentiers and property owners had suffered a great deal; so had country landlords in many cases, although since Thermidor, Year III, half of farm rents had been payable in grain. The bourgeoisie, at least, had monopolized the greater part of what national property remained, although purchasers had been asked to pay a quarter of the agreed price in metallic currency, in violation of the contract. In the course of the winter, the workers had suffered even more, because their wages had been incapable of keeping up with the fantastic rise in prices. This rise had exceeded what the fall in the value of the *assignat* would have entailed: in December 1795, bread was selling in Paris at fifty francs a pound, or seven sous in metallic currency, whereas at the height of the food shortage of 1789 it had not exceeded four. The bargemen and stevedores in the ports, the best paid of all the workers, used to earn between six and nine livres, according to Lecoulteux, and now did not earn as much as 350.

To high prices was added a food shortage, because the peasants would no longer sell their produce except in return for metallic currency, and the harvest had been a poor one. On 7 Vendémiaire, Year IV (September 29, 1795), the Convention had confirmed the maintenance of controls, with the exception of maximum prices; grain could be sold only at a market, and a district could obtain it by means of requisitioning. But since the district administration had been abolished, the canton municipalities, which were composed of farmers and farm workers, put up a stubborn resistance to the towns which was scarcely weakened by the sending out of bailiffs. At the end of the winter, they stopped all supplies. The Directory helped the big cities by means of grain provided by the land tax, half of which was also payable in grain; they were supplied above all by foreign producers, for which the bourgeoisie furnished advance payments, thus increasing its influence still further. Moreover, at a time when the merits of freedom were widely lauded, circumstances made it necessary to enforce food controls much more strictly than in Year II.

In Paris, a great many people would have starved to death if the Directory had not continued the food distributions begun by the Committee of Public Safety, though limiting them to bread and meat. Theoretically, it provided one pound of bread a day in return for four sous in *assignats*, in other words for nothing, but the lack of money cut the ration to seventy-five grams; it was made up with rice, which it was impossible to cook, for there was a shortage of wood too. In Year IV, there was an increase of 10,000 deaths in the department of the Seine. Yet expenditure was enormous: nine million francs a day in December, 1795.

The general poverty maintained endemic agitation in the working class, which was perpetually trying to bring its wages up to the level of prices. Hostility to the rich was revived by the luxury which speculators, fops and *merveilleuses* flaunted impudently. The people's irritation turned against the Directory, against the men who had abolished the *maximum* and crushed the *sans-culottes* in Prairial; more and more frequently, people were heard to say that in Robespierre's time they had at least had bread to eat. This is what made the Jacobins a force to be reckoned with. Not content with thwarting the bankers' plans, they discussed at the Panthéon the restoration of the *maximum* and a ban on currency speculation. The Directory, on the other hand, was planning to abandon the poor to their fate and announce the suppression of food distributions except for the destitute. As in 1793, as in Prairial, the Jacobins could take advantage of a hunger riot.

The dates are conclusive. The food distributions were to stop on 1 Ventôse (February 21, 1796); feeling was so strong that they had to be continued. On the third, the plan for an issuing house was defeated. On the seventh, the Directory ordered the Jacobin Club to be closed, banning a few Royalist gatherings as well in order to save its face. The sentence was executed without a hitch the next day by General Bonaparte, who had been in command of the home army since Vendémiaire; hitherto he had made a great display of Jacobinism, but he had been asking for the army of Italy, and was in fact given it on the twelfth. Having broken with the Jacobins, the Directory started dismissing their supporters and harrassing their papers. Outlawed once more, they resorted to conspiracy. The Thermidorian adventure began all over again.

This time, however, the activity of the Jacobins assumed a new appearance, because since January Babeuf's friends, especially Buonarroti, had obtained considerable influence in the Club, and in March Babeuf himself became the leader of the conspiracy. Now Babeuf, who was an even fiercer critic of civil equality than the Jacobins, and who considered political equality insufficiently effective, wanted to institute actual equality, with the result that the Jacobin plot is known as the Conspiracy of the Equals: he was a Communist, and with him Socialism, hitherto a utopian doctrine, became a political fact.

The son of a poor exciseman, married to an illiterate servant girl, Babeuf was well acquainted with the life of the poor. Becoming a Feudist, he had come in contact with the peasant community of Picardy where communal habits were still strong, as was the spirit of resistance to the big farmers with their ever-increasing power. Educated no one knows how, he had read a great deal, and as early as 1787 he had shown a certain sympathy for Communism and actual equality. So far this was only a theoretical preference and it was the Revolution which, by achieving civil equality, accelerated the progress of his thought; yet in 1791 he still considered it impossible to call for the agrarian law in public. The experiment of Year II took him further forward by showing him that the State could control the economy, and yet in Year III, he still hesitated to take direct action and confined himself to proposing to his friends the creation of a Communist association which would win over public opinion by its example. But in the course of the winter, exasperated by the terrible spectacle of poverty and by the treachery of Barras, Tallien, Fouché, and many others, forced by the Directory's persecution to go into hiding like Marat, and convinced by the failure of the compulsory loan and by the intrigues of the financial world that there was nothing to be hoped for from legal action, he came round to the idea of overthrowing the old world by violence.

Babeuf's Communism bore the mark of its time: it was aimed at distribution, not at production, the individualism of which had not yet been destroyed by capitalist concentration. The peasant would go on tilling his field, but as it would henceforth be the property of the nation, he would carry his harvest to the public warehouse. However, Babeuf differed sharply from previous Utopians, who had all been more or less inspired by moralizing and asceticism and who had envisaged little more than a rural community. It was to the self-interest of the proletariat—"its best guide" —that Babeuf appealed in order to awaken it to an idea of justice. He also counted on industry to spread abundance, and praised the machine which, in the service of the community, would lighten men's work; he pointed out that individual production was incapable of keeping pace with consumption. On the subject of consumption he was categorical: no trade or profession should receive preferential treatment; all stomachs were equal; Babeuf, in fact, was an *ouvriériste*, with no regard for the "intellectual." Nor was he a democrat in the political sense of the word; the Convention's recantations had inspired him with an incurable distrust of politicians, nor did he rely on the enslaved people whom it was in fact the revolution's task to set free. That revolution would be carried out by the dictatorship of the minority, instituted by violence. It is probably in this idea that Babeuf's historical importance lies: he arrived at a clear concept of that popular dictatorship of which Marat and the Hébertists had spoken without defining it; through Buonarroti, he bequeathed it to Blanqui and then to Lenin, who turned it into reality.

However, Babeuf's importance in the history of Socialism and his pre-eminent part in the Conspiracy of the Equals should not lead one to imagine that this conspiracy was fundamentally Communist in nature. Babeuf and his friends represented only a small minority of its members. The Panthéonists belonged to the bourgeoisie, and some of them, such as Amar and Le Peletier, were rich men; the subscribers to the *Tribun du peuple* belonged to the same class. The Jacobins' aim was political: they wanted to take their revenge on the Royalists and Thermidorians who had outlawed them, regain power and re-establish democracy. In all this, they were in agreement with Babeuf's supporters. But, once victory had been won, a break would have been inevitable and Babeuf would have been defeated. As for the proletariat, Communist propaganda did not have time to affect it and it remained indifferent.

It took a month for the plan for an insurrection to take shape. On 7 Germinal (March 27), Buonarroti was given yet another mission by the Directory to go and stir up a revolution in Piedmont. He did not leave Paris, for on the tenth Babeuf formed his Insurrectional Committee and Buonarroti joined it, together with Darthé and Le Peletier who were pure Jacobins, while others grouped around members of the Convention—Drouet, Amar and Lindet— still remained on one side. The Committee appointed an agent for each of the twelve arrondissements in Paris to direct its propaganda, which suddenly became very active in the form of pamphlets, posters, songs, and demonstrations. Military agents were also appointed to undermine the loyalty of the garrison, and especially of the Police Legion, which had been created after the *journées* of Prairial.

Circumstances remained favorable for the agitators. On 5 Germinal (March 25), the Directory, while continuing food distributions, raised the price of the ration considerably; on the fifteenth (April 4), rents became payable in *mandats*, but as mass expulsions would have followed on quarter-day, the Directory was obliged to make an exception of verbal leases which remained payable in *assignats*. La Revellière was terrified. Reubell hesitated to give the signal for repression, dreading a new White Terror; Barras tried to calm Babeuf and his supporters. It was Carnot who took the matter in hand, and from then on he persecuted the Jacobins with a somber fury. This volte-face surprised everybody. The reason for it is probably that Carnot had never ceased to be a conservative bourgeois who had rallied to the Mountain to finish with the counter-revolution and also out of ambition, but who had never approved of the social policy of Year II. But it is also that he had a despotic character which was infuriated by opposition: he outlawed the Jacobins of Year IV as he had helped to outlaw Hébert, Danton and Robespierre. At his suggestion, the Ministry of Police, taken from Merlin who returned to the Ministry of Justice, was entrusted to Cochon. On 27 Germinal (April 16), the Councils decreed the death penalty for anyone trying to bring about the restoration of the Monarchy or a return to the Constitution of 1793. Against the press, the Directory obtained, on the twenty-eighth, only an anodyne measure—the obligation

that the printer give his name at the end of each publication—but the law passed the day before made it possible
to prosecute journalists. Troops started circulating in Paris
to break up crowds. The Police Legion having fallen under
suspicion, it was decided to send it to join the armies,
whereupon it mutinied on 9 Floréal (April 28).

The Babouvists decided to take advantage of the opportunity offered. On the 11th, the Committee summoned its
agents and appealed to the members of the Convention.
The measures to be taken to obtain power caused no difficulty, nor did those to be adopted afterwards; there was
nothing Communist about them, and they resembled
those of Year II. But Babeuf wanted to entrust the government to the Insurrectional Committee, admittedly attaching an assembly to it, but one elected by the rebels on
the Committee's advice. The members of the Convention adhered to the principle of representative democracy
and wanted to recall the Convention; the most they could
obtain was to be incorporated in the assembly. The two
sides did not come to an agreement until 18 Floréal (May
7). What would have come of this enterprise? Nothing but
a new Prairial. The Directory had an even firmer grip on
the reins of power than had the Committee of Public Safety.
For the Jacobins, this was the worst mistake they could
have made.

What is more, they had delayed too long; The Police
Legion was dissolved on 11 Floréal without any serious incidents. They had been betrayed too: Grisel, one of the
military agents, had sold his friends to Carnot. Babeuf
was arrested on the twenty-first (May 10), as were Buonarroti and Drouet; all the Committee's papers fell into the
hands of the Police, and the Directory issued 245 warrants

for the arrest of the persons who were mentioned in those papers, often unknown to themselves. Although there had been no disturbance of the peace, the country's rulers were still in the grip of fear, and by railing against their prisoners, with the help of the papers, they terrified the bourgeoisie. All the more so in that in Prairial the monetary and economic crisis roused the workers once again; the Directory obtained authority to call up another 10,000 men.

All the same, the prosecution made only slow progress. Barras would have liked to reduce it to the minimum, and part of the Left, under the influence of Sieyès, refused to support the Directory. They were afraid of a new White Terror and the advantage which division among the Republicans would give to the Royalists. Carnot would have done honor to his own character if he too had shown some regret and reluctance to outlaw those who had previously fought by his side for the Republic. It was he, on the contrary, who adopted an inflexible attitude, and the majority of the Directorials joined with the Right to support him. But Drouet was a representative of the people, and the detailed procedure laid down for such an eventuality had to be observed; then again, the High Court existed only on paper and had to be organized. It was only during the night of 9-10 Fructidor (August 26-27), that the accused were taken in iron cages to Vendôme, where the High Court had been summoned. Drouet was not among them; he had just succeeded in escaping.

Up to the last minute, the Directory had been afraid that an attempt would be made to release them, and it was true that certain Jacobins had not given up the idea of direct action; they remained in communication with confederates in the army, and during the night of 23-24 Fructidor (Sep-

tember 9-10), they presented themselves at the Grenelle
camp and called on the troops to fraternize. Once again
they had been betrayed; Carnot was fully informed and
this time had refrained from taking preventive action in
order to have the opportunity of carrying out a bloody repression. The Jacobins, charged by the cavalry, left some
dead behind; a great many of them were arrested and the
Councils authorized domiciliary visits to search for the
others. In order to have punishment meted out quickly,
the Directory proposed that the prisoners be handed
over to a military commission. It is true that there were a
few soldiers among them, but a law of 22 Messidor (July
10) had just reserved for ordinary justice any trial in which
civilians were involved; the law of 30 Prairial, Year III,
which was cited as a precedent, was specifically concerned
with the Vendeans and the Chouans. However, the Councils went ahead notwithstanding. The Directory even
wanted to allow the accused only one barrister for them all;
it did not get its way in this. The Military Commission of
the Temple had thirty of the accused shot, including
three former members of the Convention. Subsequently
the proceedings were declared illegal by the Court of Appeal, on appeal by those sentenced to other penalties.

As for the Vendôme trial, it did not begin until the end
of February, 1797, and lasted three months. Darthé withdrew into haughty silence, while Babeuf, less stoical in
his attitude, pleaded that his writings had not been followed by a single act. The rest of the accused stood up to
the judges and indulged in stormy demonstrations. The
jury acquitted them all of the accusation of conspiracy.
But the judges, illegally altering the indictment, called for
the enforcement of the law of 27 Germinal and obtained

an affirmative verdict for some of the accused. Darthé and Babeuf, sentenced to death, tried to commit suicide and were carried bleeding to the scaffold on 8 Prairial (May 27, 1797). Others remained in prison until the Consulate. They were not the only victims. A schoolteacher of the department of the Ain was guillotined under the law of 27 Germinal, as a supporter of the agrarian law.

The consequences of the new White Terror had appeared by the summer of Year IV. The juries acquitted the Vendémiairists, and one of them, the deputy Vaublanc, had been allowed to take his seat. In the theaters, patriotic songs had been abandoned. Benjamin Constant, whom Madame de Staël had pushed into politics, was recommending in his writings the formation of a great conservative party under the protection of the Directory. The Feuillants were received at the Tuileries and even dined there. Carnot considered that his triumph was complete and scribbled angry notes on the letters which his friend Garrau, a former member of the Convention, sent him from Italy to put him on his guard.

As Benjamin Constant had pointed out, this new trend implied concessions to the Right. The Directory, pressing on with the purge, dismissed all those whom the reactionaries denounced to it and replaced them with their candidates. In Provence in particular, radical changes were carried out. Fréron was recalled, the communal elections of Marseilles annulled, and the municipality appointed by the Directory; with a view to putting an end to civil war, the town was placed under martial law, but the command of the military division was given to the Royalist Willot, so that the White Terror could rage without let or hindrance. In the Councils, the Right asked at one and the same time for restrictions on the amnesty of 4 Brumaire and the repeal of the law of 3 Brumaire. There were confused debates for over three months. The new majority persisted in its onslaught on the Jacobins, but the old majority formed up again to uphold the law of 3 Brumaire. Finally, for the sake of peace and quiet, it was agreed to keep it as well as the amnesty, but extending exclusion from public office to those who had benefited from the amnesty. The law was passed on 14 Frimaire, Year V (December 10, 1796). However limited the success obtained by the Right was, it was nonetheless a harsh blow for the Jacobins at the approach of the elections. Carnot would have liked a reconciliation between the Republic and the Church to speed up the political compromise, and for a moment this seemed a possibility. Bonaparte was conquering Italy and had granted the Pope an armistice: at the end of July, Count Pierachi came, on behalf of Pius VI, to negotiate a peace with the Directory, at the very moment when the latter was deciding to make no attempt to destroy the Papal States. But it insisted that Pius VI revoke all his decisions on French affairs since 1789. This was asking the impossible; on the other hand, a *de facto* agreement was realizable, for Pierachi had with him a bull *Pastoralis sollicitudo*, calling upon the clergy to recognize the government of the Republic; but Pierachi kept it to himself, probably in the hope of obtaining in advance a few free concessions from the Directory. He was expelled and the negotiations broken off. The bull was handed over in any case to the Directory, which published it; the result was a tremendous controversy, the Royalist priests asserting that it was a forgery and declaring that even if it was genuine they would not obey, while the *soumissionaires* exulted.

The Right did at least obtain the repeal, under the afore-mentioned law of 14 Frimaire, Year V, of the article in the law of 3 Brumaire, Year IV, which ordered the enforcement of the repressive measures of 1792 and 1793 against the priesthood. It remained to be seen whether these measures themselves were repealed at the same time. The Republican administrations denied that this was the case, and, for example, kept those priests who had been sentenced to reclusion in prison. In practice, however, the clergy were treated gently. Cochon recommended the Directory's commissioners not to trouble quiet priests with oaths and declarations, at least for the moment.

Control of public worship was abandoned with all the more reason. In an article published on 6 Messidor, Year V (June 24, 1797), the *Annales de la religion* would report that, out of the 40,000 parishes of old, nearly all had revived public worship. Since the clergy's influence was bound to be exerted in favor of the Right in most cases, this was of great importance at the approach of the elections. The same was true of the repatriated émigrés, whose numbers continued to grow. The sale of national property slowed down at the same time. On several occasions, the Left complained that people who had submitted tenders had been unable to obtain their contracts. Finally, on 21 Pluviôse, Year V (February 8, 1797), Lamarque explained that Ramel had given orders to this effect under a host of pretexts which he could not judge, since only the Legislature could grant exceptions. This was neither more nor less than the truth.

La Revellière's anticlericalism was finally aroused, and this drew him nearer to Reubell and Barras. Starting in Brumaire, the Directory forwarded to the Councils thousands of documents reporting the violation of the laws on religious worship and the anti-Republican activities of the clergy. On 15 Pluviôse (February 3, 1797), the Directors signed the famous letter to Bonaparte in which they declared that the "Roman religion" would always be the "irreconcilable enemy of the Republic," and that it was therefore desirable "to destroy the center of the Roman Church," in other words "the papal government." Bonaparte took no notice and signed the Peace of Tolentino, but the "triumvirate" had nonetheless condemned the policy adopted towards the Papacy the previous July.

Since the beginning of the winter, the Right had had another reason for discontent. Peace had seemed close for a moment. Negotiations with the English had taken place at Lille, and, since the invasion of Germany had failed, Carnot had succeeded in having overtures made to Austria; in foreign policy too, he was now following the Right. These hopes had been disappointed, and in January, 1797, the victory of Rivoli gave reason to suppose that the spring campaign would make the Republic's triumph complete.

Moreover, the relations between the majority and the Directory gradually became strained. The Right took the attack onto ground where the Left, for its part, had its own reasons for opposition. Once again, the Directory had complained of the excesses of the press, and it seemed as if the deputies were going to give it satisfaction, for on both sides they made similar complaints about the opposing papers. However, when Daunou put forward three motions on peddling, the repression of slander and the founding of an official paper, the last two motions were rejected after protracted debates. The Right, which controlled most of the papers, did not want to interfere with them on the eve of the elections; the Left was upset when it was reminded that freedom of the press was the bastion of its opponents; both sides were worried about the increased authority which Daunou wished to confer on the Directory. The Councils' jealousy of the latter was revealed once more in connection with the reform of the gendarmerie. They passed this measure only after depriving the Directory of the choice of some of the officers; similarly, they refused to set up an agency for direct taxation, which would have removed the responsibility for the latter from the local authorities and transferred it to officials chosen by the government.

These were some of the symptoms of the crisis which the elections were going to provoke. Another sign of that crisis was the activity of the Royalists, which was increasingly obvious and seditious. It was not without reason that the "triumvirs" took fright. It was too late. The persecution of the Jacobins had opened the way for the revenge of Vendémiaire, all the more so in that the financial situation, which was appalling, made it easier by turning everybody against the government.

CHAPTER FOUR

The Finances of the Directory

It is much more difficult to return to metallic currency than to abandon it. The Directory found this out to its cost, and it owes a good deal of its unfortunate reputation to the difficulties of the operation.

The collapse of the *mandat* had led to another general moratorium. All contracts had once more been called in question, and until the end of the Directory, law after law was passed in attempts to reconcile as far as possible the contrary interests of creditors and debtors. This uncertainty was added to that which resulted from the laws on the émigrés and their relatives, and to that which surrounded the fate of the national estates, to discourage the spirit of enterprise and irritate public opinion.

Then again, the country areas were extremely disturbed. The food shortage had cruelly affected the peasants who did not harvest enough to live on—that is to say, the great majority—and with all the more reason the day laborers. As always happened in such cases, the number of beggars and tramps had increased and many of them had taken to brigandage. This evil had become far worse during the course of Year IV; bands of *chauffeurs*—who roasted their victims over fires in order to force them to give up their money—ravaged many regions. It was not very easy to distinguish between them and those who looted and killed in the name of the King and religion. On 27 Floréal, Year IV (May 16, 1796), the Directory ordered flying columns to be formed from the National Guard to attack both sorts, and on 15 Germinal, Year V (April 15, 1797), the Councils laid down the death penalty for brigands. But the evil, fostered by the economic crisis and the resulting unemployment, was to continue through the Consulate up to the time of the Empire.

If the crisis was prolonged, the reason once again was of a monetary nature. Metallic currency reappeared only very slowly, and never regained the volume of circulation that it had reached at the end of the *ancien régime*. After inflation, therefore, came deflation: prices fell sharply, all the more so in that the harvest of 1796 was excellent. This was good for the maintenance of law and order; the workers who remained in employment defended their wages with some success and the fall in food prices made life less difficult for them. But a fall in prices discourages production, and it had this effect until the end of the Directory.

These were all deplorable circumstances for a government which had to reorganize its finances, at a time when the continuing war was already making its task extraordinarily difficult. In Thermidor, Year IV, it had outlined the program which was called for to the Councils, discovering the extent of ordinary expenditure and war expenditure, making sure that the normal budget was balanced by means of taxation, and financing the war effort by means of exceptional financial measures. La Revellière, in his memoirs, stresses the efforts the Directory made to persuade the Councils to take action, and expresses justifiable indignation that it should have been ignored. Either the Five Hundred referred the *messages* to commissions which would never mention them again, or else those commissions eventually produced fragmentary plans which were endlessly debated; and, when some result was achieved, the Ancients often called the whole matter in question again. The debates revealed an ignorance which was surprising and doubtless sometimes spurious. The Councils expressed indignation, after having voted the sums asked for, at being told that the troops had not received their pay, that the government officials had not been paid, and that the hospitals were in a state of complete destitution. It was pointed out to them that it was not enough to vote sums for the Treasury to be able to find the money, and that the taxes themselves could not provide it if they were not voted in time. It was all in vain. This incapacity was linked with political motives: the Right made no secret of its hope of forcing the Directory to make peace for lack of money; the Left alleged that the Ministers did not provide accounts—which was true—and out of jealousy of the Executive did not scruple to hinder its activities; both sides pandered to the electors or to some interested group.

Nobody ever knew exactly how much the country's ordinary expenditure amounted to because the estimates of the various Ministries were passed by fits and starts throughout the year, a practice which made it possible to dispute the size of a deficit or even to maintain, as did Gibert-Desmolières, that there was a surplus. Then again, the taxes were voted belatedly: the land tax for Year V was voted on 18 Prairial (June 6) and the *mobilière*, which had been completely overhauled, only on 14 Thermidor (August 2), when the year was nearing its end. The drawing up of the registers—which was intrusted to municipal councilors who were in no hurry to pay, were often hostile and even more often incapable—aggravated delay. Until Year V, payment of the land tax was complicated by the obligation to pay half in grain, unless it could be proved that the harvest had not exceeded consumption. The tax collectors, appointed by the municipalities, were reluctant to exert pressure on the taxpayers in the midst of universal poverty; they themselves kept what they had received as long as possible in order to obtain interest from it. The Directory proposed setting up in each department an Agency of Direct Taxation composed of government officials, but without success, as has been seen. It did, however arrange that, for the time being, the registers should be copied from those used the year before; that payment should be made in installments; that the property of tax collectors should be treated as a surety for the collection of the taxes; and that they should be given authority to send bailiffs to the houses of recalcitrant taxpayers. But these means of enforcement were not applied until the eighteenth of Fructidor. In spite of everything, the results were not as contemptible as has been said. At the beginning of Year V, for example, the Puy-de-Dôme had paid ninety-three per cent of the land tax of Year III and seventy-two per cent of that of Year IV; however, the *mobilière* was much more in arrears, because right from the start it had oppressed the peasant to the benefit of the bourgeoisie.

Under the *ancien régime* the direct taxes were also paid belatedly, but the indirect taxes insured a daily revenue. This is why the Directory insisted that they be re-established, especially since the direct taxes did not provide enough money. The stamp duty was increased; the Five Hundred agreed to raise the duty on imported tobacco, to create a monopoly in powder and saltpeter, and to tax the salt mines; but the Ancients rejected all these measures. A toll was instituted for the upkeep of highways, but without any result, because the law which was to fix the amount was not passed. Only a tax on salt would have been really effective, but hardly anybody wanted it, either the Right or the Left, and it must be admitted that the country would not have tolerated the re-establishment of the *gabelle*: Napoleon himself would wait a long time before venturing to reimpose it. As for the country's extraordinary expenditure, only imaginary estimates of it were ever made. In order to meet it, the most important source of income was the sale of national property. On 18 Fructidor, Year IV (September 4, 1796), the property which came from the Belgium monasteries was put on sale, and a law of 16 Brumaire, Year V (November 6) re-established auction sales. In two years, the sales figures rose to 200 million francs, but the part payable in metallic currency or bills did not exceed three-eighths of the estimate; for the rest, "dead bills" were accepted, in other words, requisition bonds and deeds of outstanding debts, which produced no money.

The Directory was consequently still hard-pressed. No government, in a period of deflation, could have obtained enough money from the country through normal channels to pay off arrears and finance a war. What was needed was a controlled economy, a loan, or paper money, until the problem could be solved by the exploitation of conquered countries. A controlled economy was out of the question, and a loan was impossible, but people went on thinking about paper money; and indeed a moderate issue would have been all the more reasonable in that it would have stimulated the economy. In Frimaire, Year V, Ramel brought together some merchants from the principal commercial centers and some Parisian bankers; they refused to found a national bank as long as the political crisis had not been solved. This was a declaration of war by the businessmen of France upon the Directory. Other channels were explored. On 11 Nivôse (December 31, 1796), Réal, in a report on the Mortgage Code, made it possible for landowners to "liberate" their property by creating *cédules* which were transferable by endorsement. The motive behind this measure is obvious: it would have been possible to impose on landowners a compulsory loan payable in *cédules*, which would have become a new currency. Jourdan (of the Bouches-du-Rhône), one of the leaders of the Right, denounced the idea in an impassioned speech, and the proposal was rejected. On 9 Germinal (March 29), the Directory put on sale a certain number of Parisian properties which could be purchased exclusively in *rente* certificates, under the pretext of amortizing the

debt; in reality, if the attempt had succeeded, these certificates would have become a currency and they could have
been increased in number to pay for national property.
Once again, Jourdan stepped into the breach, declaring
that he did not want the Directory to be given this means
of prolonging the war indefinitely; going further, he recalled
that the Great Book mixed up legitimate rentiers with
contractors whose usurious debts had been paid in *rente*
certificates, and he called for a revision of the National
Debt. The sale of the Parisian property was approved, but
the Directory left it at that. In these circumstances, there
was nothing left for it but to imitate the King who, in similar cases, used to resort to expedients known as "extraordinary affairs." This is what it did.

It rejected the idea of a controlled economy, but it retained requisitioning without any law authorizing it to do
so. It had scarcely been installed in power before it had
ordered the use of requisitioning; the system provided it
with grain and fodder, horses and cattle, not to mention
wagons and their drivers; price control was not restored,
but payment was made in vouchers which the government
took back in acquittance of taxes or in return for national
property. This was not enough, and, as the Thermidorians
had done, the Directory turned for help to the financiers
who, alone, had enabled the *ancien régime* to wage its
wars. In the course of Year IV, the ministers placed contracts with the "commissaries," while the Treasury, in
order to obtain metallic currency or advances, came to an
understanding with the *faiseurs de services*, who were
also bankers and merchants. As far as the "commissaries"
were concerned, the Directory finally realized that an excessive number of contracts made supervision impossible

and, by putting the purchasers in competition with one another, fostered a rise in prices. On 3 Nivôse, Year V (December 23, 1796), it decided to entrust the provisioning of all the armies and the navy to a small number of specialized companies. In other words, it favored capitalist concentration, pleading too that these companies, with greater funds at their disposal, would provide better service, and, buying in bulk, would cut down expenses. But in the existing state of the economy, there were no financiers sufficiently powerful to take on such responsibilities and the undertaking had to be subdivided much more than had been hoped.

The contractors paid in advance; this was indeed their *raison d'être*. Yet they themselves had to be paid in the end. As a result, as long as inflation continued, they frequently abandoned their responsibilities, being unable to carry them out with the assignats and *mandats* which were given them at par. Although constantly condemned, the executive agencies of Year II therefore remained in existence for a long time, since these deficiencies had to be provided for. After the return to metallic currency, the difficulties were of a different sort, but the general situation was not much improved.

As early as 1795, shortage of money had obliged the Directory to establish an order of payment: three times a month, on the advice of the Ministers, it made a note of the most urgent debts and distributed the funds which it hoped to have at its disposal during the next ten days. In October, 1796, the Councils legalized this expedient, on the understanding that the armies and the navy would have preference; the Directory added that until further notice no account would be taken of arrears. This did not mean, however, that the favored contractors were out of trouble, because, as far as the contents of the Treasury were concerned, the Directory was in the same position as the *ancien régime*. In Paris, the revolution had brought about the unity of the Treasury, but its bookkeeping was so involved that it was incapable of presenting a financial statement or of rendering accounts. The provincial tax collectors were not kept under close supervision, and moreover communications were too slow for the Treasury to be informed every ten days about their returns. The Ministers gave the contractors warrants for payment to be redeemed by the Treasury, and Ramel gave them *rescriptions* or bonds to be redeemed by the tax collectors. But when these warrants and bonds were presented, the coffers were often empty, or alleged to be empty. The government would then help the contractors to the best of its ability. Assets belonging to the Republic were lodged with them as security, and they pledged them to obtain credit; the Regent, the most famous of the crown diamonds, was thus entrusted to Treskov, a Prussian merchant who supplied horses, and deposited as security in the Bank of Berlin. Much use was made of the Batavian *rescriptions*, bonds provided by Holland to cover what was still due of the war indemnity inscribed in the Treaty of The Hague, which was to be paid in annual installments in accordance with an agreement of 1796. Accommodation bills, the so-called *cavalerie*, which were in constant use in the commercial world of that day, were also employed. In every case, the Treasury undertook to provide for the bills when they fell due, even if it had to begin again. Sometimes, authority was given for the raw materials or articles which the creditor could use to be removed from the State warehouses.

The contractors began to grow weary of all this. That is why the law of 16 Brumaire, Year V, authorized the acceptance of ministerial warrants in payment for national property. Paulée, for example, acquired over 600 hectares in the department of the Nord, and was authorized to buy property to the value of sixteen million francs in Belgium. All the same, at the beginning of 1797 the Five Hundred were informed that the contractors refused to continue their services unless they were given effective guarantees. As a result, the Councils authorized the so-called *délégations:* The Directory surrendered to its creditors specific parts of the Republic's receipts, notably cuttings in the national forests or the yield of taxes in certain specified departments, thus re-establishing the much-criticized *anticipations* of the *ancien régime,* which the Constituent Assembly had forbidden. Even so, the security was never satisfactory, since the yield of a tax remained problematical. In many cases, the creditor was forced to ask for a fresh assignation, and, as a paradoxical consequence, he would not hesitate, in order to obtain the assignation which struck him as the best, to pay the Treasury a certain amount of cash.

Irregularly paid and never sure of being paid at all, the contractors covered themselves by raising their prices. The Directory never tired of telling the Councils that things would go on like this until they provided for the replenishment of the Treasury. Nor was this all; the contractors pleaded that they had no option but to hold the State for ransom because they themselves were held for ransom by the State's own agents: the Treasury employees and the tax collectors demanded a commission before paying them; the war commissioners and the warehousemen refused to sign receipts when deliveries were made, except on the same condition. The contractors were therefore not all swindlers, in spite of current opinion, but they were businessmen: they took advantage of the situation to increase their profits when they could. Nor is there any doubt that many of them did not scruple to resort to illegal intrigues. While complaining about the Republic's agents, they were the first to bribe them in order to get their fraudulent deliveries accepted; similarly, they did not hesitate to tempt politicians or to win over those who approached them in order to obtain leonine contracts.

Under every form of government, monetary and financial disorder engenders corruption, and it is in order to praise Bonaparte—who, however, did not succeed in putting a stop to it—that such corruption has been depicted as the Directory's exclusive privilege; but it cannot be denied that the political world exposed itself to suspicion at that time, and that in several cases the suspicion was justified. The Directory and the Ministers were largely responsible for this state of affairs: contracts were not allocated in public to the lowest tenderer, but in the secrecy of government offices; with the *faiseurs de services* who provided currency, foreign bills or advances, it was indeed impossible to deal in any other way; then again, the decadal order of payments gave the government a despotic power of discrimination among creditors, and the same could be said of the delivery of assignations by means of *rescriptions*, and of the *délégations*. The politicians were no less exposed to suspicion. Some made fortunes, legally no doubt, but to the indignation of the public; Lozeau, for example, by speculating in salt; Rovère, Le Paige and Abolin by dealing in national property; and Gérard by financ-

THE *Directory*

ing the Tivoli Gardens and Ruggieri's firework displays. How could anyone fail to think that they might well use their positions to help their interests and sell their support to businessmen? In the provinces, the members of the local administrations and the Directory's commissioners were similarly suspect. There is no doubt, for example, that Tallien and Fouché, Barras and Talleyrand made money out of everything. Barras was openly associated with Ouvrard, the biggest speculator of the age and general contractor to the Navy, to whom he passed Madame Tallien when she started costing him too much; and when Talleyrand learned that he was a Minister, his first reaction was to exclaim: "I must make a huge fortune!"

A host of scandals, big and small, revealed the evil. The most famous concerned the Flachat Company and the Dijon Company. The former supplied the Army of Italy. Unable to secure payment, it obtained the revenue of the war taxes, as well as the proceeds of the sale of the English merchandise seized at Leghorn. Bonaparte maintained friendly relations with it at first, but it did not trouble to redeem his orders for payment, and it was not long before he denounced its malpractices. The Directory ended up by summoning its directors before a court-martial; they challenged the competence of the court, then escaped. Now it so happened that one of Flachat's partners was Laporte, a former member of the Convention and a friend of Reubell's; it is easy to guess what inference the public drew. The case of the Dijon Company, which served as a cover for the financier Hinguerlot, compromised Ramel and the Treasury. He had been instructed to speculate for a fall in the *mandats* to justify their demonetization. When the operation had to be liquidated, the government joined issue with the company; there followed a prolonged lawsuit, which the company won, as well as stormy debates in the Councils. There can be no doubt about Hinguerlot's fraudulent maneuvers, but the fact remains that the government had conspired to debase its own currency and that the swindler had obtained help from some unexpected sources.

Quite apart from the discredit which the shortage of money, by its demoralizing repercussions, cast on the Directory, it directly compromised it in the eyes of the electoral body by harming private individuals, already seriously affected by the monetary crisis. The peasants, paid in requisition bonds, were forced to sell them cheap in order to obtain funds. The rentiers were in an even worse plight: the Directory had dared to promise them only a quarter of the face value of their dividend coupon in metallic currency, but it was unable to find even that; they were accordingly given "quarter bonds," payable in metallic currency when the Republic could manage it, and "three-quarter bonds" which could be used for nothing but the payment of taxes or the purchase of national property. In order to live, they had to sell them to the first speculator they met.

Then again, the whole country suffered from the dilapidation of the public services. The government officials were paid only at irregular intervals; the gendarmes sold their horses, which they could not afford to feed, at a time when brigands were scouring the country; the roads fell into disrepair. To relieve the budget, the cost of the courts, the central schools and public assistance had been transferred to the local administrations; they met this cost only by means of a special rate, which was limited and inadequate, and which was as slow to come in as the taxes.

The taxpayers showed no great eagerness to fulfill their obligations; they nonetheless lent a ready ear to the Royalist opposition which imputed to war, waste and corruption, in other words to the Directory, all the evils of which the financial crisis, so complex in its origins, was the inexhaustible source.

The Elections of Year V; the Conflict Between the Directory and the Councils

The anti-Jacobin repression and Bonaparte's victories, by consolidating the Directory, had favored reconciliation with the Republic to such an extent that the King's representatives—the Paris Agency, directed by the Abbé Brottier—thought fit to make advances to the Constitutionalists, some of whom, it was said, were thinking of the Duc d'Orléans. The link was arranged by Dandré, a former Counselor to the High Court of Provence and an influential member of the Constituent Assembly, who was a supporter of legal action. The Agency recommended meeting its interlocutor's wishes, but Louis XVIII—who, obliged to leave Verona, had ended up by finding refuge with the Duke of Brunswick at Blankenburg—remained intractable. All the same, it did not escape him that the election of a right-wing majority would open favorable prospects for him; without giving up the idea of using force, he approved the making of plans to fight the elections.

The activity of the Royalists therefore took on an increasingly ambiguous character, with the Absolutists and Constitutionalists, Chouans and politicians acting together, while retaining their preferences and mental reservations. In the summer of 1796, the Paris Agency had founded an association called the "Friends of Order," which was supposed to unite all the Directory's opponents in the constitutional sphere, and inside which a smaller group of "Legitimate Sons" was to be recruited, whose members would be initiated in the plans for a Restoration and in the preparation of an insurrection. Dandré, who also wanted to found an association to fight the elections, adopted the Friends of Order, which came out into the open under the name of the Philanthropic Institute, incidentally keeping as its leader Despomelles, a member of the Paris Agency. In the Sarthe, the Institute was organized by Rochecot, a Chouan. At Bordeaux, its leader was a creole, Dupont-Constant, but he was backed up by a committee dedicated to violent action. Moreover, Dandré remained in touch with the Swabian Agency, which was directed by Précy, who had been in command in Lyons in 1793, and which gave orders to the conspirators in the east and south. The funds were provided by Wickham, the English agent in Switzerland, with the approval of Grenville and Pitt. The English, while not discouraging the advocates of insurrections, considered that the Monarchy would only be restored in

France in a constitutional form, and this was also the opinion of the Genevese Mallet du Pan and Francis d'Ivernois, the leading publicists of the counterrevolution. It was with English money that Dandré organized a personal police force and postal service and founded newspapers, notably the *Mémorial*, to which La Harpe and Fontanes contributed. The Anglo-Royalist plot which the Directory denounced therefore existed in reality: only it must be remembered that many people played its game without knowing that they were doing so. It is important too not to exaggerate the size of the Royalist organization: the military resources at the conspirators' disposal remained very slight, and the Philanthropic Institute does not seem to have played a considerable part in the elections, having been formed so far in only a few departments. The reactionaries' success was due above all to the electors' lively discontent, whose complex causes have been mentioned already.

Moreover, it soon became obvious that unity of action was far from having been achieved. The King having criticized the Paris Agency's complaisance towards the Constitutionalists, it returned at an unfortunate time to a policy of conspiracy. One of the Royalists' hopes had always been to win over some general or other. They had unsuccessfully put out feelers towards Hoche, before trying to murder him; but in the Army of the Rhine and Moselle, Moreau was a friend of Pichegru's and it was Régnier, his chief of staff, whom Mathieu Dumas had approached to obtain a commander and recruits with the right ideas for the Guard of the Legislature. The Paris Agency approached this commander, General Ramel, and believed it had won him over, as well as Malo who was in command of a regiment of dragoons. However, they ended up by warning the Directory, and it was as well for them that they did so, for the Directory had already been informed by the Prince de Carency, the son of the Duc de la Vauguyon, who had only recently been a Minister for Louis XVIII. Brottier and his accomplices were arrested on 11 Pluviôse, Year V (January 30, 1797). They were charged only with enticement, so that they could be summoned before a court-martial; they challenged its competence and lodged an appeal. The military commission itself referred the matter to the Five Hundred, where there was a lively debate; but the Directory had forestalled this move by forbidding communication of the documents in the case to the Court of Appeal, whose jurisdiction did not extend to military law. The Five Hundred gave way. The judges, however, felt that they were being intimidated, for they convicted only four of the accused, and sentenced them only to imprisonment. But in the course of the preliminary examination, one of them, Duverne de Presle, had revealed everything he knew about the activities of the Royalists. The Directory kept his confession secret. It would publish it only on the eighteenth of Fructidor in order to denounce the Anglo-Royalist plot. In any case, the Paris Agency was promptly reconstituted under the name of the Royal Council, under the Duc de la Tremoille, assisted by the Abbé de Lamare.

The affair brought no benefit to the Directory; Royalist propaganda represented it as a police plot and went on as before. The priests, while operating in their own interests, were its most active auxiliaries. The local administrations, most of the time, helped it to the best of their ability by expurgating the electoral registers and by allowing the Republicans to be excluded from the primary assemblies. The

Directory reacted feebly. A decree denied the right to vote
to all who were inscribed on the list of émigrés, but a law
confirmed it for those who had been provisionally struck
off. The Councils were asked to impose on all electors the
oath of hatred for the Monarchy and the Constitution of
1793; they confined themselves to asking for a promise
which drew hilarious comment from the Royalist papers.
The number of voters was greater than in Year IV, but not
much greater, at least in the country districts: twenty-eight
per cent in the south. Barely a dozen departments retained
Republican representatives, and only eleven members of
the Convention survived, several of whom were Royalists.
Some elections were characteristic: Willot in Marseilles,
Imbert-Colomès in the Rhône. The department of the
Seine elected only Monarchists, including the Comte de
Fleurieu, the former tutor to the Dauphin. Pichegru had
been elected in the Jura, and Royer-Collard in the Marne.
The right-wing majority, now specifically Royalist, appeared
overwhelming.

The elections immediately had serious repercussions.
Bonaparte having signed the peace preliminaries shortly
afterwards, at Leoben, the Directory was obliged to ratify
them under pain of exasperating public opinion and irritat-
ing the general, whose support was seen as a possible means
to salvation. In the Five Hundred, the Right started to act
boldly: on 15 Floréal (May 4), it secured the repeal of the
law of 3 Brumaire, Year IV, although admittedly the
Ancients refused to confirm it. Inside the Directory, the
split became final. Reubell thought that the Directory
could take the left-wing majority in hand again by speaking
openly: he wanted to ask it to annul the elections and
adopt fresh exceptional measures, in other words carry out

the *coup d'état* which would take place on 18 Fructidor, but by parliamentary methods and without having recourse to the army. Carnot categorically opposed this suggestion; in his eyes the government's duty was to bow to the legally constituted majority. In the Five Hundred, somebody proposed that the Councils in office should institute a check on the powers of the newly elected members, an operation which would have made it possible to eliminate at least some of them; this device, which would be used in Year VI, was rejected this time.

The immediate question was who was to leave the Directory; if La Revellière, Reubell or Barras was indicated by the ballot, the majority would change sides. Reubell suggested insuring the election of a Republican by anticipating the expiration of the prescribed period by means of the resignation of one of the Directors whom the present Councils would have to replace, but this ingenious device assumed that the Five were in agreement. Couldn't the ballot be gerrymandered? This was what the Royalists feared, and the Right had a law passed which made it public. Chance saved the Republic: it was Letourneur who left.

Meeting on 1 Prairial (May 20), the Ancients elected Barbé-Marbois as their president, and the Five Hundred elected Pichegru as theirs. Acting together, they recalled the deputies who had been excluded under the law of 3 Brumaire, and then elected to the Directory Barthélemy, the Republic's representative in Switzerland, where he had negotiated the treaties of Basle. It was not a good choice; cold-shouldered by the triumvirs, and regarding Carnot as a scoundrel because he was a regicide, Barthélemy, who in any case had little talent, soon resigned himself to impotence. The majority was led by the Clichy Club, to which several hundred deputies belonged, and above all by a much smaller group which met at the house of Gibert-Desmolières. It soon became obvious that the majority was as complex as the interests and sentiments which had brought about its election. The "White Jacobins," as Thibaudeau called them, who wanted to set about restoring the Monarchy without delay, did not control it. They were outnumbered by the Constitutional Monarchists who distrusted them, and above all by those deputies collectively known as the Belly, who were chiefly inspired by hostility towards the members of the Convention, and who, though sympathetic to the Monarchy, preferred to devote their attention to improvements which were immediately realizable; both groups, shrinking from violence and the harm it would cause, envisaged a provisional agreement with the Directors which would make it possible to wait peacefully for the elections of Year VI. The conservative Directorials such as Thibaudeau and Doulcet were inclined to help them. If the "White Jacobins" had had a leader, they could probably have prepared a *coup d'état* without the majority daring to stop them; they counted on Pichegru, who still enjoyed considerable prestige in the army, his treason remaining unknown; but he was not the man they thought he was. Pleasure attracted him even more than power; he seems to have been ill at ease in this political world with which he was unfamiliar; he may have wondered whether the government had not got proof of his treason; and finally, he was not sure what his fate would be under a restoration. In short, until the eve of the eighteenth of Fructidor, he tended towards a policy of temporization. The impotence of the majority is reflected in the correspondence of Mallet du Pan, who refers scathingly to the violent individuals whose mad audacity may compromise everything, and despises the Constitutionalists who lack courage and are unwilling to take any risks. Who, then, could be relied on? The "Anglo-Royalist plot" confined itself to trivialities. The Left, moreover, stood up to it, and several times, especially in the Ancients, defeated its opponents or at least forced them to postpone their plans.

The attention of the Right was drawn first of all to the situation in Santo Domingo and the administration of Commissioner Santhonax, who was attacked with incredible violence. The misfortunes of the settlers were brought up and it was decided that they should be repatriated at the Republic's expense. In reality, the disagreement was about the slavery of the Blacks, and no attempt was made to conceal the fact, although nobody dared to call for the restoration of slavery. The Directory had softened the blow by spontaneously recalling its commissioners. As there could be no question of introducing constitutional government into the colonies, the moderates allowed themselves to be persuaded to authorize the government to send out new agents.

The law of 3 Brumaire, Year IV was then considered, and was repealed almost without discussion. The majority incidentally made a point of showing its impartiality by also repealing the disqualification which the law of 14 Frimaire, Year V had imposed on those who had been amnestied, and it refused to listen to the extremists who had once again suggested revoking the amnesty itself.

On the clergy and religious worship, discussion was more prolonged, and in a few respects the majority changed sides.

Right from the start, countless petitions had pleaded the cause of the priests and had inflamed passions. The Directory itself had suggested that the situation should be clarified: were the repressive laws of 1792 and 1793 abrogated or not? At the same time, on 28 Prairial (June 16) Camille Jordan had presented a report on the subject of freedom of worship; it was regarded as symbolic because it asked that the clergy should henceforth be dispensed from oath or promise, and that the ringing of bells should be authorized, thus earning the author the nickname of "Jordan-les-Cloches." At bottom, his proposals were very moderate, for he agreed to the confinement of religious worship to church premises and agreed to penalties against ecclesiastics who used religion as a political weapon. But he had been unable to refrain from inveighing against his opponents, and on 20 Messidor (July 8), General Jourdan retorted by evoking the memory of the Republicans who had fallen in the civil war stirred up by the priests, whereupon Lemerer added to the tumult by praising "the religion of our fathers." Finally, the laws of 1792 and 1793 were formally repealed on 26 Messidor (July 14). But Boulay de la Meurthe insisted that the declaration of submission to the laws should be maintained, and, in spite of the obvious partiality of the president Henry-Larivière, this was agreed to in principle, on the twenty-eighth, by 210 votes to 204. The Ancients postponed their approval of the repeal of the repressive laws until 7 Fructidor (August 24); in any case, the text of the declaration remained in the works, and the law of 7 Vendémiaire, Year IV had not yet been retouched when the *coup d'état* occurred. Fierce attacks by Gibert on secular education, which Bailleul defended, and others on divorce, which Henry-Larivière condemned in the name of the Catholic Church, only served to make the atmosphere stormier and stormier.

For the émigrés, the results were not very effective either. A further stay of execution was granted to the Alsatians, with an extension of the amnesty to the nobles, but the Ancients rejected the resolution. They left in abeyance the one which had once again authorized the Toulon rebels to return to France, and yet another which dispensed the relatives of émigrés from all the laws directed against them. Agreement could be reached only on the émigrés whom a storm had shipwrecked on the coast near Calais, and who for two years had been sent from one court to another, none being able to bring itself to enforce the law which condemned them to death. It was decided that they should be re-embarked on a ship bound for a neutral country.

The relative impotence of the majority might have calmed the Republicans' fear if reaction had not been unleashed in the country. The administrations, now almost universally hand-in-glove with the Royalists, were systematically letting the Republican legislation fall into abeyance and reducing the commissioners to inactivity; the courts were displaying an obvious partiality; the Philanthropic Institute was multiplying its offshoots in most of the departments; nearly all the outlawed priests had openly reappeared; the émigrés were returning without let or hindrance; one and all were venting their fury on the purchasers of national property; violence was increasing even in Paris; in Provence, the Directory instructed Bonaparte to protect the Republicans, and he sent Lannes there with some troops from the Army of Italy.

To meet the growing danger, the Republicans tried to

regroup themselves. In Paris, a Constitutional Club met in Messidor, not at the Hôtel de Salm, as is usually said, but at the Hôtel de Montmorency, in the Faubourg Saint-Germain. Others were formed in Paris—about forty, it is said—and in the provinces, especially in the south where the need was particularly pressing. The Constitutional Club which had set the movement on foot had been created by Directorials; Benjamin Constant was the oracle of the Club, together with Sieyès and Talleyrand. But the Directory suspected, not without reason, that the Jacobins would come to the forefront in most of the others, and it was probably for this reason that it refrained from defending them when they were denounced on 24 Messidor (July 12) as preparing a demonstration for July 14: on 5 Thermidor (July 23), the clubs were closed, although they were authorized by the Constitution.

In all this, the Directory had shown itself as conciliatory or resigned. The Right drove it to extremes by trying to deprive it of the means of governing. It re-established co-optation in every case of a partial vacancy in the administrations; it gave orders for a complete change of personnel in the central offices of the big towns after each municipal election; it forbade the proclamation of marital law except in the case of investment by the enemy or by rebels. Above all, Gibert-Desmolières set out to deprive the government of the few resources that the financial crisis had left it.

He was guided by the Treasury, which had been a nest of counterrevolutionaries since the beginning of the Revolution; in constant conflict with the Directory, and threatened on account of its part in the Dijon Company affair, it was trying to re-ingratiate itself. In 21 Prairial (June 14), for two and a half hours, Gibert reeled off a report which recommended suppressing *anticipations*, rejecting ministers' warrants in payment for national property and consolidating them officially as Treasury scrip, entrusting the Treasury alone with purchases of metallic currency and bills and with all loans and pledges, and finally, conferring on it the power to endorse orders for payment and to divide the funds available among the various services as it thought fit, without preference for the armies or the navy. If these proposals were approved, the Directory would be deprived of all the expedients which had enabled it to govern somehow or other until now, and, most important of all, it would find it impossible to finance the war effort. Yet peace had not been concluded. It was in fact precisely to force the Directory to make peace at any price that the Right wanted to reduce it to impotence, and on 30 Prairial, it passed the articles concerning the powers of the Treasury. The Left protested indignantly; on 1 Messidor (June 19), in the Five Hundred, the tumult reached its highest pitch and deputies came to blows. However, Thibaudeau and his friends had also protested against the attack being made on the government's authority, and their arguments had created an impression; it was stipulated that the Treasury would have to give precedence to military expenditure. This reservation did not strike the Ancients as adequate; they rejected the resolution. This was a counter-thrust: Gibert's campaign continued, but its only result was to persuade the Directory to make an end of it all.

In the meantime, while undermining the government's authority, the reactionaries also tried to enter it by getting the Ministers changed in accordance with their wishes. Carnot joined Barthélemy in approving this method of insuring that the regime should become parliamentarian.

They tried in vain to detach La Revellière from Reubell, but Barras, it seems, gave his assent; it is even alleged that he was negotiating with the King's envoys. In fact, he was playing a double game. As soon as the Councils had assembled he sent one of his deputy friends, Fabre de l'Aude, to ask Bonaparte for his help if necessary; Fabre returned at the beginning of Messidor with an encouraging report and a document taken from the papers of Antraigues, a Royalist agent in the Tsar's pay who had just been arrested. This document was the account given him by Montgaillard, the Prince de Condé's agent, of his relations with Pichegru. Perhaps Barras was irritated at the discovery that he was not the only instrument of the Restoration. In any case, he immediately went into action, and, since Bonaparte was too far away, appealed to Hoche, who was now in command of the Army of the Sambre and Meuse. On 13 Messidor (July 1), the general dispatched some troops who were ostensibly supposed to be going to Brest to reinforce an army bound for Ireland, but who in fact made for Paris.

They were approaching the capital when, on the 26th, the Directors, of a common accord, proceeded to take a vote on the purging of the Ministries. To Carnot's disappointment, Barras voted invariably the same way as La Revellière and Reubell. The ministers dear to the Right —Bénézach, Cochon and Petiet—were dismissed. True, Delacroix and Truguet were also dismissed, but Ramel and above all Merlin, who was particularly detested by the Royalists, retained their positions. Among the new appointments, two caused a sensation. Talleyrand took over the Ministry of External Relations; Madame de Staël had introduced him to Barras, who had agreed to support him

—they were born to understand each other. The Ministry of War fell to Hoche, and the full meaning of this choice became apparent when Petiet informed the reactionaries of the approach of the troops. There could be no doubt about it: a *coup d'état* was imminent.

The intervention of the generals was in fact going to solve the crisis, bring the Republic back to a dictatorship, and at the same time place it at their mercy. But the regime was not the only thing at stake; the Republic's foreign policy was also involved, for Bonaparte was taking a stand against the Councils only in order to make himself arbiter of war and peace.

CHAPTER SIX

The Directory
and the Coalition

Thanks to the armies of the Revolutionary government, the Thermidorians had occupied Belgium, Holland, and the Left Bank of the Rhine. Prussia and Spain, abandoning the Coalition, had negotiated with them at Basle. But England and Austria remained in arms, and in 1795 the reverses suffered in the autumn campaign had brought the Germans back into Palatinate. The Thermidorians had been unable either to make peace or to wage war. In Year VIII, the same would be said of the Directory.

It was not impossible to defeat Austria, who could not count on receiving any effective help from her allies. True, the French armies were in a pitiful state: between October, 1794, and January, 1796, their strength fell from 750,000 men to 410,000, largely through desertion; however, by various shifts and devices, the Directory was able to send them into enemy country in the spring of 1796. Moreover, Austria too was in a bad way; if she gave in, England might one day end up by wearying of the fight; but there could be no hope of this unless there was a durable peace on the Continent, and that depended on the frontiers which the Republic wanted to obtain for France.

Only accomplices of foreign governments wanted to return to the frontiers of 1789; the advocates of the "former limits," such as Mathieu Dumas, usually suggested that they be improved: France should keep Avignon, Savoy, and part of the Netherlands. The Thermidorians had gone further: they had annexed Belgium. They maintained that this union with Belgium had been implicitly ratified by the plebiscite on the Constitution, and moreover that this Constitution forbade any dismemberment of the national territory. Of these two assertions, the first was debatable and the second false, for the ban applied only to secret treaties. However, the Directory adopted them as its own and steadfastly insisted that the "constitutional limits" were sacrosanct. As a result, the only question that remained was to know whether the French should advance to the country's "natural frontiers"—which, as matters stood, meant as far as the Rhine. The Thermidorians had confined themselves to keeping the future open by forcing Prussia to promise her eventual support for the cession of the left bank of the Rhine for the Empire. Opinions were far from being unanimous, even in the army: Kléber, for example, repudiated the French conquests, but the Royalists were violently hostile to the natural frontiers policy, and as a result the Republicans came to support it. This is what the Directory did. Carnot, who had spoken in 1793 in support of the natural frontiers and, more recently, of the union with Belgium, had rallied to the "former limits" since he had joined up with the Right; but Reubell, who was in control of foreign affairs, was the staunchest advocate of annexation, and his colleagues followed him. There was no lack of reasons for disputing whether this decision was lawful and above all whether it was wise. The Thermidorians had promised prosperity and liberty; peace was therefore indispensable to them. The natural frontiers policy was bound to make that peace more difficult and more fragile.

Was it at least compatible with a peace of some duration? It has been argued that it was, but without convincing proof. Austria was not insistent on retaining Belgium; like Prussia, she was reluctant to give up the left bank of the Rhine and thus compromise herself in the eyes of the Germans, but both countries were ready to accept the situation if they could obtain some compensation. England, since the reign of William of Orange, had made it a principle to prevent France from conquering the Netherlands, but by herself she was incapable of taking them back from her. True, if the English and the Germans gave way, that did not mean that they would never return to the attack. But that was not the question for the Directory; all they wanted to know was whether the Republic had a chance of obtaining recognition for the natural frontiers and of keeping them long enough to put herself in a position to defend them successfully. There can be no doubt that the answer was in the affirmative. But on two conditions: first of all it was essential that Prussia should find compensation in rounding off her frontiers in Germany, Austria in extending her territory in Italy, England in the undisputed domination of the seas and the acquisition of colonies; secondly it was essential that France should be satisfied with these frontiers and should not try to extend them.

These conditions were difficult to fulfill. When they had declared war, the Girondins had promised to liberate the oppressed peoples; La Revellière could not forget this, and the Italian and Swiss refugees still less; it was intolerable, they argued, that the Republic should return to the foreign policy of the *ancien régime* and come to terms with the "tyrants," allowing them to share out nations like cattle. Moreover, this hatred for the new France was constantly being revealed; the safety of the Republic depended on her dethroning them—if not in the whole world, at least in Europe. Every time that danger revived the revolutionary spirit, the elements it contained of national interest and romantic enthusiasm were reawakened too. Now, if France insisted on dominating Germany and Italy, it would be impossible to come to terms with Austria; before long the Coalition would re-form again, and the result would be perpetual war. Under the influence of Reubell, who was resolutely hostile to such a development, the Directory, for several months, maintained that it wanted no conquests beyond the natural frontiers except in order to obtain recognition of those frontiers in exchange. These very conquests increased the danger. The Directory made it a principle that its armies should live at the expense of the occupied countries, and should even send it part of their loot; it had already been observed in Belgium and the Rhineland that the population did not appreciate such costly liberty and that France could entrust the government of those regions only to revolutionaries; when peace was concluded, would they be handed back again to their enemies? Then again, the example of Dumouriez gave grounds for fearing that there might be generals who would carry out a personal policy in the occupied countries and proceed to make new conquests with the support of greedy contractors. The Committee of Public Safety had provided against this danger by subordinating the generals to the representatives on mission. The Directory replaced the latter with commissioners to the armies: Joubert and Alexandre for the armies of the North and of the Sambre and Meuse, Haussmann for the Army of the Rhine and Moselle, and Saliceti and Garrau for the Army of Italy. But in theory it granted them only a right of supervision. True, it was not long before it also entrusted them with a task of collecting war taxes, authorizing the conclusion of armistices, and putting down looting. It was inevitable that they should enter into conflict with the generals, the sole masters of the armies. Behind the representatives, there had been the revolutionary court; behind the commissioners, there was only the tottering authority of the Directory: they were sacrificed, and the generals did as they pleased. However, it was an unforseeable chance which determined the course of events. According to Carnot's plan, it was the armies of the Sambre and Meuse and of the Rhine and Moselle, under Jourdan and Moreau, which were to deal the decisive blow by marching on Vienna; those of the Alps and of Italy, under Kellerman and Schérer, being much weaker, were to conquer, if they could, northern Italy as a form of surety. But on 12 Ventôse, Bonaparte was substituted for Schérer.

He was born at Ajaccio in 1769, just after Corsica had been occupied by the French. His father, who accepted

French rule at an early date, obtained recognition for his nobility, and Napoleon was accordingly able to enter the Brienne Academy, and then the Military Academy, which he left as a second lieutenant in the Artillery. Poor and without any prospects, he owed everything to the Revolution, but, hating the French, he saw nothing in it at first but an opportunity to liberate Corsica and to play an important part there under Paoli. But the latter preferred the Posso di Borgo clan to the suspect Bonapartes, and when he broke with the Revolution and called in the English, the Bonapartes were expelled. It was then that Napoleon really naturalized himself in the service of the Montagnard Convention; he distinguished himself at the siege of Toulon and in the Army of Italy, in which he inspired the brilliant operations of Saorgio and Dego. Arrested for a while as a Robespierrist, and reduced to inactivity, he was put back into the saddle, on the thirteenth of Vendémiaire, as a result of the decisive support that he gave to Barras. Before leaving for Italy, he married Joséphine de Beauharnais, who had been the latter's mistress. It is hard to believe that he was ignorant of this, and that the influence she had retained did not help him; but he was passionately in love with her and there can be no doubt that Carnot appointed him deliberately.

Bonaparte had read Guibert, the prophet of the new war whose theories the Revolution had made applicable without Carnot or any general fully realizing the consequences. His genius was to derive a doctrine of war from them and to practice it with a mastery which has known no equal. In the Army of Italy, he had also studied—and what is more, on the spot—Maillebois' campaigns and Bourcet's book on mountain warfare. In his notes to the Committee of Pub-

lic Safety in Year II and Year III, and in the instructions
for Schérer which he inspired, the essential features of the
Italian Campaign were already clearly delineated: it was
necessary to aim at Austria, to put Piedmont out of action
first of all in order to conquer Lombardy in safety, then,
ignoring the peninsula, to march on Vienna across the Alps.

The Army of Italy occupied a large part of the Genoa
Riviera and, since Schérer's victory at Loano, held the
upper valley of the Tanaro, as well as the passes toward the
two Bormidas. Bonaparte assembled 38,000 men to fall
upon Colli's Piedmontese, whose active strength could not
exceed 12,000 men; Beaulieu's 35,000 Austrians, still scattered in their winter quarters, seemed unlikely to be able
to help him. In fact, when Saliceti sent a brigade toward
Genoa, whose government he wished to intimidate in order
to extract money from it, Beaulieu hurried up to stop him,
but this step prevented him from concentrating his troops
and helping Colli or his own subordinate Argenteau, whom
he had ordered to cut off the French troops' retreat. Bonaparte began by getting rid of the latter, who was routed
at Montenotte on April 12, driven out of Dago, and thrown
back on Acqui. At the same time, Augereau was driving
the Piedmontese out of Millesimo, while Serurier was de-
scending the Tanaro; attacked on the sixteenth at Ceva
and on the eighteenth at San Michele, Colli inflicted some
bloody reverses on his opponent; but, with his flank constantly being turned, he had to retreat every time, and after
finally being hustled out of Mondovi on the 21st, he fell
back to cover Turin. The Piedmontese revolutionaries
started agitating. The Court took fright, and on the twenty-
eighth, an armistice was signed at Cherasco. Beaulieu had
withdrawn to the north of the Po, behind the Ticino. Bona-

parte took him in the rear by forcing the passage of the Po at Piacenza, but Beaulieu, suspecting the danger, was already in retreat. He escaped, leaving only a rear guard on the Adda: at Lodi, on May 10, the bridge was taken by force. Retracing his steps, Bonaparte entered Milan. After the King of Sardinia had signed a peace treaty on May 15, ceding Savoy and Nice, he set off again and without meeting any opposition reached the Mincio, which he crossed at Borghetto on May 30. The siege of Mantua began. Since Beaulieu had failed to respect the neutrality of Venetian territory, a convention handed Verona over to the French, and granted them right of way. The Dukes of Parma and Modena obtained armistices; Bologna and Ferrara were occupied without a shot being fired.

In Milan, Bonaparte's policy had already taken shape. He had allowed the formation of a club, promised independence and given the National Guard the tricolor cockade of Italy. But he had also demanded an indemnity of twenty million francs, payable by the rich; Saliceti took possession of the public coffers and the pawnshops which, in that region, served as safe deposits; the army lived off the country. The contradiction became immediately apparent: the revolt broke out and was harshly suppressed, especially at Pavia. France could therefore count only on the Italian Jacobins, whose declared object was to revolutionize the whole of Italy in order to make it a unified republic. The Directory announced entirely contrary intentions: the Italian conquest was simply a pawn which had to be thoroughly exploited before it was handed back. It was so preoccupied with the question of booty that it ordered Bonaparte to leave Kellermann standing guard over Lombardy, and to go and hold the peninsula for ransom. At a moment when the Austrians were going to return to the attack, this order was ridiculous, and it had the further drawback of allowing Bonaparte to test his strength without any risk to himself: he offered his resignation and the Directory promptly capitulated. Admittedly, its wishes were partly satisfied. The Pope and the Dukes of Parma and Modena were forced to pay heavy indemnities, as well as to hand over manuscripts and objects of art chosen by a special commission. A division occupied Leghorn, the main center of British trade.

Bonaparte seems to have extracted about fifty million francs from Italy, and the Directory received about ten million. But the general's emancipation was only accelerated as a result. After conquering Italy, his dominating genuis brooked no impediments in that country. His army became his chattel; it lived as it pleased in a land of milk and honey, and he had granted it half its pay in metallic currency, which the Directory could not obtain for the others. He had gathered around him a horde of contractors and individuals with an eye to profit—like Haller, who became the Paymaster to the Army, or like that Hamelin, whom Josephine had brought along in return for an allowance, and whose memoirs are so enlightening. What did he intend to do with Lombardy: Make it a fief where he would settle down after the war? Whoever thought that did not understand his nature. He was the man of the moment endowed with an unequaled realism, but an object attained was never anything but the means of aiming at another which his ardent imagination had already conceived. On the evening of the Battle of Lodi, he had become aware of himself: "I saw the world sinking beneath me as if I had been swept up into the air."

The Directory did not worry, for it was a good summer for the Republic. Instead of concentrating the forces intended for the invasion of Germany, Carnot had ordered Jourdan and Moreau to operate separately; however, the drawbacks of this procedure did not appear right away. Jourdan having taken the offensive on May 31, to the right of the Rhine, the Archduke Charles repulsed him without evacuating the left bank; but at the news of Bonaparte's victories, Wurmser, who was facing Moreau, was sent to Italy with some of his troops. Charles, left in sole command, abandoned the Palatinate, and when Moreau had finally crossed the Rhine, on June 24. Jourdan returned to the attack. While Wartensleben fell back before him as far as the Naab, Moreau drove the Archduke back toward Bavaria, and ended up by reaching Munich. In Italy, Wurmser enjoyed no success. His troops, coming down from the Tyrol on both sides of Lake Garda, were beaten at Lonato and, on August 5, at Castiglione. Returning to Trent, he hit on the idea of trying to reach Mantua by the valley of the Brenta; but Bonaparte was already in pursuit, and on September 15 he was forced to take refuge in the fortress. The Directory had just concluded an alliance with Spain, thus depriving the English fleet of the bases which had enabled it to dominate the Mediterranean. It left that sea after evacuating Corsica, which the French reoccupied in October; Bonaparte was thus safe from British intervention. Moreover, since July the French had been planning a landing in Ireland in co-operation with Wolf Tone, who was preparing an insurrection there. This succession of blows persuaded Pitt to offer to negotiate, and the Directory agreed to hold a conference at Lille.

Meanwhile Bonaparte was going his own way. Saliceti

and Garrau, both good Jacobins, were helping him in this
without worrying about their government. A Lombard legion had been created; the senate of Reggio asked for help
against the Duke of Modena. Bonaparte repudiated the
armistice and, in agreement with the commissioners, summoned a congress which, on October 15, grouped Modena
and the Legations taken from the Pope in a Cispadane
Republic. The general nonetheless wanted to rid himself of
the commissioners. Already Italy was becoming exhausted
and the army's condition was worsening again; Saliceti
having been sent to Corsica, Garrau remained as the sole
target for recrimination. On October 25, Bonaparte took
a decisive step: he put Baraguey, who was in command in
Lombardy, in control of the whole administration of the
country, without any mention of the commissioner.

Meanwhile the Republic's affairs were now taking a turn
for the worse. The Armies of Germany having made no
attempt to link up, the Archduke left Latour facing Moreau, joined Wartensleben, and marched on Nürnberg.
Jourdan, taken in the rear, retreated; the slowness of his
adversary enabled him to regain the Lahn with only slight
losses, but there he was attacked and routed, and he re-
crossed the Rhine at the end of September. Moreau had
only belatedly realized the danger he was running. Returning to the Black Forest, he learned that Charles was hurrying up to cut off his retreat and had to turn off along Hell
Valley; his adversary was incapable of either concentrating
his forces or of making haste, and he was able to cross the
Rhine at Hüningen on October 26. The Austrians were
now free for the most part to go into Italy; instead they
stubbornly persisted in trying to take the bridgeheads of
Kehl and Hüningen, which the French defended through-

out the winter. All the same, a new commander, Alvinczy, took the offensive against Bonaparte, reached the gates of Verona, and repulsed every attack at Caldiero; however, as a result of the furious fighting at Arcole between November 14 and 17, Bonaparte succeeded in forcing him to retreat, but he had narrowly escaped disaster and the moral and material condition of his troops was pitiful. Soon afterwards, on December 19, Malmesbury, Pitt's envoy, not receiving the full powers with which the Directory had insisted that he should be furnished in advance, was asked to leave France. The Irish expedition, which had been placed under Hoche's command, had just set sail: it was scattered by a storm and returned to port in discomfiture. Then, on February 14, 1797, Jervis defeated the Spanish fleet off Cape St. Vincent and obtained access to the Mediterranean once more.

Bonaparte was thrown into relief as much by the setbacks of the other generals as by his own victories; he remained the Directory's only hope. After all, the defeated generals had not been much more docile than he. Kléber and Bernadotte had had the impudence, in full retreat, to tender their resignations to Jourdan and abandon him. Beurnonville, who took Jourdan's place, came into conflict with Commissioner Alexandre. Moreau had granted an armistice to Württemberg without consulting Haussmann, and returned to France on the worst possible terms with the latter. The Directory, thoroughly disheartened, dismissed the commissioners to the armies. Everywhere, the generals were left in sole command. Then again, the setbacks of the autumn had given a hold to Carnot and his friends to the Right. Already, he had secretly tried to get in touch with Thugut; in November, he insisted that Clarke, the head of his military office, be sent to Italy to negotiate an armistice. Ordered to investigate the state of the army and the conquered region as well, Clarke was rapidly won over by Bonaparte; moreover, the Directory, while confirming its intention to exchange Lombardy for the Rhineland, instructed Clarke to consult Bonaparte about the peace conditions.

Soon matters improved once more. Alvinczy had descended the Adige with 50,000 men, while Provera was advancing from Friuli towards Mantua. On January 14, 1797, on the Plateau of Rivoli, Bonaparte repulsed the Austrian columns which attacked him and drove them back into the mountains; the next day, Joubert scattered or captured what remained of them. On the sixteenth, Bonaparte, who had immediately set off again with the Masséna division, forced Provera to capitulate. Mantua finally surrendered. The excitement of victory combined with the reaction inspired by the Brottier conspiracy to divert the Directory from the path it had invariably followed until then: Clarke received orders to defend the Cispadane Republic, and on 15 Pluviôse Bonaparte was sent the famous letter, already mentioned, which urged him to destroy the temporal power of the Papacy. However, a rectification followed before long. Bonaparte and Clarke, having asked for permission to give a constitution to Lombardy, were merely authorized, on April 7, to create a provisional administration, emanating only from the general and not committing the Directory. Then the Army of the Sambre and Meuse, now under Hoche's command, crossed the Rhine again on April 16 and 18, and was soon in front of Frankfurt; on the twentieth, Moreau also crossed the river. An order was sent to Clarke to postpone any armistice; Germany was going to become the main theater of war again. It was too late: Bonaparte had already cut the Gordian knot.

After the fall of Mantua, he had marched on Rome, but without meaning to go very far: Clarke having shown him his orders, he knew that if he did not sign the peace himself, it would return Lombardy, and he regarded the surrender of Lombardy as an insult to himself. He therefore had to reach Vienna before the Armies of the Rhine. He lost no time in coming to terms with the Pope at Tolentino, demanding only a few million as well as Avignon and the Legations. On March 20, he took the offensive. Superior in numbers this time to the Austrians, who were now under the command of Archduke Charles, he reached the Tarvisio without much difficulty, from which point the Masséna division advanced as far as the foot of the Semmering: at Leoben, on April 7, Thugut's plenipotentiaries presented themselves to treat for peace. It was Bonaparte who, as early as March 30, had sent the Archduke an offer to negotiate. If he had been eager to forestall the armies of the Rhine, he was nonetheless worried by their inactivity, which could give the Austrians time to overwhelm him— all the more so in that his rear was no longer safe. It seems that, considering that it would be impossible to carry out his plan without offering Austria a bait, he had decided, even before taking the field, to offer her part of the Venetian States; in March, his subordinates provoked a revolution at Brescia and at Bergamo, and it is difficult to believe that they would have ventured to do this without his permission. Next, they tried to stir up the Terra Firma against the Most Serene Republic, but it was against the French that the peasants, irritated by the military occupation and indoctrinated by the clergy and nobility, took up arms. On

April 17, the garrison at Verona was taken by surprise and some of the troops were killed. Bonaparte was now in a very hazardous position. No less than the desire to appear at all costs as the peacemaker, and no less than the pride which attached him to his conquests, it explains the extraordinary choice which he offered Thugut: either Istria, Dalmatia, and the whole of the Terra Firma as far as the Oglio, though with the exception of Venice, if he ceded Belgium; or else just Venetia and then only as far as the Tagliamento, if he abandoned the Rhineland as well as Belgium. This was tantamount to dictating Thugut's reply. Without any authority, and without consulting Clarke whom he had been careful to send off to Turin, Bonaparte signed both the armistice and the preliminaries of the peace of Leoben on April 18. By this treaty the Republic went beyond its natural frontier of the Alps and, following the scandalous example of the Polish partitions, sacrificed an independent state to its own convenience, handing Italians over to Germans; and all this without reaching the Rhine, the "natural frontier" that it considered the most important of all.

Bonaparte had immediately sent off couriers to halt the armies of the Rhine, and had taken care to see that the news of the treaty spread before the Directory itself knew the terms. Immediately after the Royalist elections, could the Directory defy both public opinion and the general? It did not dare to do so, and ratified an agreement which dishonored the Revolution. Installed at Mombello, in the palace of the Crivellis, Bonaparte now appeared to the whole world as a true sovereign. He raised Lombardy to the dignity of a "Cisalpine Republic," gave her a constitution, joined Valtellina to her and tried to persuade Valais to grant her

a road to France by way of the Simplon Pass, but in vain
—a failure which promptly gave him the idea of interven-
ing in Switzerland. He had also thought of extending the
Cisalpine Republic as far as the sea by dismembering the
Republic of Genoa, but the Genoese patriots forestalled
him by carrying out their own revolution which they placed
under his protection.

His imagination turned toward the east: out of the spoils
of Venice, he had retained the Ionian Isles in order to get
in touch with the Ottoman Empire, and he suggested to
the Directory that he should seize Malta. However, the
final treaty with Austria still had to be concluded, and he
had explained that he hoped to take advantage of it to keep
Mantua and to obtain the Rhine. He had declared war on
Venice of his own accord on May 2; on the twelfth, the
democrats in Venice had overthrown the oligarchy and let
in the French; on the sixteenth, Bonaparte had negotiated
with the representatives of the government which had
ceased to exist, a device which had enabled him to avoid
recognizing the new government. Now in a position to
hand over Venice herself, he reopened negotiations with
Thugut. The latter raised no objections to ceding the Rhineland, counting on obtaining not only Venice, but also the
Legations. Discussions opened at Udine.

Abandoned by Austria, horrified by the mutiny of her
sailors, and at grips with the Irish, England, for her part,
had sent Malmesbury back to Lille, where negotiations had
been resumed on July 7. The Directory made some large
claims, but its chief demand was neither more nor less than
that the English restore to France and her allies the colonies
they had seized. This did not appeal to Pitt, who wanted to
keep at least Ceylon and Trinidad. The Directory, however,

had not said its last word, for it exerted strong pressure on Holland to persuade her to cede Ceylon. But at Lille as at Udine, the negotiations came to nothing. This was because Thugut and Pitt knew what was happening in Paris.

The generals of the Republic had never ceased to be abused by the newspapers of the Right. Now they were subjected to attacks in the Councils too. Disposing of the resources of the conquered countries as they pleased, without furnishing accounts to anyone, they lent themselves to criticism; Hoche was accused of having set up a Black Fund in order to prepare for a *coup d'état*. But it was the Venetian affair which set the cat among the pigeons. The "Veronese Easter" had reduced the Right to silence for a moment; but shortly afterwards the *Quotidienne* published some letters from Mallet du Pan, a publicist in the pay of England and Austria, stigmatizing its shameful inertia. On 5 Messidor (June 23), Dumolard, in a passionate speech, made out a well-founded indictment of Bonaparte. Of foreign inspiration, it nonetheless allowed the Directory to consider the Anglo-Royalist plot as being also an Austrian plot. Pastoret, for his part, bitterly criticized the measures taken against those neutral countries which placed themselves at the service of English trade, on the ground that France was thus running the risk of war with the United States. Dandré went further: he promised Wickham to help British policy, admittedly reserving the right to protect French interests, though it is not clear how he interpreted those interests. Thugut tried to take advantage of feeling on the Right and sent to Paris an envoy who, in August, met Carnot and Barthélemy; they declared that they were powerless to help, since the triumvirs no longer consulted them. At Lille, Maret, one of the Directory's representatives, advised Malmesbury to play for time, since the victory of the Councils was imminent; he was hand-in-glove with Talleyrand and, thanks to him, was able to reveal to the English the conditions of the treaty just signed with Portugal. Some suspicious individuals, who claimed to represent Barras and Talleyrand, offered their services for money. Pitt too decided to wait.

After the elections of Year V, a close connection had thus been established between the foreign policy of the Republic and its internal situation. If the Directory succumbed, the Republic's foreign enemies would triumph at small cost to themselves. But the Right, by attacking the generals, had dictated their attitude. After reading Dumolard's speech, Bonaparte exploded in fury. In reality, he played a double game as usual: he went on corresponding with Carnot, and, on the advice of his aide-de-camp Lavalette, who had come to Paris, he did not send the Directory the three million francs he had promised. But Hoche was incapable of such devices, and, since he was within reach, it is he who would have carried out the *coup d'état* if the Directory had been more cunning. Would the fate of the Republic have been different as a result? It is pleasant to think so, although the pestilential influence of the war of conquest may not have spared even Hoche. With Marceau and Kléber, he has remained dear to Republican tradition on account of his gay and generous impetuosity, his youthful lower-class enthusiasm for the Revolution. Around the memory of the soldier-citizen, whom death carried off a few days after the eighteenth of Fructidor, there float those Beethovian strains which express a regret for a noble hope left unfulfilled. It is to him that the *Eroica* should have been dedicated.

The soldiers followed their generals. Many of them retained a fierce loyalty to the Revolution and to the Republic which now incarnated it. Having shed their blood for these ideals, they considered themselves entitled to protect them against the civilians who elected Royalists: Revolution and Republic were their property. Yet there must be no illusions on this score: the armies also followed the example of their leaders, and the proof of that can be seen in the fact that the Army of the Rhine and Moselle imitated to only a limited degree those of Italy and of the Sambre and Meuse. Moreau had kept secret the correspondence of Condé's envoys, which had been captured in an Austrian wagon and which revealed the treason of his friend Pichegru; during the campaign, he had treated respectfully émigrés caught bearing arms; and he shut his eyes to Royalist propaganda. The transformation of the armies explains the growing ascendancy of their generals. Since Year II, the soldier had been increasingly reduced to passive obedience; he no longer took part in the election of his officers; the jury no longer played any part in military law; since the law of 13 Brumaire, Year V (November 3, 1796), there had no longer been a soldier among the judges; and the merging of volunteers and conscripts had subordinated both to the discipline of the line. Then again, it can be argued that the soldiers of the Directory, distinguished by the desertion of their fellows, were in a sense volunteers. They had remained because they loved war and its adventures, or because they would not have known what to do outside the regiment; little by little, they became separate from the rest of the nation, all the more so in that, since the *levée en masse*, there had been no more conscription. Professional soldiers, and encamped on foreign soil into the bargain—how could they have failed to turn to their commanders?

But they never became a Pretorian Guard. The Republic never knew a *pronunciamiento:* soldiers and generals only carried out a *coup d'état,* on the eighteenth of Brumaire as on the eighteenth of Fructidor, in response to an appeal by the bourgeoisie.

CHAPTER SEVEN

The Eighteenth of Fructidor

The Right was getting ready to suppress the political societies when, on 28 Messidor (July 16, 1797), it learned of the dismissal of the ministers it trusted; like the dismissal of Necker in 1789, the event seemed to herald a *coup d'état*. Anxiety grew when, the following day, Petiet revealed that troops were approaching the capital; two days later, the deputies known as inspectors of the hall, whose duty it was to police the constitutional precinct of the Councils, confirmed that some cavalry regiments were reported to be at La Ferte-Alais, near Corbeil, a place which appeared to be within the constitutional belt. Pichegru and

331

his friends had gone to ask for explanations, and countless groups discussed what measures should be taken. The indictment of the triumvirs seemed the only effective step. But what if they resisted? It had to be admitted that force was on their side. Nonetheless, it seems that Pichegru and Vaublanc came to an agreement with Carnot, who was then president of the Directory. Called to the bar, he was to throw the blame on the triumvirs, and an indictment would have followed; perhaps Rochecot, who was then in Paris with a band of Chouans, vainly proposing to take the Directory by force, would have intervened. But when, on 2 Thermidor (July 20), the message arrived which, without explaining why the troops had been sent, attributed their presence so close to Paris to a mistake, it was noted that Carnot had signed it. This was because Barras had shown him the document sent by Bonaparte which furnished proof of Pichegru's treason. Carnot, utterly taken aback, had changed his attitude; shortly afterwards, on the anniversary of the tenth of August, he made it clear in his speech that he would not lend himself to a Restoration. This *coup de théâtre* threw the Right into confusion.

The triumvirs, for their part, were not ready. Arriving in Paris, Hoche had been taken to task by Carnot; having imagined that the Directors were in agreement, he did not know what to reply and flew into a temper against Barras who had earned him this humiliation. Then Willot pointed out that, since he was under forty, the general could not be a minister, and a substitute had to be found. The Directory allowed the clubs to be suppressed without making any comment and Barras sent Fabre de l'Aude to propose an agreement to Pichegru. The offer was rejected, but on 8 Thermidor (July 26), Pichegru, in the conclusion of his report, confined himself to laying down the limits of the constitutional belt, in order to avoid any future error, and to banning any movement of troops from one military subdivision to another without a decree from the Directory.

This was only an interlude. It was not long before news came of the threatening proclamation which Bonaparte had read out to his soldiers on July 14, and the still more violent addresses from different divisions of his army; the Army of the Sambre and Meuse lost no time in sending similar addresses. On 3 Thermidor (July 21), the Directory had legalized the movement of the troops in a decree ordering reinforcements to be sent to Brest: they set off again under Hoche, who had left Paris after a reconciliation with Barras. His friend Chérin was put in command of the Directory guard, and it was he who prepared the *coup d'état;* Augereau, sent to Paris by Bonaparte and appointed commander of the seventeenth military division, undertook to carry it out. Under various pretexts, detachments, arms and munitions came into Paris. Money was scarce: Hoche provided a little and so, probably, did the contractors whom the Councils' attacks had ranged behind the government. Retired officers arrived from all sides and the hunting of "black collars," in other words fops, started again in Paris.

The Right, on the recommendation of Willot and Delarue, replied only with fresh demands for explanations about the approach of the troops and the seditious addresses of the armies. At this the Directory openly took the offensive, with its message of 23 Thermidor (August 10). Explaining, this time, the march of the troops by the preparations at Brest and thus assuming responsibility for it, it reduced the incident, as it had done from the beginning, to an insignificant mistake in the mapping out of a route.

333

As for the addresses, though they were doubtless illegal, the indignation which had dictated them was legitimate. Who were the real culprits? The counterrevolutionaries who murdered Republicans and those who, in the Councils, did their best to support them, while reducing the government to impotence by leaving the Treasury empty. Then the presidency fell to La Revellière, and on 10 Fructidor (August 27), receiving the envoys of the Cisalpine Republic, he made a speech that was even more provocative: "The Directory will not treat with the enemies of the Republic."

The majority, growing increasingly anxious, went on discussing without coming to any decision. On 25 Thermidor (August 12), it had admittedly authorized the reconstitution of the crack companies of the National Guard, the riflemen and the grenadiers: this was in order to rearm the bourgeoisie of the big towns so as to repeat the *journée* of Vendémiaire. Pichegru declared that the arsenals would provide the necessary arms and equipment, but in spite of Carnot, the triumvirs did not give effect to this law. The Five Hundred passed a resolution to reinstate in the gendarmerie the officers who had been excluded as suspects since 1791. The Ancients rejected it.

Two other resolutions would undoubtedly have been effective: the Guard of the Legislature was to be placed under the discretionary authority of the inspectors of the hall and removed from that of Augereau and the Directory; and retired officers would only be able to draw their pension in their place of residence, a measure which would oblige them to leave Paris. But the Ancients postponed a decision and the Five Hundred showed no greater diligence in respect of two other points: guarantees to be given to officers against the right of dismissal, which was invested

334

in the Directory, and the attribution to the criminal court
of the Seine of all trials for offenses against the security of
the State.

The inspectors of the hall, usurping powers which transformed them into a sort of executive committee of the
majority, could have organized means of action; Rovère
formed a police force and Willot recruited volunteers. For
his part, Dandré distributed arms, kept the Philanthropic
Institute on the alert, and asked Wickham for money.
Pichegru ended up by agreeing to have recourse to the
Chouans. As anxiety grew, it was decided on 17 Fructidor
(September 3) that Vaublanc should demand an indictment. This would inevitably have been the signal for action. But the Directory acted first.

In the night of 17-18 Fructidor, the triumvirs, after summoning the ministers Augereau and Chérin, made final
arrangements; at dawn, the alarm gun was fired and the
city was placed under military occupation. Posters denounced the Anglo-Royalist plot and backed up the denunciation with Duverne de Presle's revelations and An-
traigue's document. A decree announced that anyone who
tried to instigate the restoration of the Monarchy or of the
Constitution of 1793 would be shot without any form of
trial. A group of deputies, led by Pastoret, presented itself
at the Tuileries and was dispersed. Nobody tried to take
up arms. Right at the start, Pichegru, Willot and Ramel
had been arrested at the Tuileries by Augereau. A few
others, including Barthélemy, who refused to take flight
as the triumvirs had hoped he would, were taken with them
to the Temple. Carnot, whom they hated, had managed to
make his escape.

The Councils had been transferred to the Medical

School and to the Odéon, where nothing was ready for them. By the time a quorum had been formed, it was late in the day. Most of the deputies were in a state of consternation, even the Left being unable to avoid the realization that the Constitution had been struck a mortal blow. But it was too late to hesitate. During the night the Five Hundred passed the exceptional law proposed by the triumvirs, and the Ancients ratified it on 19 Fructidor, Year V (September 5, 1797). On the twenty-second, they passed a second law against the press. A few other laws followed later.

Altogether, forty-nine departments had their elections totally annulled, and others their representation cut down. The south of France, except for Provence, was the least affected. During the following months, the Directory also dismissed a great many administrations. Sixty-five individuals were sentenced to transportation to Guiana, including Carnot, Barthélemy, Ramel, forty-two members of the Five Hundred, eleven members of the Ancients, and three of the accused in the Brottier conspiracy. Fifteen of them, joined voluntarily by Barthélemy's valet, were taken away on the twentieth in iron cages. Two others went the same way a little later. Eight died in Guiana, including Gibert-Desmolières, Tronson-Ducoudray, Aubry, and Rovère. A few escaped, notably Pichegru. The others did not return until after the eighteenth of Brumaire. Altogether, 177 deputies were eliminated and their places left vacant. Of those who had been spared, some retired from public life: Dupont de Nemours resigned; Doulcet went on leave; the others, Thibaudeau for example, withdrew into silence. The opposition did not disappear, but it was decapitated and reduced to a minority.

The émigrés, even those who had been provisionally struck off, were given a fortnight to leave France under pain of death. The law of 3 Brumaire, Year IV was revived, and indeed aggravated; the relatives of émigrés were deprived of the right to vote. The repeal of the laws of 1792 and 1793 against the clergy was annulled, and the deportees who had returned to France were ordered to go back into exile; but the death penalty which those laws imposed upon them and which, as the Directory had pointed out several times, had led the courts to prefer acquittal to conviction, was replaced by deportation to Guiana. In return, the Directory was given the right to sentence any priest to deportation by an individual decree; moreover, in confirmation of the law of 7 Vendémiaire, Year IV, the promise of submission to the laws was replaced by the oath of hatred for the Monarchy and the Constitution of 1793.

The clubs were authorized once more, but the press was hard hit. Forty-two papers had been suppressed and their proprietors, editors and staff condemned to deportation, a fate which, it is true, nearly all escaped. The press was placed for a year at the disposal of the police, as was permitted by the Constitution.

The authority of the Directory increased considerably. In the majority of departments, as a result of dismissals and the annulment of the elections, there were vacancies in the courts and the administrative bodies: the Directory was given authority to fill these vacancies, in the administrations until the elections of Year VI, and in the courts until the normal end of the mandate. The Court of Appeal was likewise purged; only the Treasury escaped, probably because Ramel had been compromised with it in the Dijon Company affair. Finally, the Directory resumed the power to proclaim martial law when and where it thought fit.

The eighteenth of Fructidor consecrated the failure of the constitutional and liberal experiment attempted by the Thermidorians: the Republic had returned to a dictatorship, and since it was the Directory which had taken the initiative, it was the Directory which benefited as a result. The authority of the Legislature, already very limited, would be reduced still further, a state of affairs to which the deputies resigned themselves no more than the Convention had done after the thirty-first of May. Of further-reaching but no less decisive consequence was the influence implicitly attributed from now on to the army and its generals: the soldier had saved the Republic, and he regarded it more than ever as his property. Moreover, he was immediately assured that his importance could only grow in the future, because the eighteenth of Fructidor also set the Republic on the road to a new war.

It was inevitable that the foreign policy of France should be affected by the *coup d'état*, since the Royalists' collusion with the enemy was one of its contributory factors. Reubell immediately resumed supreme control of foreign affairs; the diplomatic staff was changed and Talleyrand took refuge in submission. At Lille, new plenipotentiaries called upon Malmesbury to restore unreservedly all the colonies of France and her allies, and negotiations were broken off as a result. In the Rhineland, Hoche being dead, the plan that he had supported for a Cisrhenan Republic was abandoned. As Thugut, now resigned to treating for peace, had sent Cobenzl to negotiate with Bonaparte, who was installed near Udine, in the Castle of Passariano, the Directory indicated that it wanted the Rhine frontier, and, since the Republic of Venice was to be restored, granted Austria only Istria and Dalmatia. Preparations for a winter campaign were set on foot. Bonaparte admittedly expected to improve the conditions provided for at Leoben, but he was well aware that a winter campaign could be waged only in Germany, and he had no intention of being thrust into the background by a *coup d'état* which he had helped to bring about. Setting himself up as arbiter, he offered Thugut, of his own accord, the Venetian territory as far as the Adige, except for the Ionian Isles; in return, he demanded Austria's support for the cession of the left bank of the Rhine, which was to be negotiated at Rastatt with the Empire, but was to exclude the region of Cologne. Cobenzl ended up by agreeing, and the treaty was signed on October 18, 1797, at Passariano, although it bears the name of the little village of Campo-Formio where the ceremony had originally been planned to take place. The Directory was utterly dismayed; but, apart from the fact that after the *coup d'état* it had countless difficulties to overcome, how could it break with the imperious general, who now had no rivals? Hoche was dead; and Moreau, who at the very moment of the eighteenth of Fructidor had decided to hand over the papers which compromised Pichegru, had been put aside as being more than unreliable. The treaty was ratified.

The Venetian iniquity was thus confirmed and even amplified, since Venice too had been handed over to Austria. Moreover, from the diplomatic point of view, the Rhineland provisions were disastrous. Thugut had retained the region of Cologne for the Empire, because it was there that Prussia's possessions were situated, with the result that that country would not be entitled to any indemnity; it could therefore be expected that in the Diet she would oppose the cession and would also draw away from France. A fresh offensive was thus likely on the part of Austria, whose Italian ambitions had been partially disappointed.

Nothing was more calculated to suggest fresh encroachments beyond the natural frontiers, which indeed had not yet been reached in the region of the Rhine. If the war was to be resumed—and in point of fact it was still going on with England—it was important that France should be sure of the countries which she had taken under her protection and which served her as a glacis; the Batavian Republic and the Cisapline Republic were not slow to become aware of this. In order to link the latter to France, Bonaparte thought of taking over Valais, though it was even simpler to invade Piedmont. Everywhere the Directory's new ambassadors—Delacroix at The Hague, Ginguené at Turin, and even Truguet at Madrid—started speaking like masters.

Nor was that all. Although officially no appeal had been made to the Jacobins, the *coup d'état* of the eighteenth of Fructidor had been carried out with their help; and, by insistently denouncing the Royalist peril, the Directory had reawakened the revolutionary spirit and at the same time aroused the enthusiasm for universal propaganda and war to the death against the tyrants which was virtually inseparable from it. It was in Year VI that the Republicans began priding themselves on belonging to the "Great Nation" whose mission was to free the world. La Revellière was susceptible to this idealism; Barras' greedy, restless spirit was not averse to upheavals; Reubell joined with them in welcoming the prospect of the fall of the Papacy, and, linked as an Alsatian with the democrats of Basle, he was predisposed in favor of intervention in Switzerland. Finally, it went without saying that generals and contractors, out of natural inclination and personal interest, would everywhere give their support to the propaganda which made them indispensable.

Less than six months after the eighteenth of Fructidor, the French were in Rome and at Berne with the approval or at the instigation of Bonaparte, who shortly afterwards would finally provoke, by setting off for Egypt, the formation of the Second Coalition.

CHAPTER EIGHT

The Directorial Terror

If the government of the second Directory, as the historians call it, was regarded as a dictatorship, that is not only because it was a "revolutionary" government, established in violation of the Constitution, but also, and rather, because the eighteenth of Fructidor inaugurated a new Terror. It remains to be seen whether the Directorial Terror revived the "coercive force" with the same severity which made the Committee of Public Safety omnipotent.

The revolutionary court was not re-established, and Bailleul proposed in vain the creation of a special court for the crime of conspiracy. However, there could be no question of using the High Court, which was slow and unreliable; the Directory had recourse when necessary to the criminal courts. It was the criminal court of the Seine which sentenced the Royalist singer Ange Pitou to deportation, and that of the Rhône which sent Allier and Surville to the scaffold, but this jurisdiction was not reliable either. Every dictatorship, and the Terror which is its indispensable complement, presuppose an exceptional jurisdiction. Against the Grenelle rebels, the Directory had already had recourse to military justice; widespread use had been made of it in Year II and it remained competent to deal with émigrés and deportees. The disturbances which followed the eighteenth of Fructidor made it possible to extend its use to a considerable degree. These disturbances were serious only in a few places—at Pont-Saint-Esprit, where the Baron de Saint-Christol was in complete control for two days, at Carpentras, at Montauban—but these rebellions provided an opportunity to set up a large number of military commissions. Then again, the Directorial dictatorship, like all dictatorships, was a police regime. Passports were reintroduced. The Legislature did not authorize domiciliary visits until Messidor, Year IV, and then for only a month, but the Directory went ahead without its permission; roundups were also carried out in the country districts. Under the Constitution, the Directory could order arrests through administrative channels under the pretext of conspiracy, but its commissioners did not possess this right, any more than did the departmental or municipal administrators; yet this is what they did, with or without the authority of the Minister of Police. They even drew up lists of suspects to be imprisoned should the occasion arise; these prisoners were released after varying times without even having been interrogated. Postal secrecy was not respected any more than individual liberty. As for the freedom of the press, it was officially suspended; the censorship was not re-established any more than it had been in Year II, but the Minister of Police had a census of papers carried out, and on the basis of his reports, the Directory suppressed a considerable number of them—sixteen at once, for example, on 27 Frimaire, Year VI (December 17, 1797). Admittedly they soon started reappearing under other names, but, reduced to extreme prudence, they had become insipid; moreover, many of their contributors were affected by the deportation order decreed on 22 Fructidor. Books were likewise seized. As for the theaters, Audouin, in April, 1798, got the Five Hundred to confer on the Directory the right to control them. Lamarque had protested against this increase of power for the Executive; nonetheless, he had asked for a law to fix the number of theaters and impose a host of restrictions on them. The Ancients rejected the resolution, but the Five Hundred did not take up Lamarque's plan, so that the police retained their arbitrary powers; in January, 1799, the Central Administration of the Seine gave orders for the existing repertory to be submitted to it and for all new plays to be presented to it in future.

Finally, administrative pressure increased as a result of the fact that dismissals and the annulment of elections reinforced centralization. In the Sarthe, for example, out of 807 agents and assistants, 584 had had their election quashed. Some of them were irregularly reinstated by the remaining minority; but the Directory dismissed another 290, so that in the end 599, or three-quarters of the total, were replaced, generally speaking to the satisfaction of the central power.

Two categories of individuals were the special targets of the Directorial Terror: the émigrés, as well as their relatives, and the priests. The case of the émigrés was clear, but, in the Councils themselves, attention was drawn several times to the danger of excessive repression. There were a good many errors in the list; the Directory had full power to add to it and was extremely slow to strike names off. Meanwhile it opposed any attenuation of the law of 19 Fructidor, maintaining that in cases of dispute the courts should suspend sentence until an administrative decision was reached: it is true that the military commissions acted with circumspection and that more than once the local administrations intervened in favor of the accused. However, the commissions had at least 160 people shot, including a few women, principally in the southeast, and in most cases during Year VI. To these must be added the death sentences passed by the criminal courts, which have not been counted. But emigration was not always the only ground for indictment: Rochecot, Trion, Allier, and Surville were also conspirators and rebels. As for the law of 3 Brumaire, Year IV, it henceforth caused less controversy. It was enforced against only one deputy, after which it was not mentioned again in the Councils; but this was because the persons concerned, taking the hint, henceforth took refuge in abstention. The relatives of émigrés continued to be unable to dispose of their property unless they agreed to a division of the anticipated succession, the Ancients having rejected the resolution which, before the eighteenth of Fructidor, had repealed the law of 12 Floréal, Year III.

The situation of the clergy was not as clear as that of the émigrés. In December, Chollet told the Five Hundred that there was still uncertainty about the laws of 1792 and 1793, since some people considered that they were still in force; he protested at the possible enforcement of the death penalty against deportees who had returned to France, and went much further in proposing that nothing more should be required of the clergy, even the non-juring priests, than the oath of hatred for the Monarchy. He did not win his case; Delbrel, however, obtained a decision that a commission would examine the modifications called for by considerations of humanity. There was no further mention of the subject; when, in Year VII, Briot demanded that all deportees should be considered as émigrés, his proposal was rejected. This suggests that the Five Hundred implicitly confirmed the substitution of deportation to Guiana for the death penalty in the case of deportees who had returned to France. Moreover, in Year VII, Duval, the Minister of Police, indicated in a circular that deportees who had returned home were liable only to deportation to Guiana. Unfortunately for them, many administrations had entered them on the list of émigrés, and as a result 41 were executed. Many others might have suffered the same fate, but the military commissions acquitted them or at least hesitated, in which case the administrations, on being consulted, frequently declared that the deportee, having left France in obedience to the law, could not be considered an émigré. The aforementioned circular by Duval confirmed that this was the case if the accused was listed with the endorsement "deportee," and that if this endorsement was missing he was entitled to dispute the inscription. Moreover, the example of Finistère reveals that the law of 19 Fructidor was enforced in an arbitrary fashion: some deportees who had returned to France, and who had complied with the law by asking for their passports, were promptly sent off to Rochefort, and some of them were put on ships for Guiana; another man was shipped off as liable to deportation without any sentence or administrative decree stating this to be the case.

Again, the priests who had taken the required oaths could be sentenced to deportation to Guiana by a Directorial decree; they were particularly exposed to this danger if they now refused the oath of hatred for the Monarchy. The government's obligation to issue a special decree for each individual was an illusory safeguard, and, in the case of the Belgian priests, no attention was paid to it: 9,234 of them were sentenced *en masse*.

In the rest of the Republic, between seventeen and eighteen hundred priests seem to have been sentenced, either as deportees who had returned to France or by Directorial decree. But very few of them set sail for Guiana. One of the ships was captured by the English; two others went off with 263 priests, of whom 156 died in Guiana. Of the others, 920 remained on the Isle of Ré and 192 on the Isle of Oléron, including 348 Belgians and one Rhinelander. Out of nearly eleven thousand priests liable to deportation, therefore, only a little over a tenth were arrested and only twenty-five in every thousand were eventually transported. Moreover, those who were infirm or over sixty years of age were interned in special houses. The life of the interned priests on the islands and on the mainland was very hard, and death claimed a considerable number of them, a fact which can be partly explained by their age.

Instituted on the eighteenth of Fructidor, the Directorial Terror was aimed at the Royalists, and it cannot be denied that it was quite effective: until Year VII, they were unable to attempt any serious insurrection. "Surveillance reached such a pitch," wrote Tercier, the Chouan of the Sarthe, "that there was no longer any safety anywhere." Allier and Surville, who had taken command of the Royalists in the Ardèche, were speedily defeated and executed. However, armed bands continued to roam the countryside without being easily distinguishable from brigands proper. Consequently, on 13 Nivôse, Year VI (January 18, 1798), a new exceptional law referred acts of brigandage liable to the death penalty to the military commissions, if they had been committed by two or more persons, though it left the preliminary examination to the ordinary magistrates. This was a considerable step toward provostal justice and clearly pointed the way toward the extraordinary courts of the Consulate.

If it had been left to certain members of the Directory, the coercive measures would have gone much further. In 1798, a proposal was put forward to make the wearing of the tricolor cockade compulsory, a measure which would have vastly increased the number of suspects. Then again, Sieyès advised the Directors to expel all the nobles from the Republic, a suggestion which was in accordance with what he had written in 1789: without them, the Third Estate would still remain the nation and indeed would be far better off as a result. The sans-culottes had often called for the general prescription of the enemy class, without the Committee of Public Safety ever agreeing to their demand. Sieyès now went further than the Committee; in advocating the most extreme measure of the Terror, he appears as the incarnation of the Revolutionary bourgeoisie, as fanatically opposed to the nobility as to democracy. La Revellière and Reubell protested indignantly, but Sieyès

nonetheless got Boulay de la Meurthe to put forward his
motion in the Five Hundred, on 3 Vendémiaire, Year VII
(September 24, 1793): the nobles were to be denied citizenship unless they obtained naturalization under the
same conditions as foreigners; exceptions would be made
in the case of those who had rendered service to the Revolution; many nobles, on account of their offices or dignities
under the *ancien régime*, would be exiled and their property liquidated, the proceeds being sent to them in the
form of goods, after the deduction of an indemnity for
the benefit of the nation. Feeling ran so high that Boulay
declared on the twenty-ninth that he would not press the
demand for exile. Although opposition continued, for example in the *Moniteur*, the deprivation of citizenship nonetheless became law on 9 Frimaire (November 29).
However, for the law to be properly enforced, the Legislature would have had to indicate how exceptions were to
be granted, and this it never did. Consequently the cases
when it was applied to nobles seem to have been extremely
rare.

The dry guillotine, as transportation to Guiana was
called, left unpleasant memories, but the Directorial Terror was not particularly bloody, and above all—showing
greater shrewdness than the Jacobin Terror—it aimed only
at certain clearly defined categories. In reality, many of
its measures served several purposes; the Directory could
turn them against adversaries of every shade of opinion,
and it did not fail to do so. However, the mass of the population never felt threatened as it had by the Law of Suspects. Moreover, the repression remained purely governmental; the Directory did not re-establish the revolutionary
committees whose activity, all the more effective in that

they possessed a detailed knowledge of local conditions, had opened the way to personal hatred and extortion and thus created irremediable divisions throughout the country. It should be added that in time a growing repugnance was shown for the harsher measures; no law was passed to aggravate the Terror until, in Year VII, the Royalists' collusion with France's enemies abroad reawakened the country's anger; after August, 1798, nobody left for Guiana, and after March, 1799, only one execution of an émigré was recorded.

If a Terror is indispensable to any dictatorship, it cannot make up for the incapacity of the rulers and for bad organization to insure effective government. The changes which had been effected in the ruling personnel of the Republic had not increased its value. Carnot and Barthélemy had been replaced by François de Neufchâteau, who had been looking after the Ministry of the Interior for six weeks, and Merlin de Douai, who left the Ministry of Justice. Of the Ministers of Year IV, only Ramel was left, and, as experience showed, the change had not been beneficial: only the Belgian jurist Lambrecht, who took the place of Merlin, was a man of any eminence. Moreover, the Executive, retaining its collective nature, remained exposed to internal disruption like the Committee of Public Safety. But the fundamental defect of the new dictatorship was that it left the Constitution as it was, without even suspending it as had been done in 1793.

This was not because the Directorials were all unaware of the distinction between the constitutional regime, which belongs to a time of internal and external peace, and the exceptional government, which extraordinary circumstances make it necessary to install in its place. On 19

Fructidor, the Directory itself had pointed out to the Ancients that "it was impossible to apply the ordinary rules to an extraordinary case unless one wanted to play into the enemy's hands"; Cabanis in Year VI, and Berlier in Year VII, argued forcefully that the constitutional guarantees could not be strictly observed as long as the Revolution had not been completed. The Monarchists had naturally protested indignantly at this relativity which the Montagnards had invoked to justify the Revolutionary government. Portalis had, however, mitigated the condemnation by adding that, if exceptional measures were necessary, they had to be provided for by the Constitution. But what if the latter was silent? And what if, as was the case, a delay of seven years was required before it could be revised? There was therefore no lack of people who argued that, since it had been violated on the eighteenth of Fructidor, it would be better to change it in order to give the dictatorship an appropriate organization. But, characteristically, the idea that occurred to one and all was not to introduce into the Constitution the possibility of suspending it wholly or partly for a time, after the manner of the Montagnards, but to effect a permanent transformation of the constituted powers in an authoritarian direction. Immediately after the *coup d'état*, there had been a rumor that the Directory was going to adjourn the Councils; it was denied. Soon afterwards, Boulay asked if it would not be advisable to institute a regular procedure in the event of conflict developing once more between the Directory and the Councils, a suggestion which was doubtless a hint that the Directory should be granted the right of dissolution. In November, Laussat, in the Ancients, called for a strengthening of the Executive. The Councils did not see things this way, but they envisaged an extension of their powers by the postponement of the elections. La Revellière tells how a delegation approached the Directory on the subject, and Barras adds that a similar approach was made in Ventôse, Year VI; according to this plan, only vacancies would have been filled, and the elections would have been put off for ten years. The most coherent projects seem to have been drawn up by Sieyès, with Talleyrand's help and probably also that of Madame de Staël and Benjamin Constant, who on several occasions praised Cromwell and Robespierre for having made the Executive preeminent. Lauraguais, one of Barras' relatives, kept him fully informed. Talleyrand told Bonaparte that Sieyès was proposing to go and see him, and we have the general's reply: he recommended depriving the Executive of the right to conclude peace or declare war, as well as the power to vote taxes! "The government's power, with all the latitude I give it, ought to be regarded as the real representative of the nation."

For the moment, nothing came of all this. The majority would have been quite willing to perpetuate itself, but had no intention of abdicating. The Directory, having had the *coup d'etat* legalized by the Councils, had not dared to ask them at the same time for a fresh increase in power. Besides, its members were not in agreement; La Revellière naïvely boasts of having maintained the Constitution by means of a trick, and his friend Daunou maintained that the eighteenth of Fructidor was "a purely conservative act." Reubell and Barras had no taste for these sophistries. But the former was suspicious of the latter, and even more so of Bonaparte. As for the economic organization which had enabled the Committee of Public Safety to maintain the currency and supply the armies, the Directorial bourgeoisie ruled it out as a matter of course, and, at a time when the armies were living on the conquered countries and the new political era seemed to promise a restoration of the nation's finances, it had no lack of arguments.

Therefore, no matter how much circumstances had increased the powers of the Directory, it remained defenseless in the face of the Councils and the Treasury. In the departments, administration remained unstable. But all the results of the eighteenth of Fructidor were going to be called in question—this was the essential point—by the annual elections, and, to begin with, no later than the following March.

At least it seemed for a few months that the unity of the Republicans had been restored. The declaration of ineligibility which the Convention had applied to some of the Montagnards was repealed. The Directory once again included a good many Jacobins in its appointments and took care not to offend their papers. A few legislative measures were taken to please them. The Santo Domingo elections having been validated, Sonthonax took his seat, while the law on the return of the settlers was annulled. Plans were made for a reform of the judiciary, in view of the constant denunciations of the partiality of the courts. There was no fixed term for the electoral mandate of the judges, prosecutors and clerks of the criminal courts: a law remedied this defect and entrusted the Directory with the task of finding replacements for those who had been elected in Year IV. Another law provided for revision of the list of jurors in those departments where the elections had been annulled. What the Jacobins wanted most of all was for a process of reconsideration to be made available to Republicans who had reason to complain of Royalist judges: the Directory took a favorable view of this request, but the Councils considered that it would be difficult to produce a legal definition of a reasonable claim, and pointed out that criminals might take advantage of the provisions. Distrust of the terrorists came to the surface now and then. The apologists of the eighteenth of Fructidor never spared them their invective. When Lamarque obtained for the acquitted terrorists of Vendôme the indemnity laid down by a law of the Convention, the Ancients rejected the resolution. In Frimaire, Rabaut expressed alarm at the Directory's Jacobin appointments.

However, until the end of the winter, the Directory did not seem to suspect that the danger lay with the Left, and there is reason to believe that it was chiefly preoccupied with the generals. Augereau had been given command of the armies of the Sambre and Meuse and of the Rhine and Moselle, joined together under the name of the Army of Germany; he complained loudly of ingratitude, for he wanted a place in the Directory; soon it was alleged that he was plotting with the Jacobins of Strasbourg, and he was sent to the Pyrenees under the pretext of preparing an expedition against Portugal. Bonaparte, after playing a double game, was irritated that the eighteenth of Fructidor had not opened the gates of power to him; the Directory had been obliged to send him Botot, Barras' secretary, and to let him arrange the Treaty of Campo-Formio as he wished, so eager did he seem to throw in his hand. From Italy he went by way of Switzerland to Rastatt, to open negotiations with the Empire, and then went to Paris, where he was solemnly received on 20 Frimaire, Year VI (December 10, 1797). His attitude was cold and haughty;

in reply to Barras' speech he made the famous comment: "When the happiness of the French people is based on better organic laws, the whole of Europe will become free." During the following months, he was nonetheless consulted on foreign affairs, and, more than anyone else, he got the Republic to bog itself down in the path which he had done so much to make it take.

CHAPTER NINE

The War Against England and the Resumption of Propaganda

At Campo-Formio, France had made peace with the great Continental powers; but the war against England was still going on, and since 1793 this duel had caused her considerable harm. Compelled to conquer on land if she were not to perish, she had, as past experience should have enabled her to foresee, been obliged to give up ruling the seas, or at the very least maintaining a balance of power at sea—all the more so in that the emigration of officers, indiscipline, the shortage of money and the treachery of

Toulon had ruined her navy. After the 1793 campaign, England on the contrary had neglected the Continent where she did not reappear until 1799; confining herself to keeping the struggle going with her subsidies, she had devoted the greater part of her resources to naval and colonial warfare. The French squadrons hardly ever left port; true, the British blockade was frequently interrupted, especially in winter, but even so they moved about only stealthily and did not look for a fight. The shipowners, as usual, had fitted out privateers from which great things were expected; but the English, grouping their merchant ships together in escorted convoys, were less and less afraid of commerce being destroyed, whereas France's shipping trade was gradually wasting away.

Separated from her colonies, she had seen most of them fall into the enemy's hands or break away from her. At Santo Domingo, after Sonthonax had been recalled, General Laveaux, keeping only a few towns in the north of the island, had rallied to his cause Toussaint L'Ouverture, one of the Negro leaders, who, with the help of Rivaud, a mulatto who had held out in the south, had fairly quickly forced the English to evacuate the island. But it was not long before he made himself master of the colony; Laveaux and Sonthonax, returning on mission, were sent back to France under the pretext that they had been elected deputies; while General Hédouville, who replaced them, would soon leave in his turn. Toussaint, who incidentally displayed a truly statesmanlike genius, did not break with the Directory, but the authority of the mother country was no longer anything but nominal. In Guadeloupe, Victor Hugues, who had reconquered the island in 1794, was managing to hold out; the other West Indian islands—Tobago,

Saint Lucia and Martinque—were lost; the same was true
of Dutch Guiana and of Trinidad, which belonged to Spain.
The French islands in the Indian Ocean were still safe,
but the Île de France, refusing to abolish slavery, had
forced the Directory's commissioners to re-embark.

It was the West Indies which supplied France with most
of the colonial produce—especially sugar—which she distributed to her neighbors; her trade could not make good
the loss of them and, as for the rest, while peace on the
Continent reopened markets to it, it could not benefit
greatly from them without maritime transport. Its fate
therefore depended to a large extent on the help which it
could obtain from neutral shipping, which in turn depended on the British blockade. The English refused to
allow neutral flags to cover enemy merchandise, and, in
order to seize that merchandise as well as contraband of
war, arrogated to themselves the right of search on the
high seas. In reality, they granted all sorts of licenses which
considerably attenuated the harshness of these rules, because they were aimed much less at ruining the enemy's
military power than at enabling the English merchants
to earn money in his place. From this point of view, there
was no objection to even selling to the enemy in order to
obtain his currency; the blockade was mercantile rather
than warlike. The neutral ships were indispensable to
traffic with the enemy; besides, English trade was too
considerable to do without them, and political considerations often led to the making of concessions. They were
therefore given licenses on condition that they came into
an English port to have their cargo inspected and to pay
taxes. They protested in the name of "the freedom of the
seas," but one and all—Hanseatics, Scandinavians and

Americans—submitted, especially since they were making large profits. The disputes were above all concerned with colonial produce. In peacetime, France, like the other powers, reserved trade with her colonies for herself, but when at war with England, being unable to reach them, she suspended her exclusive rights and opened their ports to neutrals. England forbade the latter to take advantage of this permission, and reserved the trade with the enemy colonies for her own shipping. On this point too, a compromise had been reached: in 1794, after the United States had agreed to close their ports to the French privateers, they were allowed in exchange to import and re-export French colonial produce; the European neutrals had been given permission to go and fetch that produce to ship it either to their own ports or to England.

During the American War, France had respected the freedom of the neutrals, and the latter asked for nothing better than to help her as far as British controls would allow. But the Convention, adopting a policy of reprisals, had applied the same principles as the English, and thus harmed the neutrals; under the influence of the protectionists, it had even forbidden the admission of English merchandise and passed a "navigation act" forbidding foreign ships to bring anything into France except produce from their own countries. In fact, finding it impossible to do without the neutrals, the Committee of Public Safety had quickly returned to an opportunist policy similar to that of the English, and the Thermidorians had followed this by reviving the treaties of trade and navigation. All the same, the ban on British merchandise remained, and on 10 Brumaire, Year V (October 30, 1796), it had been aggravated by a law which branded a great many goods as English, whatever their real source, and for the rest called for the production of a certificate of origin issued by the appropriate consul. Domiciliary visits hàd followed and, as in 1793, British subjects had even been arrested. In the course of the following summer, the Directory informed the neutral countries that it would seize their ships, even on the high seas, if they continued to comply with England's requirements. However, until the eighteenth of Fructidor, it does not seem that in practice they ceased to place themselves at the service of French trade. Theoretically, France had done everything to make the English blockade as impervious as possible to the enemy's will, but the need to export and to obtain certain raw materials had likewise forced her to make certain concessions.

Confronted by these results of the English war, thoughtful Frenchmen, however preoccupied they might be with hostilities on the Continent, were obliged to admit that France and England had probably arrived at the last act of the "Second Hundred Years' War," begun under Louis XIV for the control of the high seas and of the world. Most of their compatriots, being countrymen, did not bother their heads very much about such problems, but they hated the English as traditional enemies and accused "perfidious Albion" of having taken the lead of the counter-revolutionary crusade, and having subsidized the Coalition, in order to satisfy her selfish greed with impunity. They did not believe her to be invincible for a moment. At that time of wooden sailing-ships, coal and iron had not yet given the English that superiority which would make competition impossible; and seaboard conscription was a better source of recruits than the press-gang. Then again, England had no national army and employed only mercenaries; while there could be no question of sending Republican troops to conquer India or the West Indies, the idea of landing them in England did not seem impossible, nor did that of winning over Ireland, which was always ready to rise in revolt; an attempt made in December 1796 had failed, but that had been due to a storm and not to the enemy fleet. The economic war too, right from the start, had seemed full of promise. For the French the strength of a State lay essentially in its peasants and its agriculture; the state of production, the influence of the Physiocrats, and the example of the Roman Republic—all combined to fill them with contempt for the modern Carthage whose life depended on an export trade built on the artificial and fragile scaffolding of credit. She had only to be prevented from trading with the Continent and she would be reduced to bankruptcy, starvation, and revolution.

When the eighteenth of Fructidor reawakened the old revolutionary ardor, it was therefore not simply the spirit of propaganda which it benefited: the conclusion of peace on the Continent also enabled it to turn against England, all the more so in that the alliances with Spain and Holland inspired boundless hopes. In a circular of Nivôse, Year VI, Talleyrand—the Anglophile!—inveighed against the tyrants of the world, the vampires of the sea, which the Republic was going to exterminate for the benefit of civilization and in order to liberate the oppressed nations, thus earning the latter's undying gratitude. These bellicose accents undoubtedly awakened a response; The Directory was able to float a loan of eighty million francs, and inventors came forward with proposals for dirigible balloons and even submarines. The Irish, who had risen in revolt in 1798, had been crushed; nonetheless, an invasion of England was decided on. About fifty thousand men were moved to Brest, and Bonaparte was given command of the "Army of England"; he seems to have taken the plan seriously for a while. At the same time, the economic war took on a new character. On 29 Nivôse, Year VI (January 18, 1798), a law putting the Directory's threats into effect made it possible to seize those neutral ships which had complied with English requirements or on which any article of British origin was found, even if it were only a sailor's knife or the captain's cutlery. This harshness seemed incredible; it increased the number of prizes, the privateers enthusiastically making themselves the instruments of the law. The merchants who saw the neutrals deserting the French ports, and the consumers who were deprived of colonial produce, protested, but so also did the manufacturers: this was not how they understood protection. They were quite willing to have a ban on manufactured goods which competed with their own, but they wanted to receive the raw material they lacked, especially cotton: and they approved of the "Continental blockade" —for the Napoleonic method would be nothing else— provided it remained mercantile like the British blockade, and did not become warlike at their expense. In the event, exceptions to the law of 10 Brumaire, Year V, had to be made in the case of tools, agricultural implements, and calico intended for printing. And at bottom, the Directory really considered that a policy of opportunism remained necessary: it asked the Councils to restore its jurisdiction over prizes of war, unwisely transferred to the ordinary courts, so that it could regulate the enforcement of the blockade to suit the complicated interests of the Republic.

Even so, the policy which had been adopted seriously

weakened French exports and had a deplorable influence on external relations. The United States jibbed and took retaliatory measures against French shipping, so that the two republics found themselves practically in a state of war. However, the Americans agreed to negotiate, and Talleyrand took the opportunity to ask their envoys for a jug of wine; when the latter's correspondence was communicated to the Senate and made public in the spring of 1798, a terrible scandal resulted. Then again, the economic war, interpreted in this way, could not have its full effect except if the whole Continent co-operated, a state of affairs which could only push France into the policy of conquest already encouraged by the spirit of propaganda. The completion of the conquest of Italy and the seizure of the Hanseatic ports and Hanover, in order to close Germany to English trade, were consequences which naturally recommended themselves to the advocates of total war. The annexation of Mülhausen and Geneva took place in 1798; it can be explained, at least in part, by the desire to suppress two centers of smuggling.

Alone now in face of a bigger and threatening France, England became aware of her perilous position, and the war, for her, began to become a national affair. The preparations for an invasion, however, were soon abandoned. From Holland and Spain the Directory obtained nothing. In 1797 Jervis had beaten the Spaniards off Cape St. Vincent; he blockaded Cádiz, and Nelson's squadron entered the Mediterranean; Brueys declared that he was incapable of bringing the Corfu squadron to Brest; Duncan routed the Dutch at Camperduyn. The military leaders were skeptical about the chances of success. On 5 Ventôse, Year VI (February 23, 1798), on his return from an inspection in the west, Bonaparte decided to abandon the project. It had no other consequences but the dispatch, in August, of a small expeditionary force to Ireland: General Humbert succeeded in landing, but was soon surrounded and had to surrender.

There had been no lack of reasons to justify the abandonment of the scheme: the navy could not guarantee the crossing, and, moreover, the Republic was not sufficiently sure of peace on the Continent to deprive itself of an excellent army and its best general. But Bonaparte had added that, if negotiations for peace were not opened with England, the war had to be taken to Egypt, and there was not a single one of the arguments against the invasion of England which did not apply, with even greater force, to this new undertaking; there were also several others which condemned it in its own right.

That Bonaparte's imagination should have flown after Alexander toward an almost legendary Orient was only to be expected after the occupation of the Ionian Isles, the expression of his views on Malta, and the dispatch of an agent to Ali-Tebelen, the Pasha of Janina; nothing could be less surprising. He would certainly have preferred to conquer England, if that had proved possible. As soon as that plan had to be given up, the Orient returned to the foreground. For Bonaparte could not remain idle without running the risk of compromising himself in political intrigues which were still premature, and without peace dimming his prestige. If his choice fell on Egypt, that was probably due to Talleyrand, and there is some mystery about the part played by the latter. True, Egypt had occupied a place in French tradition since the Crusades, and in the trade of Marseilles since the Capitulations; the mer-

chants had been complaining for years about the Mamelukes, the mercenaries who exploited the country under
the nominal authority of the Sultan; and the consul
Magallon maintained that an invasion would be sure to
succeed. Egypt, moreover, was on the way to India,
where Tippoo was still defending Maisur against Welles-
ley. In Messidor, Year V, speaking to the Institute, Talleyrand had advocated the resumption of colonial expansion,
and Egypt was one of the most splendid preys anyone
could wish for. But it could not escape Talleyrand's notice
that an agreement with England, which he had always
wanted, would be impossible if, while insisting on keeping
the natural frontiers whose acquisition he himself approved
—even though his admirers have suggested the contrary—
the Republic also undertook an overseas conquest that
might alarm its rival; and none was more calculated to do
so than that of Egypt. Then again, one of the principles
of the Republic's policy had been to abstain from any intervention in eastern Europe, and it was by keeping silent
on the Polish partitions that it had been able to detach
Prussia from the Coalition. By conquering Egypt, on the
other hand, it risked provoking war with Turkey, for it was
in vain that Talleyrand maintained that the Sultan did not
care about such an illusory possession; worse still, it meant
reopening the Eastern question without the consent of Russia, thus arousing her enmity and inciting her to fight the
French, which was something she had always avoided. Talleyrand was closely associated with Bonaparte; was he
simply trying here to serve him to the detriment of the
nation? That is possible. But, since he was in the habit of
selling himself to the highest bidder, it has been suggested
that he might have undertaken to divert toward Egypt the

army that was threatening England with invasion, and to provoke the formation of a new Coalition, as he would against Napoleon. The Directory had reason to suspect him: a letter from Madame Grand, his mistress, to a London correspondent, maintaining that Piedcourt (Talleyrand suffered from a club foot) wanted to "help his English friends," had been intercepted; the lady was arrested and then released. It must be assumed that, on the eve of the dreaded elections of Year VI, the Directory considered it out of the question to force Bonaparte and Talleyrand into opposition; but that it should have adopted their rash proposal for a reason of that sort tells heavily against it.

Even if it had rejected the plan of an invasion of Egypt, peace on the Continent would still have been necessary if it was to wage war on England with any chance of success. Everything, however, simultaneously impelled the Directory toward a policy of invasion which could only compromise peace: the influence of the generals and the contractors, the revolutionary ardor which it itself shared, the vague desire to deprive England of her markets in order to monopolize them, and even the temptation to secure all possible guarantees in anticipation of a new war. The enslavement of the sister republics soon became obvious. It was important that Batavia should have a stable government, capable of helping her protector, and this was far from being the case. True, the provisional rulers, who had been in power since 1795, had submitted a constitution for popular ratification in August, 1797, but a coalition of the supporters of the House of Orange and the unitarian democrats had rejected it. After the eighteenth of Fructidor, Delacroix, the French envoy to The Hague, came to an agreement with the latter to propose a *coup d'état* to Paris.

Daëndels, who was in command of the Dutch army, and Joubert, the commander of the occupation forces, had promised their co-operation. On 3 Pluviôse, Year VI (January 22, 1798), the Batavian Assembly declared itself to be a constituent body, and, after purging itself, drew up a new constitution which, this time, was accepted. It was just as necessary to make sure of the Cisalpine Republic. On 3 Ventôse (February 21), the Directory concluded a treaty of alliance with it which prolonged the occupation of the country by a force of twenty-five thousand men at the expense of the new republic; at the same time a liberal trade agreement was signed, but this did not prevent the Cisalpine Councils from rejecting both treaty and agreement, as impossibly onerous. The regime in power had been instituted by Bonaparte without either popular ratification or French approval; the Directory therefore considered itself as much at liberty to intervene and change it as it had been in Holland. The Councils were purged and arrests carried out, after which the treaties were ratified.

Bonaparte's conquest, incidentally, was the parade-ground of the advocates of propaganda, and it was chiefly around the Cisalpine Republic that the latter exerted their influence. There, coming from all parts of Italy, and joining up with the generals and the contractors, there gathered all those who dreamed of turning the peninsula into a unitarian republic. The Cisalpine conservatives themselves considered that in return for the alliance with France their country should be enlarged at the expense of the Pope and Piedmont. Cisalpine bands kept entering the Marches and it was hoped that in Rome the revolutionaries would take action. They did in fact start a riot on December 28, 1797, but their adversaries got the upper hand and, holding the

French responsible, threatened the Embassy, which was then under Joseph Bonaparte; in the brawl that followed, General Duphot was killed. The Directory's hostility towards the Papacy was too fierce for it to miss the opportunity. Berthier, who was now in command of the Army of Italy, received orders to march on Rome, and Bonaparte encouraged him. However, the Directory had no intention of letting the Roman Republic become a new Cisalpine Republic for Berthier, and it immediately sent a Civil Commission to organize it, which was joined by Daunou and Monge. Berthier, in any case, found the task he had been given repugnant. Arriving outside Rome on 11 February, he was nonplused when Pius VI accepted all his conditions; the revolutionaries having proclaimed a republic in the Forum, in the midst of a crowd of onlookers, and called in the French, he occupied the city, sent the Pope off to Sienna, and let Masséna take over. The Commission proclaimed a constitution, drawn up by Merlin, which, until the end of hostilities, submitted the laws and the actions of the "consuls" to the ratification of the French general, so that the Roman Republic immediately became the least free of them all. It was also the most heavily ransomed: Haller, the contractors, and the generals had started looting right from the beginning. The junior officers protested indignantly and, when Masséna arrived, mutinied; this general was reputed to be one of the boldest of looters and they bore him a long-standing grudge, since most of them belonged to the regiments which Moreau had sent to Bonaparte, under Bernadotte's command, at the beginning of 1797, and which had come to blows with his division. The Commission was unable to restore order, and finally the Directory was obliged to appoint a new commander:

Gouvion-Saint-Cyr, one of Moreau's lieutenants. The Roman Republic thus began under the most unfavorable auspices.

It was from Bonaparte, determined to join the Cisalpine Republic to France by way of Valais, that the decisive impulse came which led to the creation of the Helvetian Republic. Switzerland was then only a confederation of independent cantons, governed by privileged bourgeois patriciates which, having gained control over some part of the country, treated the inhabitants as subjects: this is how the Vaud region had become a sort of Bernese colony. The Swiss patriots, notably Ochs of Basle, wanted both to create a unitarian republic of which every Swiss would be a citizen, and to overthrow the oligarchy. Unwilling to count on an insurrection, they hoped that France, without occupying Switzerland, would behave in a sufficiently threatening way for the oligarchy to collapse. The Directory had no lack of grievances against the latter, but it had secured the expulsion of Mallet du Pan, Wickham and the émigrés; an agreement was under consideration giving France the Jura territories and the town of Bienne; these she claimed as dependencies of the bishopric of Basle, which had become the department of Mont-Terrible. So far, the suggestions of the Swiss democrats had not met with any response, any more than the claims made by Laharpe, a native of Vaud—claims based on a sixteenth-century treaty by which France, while recognizing the rights of Berne over the Vaud region, had nonetheless guaranteed the latter's liberties. The affair was set in motion on December 8, 1797, at a dinner at Reubell's which brought together Bonaparte and Ochs. Soon afterwards, Ochs began a campaign to get the cantons to accept a constitution drawn up by Merlin and Reubell. Several cantons gave their assent. At the same time, a division of the Army of Italy had been moved to the frontier of the Vaud region, though with orders not to cross the border unless it was attacked. But as the inhabitants of Vaud had lost no time in giving their support to the new constitution, the Bernese sent a few troops to attack them: the French commander despatched an envoy to parley with them, and in the darkness he was fired at by mistake; the Vaud region was immediately occupied. So far the situation was not irremediable. All of a sudden, in the night of February 13-14, 1798, the Directory ordered its troops to march on Berne, probably at Bonaparte's suggestion. Brune advanced from Lausanne, and Schauenbourg from the Jura; the town was occupied after some fairly severe fighting. The Directory immediately appointed a civil commissioner, a former member of the Convention called Lecarlier, who was given Rapinat, Reubell's brother-in-law, as his assistant. They enforced the constitution, seized the Treasury of Berne, imposed a levy of fifteen million francs on the cantons, and tried to put an end to arbitrary requisitioning and looting; but they had to put down the insurrection of the highlanders of Schwytz, Uri and Unterwald, as well as that of Valais. The Bernese, showing greater cunning, bribed Talleyrand and obtained a treaty which reduced their levy. Lecarlier, who had been appointed Minister of Police, had just been succeeded by Rapinat, who flew into a rage and refused to enforce this treaty, thus incurring the wrath of the Swiss Directory: on 28 Prairial (June 17), without consulting Paris, he carried out a *coup d'état* which broke all resistance. The Helvetian Republic was not beginning very much better than the Roman Republic.

Piedmont only narrowly escaped the same fate. In 1797, the King of Sardinia had ruthlessly repressed a revolutionary movement, and, after the eighteenth of Fructidor, had lost no time in ratifying the treaty of alliance with France which until then he had left in abeyance. However, Cisalpines and Genoese were impatient to extend their territories at his expense. The representative of France, Ginguené, had no sooner arrived at Turin than he set about helping them, and Brune, appointed commander of the Army of Italy, allied himself with the Jacobins in Milan; soon afterwards, armed bands entered Piedmont. For months, the Directory posed as a mediator; finally, after Ginguené had succeeded, on 9 Messidor (June 27), in imposing on the terrified King a convention which handed over the citadel of Turin to the French, it thought fit to keep this prize.

Austria could scarcely have been expected to view this extension of French influence with equanimity. Not that Thugut expressed any indignation at it; still looking for an opportunity of self-aggrandizement in Italy, he simply bided his time. At Campo-Formio, it had been agreed that, if France made fresh acquisitions, Austria would be entitled to compensation. It is true that the Roman and Helvetian Republics were supposed to be independent. But at Rastatt, the Directory exceeded the provisions of the Treaty of Campo-Formio. Reubell regretted that the Cologne region should have been left to the Empire, and, from the point of view of general policy, the Directory could not give up its claims to that region without alienating Prussia which, ceding nothing more, would not be entitled to any of the annexations she was planning in Germany; this was playing into the hands of Austria, which had in fact wanted to foil her rival. Consequently Treilhard, who had taken

Bonaparte's place at the Congress, demanded the whole of the left bank of the Rhine and obtained a general agreement from the Diet on 19 Ventôse (March 9). Cobenzl immediately asked for compensation. Treilhard's retort was as surprising as it was categorical: the Cologne region, having been under military occupation for a long time, could not be regarded as a new acquisition. In these circumstances, war was in sight. It seemed imminent when, in April, Bernadotte, the French Ambassador in Vienna, was attacked by rioters after hoisting the tricolor flag, and, failing to obtain suitable redress, left the city.

However, it was postponed. Neither Thugut, who was not ready, nor the Directory, which was preoccupied with the current elections, was prepared to begin hostilities. Moreover, the wind had changed once again in Paris: the Directory had just broken with the Jacobins, and for a moment it seemed likely that its foreign policy would be modified as a result.

The New Anti-Jacobin Reaction; the Twenty-Second of Floréal, Year VI (May 11, 1798)

After the eighteenth of Fructidor, the elections of Year VI had soon become the major preoccupation of the Directory and the Councils. A great deal was at stake, for what was involved was not strictly speaking a partial change of representatives, since the recent exclusions had greatly increased the number of unforeseen vacancies: there were 437 deputies to be elected. The disappearance of the last third of the "perpetual" members of the Convention made the situation still more serious. Until Pluviôse, the Royalist peril remained the overriding problem. Since the suspension of the elections had not been agreed, the Directory resorted to other expedients, which were no less contrary to the spirit of representative government and which, for that reason, had been rejected in Year V. The law of 12 Pluviôse, Year VI (January 31, 1798) charged the existing Legislature with the task of checking the credentials of the newly elected deputies; thus the outgoing deputies would purge their successors! Another law, that of 24 Pluviôse (February 12), stipulated that the election of the new Directory should take place on 27 Floréal (May 16), a measure which likewise allocated it to the existing Legislature: whatever the new majority might be, the Directory would nonetheless remain entirely Republican.

Gradually, however, it became apparent that not many Royalists would vote in the elections: the new Terror would intimidate them. Some of them advocated abstention, the law of 19 Fructidor having imposed upon the electors the oath of hatred for the Monarchy; many of them would be excluded by the law of 3 Brumaire, Year IV, and the one which had just been passed against the nobles; in Ventôse, yet another law excluded all those who had rendered services to the rebels. Nobody could have any illusions about the prestige of the Directory and its minions. Was there not reason to believe, therefore, that the effacement of the Royalists would benefit the Jacobins most of all? In the provinces, the Constitutional Clubs were chiefly directed by them and, thanks to the new appointments, there was no lack of administrators and commissioners to favor them. In Côte-d'Or there were nine clubs, and in the Sarthe twenty-five. The Le Mans club organized what was known as an *ambulance* or perambulation: every tenth day, it went in procession to the seat of some canton where colleagues and friends had prepared a fête, concluding with the foundation of a new club which in its turn propagated itself in the neighboring communes. The ban on affiliations could not prevent them from acting together. The result was a ready-made election "machine."

But apart from this propaganda, it may be that the proposals made by Pons de Verdun in the Five Hundred, on 22 Nivôse (January 8) and again on 3 Ventôse (February 24) greatly contributed to shifting the danger back to the Left in the eyes of the Directorials. To take part in the primary assemblies which opened on 1 Germinal, it was necessary, according to the Constitution, to have one year's residence, dating from inscription on the civic register; in Year V, the Republican majority had realized that, the previous year, its supporters had been unable to demand or obtain inscription on account of the White Terror, and it had decided that all who entered their names up to 30 Ventôse should be deemed to have done so a year before. Adopted only five days before 1 Germinal, this measure had had no effect. Pons asked for it to be revived. As it was bound to benefit the Jacobins most of all, it is significant that the Ancients should have rejected, on two occasions in Year VI, a resolution which had struck them as legitimate in Year V. Pons also wanted favorable consideration to be given until 30 Ventôse to those citizens who offered to pay the tax of three days' work in order to become eligible to vote. Again it is significant that Régnier should have cried: "Anybody would think that Pons regarded as good Republicans precisely those people who don't pay taxes"; and that Pilastre, one of La Revellière's friends, should have protested that in Year V there had probably not been as many as fifty men in the whole of France who had acquired the right to vote in that way. To understand the rejection of Pons' proposal, it is sufficient to recall that the Constitution restricted voluntary registration to the month of Messidor, and the full meaning of these acrimonious remarks becomes apparent: Pons had annoyed the Directorials with an ingenuous movement in the direction of universal suffrage. Thus, at the very moment when laws were directed against the Royalists, an anti-Jacobin reaction began which was to turn them to its own purpose.

La Revellière was thoroughly alarmed, for he had been warned that terrorists were planning to assassinate him during the walk that he took nearly every day to the Jardin des Plantes, to see his friend the botanist Thouin. Merlin, for his part, out of fear too or as a deliberate policy, revived Carnot's role with the same stubborn hatred for those whose views he had represented in 1793. Once again, the Directory repeated the accusation, which, in Year II, had enabled the Committee of Public Safety to crush simultaneously the extremists of both Right and Left: it denounced both branches of the counterrevolutionary conspiracy, that of the White Cockade and that of the Red Cap. In point of fact, there was no danger that the electors would choose terrorists, but by confusing the democrats with them, the Directory was sure of creating an impression, for what the bourgeoisie dreaded was not only the Terror but also the social democracy of Year II. "Social fear" was therefore a valuable help to the Directory. The *Moniteur* alarmed landowners by reporting "posters in which shameless anarchists preached the leveling-down and the equality of Robespierre; and promised to give those who have not, the property of those who have." On 9 Ventôse (February 27), at the Constitutional Club, Benjamin Constant called on property owners to rally to the Directory:

The Revolution was carried out to insure liberty and equality for all while leaving the property of each inviolate. It has
therefore undertaken to defend that property . . . ; all the
government's powers, all the legislators' measures must aim
at maintaining it, consolidating it, surrounding it with a sacred barrier.

In reality, those who have been called the Neo-Jacobins
were not communists any more than they were terrorists,
but it is true that they were quite capable of partially
reviving the social democracy of Year II, and this was what
had to be avoided at all costs. "Whoever outlaws wealth
conspires against mediocrity," added Constant. Well said!

It was in vain that Barras protested at the division which
was going to be created once more among the Republicans,
for his colleagues had ulterior motives. For Reubell—and
probably also for Merlin, who was no less authoritarian—
the main object was not so much to exclude the democrats
as to provide the Directory with a docile majority. In spite of
the solidarity of the Fructidorians, the Councils' hidden
jealousy of the Executive had been awakened a good many
times. Lamarque had deplored the fact that the legislators
should be "so to speak effaced from the political body."
Since the Directory had annulled the lists of jurors drawn
up by the central administrations it dismissed, the legality
of its decrees had once more been disputed. It had been
refused the right of dismissal with respect to the judges,
prosecutors, and clerks of the criminal courts. It had also
been refused control over the theaters. In the course of
financial debates, criticism was beginning to be made of
government extravagance. La Revellière claims, incidentally—and this is quite probable—that Chénier, Baudin,
Camus and many others had gone into opposition because

they had not obtained the privileges or the consideration to which they felt they were entitled, and that all the deputies were annoyed at having no influence in the ministerial offices. Nothing illustrates this conflict better than the affair of the cloaks. The Constitution prescribed for the deputies, as for the Directors, an official uniform and, in January 1798, this uniform was being made in Lyons when the police of that city confiscated the material as being of English origin. A storm of indignation broke out in the Councils at this attack on the majesty of national representation, and a law was passed requiring the Directory to order the restitution of the material. The government saw that, if the Fructidorians showed little gratitude to it, the future majority might be even less docile. One can therefore form only an imperfect idea of its intentions and the resulting consequences if one imagines that the Jacobins, such as Dubois-Crancé or General Jourdan, were the only ones to cause it concern; it was no less anxious to outlaw independents such as Lamarque, a former Girondin. Apart from the fact that every government is naturally drawn to a policy of this sort, it was bound to recommend itself once the Directory had returned to a dictatorship without suspending elections. The Committee of Public Safety had broken all resistance in the Convention, and Bonaparte, as First Consul, would declare bluntly: "There must be no opposition."

Having made up its mind, the Directory prepared for the elections with much greater care than in Year V; besides, this time it had a much wider range of means at its disposal. Merlin increased the number of dismissals; first of all, Sotin, Minister of Police of the eighteenth of Fructidor, suspected of Jacobinism, was replaced by Dondeau, one of this Director's tools. Envoys were sent out to spur on the commissioners in secret: for this purpose, inspectors were used whose official function was to supervise the enforcement, now begun at last, of the highway toll; they were provided with funds, and also with a list of the candidates approved by the Directory. Intimidation was also used: certain administrations and commissioners carried out arrests of suspects; Lyons, Marseilles and several other towns were placed under martial law. But Merlin's favorite expedient, one very characteristic of his crafty mind, was to turn the law of 12 Pluviôse against his adversaries, by systematically organizing secessions which would enable the present majority to validate whomsoever it pleased. These secessions were therefore a common feature of the elections of Year VI. In Paris, for example, the electoral assembly of the Oratoire, which was almost entirely left-wing, saw Merlin's confederates withdraw to the Institut, where they finally gathered together 212 electors out of 609. These maneuvers were not always successful. In the Sarthe, the Central Administration fought only the Royalists, and allowed the clubs' delegates to hold a meeting on 5 Ventôse (March 5) to draw up the list of candidates; the same day, the Directory suppressed the clubs and their newspaper, and dismissed three members of the Central Administration as well as several other officials. The left-wing list nonetheless went through unaltered. However, the fact remains that a majority of Directorials was elected; but, in order to obtain the exclusion of the opponents it feared, the Directory was obliged to terrorize the population, and the elections were said to have been execrable.

The Councils set to work checking them in accordance with the regular procedure; this operation was not expected to be completed before 1 Prairial, in which case the deputies who had not been invalidated would take their seats. In order to exclude the "wild beasts," as Creuzé-Latouche called them, it was suggested before long that the method should be changed; Régnier asked that the "brave seceders" be encouraged. Lamarque defended the majority principle: the Directory's confidants retorted that, first of all, since the electors had taken an oath of hatred for the Monarchy and the Constitution of 1793, they could not have elected Royalists or Jacobins without perjuring themselves, in which case the election was null and void; and that secondly, in order to exclude unworthy persons, the Legislature had an implicit right of censure over the newly elected deputies, a right which was justified chiefly by examples taken from the United States. When a message was sent to the Directory asking for any information it might have, the Left did not fail to point out that this would enable it to dictate a choice of deputies, so that the deviation from the majority principle would end up by giving the government power to purge the Legislature, a state of affairs which was the negation of the representative system.

On 13 Floréal (May 2), the Directory replied by denouncing the conspiracy of the Royalists and the Anarchists, and, on the fifteenth, the Five Hundred, after validating the elections made at the Institut for the department of the Seine, suspended the operation. As far as the majority was concerned, that was the end of the matter. Its leaders, Bailleul and Hardy, joined with the Directors to draw up a hurried list of exclusions, and, on the eighteenth, asked the Council to adopt it *en bloc*. General Jourdan made an eloquent protest, asking for each item to be examined and voted upon separately, but his adversaries urged the hesitant Assembly to bar the way to the Terror. "The guillotine is ready," Crassous is alleged to have said, according to Barras; "do you want to mount the scaffold?" The reply went without saying. The Ancients ratified the list without turning a hair.

The law of 22 Floréal, Year VI (May 11, 1798) validated the elections in forty-seven departments out of ninety-six. It excluded the deputies in eight departments where there had been secession, so that their seats remained vacant; in nineteen others, the seceders were preferred on account of their political color. Elsewhere, one or more representatives were disqualified; what is more, over sixty administrators or judges were set aside. Altogether, 106 deputies were expelled, including Lamarque himself; about sixty members of the opposition seem to have escaped. The elections did not by any means present the threatening appearance they were alleged to have, but the majority loyal to the Directors had no doubt been reduced, and, if the minority had not been left without leadership, it might well have embarrassed them. The governmental character of the *journée* becomes even more obvious when it is realized that sixty-eight commissioners and seventeen other officials nominated by the Directory figured among those admitted, as well as 106 administrators and judges, many of whom it had probably also chosen, so that over 150 deputies had used their official positions to impose themselves on the electors and could be regarded as government agents. Although the twenty-second of Floréal seems to have run counter to the eighteenth of Fructidor, it confirmed the latter by aggravating that subjection of the Legislature which was to be one of the essential features of the Napoleonic regime. The intrusion of government officials would indeed vitiate the representative system until 1848.

A few measures followed for the benefit of the Executive; it was given authority to fill any vacancies in the ranks of the judges, prosecutors and clerks of the criminal courts until Year VII, and similar authority with respect to the magistrates elected in Year V. As for the change in the personnel of the Directory, it took place on 27 Floréal, in accordance with the law of 24 Pluviôse: the place of François de Neufchâteau was taken by the jurist Treilhard, a regicide and former member of the Constituent Assembly. He had left the Legislature on 1 Prairial, Year IV, and it could therefore be argued that he was not eligible, but in Ventôse it had been maintained that the interval of one year had to be counted from the resignation from office to the return to office and not to the election, without anybody raising any objection. Treilhard's accession did nothing to enhance the prestige of the Directory, for it meant yet another lawyer to sit with "King" Barras—an arrogant lawyer, what is more, who would soon increase the number of malcontents.

The Directorials were well aware that, having broken the unity of the Republicans, they ran the risk of seeing the Royalists raise their heads again. To guard against this danger, they authorized on 18 Messidor (July 6) domiciliary visits for a period of one month, incidentally without much result, and they took active measures against those citizens liable to deportation who had so far escaped; the law of 19 Brumaire, Year VII (November 9, 1798) made it possible to inscribe those who did not give themselves up on the list of émigrés. In point of fact, most of the trouble suffered by the

Directory came from the Jacobins and its own majority. On 26 Prairial, Year VI (June 17, 1798), a banquet which brought the deputies together at the Hôtel Biron ended in uproar, some of the guests having refused to drink the health of the new Directory. As for the majority, dissatisfied with itself for having excluded a good many men it esteemed, it was also dissatisfied with the government which had forced it to give way. It is significant that on several occasions the Presidents were taken from the Left: Pérès de la Haute-Garonne, Savary, General Jourdan and General Marbot. Denunciations against speculators and against Schérer, the Minister of War, became frequent. Bonaparte's brothers, Joseph and Lucien, were now deputies, and the latter distinguished himself by his violent, demagogic opposition. At the very moment when the Directory's authority seemed undisputed, its fall was beginning to be prepared.

Abroad, its dictatorship cut an even poorer figure. Having quarreled inside France with the Jacobins, it started fighting their friends in the sister republics, chiefly those in Italy, and showed considerable suspicion of the generals and the contractors who protected them. The Batavian Republic was the first to feel the effects of the twenty-second of Floréal. The unitarian democrats, who in any case were at loggerheads with Daëndels and Joubert, were denounced by the Conservative notables as dangerous anarchists; Delacroix was recalled; on 24 Prairial (June 22), the government was purged and new elections assured it of a majority. In Switzerland, Rapinat saw his *coup d'état* annulled and received orders to return to France; not having been replaced, however, he remained in office, and it was he who signed the treaty of alliance. Contrary to the reputation given him by the Directory's adversaries and France's enemies, he was an honest man who did his best to make the occupation bearable, and in fact it cost the Swiss much less than the Romans, although they complained much more. The counterrevolution was still alive: the Catholic cantons rose yet again in revolt, and in October the oligarchs let the Austrians into the canton of Grisons.

The events in the Cisalpine Republic were even more distressing. The Directory sent into that region several financial agents who were hostile to the Jacobins, unpopular with the generals whom they had been sent to watch, usually capable, but chosen among the former aristocracy and thus inevitably denounced in Paris and in Italy as counter-revolutionaries: Faipoult de Maisoncelle, a former minister; Amelot de Chaillou, the son of a former minister of Louis XV, a sometime administrator of Burgundy, and a director of the emergency fund under the Constituent Assembly; Laumond, who had succeeded him in this last post after serving in the Assay Office; and Eymar, the brother of an Abbé who had figured among the "blacks" in the Constituent Assembly. Trouvé was sent with them as an ambassador; he was a tool of La Revellière, and an ambitious mediocrity. Under the influence of some Lombard nobles, the Directory declared Bonaparte's constitution null and void, and instructed Trouvé to draw up another, which, in spite of Brune, was imposed on the Cisalpine Republic. But soon the general received compensation; orders were given for this constitution to be submitted to a plebiscite, probably on the intervention of Barras, and, as Trouvé and Faipoult protested, they were replaced by Fouché and Amelot. With the connivance of the former, Brune carried out a fresh *coup* in the night of 17-18 *October*, which expelled

Trouvé's creatures from their posts; popular ratification followed. Meanwhile, Ginguené went on agitating in Piedmont, and Brune's second in command organized a demonstration in Turin, which he probably hoped would lead to disturbances that would allow his chief to occupy the country. This time the Directory got angry; Ginguené was dismissed, Fouché recalled, and Brune sent to Holland.

It was just when hostilities were beginning, the Neapolitans having invaded the Roman Republic, that the Directory took the measure which best illustrates the policy it had followed since Floréal with so little success: on 5 Frimaire, Year VII (November 26, 1798), it re-established the commissioners to the armies; three were appointed— Rapinat in Switzerland, Amelot in Milan, Faipoult in Rome. But they received no more authority than their predecessors, and their fate was even more pitiable. Joubert, who had succeeded Brune, quickly found Amelot's supervision intolerable, and tendered his resignation; the Directory finally accepted it in January, but, remaining faithful to its policy of delay, it replaced Amelot by Laumond. Schérer, who took over command of the Army of Italy, was deferential to the government's representative, and it was partly this which drew upon him the hatred of his subordinates: he would pay dear for it in the future. As soon as he arrived in Switzerland, Masséna took no notice of the civil commissioner, who asked for his recall. But it was the army that had been given the task of repelling the Neapolitans which suffered most of all. It had been entrusted to Championnet, whose conflict with Faipoult culminated in a tremendous quarrel.

The Directory had thus to a certain extent checked the activity of the propagandists, and had prevented them from revolutionizing Piedmont; but, to turn Austria away from the Coalition, it would have been necessary to go back on previous policy and there was no question of that. After the twenty-second of Floréal, François de Neufchâteau had been sent to Seltz, in Alsace, to confer with Cobenzl; he was given orders to confine himself to the Vienna incident and to refer the question of compensation to Rastatt. There, Austria could only have asked for German territory, when it was on Italy that she had designs; for the Directory, the latter country obviously remained a private preserve.

Accordingly, it carried out no real changes in its foreign policy; the fear of premature hostilities had inspired it with a certain moderation, but hesitation is not repentance. The measures taken against the Jacobins in the sister republics were simply an internal political maneuver, the logical consequence of the twenty-second of Floréal; and the supervision that the Directory tried to impose on the generals can be seen as a necessary complement of its dictatorship. Without postponing war to any significant degree, the anti-Jacobin reaction added noticeably to the general confusion, compromised the Republic's prestige, and earned for the Directory new and formidable enemies.

CHAPTER ELEVEN

Finance and
the National Economy

In spite of certain reserves, it was during the twenty months following the eighteenth of Fructidor that the Directory enjoyed its greatest authority and was least obsessed by matters of urgency. These circumstances benefited to some extent its positive achievement, which, in so many respects, prepared the way for that of the Consulate.

Financial recovery was the first task that faced it, and, as early as the evening of 19 Fructidor, the Directory had outlined its plan for this recovery in a special message. It reduced expenditure from a billion francs to six hundred million, no doubt largely thanks to peace, but also by means of that "liquidation" of the National Debt which had been considered in the spring. The Councils adopted the measure fairly quickly. This was the famous "Ramel liquidation" or "bankruptcy of the two-thirds" consecrated by the law of 9 Vendémiaire, Year VI (September 30, 1797) for the Registered Debt, and by the law of 24 Frimaire (December 14) for annuities, pensions and the Floating Debt. One-third of it was consolidated by inscription in the Great Book, or National Debt Register; the bonds could be used for the payment of taxes and for that part of the purchase price of national property payable in currency. The other two-thirds were reimbursed in bonds which could be used to pay the rest of this price, in competition with other "dead securities." The interest of the consolidated third exceeded eighty million francs, so that the budget was lightened by twice that sum, quite apart from the fact that it was relieved in arrears.

A fiscal effort was necessary nonetheless. A few measures were taken to accelerate the collection of direct taxes. A Tax Agency was set up in each department: assessment was made the responsibility of the commissioners, with the help of assessors representing the taxpayers; the drawing up of registers was entrusted to the offices of the central commissioner, who had an inspector to help him. The commissioners had a great many other responsibilities, and they lacked the necessary technical knowledge; this unsatisfactory arrangement did not produce the results which had been hoped for. The ruthless use of bailiffs was much more effective. But direct taxation, which in any case had been slightly reduced, could not be sufficient by itself. The stamp duty was extended to newspapers and posters; the monopoly of the coaching office having been abolished, a tax was imposed on the price of seats in stagecoaches; and the tolls payable on the highways were finally regularized. But the Councils went on approving expenditure without an over-all plan, and passing finance laws so late in the year that they benefited future budgets most of all; they left the new postal tariff and the increase in registration duties in abeyance. They were still extremely reluctant to approve taxes on consumption; it took them a year just to approve a slight increase in the tax on imported tobacco. The deficit for Year VI was estimated at 250 million francs. As for the burden of extraordinary expenditure, it was thrown onto the national property, which could not support it; the chief sources of income were a loan of eighty million francs for the war against England, credits obtained from the Hanseatic ports, and the exploitation of the sister republics: the Berne treasury partly financed the Egyptian expedition. Altogether, the Directory was obliged to admit that the Councils, whatever the political color of the majority, all suffered from the same defects where finance was involved.

During the summer it insisted that the budget for Year VII be approved before 1 Vendémiaire. Its wish was not granted, but at least certain laws were adopted during the autumn which for a long time were, and in some cases still are, fundamental; the patents tax of 1 Brumaire, Year VII (October 22, 1798); the stamp duty of 13 Brumaire (November 3); the land tax of 3 Frimaire (November 23); the registration duty of 22 Frimaire (December 12). The *mobilière* was reorganized on 3 Nivôse (December 23) for the third time since the Revolution; it would be reorganized yet again under the Consulate. What is more, on 4 Frimaire (November 24), the Councils decided to create a new direct tax, the tax on doors and windows, which was fixed at a modest rate and, for that reason, was paid more regularly than the rest. The situation nonetheless remained serious. In Pluviôse, after a stormy debate during which Lucien Bonaparte violently attacked the "ungodly doctrine" of the oppressors of the poor, the Five Hundred finally agreed to tax the salt from the salt marshes at the rate of one sou for each pound produced, the salt mines in the east having been leased with authority to sell theirs at two sous a pound; but the Ancients rejected the resolution. Indirect taxation had been approved only in the form of the *octroi* or town dues; it was adopted for the hospitals of Paris on 27 Vendémiaire, Year VII (October 18, 1798). In Floréal, when Ramel estimated the deficit for Year VII at sixty-six million francs, the Councils confined themselves to doubling the tax on doors and windows. Naturally, the imminent war had resulted in some attention being given to extraordinary revenue. On 26 Vendémiaire, it had been decided to sell a fresh portion of national property up to a value of 125 million francs in metallic currency, and in Ventôse holders of estates mortgaged by the Monarchy were authorized to buy the property. But the disappointments of old were repeated.

The poverty of the Treasury therefore continued; contractors and financiers retained the whip hand, and the fame grew of Ouvrard and Hinguerlot, of Paulée and Vanlerbergh, of Seguin and Madame Lange's husband Simons; the Bodin Company and many others made themselves a reputation after the Flachat and Dijon Companies. The Directory went on paying in the same coin and submitting to the same demands: it had to agree to assignments which were often advances; the "Regent" was once again put in pawn; the Batavian *rescriptions* were pledged by the million. The corruption of the financial and military agents continued. The Directory occasionally balked: in August, 1798, several of the auxiliaries of Schérer, the Minister of War, were dismissed, including his own brother; during Year VII, there were a great many agreements which granted contractors fresh assignments only in return for fresh advances, as would be the practice under the Consulate. But it is significant that the Directory was unable to impose its will on the Treasury. When it demanded from the disbursing officials a statement of account every ten days, and decided that it would authorize expenditure only to the amount of recorded funds, in order to put a stop to malpractices, the Treasury resisted to the extent of suspending all payments, and the government finally gave in. Treason even entered into it: in Thermidor, Year VI, the Treasury, in spite of the Directory's orders, paid no money to the generals entrusted with the second Irish expedition, and thus helped to bring about its failure; one of its agents, the mysterious Vannelet, boasts of the fact in one of his letters to d'Antraigues, for whom he acted as a spy.

A good many scandals revealed the seriousness of the situation. For example, the Rochefort Company, entrusted with the task of supplying the Army of the Danube, had abandoned the task but had nonetheless retained thirty-two million francs assigned to it; the Chevalier Company was paid several million francs in national property to build ships, but did not lay down a single one; while Schérer placed a huge contract for cloth with Haegmann, a small businessman in Lille who was a figurehead for Seguin, and allowed him to obtain payment by drawing on the military warehouses, which were thoroughly plundered.

The fact remains that justice has not been done to the Directory's achievement. By assuming responsibility for the bankruptcies that were an inevitable consequence of the return to metallic currency, it smoothed the way for the Consulate, which, moreover—and this is a point that historians fail to mention—completed the liquidation of the past by means of another bankruptcy. It was the laws of Year VII which laid the foundations of the country's financial reorganization. When the Directory was unable to attain its object, it did at least indicate the necessary solution, for example the creation of an autonomous administration for direct taxation, the return to moderate indirect taxation, and the subordination of the Treasury to the Executive. Even the repeated admonitions that it addressed to the Councils helped to convince public opinion that a revision of the Constitution, giving the government the right to take the initiative, was one of the necessary conditions of financial recovery. What is more, to maintain that Napoleon managed to do without the contractors and succeeded in inculcating honesty into the whole of the administration is sheer nonsense. And, of course, the Directory's contemporaries cared even less than posterity about its difficulties; in Year VII as in Year V, the Councils, irritated by its justified reproaches, used it as a scapegoat and, this time, took their revenge by overthrowing it.

The same critics who praise the Thermidorians for having suddenly returned to metallic currency and for having abruptly abandoned a planned economy make no allowance for the invincible difficulties which deflation produced for the Directorials—who, after all, were the same men— by bringing about the ruin of credit and a collapse in prices. Metallic currency reappeared only very slowly. As far as possible, people hoarded it or bought land; the small amount of silver and copper that the Directory managed to mint disappeared rapidly; in Year IX, despite the victories of the Consulate, less than a billion francs in metallic currency was in circulation, as compared with two or three billion in 1789. Credit was accordingly rare and dear; it was impossible to obtain a loan, with security, at less than ten per cent, and the interest on a short-term loan was as much as seven per cent per month. In these circumstances, how could the Directory keep the Treasury in funds without exorbitant sacrifices, and revive the spirit of enterprise in order to enable the economy to bear the burden of taxation? True, a few businessmen had founded issuing banks. In 1796, some financiers, including Perregaux and Récamier, in association with some leading merchants, founded the Current Accounts Bank; it discounted only bills with three signatures—in other words, it used its bank notes to recover from its shareholders the commercial bills which they had discounted themselves; it was a super-bank. In order to break its monopoly, the Trade Discount Bank, which required only two signatures, was founded on 4 Frimaire, Year VI (November 24, 1797): this was a sort of friendly society which experienced some difficulty in establishing itself. Other issuing banks were founded, even in the provinces—at Rouen, for example. But, to give their banknotes wide circulation, the Republic would have had to accept them itself and thus turn them into a currency. The Directory asked for nothing better. In Year VII as before, the Councils invariably refused their consent.

To dear credit, deflation naturally adds a fall in prices. But it is impossible to estimate its influence here, because from 1796 to 1798 there were bumper harvests which helped to produce the same result. In 1798, wine was also so abundant that there was a slump; on the other hand, the drought caused a crisis in breeding, but the effect on prices was the same, because the peasants had to sell their cattle cheap. In Paris, it was calculated that corn had to sell at between twenty-two and twenty-six livres a *setier* for the farmer to cover his costs: in Year VI, it sold at between eighteen and twenty livres. Generally speaking, farm prices, from Year V to Year VII, were between a quarter and a third lower than those of 1790, which had been a year of plenty; and at certain moments the fall exceeded fifty to sixty per cent in certain markets. This fall in prices naturally had some advantages for the government: it had the troops to feed, and the police reported that the common people were delighted at having finally obtained the "three eights" that they wanted most of all: bread at eight sous (for four pounds), meat at eight sous (per pound), and wine at eight sous (per pint). But it is easy to imagine how unpopular this prolonged fall in prices made the Directory with the big farmers, the well-to-do husbandmen, and the landed proprietors, from whom most of the electors were recruited. And, to return to the question of finance, it must be admitted that in these circumstances it was no mean achievement to effect a considerable reduction in tax arrears, especially when it is remembered that, under the *ancien régime*, taxation was never less than eighteen months or two years behindhand. In the Puy-de-Dôme, at the beginning of Year VII, half the land tax for Year VI had been paid, and, on the eighteenth of Brumaire, arrears had been almost completely paid up to Year V; to achieve this result, severe measures had been necessary, which again did nothing to increase the Directory's popularity.

Nor was that all. As had always happened in the old economy, the agricultural crisis reacted on industry, for, since the greater part of the population remained rural, low farm prices reduced its purchasing power. Now the manufacturers were already finding it extremely difficult to make good the losses which fixed prices, requisitioning and civil war had caused them, while the lack of credit and the continued fall in prices discouraged the spirit of enterprise. Transport, too, was meeting all sorts of difficulties. The meager yield of the toll did not make it possible to repair the roads which had been neglected since 1792, and brigandage made them anything but safe. The country's canals were few in number and maintenance work on them had come to an end. Yet inland transport should have increased since the naval war had shut down the coasting trade.

However, external trade was even more seriously affected. In 1797, only 200 seagoing vessels were left, or a tenth of the number sailing in 1789. For a long time, the neutrals had enabled French exporters to beat the English blockade; but, in return, they imported English merchandise, and in Year VI, the Directory, determined to exclude the latter, adopted a policy toward the neutrals which led them to shun French ports. The "Islands," especially Santo Domingo, which occupied such an important position in French trade at the end of the *ancien régime,* now had scarcely any contact with the mother country. The Egyptian expedition, involving as it did a break with Turkey, closed the Middle East. The Continental war had already delivered the Swiss and German markets into English hands. In Year VIII, although France had grown much bigger, her exports amounted to only 272 million francs, as compared with almost twice as much in 1789. Close union with her vassal states and allies might have helped, and the treaty with the Cisalpine Republic seemed to have been concluded with this end in view; moreover, the Councils appeared to favor a liberal customs policy: the tariff for Year IV was lower than that for 1791. But the Directory's offices, though hostile to controls at home, remained imbued with mercantilism with respect to foreign countries, and the manufacturers—who were all, especially the cotton-spinners, protectionists—laid siege to the government; indeed, they showed great bitterness about the competition of annexed Belgium. The Directory therefore tended rather to regard the sister republics as colonies to be exploited, and in this respect as in so many others, it foreshadowed the policy of the Napoleonic regime. The customs barriers with Spain, France's ally, were also strengthened at the same time.

Finally, political circumstances increased the number of crises. The eighteenth of Fructidor alarmed the rich and reduced Parisian trade; the law of 10 Brumaire, Year V, against British merchandise encouraged speculation on a rise in the price of colonial produce, and the result was a slump in Messidor, Year VI; as of the following autumn, the prospect of another Continental war had a depressing effect on business and the situation became steadily worse.

These circumstances did not augur well for the efforts which the Directory made to help producers, and for which the chief credit must go to François de Neufchâteau. Becoming Minister of the Interior again in Prairial, Year VI, he showed in fact great zeal in all the spheres he controlled: he tried to put local finance in order, drew up a plan for inland navigation, revived the statistical operations of the

Committee for Public Safety, and took an interest in public assistance and education. If it had been left to him, agriculture would have been revived, as in England, by a policy of re-allocation, and by the abolition and division of common land; he was obliged to confine himself, like the Committee of Public Safety, to issuing instructional and stimulating circulars, and to promising encouragement. He likewise appealed to the manufacturers, whom he put on their mettle by opening, on 24 Vendémiaire, Year VII (October 15, 1798), the first national exhibition, and by announcing a competition intended to reward innovators and inventors.

In point of fact, industrial production, although it was picking up again, remained lower than it had been in 1789. Lyons had twelve thousand looms before the Revolution and only 6,500 in Year XI; Carcassonne's production had fallen from sixty thousand rolls of cloth to seventeen or eighteen thousand. Technical progress remained extremely slow, and the interruption of relations with England, which provided the new machines and the workers who demonstrated them, could only harm it. As was only to be expected, it was most apparent in the cotton industry: the "jenny" came into general use, but the "mule" remained a rarity; apart from the extension of the flying shuttle, weaving was not affected; for colored materials at least, Oberkampf put the first printing machine into service in 1797. The woolen industry and metallurgy introduced no innovations. The manufacture of chemical products increased under the influence of the laboratory, but it did not use machines. The steam engine not being in use as yet, industry remained scattered, and as before, concentration occurred only in a commercial form. Great industrialists made their appearance under the Directory—Bauwens, Richard and Lenoir, Ternaux, Boyer-Fonfrède—as well as men like the Périers, Oberkampf and Chaptal, but most of them derived their power less from their factories than from work at home. Nor were their activities narrowly specialized, for as well as manufacturing, they engaged in brokerage, transport and banking.

France was still an essentially rural country. But as such, the Revolution, in proclaiming freedom of farming, had not changed the country's habits; indeed, by increasing the number of small landowners without either capital or knowledge, it had rather tended to strengthen routine. The abolition of the tithe and of seignorial rights greatly benefited the landowner, but he used the money saved to raise his standard of living or to extend his estate rather than to improve his equipment and methods. As there was no reallocation of land (on the contrary, it was parceled out to an increasing extent), enclosure remained difficult and communal practices diminished only very slightly; but the cultivation of potatoes, oleaginous plants, chicory, tobacco, and fodder plants slowly extended—a development that gave promise of a gradual reduction of fallow land. However, it was vine-growing which, since the abolition of subsidies, had made the greatest progress. Most peasants went on producing for their own needs; the speculative spirit was foreign to them as yet.

Experience had shown that France, having undertaken a national war for the first time in the history of the Great Powers, was incapable of waging it without forcing her inhabitants to reduce a standard of living which was already very low. She was accordingly faced with a choice between making peace or carrying the war abroad. The Directory was able to maintain itself in power as long as its armies lived beyond the frontiers. By bringing them back to France, defeat was to impose on the country a burden which would make it find its government intolerable. This was also the fate which lay in store for Napoleon.

CHAPTER TWELVE

Society and
the Current of Ideas

The social structure, at the time of the Directory, still bore profound traces of the revolutionary cataclysm. In Paris, the high Church, the court nobility, the farmers general, and the law and finance officers had disappeared. A breach had been made in the bourgeoisie of the *ancien régime*; the lawyers, no longer forming a corporate body and no longer buying their offices, had diminished in both numbers and prestige; and inflation, that insidious complement of revolution, had ruined the rentiers and sorely tried the property owners. The appearance of the city bore witness to the general impoverishment: the aristocratic mansions, turned into public buildings or leased to speculators who obtained money from them as best they could; the streets obstructed with impunity by the artisans and shopkeepers, and appallingly dirty; the houses allowed to go to rack and ruin, the householders no longer even having the latrines emptied, a circumstance which, in the center of Paris, exposed passers-by to the risk of unspeakable aspersions. It was the financiers and the businessmen—the Perregaux and the Récamiers, the Périers and the Chaptals—who had done best for themselves. Their ranks had been swollen by *nouveaux riches* who had made their money in speculation; but some of these, real captains of industry, rejuvenated the strength and vigor of the bourgeoisie. On a lower level, the employees paid by the State were more numerous; the writers and actors had raised themselves in public opinion; the merchants and artisans had frequently seen their affairs prosper and had become members of the middle class. The whole remained an incongruous medley and a fresh classification had still to be carried out. Next to the salons of Madame de Staël and Madame Récamier in Paris and of Madame de Condorcet at Auteuil, which remained fairly exclusive, people of very different origins and cultures could be seen rubbing shoulders in the entourage of Barras or Ouvrard and in the society of the women of easy virtue who were attached to them: Madame Tallien and Madame Fortunée Hamelin, whose scanty attire and shameless behavior have been used by anecdotal historians to characterize the France of the Directory. In Madame Angot we may see a caricature of the *nouveaux riches* who displayed their vulgar luxury and coarse arrogance in this indulgent environment.

The provinces had not been spared. The privileged social groups of which the Provincial States, the Parlements and the Clergy formed the nuclei, had broken up. In the big cities in the south of France, the Federalist crisis had made great gaps in the upper middle class. However, very much more had been preserved. A great many nobles, such as the Marquis de Ferrières, had survived and kept their lands. Here, the rentiers were less important than the landed properietors, whose capital remained and had even increased as a result of the purchase of national property; the *nouveaux riches* were less numerous and less scandalous. It was in the departments that it was most obvious that the French people had not taken Barras and Madame Tallien as their models, but on the contrary had retained their traditional habits of stubborn thrift, of a parsimonious and oppressive family life into which individualism had scarcely penetrated, and feminism even less.

This was just as true, for obvious reasons, of the country districts. The benefits of the Revolution had gone above all to those whom one might call the peasant bourgeoisie, the big farmers and the well-to-do husbandmen. However, the number of small-holders had increased, especially in those regions where the collective purchase of national property and the division of common land had favored the humble. As a result of the breaking up of big farms, farming on a modest scale had also increased. Relieved of the tithe and of seignorial rights, the peasant landowners had become as conservative as the bourgeoisie. But it would be a mistake to exaggerate the progress of this *embourgeoisement* of the nation, which in any case is a permanent feature of the history of France. The urban proletariat remained as it was; the majority of peasants still had not enough land to live on without additional earnings; and while there were somewhat fewer agricultural laborers, they remained at the mercy of unemployment and bad harvests. All that can be said is that in the midst of general deflation the workers were successful in defending their wages, which remained one-quarter or one-third higher than those of 1790: moreover the trade guilds had reappeared everywhere. The good harvests of the Directorial years therefore afforded the lower classes a temporary respite.

This society, still in the melting-pot as it were, could claim to be conforming to the aims of the Revolution, which, by proclaiming civil equality and suppressing "corporations" of all sorts, had left no other principle of social hierarchy in existence save the power of money, with its constant fluctuations. The classes that the inequality of wealth distinguished were more clearly opposed now that the social orders had disappeared. Babeuf's enterprise and the terror which it caused the bourgeoisie are sufficient proof of this, but there were concrete signs such as dress: while wig and knee-breeches had gone out of fashion, the workers wore jacket and cap, smock and bonnet, clogs rather than shoes; from one social class to the next, the "cascade of contempt" which Cournot mentions was still flowing as steadily as before 1789.

The Constitution of Year III gave the "notables" enough authority already for the reaction to continue which had been initiated after the ninth of Thermidor, against the democracy of Year II and even against certain aspects of the work of the Constituent Assembly. The promised codification was once again postponed. In the meantime, family courts and compulsory arbitration were abolished; imprisonment for debt was re-established; and divorce and the rights granted to natural children were attacked. The sale of national property, as regulated by the law of 28

Ventôse, Year IV, transferred the greater part to the bourgeoisie, and later on the restoration of auctions enabled it to benefit from the rest. In Year IV, likewise, the division of common land had been suspended, because the farmers wanted to keep it for their flocks or to lease it cheap. Under the pretext of obtaining payments of the ground rents, of which the State possessed a great number due to the clergy and the émigrés, an attempt was even made to call in question the law of July 17, 1793, which declared them null and void when one of the articles of the contract was of a feudal nature. While this attempt was abandoned, the Directory did at least reimpose on the peasants in Brittany who held annullable estates the obligation of re-purchase of which the Convention had relieved them, and it is significant that this new law on legal tenure should have been voted in the Five Hundred before the eighteenth of Fructidor and adopted by the Ancients soon afterwards, on 9 Brumaire, Year VI (October 30, 1797).

However, the reaction did not go very far, because the notables were divided. They were divided first of all by regicide and the democratic tradition of Year II; but perhaps even more by the aggressive anticlericalism which brought most of the Directorials close to the *sans-culottes*. Not that the notables who were hostile to them were all believers, but those who remained Voltairians considered —just like Voltaire, as it happens, and on account of the circumstances, with a hitherto unknown sense of urgency —that the common people had to have a religion and that the clergy was indispensable to social order; they also believed that the civil war would never really be brought to an end until peace had been made with the clergy. The Directory, on the other hand, especially after the eighteenth of

Fructidor, pursued a policy of hostility. Admittedly those priests who were neither non-juring nor deportees, who had taken the oath of hatred for the Monarchy and who abstained from all political activity, could practice their religion, but under the threat of deportation on the slightest pretext and on condition that they refrained from any external manifestation. They were not even allowed to keep registers of Catholicity or to publish banns, while their right to refuse to marry divorcees or to bury non-Catholics was sometimes disputed; they were permitted nothing which might appear to be a repudiation of civil law.

Some Directorials, moreover, like the "tyrant Robespierre," considered that the Republic could not live without a metaphysical doctrine, and would have liked to set up a civil religion in competition with Christianity. Such were La Revellière and his friend Leclerc. The majority would have nothing of it, but an attempt was made by certain private individuals. In January, 1797, the bookseller Chemin, together with a few friends, inaugurated Theophilanthropy, a moralizing, idealistic deism which brought together, in the churches of Paris, a fair number of Republicans of all shades of opinion. La Revellière acted as their patron, but his colleagues regarded the new "pope" with pitying contempt, and indeed soon began to suspect the Theophilanthropists of left-wing tendencies. With the novelty wearing off, this religion was on the decline in Year VII; moreover, it had never reached the common people. Freemasonry, whose philosophical principles were very similar, was likewise unable to do so, but in its secret gatherings it had brought together part of the bourgeoisie in a more firmly established group. In 1796, Roëttiers de Montaleau had revived the Order of the Grand Orient, and three years later, concluded an agreement with the so-called Scottish masonry; about a hundred lodges were then opened. Freemasonry thus prepared itself for the important part it was to play under the Napoleonic regime, but it remained under suspicion of Royalism at the time of the Directory, for Roëttiers had been one of Lafayette's supporters.

If most of the Directorials refused to repeat the experiment of the Religion of the Supreme Being, they were all in agreement to impose the Republican calendar—which in 1798 had become the Almanach of the Republic—and to give at long last a regular organization to the decadal and national feasts which the Convention had adopted in principle and occasionally celebrated. After the eighteenth of Fructidor, a circular from the Minister of the Interior called upon the clergy to sanctify the *décadi*, and despite Grégoire's protests, a decree of the Directory, dated 14 Germinal, Year VI (April 3, 1798), ordered all authorities to date all official acts by the Republican calendar. The laws of 17 Thermidor, Year VI (August 4) and 23 Fructidor (September 9) instituted the cessation of work on the *décadi*, though without imposing it in the individual's home, and established a list of feast days, a measure which provoked fresh conflicts with the clergy, since even the constitutional priests often refused to transfer High Mass to the *décadi*.

The Directory's policy irritated the believers by the pulling down of crosses, the banning of processions and pilgrimages, and the sale of churches where Mass was not regularly celebrated; it pushed into the arms of the extremists priests who would otherwise have tended to accept the laws; and the Republican calendar, by disturbing everybody's habits, alienated the indifferent. Altogether, without being as violent as the terrorists, the Directorials made themselves no less unbearable.

In this way, they compromised the process of de-Christianization, which in fact was continuing of its own accord. True, the faithful asserted their belief, and the hard times brought back the lukewarm Christians who, as always happens in such cases, sought moral support or consolation in the Church; but in the midst of the common people itself there was now a minority violently hostile to the clergy, and the latter was in such a deplorable condition that the future seemed bleak. Deprived of funds, and partly reduced to clandestine, itinerant worship, it obtained hardly any recruits; already inadequate in numbers, it included many aged priests who would not have successors. The practice of the sacraments therefore became more intermittent; instruction of children was often impossible; the habits of religion faded away. What is more, the clergy suffered from its divisions. The Constitutional Church, abandoned by the Republic, remained in existence, although weakened by abdications, marriages, and recantations. It still had forty-four bishops, of whome Grégoire was the most distinguished, and in 1797 they held a national council. It numbered even more priests than we are normally led to believe; in the Sarthe, a Chouan region, at least 122 have been counted, in comparison with about 200 Papists. They still had their supporters: at Sedan, three-quarters of the population remained attached to them. Moreover, it should not be forgotten that for many people the main thing was that religious worship continue; whatever their individual preference might be, they resigned themselves to accepting the constitutional priest, for want of any other. That is why the policy of de-Christianization of Year II had been a political error, and also why the Directory would have done better to deal considerately with the priests who had linked their cause with that of the Revolution. The Roman clergy fought them bitterly, but it too was divided. The non-juring priests, whose paper was the Abbé de Boulogne's *Annales ecclésiastiques*, usually condemned the *soumissionnaires*, the most famous of whom was the Sulpician Emery, and who also had their paper, the Abbé Sicard's *Annales religieuses*. They particularly attacked the *haineux* or "haters," those who had agreed to take the oath of hatred for the Monarchy. In the Sarthe, half the Roman priests took it; it is true that half the *haineux* later retracted, but the situation did not become any clearer as a result. It should be added that, separated from its bishops, most of whom had remained abroad where some lived on English subsidies, this clergy contracted independent habits and often subordinated the Church's interests to its Royalist enthusiasm. In short, the Catholic clergy was disintegrating at the same time as it was diminishing. If it had pursued a policy of secular indifference, the Directory could have counted on time to do the rest.

From its own point of view, all its efforts ought to have been directed toward education and not toward changing the calendar. The law of 3 Brumaire, Year IV, allowed freedom of education, but at the same time confirmed the establishment of secular public schools, a measure which rendered the reconstitution of a *de facto* Church monopoly impossible. In this respect, the primary school was of capital importance. Possibly the Directory would have recognized this if it had not been short of money and personnel; however, more than one Thermidorian considered, as did Voltaire, that the common people had no time for education and that, moreover, it would be of no use to them. An opinion of this sort was even more common with regard to women, whatever their station in life. In any case, the law of 3 Brumaire chiefly concerned the higher and secondary levels intended to prepare the sons of the bourgeoisie for the liberal professions, and the Directory enforced it with this end in view. Since the great establishments of higher education, chiefly devoted to the sciences, had been founded or reorganized by the Convention, all the Directory had to do was to install the Institut which was to undertake the control of research. There remained the task of opening the "central schools"; each department was to have its own, and they did in fact have them, with very few exceptions. The local administration maintained them and appointed the masters on the advice of a jury, so that this secondary education was largely decentralized, whereas higher education, with the exception of two medical schools, had been concentrated in Paris. At the central school, the classes, divided into three successive series, each of two years, were optional; the sciences occupied a considerable place in them and were preferred. But the French language, which was not taught in all the colleges under the *ancien régime*, also occupied a place of honor; if the ancient languages were not eliminated, still they had ceased to be the basis of the educational system, and sometimes the modern languages were admitted on an equal footing. Several of these schools had remarkable masters, and some of them, those in the Doubs for example, were very successful. However, they were reproached for not providing elementary tuition, for not forming study courses, and for not maintaining supervision and discipline, so that they resembled institutes of higher education rather than colleges for adolescents. What is more, they had no boarding facilities. It was suggested that the Councils should found preparatory "secondary schools" and a "national Prytaneum" at which the Republic would maintain 1,200 scholarship students. But, in this respect again, the foundations were laid for the Consulate's achievement and nothing more. As for the primary schools, each department established a certain number, but not one in each commune; the central administration also appointed the teachers, who were selected by a jury; it likewise appointed women teachers, whereas there were no secondary schools for girls. The municipal administration had to provide premises for the school and accommodation for the teacher; but it was not obliged to pay the latter, whose school fees might be his only source of income. Recruiting was totally inadequate in both quantity and quality; and it remained inadequate, for there were no training colleges for teachers. In Year VII the Five Hundred were asked to re-establish payment of the primary-school teacher by the Republic, but in vain. Where would the Republic have found the money? Moreover, experience showed that parents were far from eager to send their children to school, except to prepare them for their first communion. The secular character of public education therefore hindered its progress, and it goes without saying that, for the Directory, there could be no question of abandoning it. Consequently there were private primary and secondary schools everywhere, which more often than not were denominational. The Directory placed them under the supervision of the municipal authorities, forbade civil servants to send their children to them, and decided to choose its agents only from the pupils of the public schools. It does not appear that these last two measures had the slightest effect, but inspection and obligatory attendance at decadal ceremonies led to the compulsory or voluntary closing of several private schools.

The experiment, having lasted barely two years, did not enable the Directory to exert a positive influence on the education of the young people of France. In any case, circumstances would not have favored it. Brought up more or less haphazardly during these troubled times, and embittered by the memory of the hardships that had darkened their early years, the growing generations were even more inclined than usual to run counter to their parents and thought of nothing but enjoying themselves. Those who were ambitious tended to turn towards the army, in which they could make a career for themselves, if they were courageous, without needing to have learned anything. One and all rejected idealism; contemporaries are agreed in recording their unscrupulous utilitarianism. The Revolution could not find cause for self-congratulation in this, but neither could the counterrevolution, for these young men had no desire to return to the *ancien régime*. It was a time when the life of the spirit was not held in particularly high honor, and indeed it had nothing original to offer.

Rationalism was, in a sense, the official philosophy. Represented by the "Ideologues," it held full sway at the Institut. Under the influence of English thought, it had repudiated apriorism and the deductive method of the Cartesians, as well as all metaphysical preoccupations, to become experimental and positivist. Destutt de Tracy's aim was to determine, by means of observation, how ideas are formed, whence the name of the School; the doctor Cabanis was working in the direction of experimental and pathological psychology. Morality for them meant a knowledge of customs and manners. Ginguené and Fauriel introduced historical and relativistic criticism into the study of literature and the arts. The sciences, which were making steady progress, served as a rampart for rationalism, whatever the personal opinions of the scientists might be, and this is why conservatives and reactionaries have always tended to cut down the scientific share of education. In 1796, Laplace had just published his *Système du monde*; Lagrange and Monge were famous; for the time being, France had no great physicists, but chemistry could boast Berthollet and several others; Haüy was creating crystallography; Lamarck, Cuvier and Geoffroy-Saint-Hilaire were beginning to teach at the Museum; while Bichat was about to publish the results of his research into tissues.

Those who hated the Revolution rejected the rationalism of the eighteenth century, even when it remained idealistic and deistic, as being responsible for the catastrophe which had overtaken France. A return to tradition and revealed religion was advocated by the philosophical turncoats: La Harpe, who had become a Fideist, or Fontanes, who invoked social utility. A similar evolution was taking place in émigré circles, and it was outside France that Bonald and Maistre published their first works in 1796. Adapting experimental rationalism to justify tradition, after the manner of Burke, they would become the masters of the counterrevolution in the nineteenth century, but the Directory's contemporaries knew nothing of them. A work that obtained speedier success was the *Mémoires pour servir à l'histoire du jacobinisme*, which the Abbé Barruel published in 1797 to reduce the Revolution to the level of a Masonic plot.

In the world of ideas, what threatened the supremacy of

rationalism most of all was Rousseau's influence, which was greater than ever, in spite of the disfavor with which people viewed his political theories. He had set feeling against reason, and had held intuition to be the true instrument of knowledge, to such a degree that it opened up the moral world and even the supernatural by means of direct contact with God. The common reader appreciated his sensual sentimentalism most of all, but his mysticism had certain links with the vague, esoteric doctrines which had abounded in the eighteenth century and which were classed together under the name of Illuminism. France had not entirely escaped these doctrines: Saint-Martin, the "unknown philosopher," was still alive; Alsace and Lyons remained two centers of mysticism. These tendencies would inspire, in Germany, a "Romantic" philosophy which later exerted a certain influence in France, without ever having been thoroughly taught there.

In France, Romanticism remained a type of feeling, a literary and artistic form of individualism, a reaction against classical art. Under the Directory, however, nobody foresaw that the latter was going to be dethroned, and Pre-Romanticism is all that one can talk about at this time, Classical literature was still highly regarded, the classical tradition being maintained by writers who were distinguished even if devoid of genius: Ducis, Arnault, Andrieux, Delille, and "Pindar" Lebrun. But it was on the decline, for the society that had witnessed its birth had disappeared and its effects were exhausted. The *nouveaux riches* and the members of the petty bourgeoisie who had not had a college education could not appreciate its inspiration and its allusions to Greek and Latin sources; they far preferred Pixérécourt's melodramas and the novels of Pigault-Lebrun and Ducray-Duménil, which were the origins of Romantic drama. Bernardin de Saint-Pierre's work *Paul et Virginie*, which dated from 1787, was still read with undiminished enthusiasm. The "troubadour style," made fashionable by the Comte de Tressan, and popularized by songs and engravings, foreshadowed the Romantic cult of a conventional medievalism. The Romantics of other countries were also beginning to be appreciated, and there was nothing to equal the extraordinary fame obtained under the Directory by Ossian's poems, manufactured by MacPherson about thirty years before.

The return to antiquity, which had characterized the end of the *ancien régime*, did not revitalize literature: Chénier's poems had remained unpublished. But it had revived memories of their college days among the orators and journalists of the Revolution, and this constantly became apparent at the time of the Directory. It had imposed itself particularly on the painters and sculptors: it was in 1799 that David exhibited his *Sabines*. However, this revival of antiquity also benefited Alexandrine art, so-called Etruscan motifs, and even Egyptian ornaments; and thus, in decorative art at least, the eighteenth-century tradition had been maintained in a parallel fashion, while acquiring elements which foreshadowed the "Empire" style. Like the "Louis XVI" style, that of the Directory was heterogeneous.

In the spiritual sphere as in politics, it was a period of transition. Perhaps it reveals, more clearly than other periods easier to characterize, that of the different tendencies which offer themselves to the mind, none is ever effaced, even when one of them seemed to have obtained final supremacy.

CHAPTER THIRTEEN

The Egyptian Expedition and the Second Coalition

Approved on 15 Ventôse, Year VI (March 5, 1798), and prepared with the greatest secrecy, the Egyptian expedition comprised thirteen ships of the line, seventeen frigates, thirty-five other warships, 280 transport craft, 16,000 sailors, 38,000 officers and troops, and also a commission of 187 scientists, writers and artists including Berthollet, Monge and Geoffroy-Saint-Hilaire. It was nearly called off again as a result of the incident in which Bernadotte had been involved in Vienna, for Bonaparte had taken the affair in hand and offered to place himself at the head of the army if war broke out. Barras even claims that he had to order him to set off. It is possible that Barras exaggerated the part he played, but it is also possible that Egypt would have lost its attraction for Bonaparte if hostilities had opened again in Europe. Whatever the truth of the matter, he left Toulon on 30 Floréal (May 19).

Progress was slow and he did not reach Malta until June 6; the Grand Master of the Order that had been installed there since the sixteenth century had allowed himself to be bribed, and handed over the island without firing a shot. Continuing on its way, the fleet only narrowly missed Nelson. He was looking for it everywhere, went ahead of it without knowing, landed at Alexandria and set off again for the Aegean Sea, while behind him Bonaparte was disembarking. After seizing the port, the army hugged the Nile, skirmishing with the Mamelukes; then, on July 21, it routed them near the Pyramids and entered Cairo. Bonaparte then pursued Ibrahim, one of the two leaders, as far as the isthmus, while Desaix was pushing Mourad back beyond Assuan. Meanwhile, Nelson had returned to Sicily, where the complicity of the Neapolitans enabled him to rest and refit; informed at last of his adversary's whereabouts, he appeared, in the evening of July 31, in the Aboukir roads, where Brueys' squadron was lying at anchor pending orders from Bonaparte to return to Corfu. On August 1, it was destroyed and its commander killed. This terrible disaster, which imprisoned Bonaparte in his conquest with no hope of returning home or obtaining reinforcements, had tremendous repercussions throughout Europe. On September 9, Turkey declared war on France and, under the protection of the victorious admiral, the Neapolitans decided to invade the Roman Republic.

In spite of all this, Bonaparte went on organizing his

conquest as if it were to be lasting; after the Cisalpine Republic, his genius found a new testing-ground here. His policy consisted in leaving the native administration in place, but under supervision; in other words, he established a protectorate. At the same time he inaugurated an embryonic representative government by instituting a municipal divan in Cairo, another in each province, and finally a general divan, all composed of notables chosen by himself: his concept of the constitutional regime was a system of consultative bodies appointed by the government, and his social policy consisted in attaching the notables to himself by entrusting them with the administration. He also fixed his religious policy in Egypt: since the population was almost entirely Moslem, he turned Moslem, he said later; in other words he displayed a profound respect for Islam and its prophet, and heaped favors upon its leaders. The enlightened despot nonetheless undertook, with relentless energy, the modernization of the country—taking sanitary measures against the plague, putting the canals back into service, creating a postal service, opening the first printing-works, setting up the first windmills, and making plans to substitute irrigation for inundation, and to link the Nile to the Red Sea. The commission he had taken with him became the Cairo Institute, and its work prepared that famous *Description de l'Égypte* which was the most lasting result of the expedition. This policy came into conflict with the Moslems' incurable mistrust, expecially as Turkey, with the help of English propaganda, urged them to wage a holy war on the French: isolated soldiers and small outposts were attacked, and the nomads never relented. All the same, the majority of the population would probably have resigned itself if the army had not been obliged to live on the country by means of taxes, levies and confiscations. To make sure that taxes were paid and his funds increased, Bonaparte demanded the registration of landed properties and the payment of taxes on changes of ownership, legal documents, and certificates of birth, marriages and deaths. The result was a terrrible insurrection in Cairo on October 21, and a bloody repression.

Besides, it was known in Egypt that Turkey was preparing to invade the country by land and sea with the support of an English squadron. At the end of the winter, Bonaparte decided to go and destroy the army which was gathering there; he set off in February, 1799, with 15,000 men, crossed the desert, and advanced as far as Acre without meeting much resistance. But the Pasha Djezzar and the émigré Philippeaux defended the town stubbornly, and after Sidney Smith had captured the ships which were bringing the siege artillery, Bonaparte finally retreated on May 20. He returned to Egypt, not without sustaining losses on the way. He had at least delayed the Turkish attack on the isthmus, but soon afterwards an army landed at Aboukir; it was destroyed there on July 25. However, there was no way out of the situation, and it was in vain that the Directory had tried to send Bruix to help. In August, Bonaparte, leaving his army to Kléber, went off to seek adventure in France.

At this time, it was nearly a year since his initiative had set the Second Coalition on foot. After the Turks, the Russians had joined in. The Tsar and the Sultan formed an alliance, and the Russian fleet was allowed to pass through the Straits to go and attack the Ionian Isles: Corfu was the last to fall, on March 3, 1799. The Egyptian expedition had thus provided the Russians with access to the Mediterranean and a position in the Ottoman Empire which they have never recovered since. The Tsar hoped for even better things: he appointed himself the protector of the Order of Malta and of the King of the Two Sicilies. The English had lost no time in giving their support to the Russo-Turkish entente; they were blockading Malta and were in control at Naples. On December 29, an Anglo-Russian alliance finally came to the main point: it was decided that they should make combined landings in Italy and Holland and that Russian troops based in Jersey should threaten Brittany.

A month earlier, either out of conceit or out of misplaced confidence in the speed of their protectors, the Neapolitans had gone ahead, under the leadership of the Austrian Mack, and occupied Rome. They had thus provided the propagandists with a supreme success. The Directory declared war on their king, and also on the King of Sardinia, who was regarded as an accomplice and withdrew to Cagliari; the whole of Piedmont was occupied without a shot being fired. Championnet had withdrawn his little army behind the Tiber. Attacked at Civita-Castellana, he routed his adversaries, re-entered Rome, and, taking the offensive in his turn, occupied Naples on January 23, 1799. He made a show of ignoring Faipoult, the Civil Commissioner. On the way, the army and a good many of its commanders had engaged in looting, and the Castle of Caserte, the Neapolitan Versailles, had been cleaned out. In Naples, all the public coffers were seized by the generals, and Championnet made it clear that he regarded himself as the Bonaparte of southern Italy: after joining up with the Liberals, he proclaimed the "Parthenopian Republic," the government of which he entrusted to them, promising to content himself with a levy of sixty million. Faipoult intervened to enforce both his own levies and the intentions of the Directory. The latter did not want another republic; it was keeping the new conquest as exchange currency and had urged that it should be thoroughly exploited, thus returning to the policy of 1796. Faipoult insisted that all prizes of war should be handed over to him, gave orders that crown property and the goods of those émigrés who had followed the King of Sicily should be sequestrated, and imposed a monthly levy upon the country. Championnet stood up to him and finally expelled him. As usual, the Directory recalled both of them; but soon, better informed, it had the general arrested and summoned before a court martial; several of his subordinates suffered the same fate or were cashiered. For the first time, the Directory was trying to bring the generals to heel: they would help to overthrow it.

The Coalition needed the support of Austria or Prussia to launch an attack on the Adige, in Switzerland and on the Rhine. Prussia showed a certain reticence; however, when the Directory sent Sieyès to Frederick William III with yet another proposal for an alliance with the Republic, the King had him shown the door. Thugut negotiated while refusing to enter into any engagements: he knew that the Tsar wanted to restore the Italian sovereigns whose spoils he coveted, and that England wanted most of all to reconquer the Netherlands, in which he was uninterested. War broke out without his having signed anything, and from the outset the Second Coalition, like the First, carried within itself the seeds of its failures and its final disintegration. All the same, Thugut prepared for war and authorized the Russians to cross Austrian territory. The Directory made this a *casus belli* on 22 Ventôse, Year VII

(March 12, 1799). Tuscany was promptly occupied and Pius VI taken to Valence where he died in August. A bloody incident fixed the character of war in the eyes of the revolutionaries. During the night of April 28, as the French plenipotentiaries were leaving Rastatt, they were attacked by Austrian hussars. One of them, Jean Debry, escaped; the other two, Roberjot and Bonnier, were killed. It is still uncertain who was responsible for these murders; in France they were seen as a manifestation of the hatred that the kings and the aristocracy had vowed for the Republic and as proof that the counterrevolution was beginning a new crusade.

Since the autumn, the Directory had been getting ready to withstand the attack. After the eighteenth of Fructidor the reawakening of the revolutionary spirit had revived the question of the general mobilization of the nation. Debry had even put forward, though unsuccessfully, a plan for the military training of French youth. On a more modest scale, Jourdan, on 23 Nivôse, Year VI (January 12, 1798), had proposed the formation of an auxiliary army of 100,000 men chosen by ballot; since this method of selection was criticized as contrary to the principle of equality, he prepared a new project which became the law of 19 Fructidor, Year VI (September 5, 1798), known as the Jourdan Law or the Conscription Law. It inaugurated compulsory military service between the ages of twenty and twenty-five, with exemption only for men who had married before 23 Nivôse, Year VI. The conscripts fit for duty were to be registered on a national list, in five classes and according to their dates of birth. If a levy was necessary, the Legislature decided on a contingent which the Minister of War called to the colors, beginning with the youngest.

Those who refused to answer the call were deprived of civic rights and even of certain civil rights. On 28 Nivôse, Year VII (January 17, 1799), another law annulled the dispensations and exemptions granted since 1793.

Immediately after the Jourdan Law had been passed, an initial levy was decided on. The law of 3 Vendémiaire, Year VII (September 24, 1798) fixed it at 200,000 men. As before, considerable difficulties arose. The registration details were incomplete or nonexistent; no provision had been made for the medical examinations, which the Minister had to leave to boards composed of fathers whose sons were affected by the Law, a fact which gave rise to scandalous abuses; it proved impossible in practice to draw up the national list of conscripts. Their number was put at 203,000, including those who had already been invalided out; 143,000 were found fit for duty, a figure which represented a huge wastage. Only 97,000 answered the call to colors, and these were sent to join the armies in isolated detachments, a practice which facilitated desertion; only 74,000, or fifty-one per cent of the total, joined their units. On 28 Germinal, Year VII (April 17, 1799), the Legislature decided that the numbers of the prescribed contingent should be made up, but it made serious alterations to the Jourdan Law: those liable to conscription were authorized to meet beforehand to find volunteers to complete the contingent or to draw lots among themselves; what is more, the conscripts marked down for call-up were allowed to provide a replacement. Nonetheless, only 71,000 men answered the summons, 57,000 of whom reached the front.

The Directory's army had become a professional army. This flood of conscripts gave it, by means of a fresh amalgamation, something of the popular character of the army of Year II. But it was not sufficiently reinforced for the opening of the campaign, and, unlike its predecessor, it did not have the advantage of numerical superiority over the enemy. Nor was it properly supplied. It was in order to clothe, equip and arm the conscripts that the Legislature put on sale, as we have seen, 125 million francs' worth of national property, and the great fiscal laws of Year VII bear witness to an effort to pay for the war; but it was a belated, inadequate effort. The conscripts were sent to the front before they were completely ready; and as for the armies, living on vassal or enemy countries which were already exhausted, they were in a state of destitution. In Italy, their principal source of supply was recently occupied Piedmont, which was thoroughly exploited.

In the over-all concept of the campaign, the spirit of the new warfare was totally lacking. The Army of the Danube, numbering 45,000 men and under Jourdan's command, was given the task of invading southern Germany. Of the 100,-000 men who were in Italy, Schérer was able to assemble only 45,000 on the Adige. Between the two of them, Masséna was to conquer the Canton of Grisons and threaten the Tyrol. The French therefore attacked everywhere at once, on a long front, instead of using Switzerland by establishing a main striking force there which could be moved at will into Italy or Germany to obtain a decision. The Austrians were set out in the same way: the Archduke Charles had 75,000 men in Bavaria; Kray had 60,000 in Venetia; and 20,000 more guarded the Tyrol. They appear to have been unaware of their numerical superiority, and waited for the Russians before committing themselves completely. Moreover, Thugut subordinated Austrian military operations to his political schemes. The campaign, slow-moving and disjointed, displayed all the characteristics of a war of the *ancien régime*.

It was Masséna who obtained the greatest success; he occupied the Canton of Grisons, but, entering Vorarlberg, came to grief before Feldkirch. Jourdan advanced as far as Lake Constance and attacked the Archduke at Stokach on March 25; repulsed, he brought his army back to the Rhine and handed in his resignation; on this front, the Archduke was unable to press forward, for Thugut sent him to invade Switzerland. Schérer carried the fortified positions of Pastrengo and Rivoli, but his attack on Verona was badly planned and tried his army sorely; attacked in his turn at Magnano, on April 5, he beat a retreat, although the battle had been indecisive, and, without trying to resist anywhere, withdrew as far as the Adda before handing the army over to Moreau. Kray was not very forceful either: he waited for Suvoroff, who brought along 20,000 Russians and assumed supreme command. This general, famous for his victories over the Turks and the Poles, was a remarkable trainer of men rather than a strategist. Between April 25 and 27, he attacked the crossings of the Adda and forced several of them, notably at Cassano; the Sérurier division was destroyed or captured; Moreau evacuated the region of Milan and re-assembled the debris of his army at Alessandria. Suvoroff staged a triumphal entry into Milan, but then dispersed a good part of his troops and waited until May 12 before attacking Moreau, without much success. All the same, the French withdrew again as far as Coni.

Moreau was counting on Macdonald who, with exceptional slowness, was bringing the Naples troops back up the rebellious peninsula. Instead of summoning Macdonald to join him, he arranged to meet him near Alessandria.

Macdonald crossed the Apennines, only to find his way
barred by Suvoroff on the banks of the Trebia. The battle
lasted three days, from July 17 to 19: having failed to break
through, Macdonald went back across the mountains and,
hugging the coast, made his way to Genoa. Moreau, who
had advanced victoriously as far as Marengo, fell back to
join him.

The setbacks in Germany and Italy led to a withdrawal
by Masséna; he had to evacuate the Canton of Grisons and,
since the Archduke had crossed the Rhine, fall back on the
Limmat. Attacked, he won the first Battle of Zürich, on
June 4, but he thought fit to cross back over the river and
abandon the town. He took up a position between the
Rhine and Lake Zug, covered by the Limmat and Lake
Zürich. But as Lecourbe had been obliged to abandon the
St. Gotthard Pass and the valley of the Reuss, he was open
to attack from the rear by an army coming from Italy.

Summer had come, and there was every reason to expect
some large-scale operations; the Coalition forces could
converge on Switzerland, crush Masséna, and enter France
through the Burgundy gateway. But nothing of the sort
happened, and for two months hostilities were, so to speak,
suspended. Italian fortresses, even Mantua, fell to Suvoroff
with an incredible rapidity which aroused suspicions of
treason; having obtained control of Piedmont, his only
thought was to install the King there and invade Dau-
phiné. Thugut was anxious to find a way of getting him to
leave Italy by sending him into Switzerland, and he suggested to the Tsar that the liberation of that country
was a task worthy of the savior of Europe; in fact, his only
concern was the political profit to be derived from this
maneuver. As in 1793, the Coalition Powers thus gave the

Republic a breathing space; however, the French armies, despite the government's exhortations, remained incapable of undertaking anything until the end of the summer, and long before then the war had provoked decisive events in France.

CHAPTER FOURTEEN

The Crisis of Year VII

At the beginning of Germinal (late March, 1799), the campaign had scarcely begun and there had been no set-back to obliterate the memory of the easy conquest of Naples. However, the elections promised to be unfavorable to the Directory, for since the autumn, well before war had been declared, its oppressive influence had been felt in the stagnation of business, the growth of taxation, and above all in conscription. True, since 1793, absentees and conscripts had been pursued, but no contingent had been called up; if there had been such an ardent longing for peace, it had been largely out of fear of a fresh levy. Now it had come. The mediocre result that it yielded bears witness to its unpopularity; moreover, it was not carried out without trouble. In November, 1798, part of the Belgian countryside rose in revolt: this "war of the peasants" lasted two months and left the country highly disturbed. In France, fear of a new Vendée insurrection had been so lively that the Directory had been authorized to suspend enforcement of the law in the west; the Chouans nonetheless acquired new strength, and in March the town of Château-Gontier was taken by surprise. Everywhere, the rebel bands were swollen by absentees and deserters, and their attacks became more frequent.

Most of the public blamed the Directory for having provoked the war, while the Jacobins accused it of having failed to make the necessary preparations, and of allowing the counterrevolution once again to play the enemy's game. The Directorial majority, conscious of the electors' anxiety and discontent, threw the responsibility on the government —as always happens in such cases—but not without a certain genuine feeling, since it was irked by the Directors' dictatorship. Resorting to the traditional diversion, the Directory denounced the partnership of Royalists and Anarchists in the enemy's service. "Just as the campaign is opening," declared the *Moniteur*, "it is at home that the first blows are struck." During the elections, at least, the Royalists lay low as in Year VI and for the same reasons: it was the Jacobins who were under attack. A circular issued by François de Neufchâteau tried to revive fear of the Terror and frighten the rich:

No more brigands in office, no more scoundrels in power. . . . Would you like to see the law of the *maximum* reimposed? Would you like to see Féraud's murderers reappear carrying his bleeding head on a pike?

In preparation for the elections, the usual methods were used: massive dismissals, instructions to the commissioners, the dispatch of special agents to a score of departments, and the organization of secessions; in the Doubs and the Sarthe, official pressure created a scandal. However, it was not as energetic as in Year VI, probably because the Directory or its officials were aware of a hostility they could not hope to overcome. Indeed, it was often enough for a candidate to be recommended by the government for him to be defeated: out of 187 who had been recommended more or less openly, 121 were beaten. Since the law of 12 Pluviôse, Year VI, was still in force, could not the device of the twenty-second of Floréal be repeated? The attitude adopted by the Councils ruled out this possibility: they systematically validated the choices of the original assemblies.

As the Directory had aimed its attack chiefly against the Jacobins, its defeat was regarded as their victory. Yet this was not the case. The Thermidorian bourgeoisie still formed the majority and it was not long before this became obvious. As it was violently hostile to the Directors, it came to an agreement with the Jacobins to overthrow them, but its political and social tendencies remained those of the government it had turned out. The crisis therefore took place in three stages: the fall of the Second Directory, the apparent triumph of the Left, and a violent and vigorous anti-Jacobin reaction.

During the weeks following the elections, the situation of the Republic underwent a disastrous deterioration. Italy was lost, Switzerland invaded, Holland threatened. At home, administration was disorganized by the Royalists' guerrilla warfare and by passive resistance to civic obligations. "Everything is going to pieces," stated a report of 18 Prairial. Hostility to the Directors increased as a result; they were clearly incapable of making either peace or war. Was this simple incompetency? To have tolerated the wastefulness which emptied the military depots and condemned the army to destitution was criminal negligence at the very least. The addresses which started coming in from the departments openly accused Schérer of treason. The generals joined in the chorus of blame in order to explain their defeats, avenge their disgrace, and avoid the prosecution to which they had rendered themselves liable. Their collusion with the opposition, already visible in the press and in speeches, is obvious from the place that the Five Hundred gave them in their lists of candidates in the course of the crisis: one of these lists included seven generals and admirals out of ten names. As of the end of Germinal, the examination of the financial measures that had become indispensable strained relations between the Directory and the Councils to the breaking point. Once again, the *rapporteur*, who was Génissieu, reduced the deficit to nothing and triumphantly recalled the credits that had been voted; Ramel once again pertinently refuted his arguments. In Floréal, a rumor began to spread that the Directory was preparing a *coup de force*: but this was impossible, since the Directory had quarreled with the generals, and the latter, defeated and humiliated, were incapable of imitating Bonaparte and Hoche.

In any case, even before the new Councils had met on 1 Prairial, chance had declared itself, contrary to Year V, against the Directors; on 20 Floréal, when they drew lots to discover which one was to retire, it was Reubell, the most intelligent member of the government, who was indicated by the ballot. Then, after the Five Hundred had proposed General Lefebvre, who was reputed to be a good Jacobin, in the first place, the Ancients, on 27 Floréal (May 16), rejected him in favor of Sieyès by 118 votes out of 205. Sieyès was known to be hostile to the Directors; it was also known that he was full of contempt for the Constitution of Year III, which had been preferred to his own, and that he wanted to change it. His election showed that hostilities had opened and indeed that there was a large majority of the Ancients in favor of revision. Barras had contributed to Sieyès' success—possibly because he was not opposed to the idea of revision, more probably to ensure his own survival now that the fall of the Second Directory seemed likely. The Trojan horse was in position, but probably few people imagined that Sieyès, the theoretician of the liberal representative system, was going to dig its grave.

Returning from Berlin, he was unable to take his seat in the Directory until 21 Prairial (June 9); ten days were enough for him to attain his object, a fact which makes one wonder whether this "revolutionary mole," as Robespierre called him, had not been at work for a long time. In the Five Hundred, Boulay, Bertrand du Calvados, Poullain-Grandprey, and Bergasse-Laziroule were his spokesmen; he probably manipulated the Jacobins through Lucien Bonaparte, and the generals through Joubert, the commanding officer of the seventeenth military division, whom he appears to have chosen as the instrument of his future *coup d'état*. All of a sudden, on 28 Prairial (June 16), Poullain-

431

Grandprey recalled that the message of the seventeenth, asking the Directory for an *exposé* of the military situation, had remained unanswered, and obtained a decision that the Five Hundred should stay in permanent session until an answer arrived; the Ancients followed their example. The Five Hundred also ordered their commissions to meet to consider what measures should be taken—an order of dubious legality—and the real discussion was thus taken outside the Assembly; then, about eleven o'clock at night, the hall filled up and Bergasse, suddenly attacking Treilhard's election, got a resolution passed which expelled him from the Directory and which the Ancients promptly ratified. The motive invoked had been implicitly rejected in Year VI, as has been seen; and besides, a month before, a deputy had been validated who was not of the legal age at the time of his election, on the ground that he would attain that age before 1 Prairial. La Revellière therefore proposed, that same night, that the Directors should not promulgate the law, but as Sieyès and Barras declared themselves in agreement with the Councils, Treilhard withdrew; on the twenty-ninth, his place was filled by Gohier, the President of the Court of Appeal, who had been Minister of Justice in Year II and was considered to be sympathetic towards the Jacobins. On the thirtieth, Bertrand returned to the attack, this time against La Revellière and Merlin, openly accusing them of misappropriation and treason; then Boulay denounced "the subjection of the Legislature" and the factious resistance which had been envisaged during the night of the twenty-eighth; several representatives called for an indictment, and Joubert and Bernadotte made threatening remarks. However, Sieyès, Barras, and the majority wanted a peaceful solution, and as it

turned out the crisis was solved behind the scenes. As early
as the twenty-ninth, Sieyès had asked his colleagues to resign; on the thirtieth, Barras, failing to overcome their
resistance, made a terrible scene. Deputies came along to
advise them to submit; finally the Ancients formed an un-
official delegation which came and begged them to give
way in the interests of the Republic. Merlin, utterly terrified, capitulated first, and La Revellière resigned himself
to following his example. On 1 and 2 Messidor, their places
were filled by Roger-Ducos, a regicide member of the Convention, then a magistrate in the Landes, proposed by
Sieyès, and by Moulin, an obscure general and good Jacobin,
chosen by Barras. All the ministers were successively replaced, not excepting Talleyrand.

The *journée* of the thirtieth of Prairial, Year VII (June
18, 1799) was therefore not a *coup d'état*: the two Directors had not dared to face a perfectly legal indictment; but
the event involved an interpretation of the Constitution
which the Directory had never accepted and which, giving
the Legislature power over the Executive, tended towards a
parliamentary system. As early as 3 Messidor, François de
Nantes, on behalf of a commission of eleven set up on 29
Prairial, presented a complex and confused project adopted
on the ninth, of which several articles, restricting the Directory's authority, emphasize this aspect of the crisis, although the Ancients postponed and finally refused ratification. However, if the thirtieth of Prairial was a ninth of
Thermidor insofar as it changed the personnel of the government to suit the Councils, it did not subordinate it or
weaken it, as the Thermidorian Committees had been subordinated and weakened: the Directory retained the duration and the authority laid down by the Constitution. It is

true that it had not gained in either prestige or unity; but Sieyès imposed his opinions on it, and, in his stubborn determination to bring about the downfall of the regime, he displayed a skill and a firmness that form a striking contrast with the feebleness he showed on the eighteenth of Brumaire.

Then again, the thirtieth of Prairial was the *journée* of the generals. Bernadotte was given the Ministry of War; Joubert was put in command of the Army of Italy; as for Championnet, he was released from prison, the charge against him was dropped, his subordinates were released and replaced, and he was put at the head of an Army of the Alps which was formed to bar the way to Suvoroff. The commissioners to the armies were finally stripped of all authority: Rapinat's resignation had been accepted, while Joubert, on his arrival in Italy, told Laumond that since he no longer had any conquered territory to control, there was nothing for him to do, and sent him back to France.

Finally, the thirtieth of Prairial was a revenge for the twenty-second of Floréal: the three new Directors were "Floréalists" and the appointment of Robert Lindet, sometime member of the great Committee of Public Safety, as Minister of Finance seemed symbolic. This impression was confirmed by the numerous dismissals which followed and the appointment of leading Jacobins such as Raisson, Chaudieu, or General Marbot who took Joubert's place at the head of the seventeenth division. The resolution of 9 Messidor abrogated the law of 19 Fructidor, extended in Year VI, which had suspended the freedom of the press; the Ancients decided to ratify this article on 14 Thermidor (August 1), but the newspapers had not waited to proliferate. It is true that most of them were hostile to the Republic, but the clubs also reopened, and they were generally dominated by the Jacobins. One report states that there were soon over forty in Paris; the most famous one met as of 18 Messidor (July 6) in the hall which the Five Hundred had left in Year VI for the former Palais Bourbon, and was therefore generally known as the Club du Manège or the Riding-School Club. The first "regulator" was Drouet, Babeuf's accomplice; 250 deputies joined the Club and there were up to 3,000 members.

That the thirtieth of Prairial was above all a victory for the Jacobins was also the impression given by the passing of the famous laws that the Left obtained immediately afterward by invoking the dangers threatening the Republic— not only because the majority was by no means insensitive to those dangers, but also because this majority, still excited by its struggle with the Directors, took a few days to realize that it was on a slippery slope leading to a new revolutionary government.

Proposed by Jourdan on 9 Messidor (June 27), the law of the tenth provided, as he said, for the *levée en masse*: all five classes of conscripts were called up in their entirety; at the same time, the system of replacements was abolished, and leaves granted since 1793 were submitted to departmental military commissions for revision. The number of men liable for conscription was estimated at 223,000, and the number of those who left for the front at 116,000. A month later, another law gave orders for the reorganization of the National Guard—a necessary measure, for flying columns could be drawn from it to fight for rebels and the brigands.

After men, it was the turn of property. Requisitioning increased again, this time openly encouraged by instructions from the Directory to the departmental authorities. Above all, the compulsory loan was reintroduced, again proposed by Jourdan on 9 Messidor, immediately adopted in principle, and fixed at 100 million francs. Considerable difficulty was experienced in fixing the conditions, which became law only on 19 Thermidor (August 6). The loan, fixed in accordance with a graduated scale, affected those who paid at least 300 francs in land tax, as well as investment incomes impartially estimated by a jury of citizens not liable to the loan, over and above 10,000 francs, though a speculative fortune could be taxed on the whole of the yield.

Then there came a repressive law, the Law of Hostages of 24 Messidor (July 12). In those departments which the Legislature declared to be wholly or partly "in a disturbed condition," the central administration was to intern hostages chosen from among the relatives of émigrés and rebels and the nobles excluded from civic rights; in the event of the murder of an active or retired government official, a soldier, or a purchaser of national property, the Directory would deport four hostages; what is more, all were collectively liable to a fine and responsible for paying indemnities to the victims' families as well as all other damages. An amnesty was offered to the rebels, with the exception of the leaders, on condition that they handed over their arms; if they failed to take advantage of this offer, they would be summoned before a military commission and executed upon identification.

Finally, that same 24 Messidor, Montpellier presented his report on the legal proceedings that the Councils, the Jacobin papers and the constant flow of addresses kept demanding against Reubell, La Revellière, Merlin, Treilhard, the ministers, and the commissioners to the armies; it concluded in favor of indicting the four Directors and Schérer. The Five Hundred accepted the report, but as the law laid down certain formalities which had to take thirty-three days before the matter was even referred to the Ancients, there was time for resistance to be organized.

At the end of Messidor, it was already strong, and on the twenty-sixth, the anniversary of the fourteenth of July, Sieyès issued an initial warning to the Jacobins. It was not that he, any more than the Directorials in the Councils, was opposed to measures of public safety, but they were all determined, whatever the cost, to keep the enforcement of such measures in their own hands; what frightened them was that the Jacobins declared that these measures would remain vain if the old revolutionary spirit was not awakened among the common people; this suggested that before long they would insist on associating the people with the government and that France would witness, at the very least, the return of the revolutionary Committees. As early as the evening of 30 Prairial, Boulay had rejected as "an atrocious slander" the suggestion that the adversaries of the defunct Directory wanted to restore the 1793 regime: "No, no, it will never rise again; there is not one of us who would not die fighting any factionists who tried to bring it back." A little earlier, a report already quoted, recommending the dispatch of agents into the provinces to infuse fresh energy into the administration—in other words a return to one of the expedients often used after the tenth of August— added: "These agents wish to be received only into the class of honest, well-to-do people . . . they must be the protectors of persons and property."

This expressive text was answered by another, by Lamarque, from the other side: "Some want the people to be used to repel the barbarians; others are afraid of using that omnipotent force, in other words they dread the mass of the Republicans more than the hordes from the north."

The *levée en masse* and requisitioning undoubtedly increased fear and irritation throughout the country, but they were liveliest in the ranks of the upper middle class, the only class affected by the compulsory loan. Moreover, the contractors had been specially singled out for attack in a resolution of 5 Messidor, admittedly rejected by the Ancients, which had forbidden anyone in official or government employment to have any connection with their contracts. However, Lindet had persuaded a certain number of contractors and bankers to accept a treasury arrangement which liquidated part of the expected yield from the loan. The former accepted assignment of the loan up to the sum of thirty million francs in exchange for the assignments on the public coffers that they possessed, which the bankers, grouped in "syndicates," accepted as security for bills subscribed by themselves in favor of the government, which had them discounted or used them in payment. Perregaux also set a good example by putting his own name down for a large contribution to the loan. But, generally speaking, recriminations and passive resistance foreshadowed failure, and little more than a third of the expected sum was collected. A considerable number of rich people left Paris after dismissing their staff; and, as an even more significant sign of the times, it was announced that some factories were going to close. There can be no doubt that a compulsory loan, especially in such circumstances, was bound to produce a reduction in business; in this panic, there was also an element of genuine fear, and it is consequently impossible to tell how far political calculation entered into it; but political calculation is always present.

The Directory and its supporters were chiefly concerned about the legal proceedings which threatened the victims of the thirtieth of Prairial, for if they were carried out, matters would not end there. Barras and above all Sieyès were already under attack. Of the latter, it was alleged in conversation and in print that he had signed an agreement in Berlin obtaining the mediation of Prussia, in return for the surrender of some or all the Republic's conquests and the restoration of the Monarchy in favor of the Duc d'Orléans or the Duke of Brunswick. It is not known whether there was any substance in these allegations; in any case they terrified Sieyès.

Most of the newspapers had immediately launched an attack on the Messidor laws, and pamphlets and lampoons joined in; the left-wing deputies and their friends did not always refrain from provocative demonstrations, such as Jourdan's toast on July 14 "to the resurrection of the pikes"; slander and abuse were used in reply. The clubs, and especially the Club du Manège, were denounced as dens of crime and conspiracy; the *jeunesse dorée* came and threatened the Manège, whose members retaliated; the two sides came to blows. In several towns, such as Rouen, Amiens, and Caen, similar disturbances occurred; at Bordeaux, blood was shed.

Although its adversaries evoked the memory of the thirty-first of May, the Left could not count on a mass movement; there was no longer any popular municipality in Paris, nor any Sections, nor any armed force other than the garrison, about 20,000 men who had been quartered in the capital since the eighteenth of Fructidor. It was insinuated that the Jacobins wanted to stir up the suburbs, but when, by some extraordinary chance, they happened to formulate a program—as did Bach, for example, on 30 Thermidor at the Club du Manège, or Jourdan, on 27 Fructidor at the tribune—none of the social elements of the policy of Year II figured in it, except for the opening of workshops for the unemployed, which was simply a measure of assistance. True, hostility to the rich was apparent in items such as the reduction of large stipends and a war tax to which they alone were liable—measures which the Legislature had in fact already adopted—but there was nothing in all this to incite the populace to take up arms, and indeed it did not budge. The only precaution that it was imperative for the government to take was to put the majority on guard against taking fresh exceptional measures and, by means of a determined attitude, to prevent it from disintegrating. This is what Sieyès set about doing right away.

On 8 Thermidor (July 26), Cornet, one of his confederates, suddenly got the Ancients to decide that no political society should henceforth be allowed within the precincts of the Legislature, as a result of which the Club du Manège moved into the church in the rue du Bac. But, after Cornet, Danton's tiresome friend Courtois had vehemently denounced the terrorists and asserted that they were planning to assassinate the Directors and summon a Convention. A commission was set up to examine the evidence; on the thirteenth, Cornet, the *rapporteur*, found nothing to report save a couple of posters that were declared to be seditious; but nonetheless he called upon the Directory to "enforce the Constitution." Two days before, the Ministry of Police had been entrusted to Fouché, and on 24 Thermidor (August 11), Marbot, who had been dismissed, was replaced by

Lefebvre. That same day, the final debate on the indictments began in the Five Hundred: it was the moment for action. On the twenty-sixth, Fouché closed the club; and on 1 Fructidor (August 18), the proposed indictments were rejected by 217 votes to 214, which suggests that they might well have been approved if the waverers had not been intimidated by the blow that Sieyès had just struck. The peace had not been disturbed, and the violent recriminations of the Left had no effect. From then on, nothing more was heard of the clubs. The break between Sieyès and the Jacobins was now absolute, and Barras, now compromised in their eyes, found himself isolated. The Left, incidentally, did not regard the battle as completely lost, and on two occasions the Royalists' rebellion and military setbacks provided it with opportunities to resume the attack.

The signal for an insurrection was given on 18 Thermidor (August 5), in the Haute-Garonne and the neighboring cantons, by ex-General Rougé and the Comte de Paulo. It was formidable, and Toulouse was cut off for a while, but it remained an isolated phenomenon; in the west, Bourmont did not appear until the end of August, and he fixed the taking up of arms for mid-October. The rebels of the southwest were gradually scattered; those who held out were routed at Montréjeau on 1 Fructidor (August 18). In Paris, feeling had run high. Destrem brought the news to the Five Hundred on 26 Thermidor, just as the club was being closed. Domiciliary visits were promptly authorized for a period of one month; subsequently, a "disturbed state" was declared in a good many cantons, though it does not seem that the Law of Hostages was effectively enforced in them. Sieyès for his part, on 16 Fructidor (September 2) obtained the deportation of the staff of thirty-four Royalist papers still affected by the law of 19 Fructidor, Year V; but he took the opportunity to hit out in both directions: the next day, another decree was issued for the arrest for conspiracy of the staff of sixteen other papers, and this time the Jacobin organs figured on the list. The majority had been so thoroughly incited against the Jacobins that it had forgotten its grievances against the Directory as a result. The Ancients accordingly rejected the resolutions of 9 Messidor which were directed against the Directory, and notably that which forbade it to keep troops inside the constitutional belt without a special law; Sieyès was able to retain them in order to carry out the *coup d'état* of the eighteenth of Brumaire.

Meanwhile, in Italy, Joubert had taken the offensive against Suvoroff, to the north of Genoa, without waiting for Championnet, who was coming down into Piedmont, to join him. On 28 Thermidor (August 15), at Novi, he was killed and his defeated army was withdrawn by Moreau. However, this fresh disaster made less of an impression than the landing by the English at The Helder on 10 Fructidor (August 27); the Batavian fleet surrendered without a fight, 25,000 Russians were landed, and the Duke of York arrived to take command. Daëndels and Brune were pushed back and thrown onto the defensive. In Paris, a new invasion was seen to be possible if the enemy pushed south fast, and there was considerable alarm. In the Five Hundred, on the twenty-seventh (September 13), Jourdan solemnly proposed that the country should be declared to be in danger. Tumult broke out, and the public galleries joined in the commotion: this was the last of those dramatic sessions that had studded the history of the Revolution. Lucien Bonaparte turned against the Jacobins, and Daunou put the majority on its guard with great political acumen, pointing out that either the declaration was merely sheer rhetoric, or else it would be invoked later on to obtain measures which the history of the Legislative Assembly and the Convention had made all too familiar. Boulay finally obtained an adjournment, which made it easy to predict the result. Meanwhile the mob had gathered at the Tuileries and everyone was wondering what Bernadotte would do. The Jacobins had gone and offered him great "authority" if he intervened in their favor. Despite all his bragging, he was afraid of risks and had decided to wait and see. But Sieyès acted boldly and, in agreement with Barras and Roger-Ducos, sent word to him that the Directory accepted the resignation he had not offered. The fact remained that the Jacobins, instead of appealing to the people, had also turned to the generals; the drama was nearing its end. On 28 Fructidor, Jourdan's motion was rejected by 245 votes to 171. However, a few days later, Garrau succeeded in getting the death penalty prescribed for anyone who proposed, supported, or even accepted any offer involving the dismemberment of the territory or a change in constitution. This was the last success the Left won.

All of a sudden, in fact, some resounding victories were obtained which completely changed the situation. Thugut had not wanted the Anglo-Russian forces to occupy the Netherlands by themselves, and had ordered the Archduke Charles to go and join them, leaving Switzerland to Korsakoff who had just arrived there with 28,000 Russians. Suvoroff would go and join his compatriot, thus leaving the Austrians in sole control of Italy. Paul I, proud of his role as liberator of Switzerland, accepted this splendid plan. The Archduke sensed the dangers it involved and tried in vain, on August 17, to crush Masséna before setting off. After a French attack had likewise failed, on the thirtieth, he had to resign himself to obeying, but he left his second in command, Hotze, on the Linth, while Korsakoff guarded the Limmat. Meanwhile, however, Lecourbe had reconquered the Gotthard Pass and the valley of the Reuss, and Molitor had advanced as far as Glaris, a move which blocked Suvoroff's way. Thus temporarily covered in the rear, Masséna, immediately after the Archduke's departure, attacked Korsakoff; the latter, surrounded in Zürich, escaped with difficulty, while Soult routed the corps under Hotze, who was killed. The second Battle of Zürich had lasted three days, from 3 to 5 Vendémiaire, Year VIII (September 25-27, 1799). Meanwhile Suvoroff had pushed Lecourbe back step by step as far as Altdorf. There, for want of a route along the lake, he had to cut across the mountains, and came up against Mortier, whom Masséna came hurrying up to support. The Russians turned upon Molitor, who, pushed back against the Linth, repulsed every attack at Näfels. Learning at last of the disaster that had overtaken Hotze, Suvoroff escaped by way of the Col de Panix, across the Tödi, and reached the Rhine on October 7 at Ilanz, whence he moved on to the Vorarlberg. The whole of Switzerland found itself once more in the hands of the French.

In Holland, the Duke of York had vainly attacked Brune at Bergen and Castricum, on September 19 and October 6. Because his troops were decimated by epidemics, he signed an evacuation agreement at Alkmaar on the eighteenth.

These victories were crowned by a piece of news which

seemed positively miraculous: on 17 Vendémiaire (October 9), Bonaparte had landed at Fréjus and was traveling toward Paris, arousing enthusiasm all the way. The return of the Invincible One completed the general conviction that the Republic had been saved. Since the beginning of the war, the sequence had always been the same: defeat called forth extreme measures; victory made them useless; in the period of peril, the Jacobins imposed themselves because they were bold and ruthless; when the danger had passed, the moderates triumphed at small cost to themselves. The reaction accordingly began. The Five Hundred appointed commissions to examine the changes to be made in the Law of Hostages and the legislation on the émigrés. The Ancients rejected the Garrau resolution. Even more significant was the report which Thibault read out on 9 Brumaire (October 31) on the compulsory loan, which he proposed abolishing by increasing direct taxation by half. The Assembly voted in favor of printing the report, and Lesage-Senault exclaimed: "The counterrevolution has been carried out." The debate continued on the sixteenth and seventeenth, and was adjourned to the eighteenth, which was the day of the *coup d'état*.

The crisis of Year VII had clearly been surmounted. The Directory was in full command of the situation; the exceptional laws were going to be repealed or modified; the rich felt reassured; the danger of invasion had passed. But for how long? After such a sore trial, was the country going to wait for the spring campaign and the elections of Year VIII to provoke a fresh crisis?

CHAPTER FIFTEEN

The Eighteenth of Brumaire

The crisis had been surmounted, but, of the perils that had produced it, not a single one had disappeared. In the spring, the war would begin again with all its hazards. And now that the armies had been brought back to the frontiers, where would the money come from? The government officials and the rentiers were crying famine, and all the public services were in abeyance. At home, the civil war had begun again. On October 14, at a signal given by Bourmont, the Chouans had seized Le Mans; then it was the turn of Nantes and Saint-Brieuc. Their successes were ephemeral; in Vendée, Travot promptly put down the rebellion, and to the north of the Loire, Hédouville was soon able to negotiate a peace; but the fact remained that the counterrevolution was still a threat. Among the politicians, the elections of Year VIII were the chief preoccupation. The reaction could play the Royalists' game; all the same, immediately after the Messidor laws, the Jacobins remained the principal bogymen. In any case, the uncertainty was nerve-racking: people were appalled at the idea that everything would begin all over again the following year. Finally, what was to be done about Bonaparte? Arriving in Paris on October 14, he showed a thoroughly Republican tact and visited the Institut like an ordinary ideologue. However, all eyes were turned on him. Nobody thought of blaming him for the Egyptian adventure; exiled by the wicked Directors, he had foiled their plot by the prodigious feat of miraculously avoiding Nelson twice over. He clearly had a lucky star, and nobody cared very much what position he was given, provided he took action. After Campo-Formio, he had been the government's adviser; now he could be entrusted with the conduct of the war as supreme commander. Would he be content with so little? Legally, he was too young to be a Director or a minister.

The need to revise the Constitution therefore became more pressing every day. Since the eighteenth of Fructidor, the number of people advocating revision had grown steadily. The triumvirs, not daring to carry it out in France, had nonetheless revealed their opinion by drawing up for the sister republics constitutions that introduced the Constitution of Year III only in a profoundly modified form. In the Five Hundred, on 2 Pluviôse, Year VI (January 22, 1798), one deputy went so far as to declare that the Con-

447

stitution contained "the seeds of death." Daunou, in approving the twenty-second of Floréal, urged La Revellière to make arrangements to obtain favorable election results "until such time as the change in the personnel of the Legislature can be made less frequent"; on 10 Brumaire, Year VIII (November 1, 1799), the *Décade* published an openly revisionist article which has been attributed to him, and it is probable that by this time he had stopped considering a constitutional procedure, since he was one of the leading Brumairians. Outside the Councils, Benjamin Constant had adopted the same attitude, immediately after the eighteenth of Fructidor, and Madame de Staël likewise, notably in the pages which have been published in our own time under the title of *Fragments politiques*. But the revisionist *par excellence* was Sieyès, seeing that in Year III he had set his own plan against the one which had been adopted. Since then, his ideas had developed, though admittedly we know them only from conversations held after the *coup d'état*, of which Boulay, Daunou, and Roederer have left summaries, which incidentally are partially contradictory.

Since an immediate revision of the Constitution was legally impossible, a *coup d'état* was necessary and Sieyès had been considering it ever since his election. Even if the majority in the Councils had thought it to be indispensable, it would never have agreed to take the initiative. The *coup d'état* would therefore have to be military and anti-parliamentarian, as on the eighteenth of Fructidor; but this time it was a much chancier affair. In Year V, the army had expelled the Royalists with a will, but now the circumstances were entirely different; true, it did not like the "lawyers," but even so, they were Republicans and even Jacobins. To obtain its support, a leader was needed who had not only a brilliant reputation but also an irreproachable revolutionary record. On both scores there was nobody superior to Bonaparte, and chance had brought him along at exactly the right moment. The Jacobins had welcomed him just as eagerly as the rest, and, it seems, were putting out feelers to him. They would not have given him a free hand any more than the Royalists, and he rejected their advances. For what he wanted to do, he had to have the economic and social power of the notables at his service, whereupon having joined forces with him, they would be his prisoners, out of fear of the counterrevolution and of democracy. Besides, it was impossible for him to hesitate: he was a mere general on half-pay—whose situation was indeed of dubious legality—and he could not take command in Paris unless he found accomplices in the Directory and the Councils. The trouble was that he could not stand Barras (there was Joséphine between them, if nothing else) and he loathed Sieyès; Talleyrand had to intervene to square matters between him and the latter. Cambacérès, the Minister of Justice, was apparently in on the secret; it seems that Fouché was not initiated, but, discovering what was going on, made himself an officious accomplice. In the Ancients, President Lemercier and the inspectors of the hall played a decisive role; the Five Hundred were a doubtful quantity, but they had been persuaded to choose Lucien Bonaparte as their President. Some of the generals, such as Jourdan and Augereau, held themselves aloof; they could not intervene if the government was opposed to the idea. Most of them, however, rallied joyfully to Bonaparte in order to gain control of the Republic; Moreau himself was so full of rancor that he was prepared to help the man who was to

449

bring about his ruin. Collot, the contractor, advanced a little money, and he was probably not the only one; on 7 Brumaire (October 29), a law had suspended the assignments that had been made to them until their accounts were audited; in the evening of the nineteenth, they were handed over to them.

To justify the enterprise, a terrorist plot was alleged; and, since the fear which the terrorists inspired had gripped the bourgeoisie since the ninth of Thermidor, the eighteenth of Brumaire, in this respect, can already be seen as the culmination of the period. This accusation, made in bad faith, did not meet with much incredulity, for since Messidor most of the papers had been making it. Madame de Staël bears witness to the extent to which the possibility of a Jacobin victory terrified people:

> I was so convinced that, in that event, one could expect the cruelest persecution, that I gathered together all the money which I then had with my men of business in order to divide it between two of my closest friends and myself, so that we could immediately go abroad. Every quarter of an hour, I received news from Saint-Cloud, and, depending on the news I received, I hastened or postponed my departure.

However, some of the representatives could be expected to ask for proof of the existence of the alleged plots; they would also object that the Directory was sufficiently well protected, as had been shown since Year IV, and that in any case it was for the Directory to ask the Councils for exceptional measures, at the same time informing them of the facts. An extraordinary meeting of the Ancients was therefore called, and it was arranged that those likely to be troublesome should be informed too late. On 18 Brumaire (November 9), Cornet mounted the tribune, and, after hearing his account of the imminent peril, those present voted the agreed measures: the transfer of the Councils to Saint-Cloud (which was legal), and the appointment of Bonaparte as commander of the troops in Paris (which was not, for only the Directory had the right to make an appointment of this sort). From that moment, the battle had been won. Already, Bonaparte had brought the generals together at his house in the rue de la Victoire; the troops immediately set off. If there had been a majority in the Directory which had refused to recognize the Ancients' unconstitutional decision, it might have found a general to set against Bonaparte. Everything depended on Barras; he allowed himself to be persuaded to leave. Gohier and Moulin were powerless, and Moreau held them prisoners until they tendered their resignations.

At Saint-Cloud, the conspirators, it seems, were counting on the Councils to proclaim the overthrow of the Constitution of their own accord; but they had not prepared a scenario, or even a text which would provide the opportunity for debate. Consequently the plot very nearly came to grief. In the Ancients, those who had been absent the day before protested; the majority hesitated, all the more so since, from the legal point of view, the initiative lay with the Five Hundred where the Left was stubbornly holding out. Bonaparte decided to intervene. Addressing the Ancients, he once again denounced the plot without making any positive suggestions, and, in reply to voices invoking the Constitution, he retorted angrily: "The Constitution? You have violated it; it no longer exists." With the Five Hundred it was worse; at his entry, uproar broke out; by what right did he enter the Assembly without being summoned? The cry of "Outlaw him!" was heard. He turned pale and left the hall. A confused discussion followed. Lucien defended his brother and, rather than take a vote on the proposal to outlaw him, left the chair; some grenadiers burst into the hall and took him outside. The two Bonapartes, on horseback, went and harangued the troops, Lucien denouncing the factious deputies who had sold themselves to England, and who had dared to hurl themselves upon their general to stab him with their daggers. The Guard of the Legislature was itself finally won over, and, while the charge was being sounded, forced the Five Hundred, who were still deliberating, to evacuate the Orangerie.

That evening, a small number of deputies, who had been gathered together with considerable difficulty, organized the provisional Consulate. Contrary to expectations, there was some resistance: it was proposed that the meeting of the Councils be adjourned until 1 Nivôse, when they would elect a new Directory. But the Brumairians won the day easily. The Councils, some of whose members were in any case declared to have been expelled, were replaced by two commissions whose function was to pass the laws proposed by the Consuls and to prepare a new Constitution. The three Consuls were Bonaparte, Sieyès and Roger-Ducos: they were said to be equal, but there could be no doubt about the true state of affairs. It was not only a day of lies —the fiction of the daggers added to that of the plot—but also a day of dupes; since the civilians had not been sufficiently docile, the soldiers had had to be given free rein, and as a result Bonaparte had promptly and finally eclipsed Sieyès. The eighteenth of Brumaire is therefore usually represented as the occasion of Bonaparte's accession to power. Nonetheless, however dazzling his reign may have been, that *journée* had a wider historical significance.

By the Constitution of Year III, the Thermidorians had tried to re-establish, in a Republican form, the liberal representative regime which the bourgeoisie had attempted to inaugurate in 1789, and which is one of the characteristic features of its preponderance. The history of the Directory is that of the gradual failure of this attempt; in point of fact, the Republic had been reduced once more to a dictatorship. Putting an end to all ambiguity, the eighteenth of Brumaire made it possible to organize that dictatorship by the abolition of elections and the omnipotence of the Executive.

The events of the period make it abundantly clear why the annual recurrence of elections should have become intolerable to the Directorials. Moreover, they had no lack of objective motives, for, if frequent elections can be seen as an indispensable corrective for a purely representative system, since they alone enable the citizens to exercise their sovereignty, it is also true that they weary the citizens themselves and are prejudicial to the efficiency of both government and administration, making them unstable and monopolizing their attention. Annual elections, however, only aggravated the fundamental defect that the Montagnards had pointed out in the electoral system: the Revolution at war could not allow its enemies to turn freedom and elections against it, by promising peace and an end to the sacrifices which it had to impose for its own safety. That is why they had suspended the Constitution until the cessation of hostilities. Without ever admitting that the hated Jacobins were in the right, Thermidorians and Directorials had been obliged to make this admission implicitly with the decree of the two-thirds, and with the violation, on the eighteenth of Fructidor, of their own Constitution. To suspend it as in 1793 did not suit them, and would have left the future uncertain. The supporters of the divine right were still too powerful, inside and outside France, for them to think of repudiating the principle of the sovereignty of the people, in the name of which the bourgeoisie had seized power. As has often happened since, they had therefore looked for a device which would allow them to falsify the enforcement of that principle, and had tried it out on the twenty-second of Floréal; but, in Year VII, it had proved ineffective. That is why Sieyès, in the Constitution of Year VIII, decided to counterbalance election by means of co-optation. Already, the Constitution of Year III had resorted to this last method in order to complete the administrative bodies; everything considered, the decree of the two-thirds and the purge of the twenty-second of Floréal were substitutes for it; and Madame de Staël had advocated it for the recruitment of the Ancients. In Year VIII, the Brumairians installed themselves in the assemblies. In the future, the people would present them only with candidates; their dictatorship became permanent.

The Montagnards had not confined themselves to suspending elections; they had also concentrated and stabilized the Executive, stretching its powers to the limit. The Constitution of Year III had granted the Directory considerable authority; it had extended this on its own account, and the Councils themselves, carried away by circumstances, had conferred supplementary powers on it—powers which were on a temporary basis, but which were renewed so often that they had become practically normal as a result. From one end of the period to the other, the Executive, by its appointment of a considerable number of administrations and courts, by the extension of its statutory powers, by its

police despotism and its contempt for the rights of the individual, had moved towards the Constitution of Year VIII.

However, the Convention had been jealous of its Committee of Public Safety and the Councils of the Directory.
These executive organs were chosen by the Legislature;
their collective character and the divisions which resulted
from it had provoked or promoted their fall on the ninth
of Thermidor and the thirteenth of Prairial. La Revellière
deplored the fact that the Constitution of Year III had not
granted the Directory the right of veto or, at the least, the
power to initiate laws, the right of dissolution, and the control of the Treasury; his colleagues shared his opinion and
had strengthened the Executive in Holland, Switzerland
and Rome. The Brumairians, restricting the power to initiate laws to the Consuls alone, dividing the right of debate
and vote among three assemblies, and instituting a constitutional check for the benefit of a conservative Senate, weakened the Legislature to such an extent that it was henceforth incapable of resistance; the subjection of which it had
complained under the Directory was made absolute. The
Consuls, appointed under the Constitution of Year VIII
for ten years, and directly invested by a plebiscite, were on
the contrary an independent power. What is more, unity
was imposed upon the Executive, since the First Consul
alone was entrusted with the power of decision. It was in
this respect that the eighteenth of Brumaire was a day of
dupes for Sieyès. Yet according to Fabre de l'Aude, he
bitterly criticized the collective character of the Directory,
as Carnot had done, maintaining that "a number of
leaders lead nothing"; but he wanted "a dual mechanism"
—"a head plus a sword to carry out what the head devises."
His opinion did not prevail. Some Brumairians doubtless

preferred to make sure of Bonaparte's favor, but men such as Cabanis and Daunou who never joined in the scramble for office, and who were sufficiently high-minded to consider nothing but the general good, must have felt that a single stable will was indispensable to the salvation of the Revolution, as Robespierre had believed. The evolution of the wartime Revolution toward a dictatorship thus reached its culminating point.

If the liberal experiment of the Constitution of Year III had turned out badly, the barrier it had set up against democracy had proved to be solid: power remained in the hands of the conservative bourgeoisie. However, the latter had considered itself in danger of Year VI and Year VII. Various remedies were envisaged, such as the raising of the franchise qualification, conditions of eligibility—above all the obligation for representatives to be landowners, as Boissy d'Anglas had suggested in Year III—and also graduality, which the Directory had introduced in Holland and Rome. But these restrictions, which would seem adequate in 1814, were not sufficient in Year VIII, because while they would bar the way to the Jacobins, the Royalists could not suffer from them. That is why co-optation was preferred. This solution bore the mark of its time: the monopoly of power was reserved exclusively for the notables, but they were at least notables. Since Year IV, a considerable volume of administrative work had been performed which, as we have seen, laid the foundations in many respects for that of the Consulate; thus it has rightly been said of the history of the Directory that, despite its detractors, it could take as its motto: *Sic vos, non vobis*. Under Bonaparte's eye, the bourgeoisie continued its work: it was the bourgeoisie that established the institutions of the Consulate and the Empire, and drew up the laws, thus fixing the limits of the society it dominated. The eighteenth of Brumaire consecrated the Revolution in the form in which the bourgeoisie had conceived it in 1789.

Yet the fact remains that it held terrible disappointments in store for that class. One was easy to foresee. In setting up a dictatorship aimed against its enemies, the bourgeoisie had not intended to abandon freedom for itself or to subject itself to despotic control; but, since the *coup d'état* had been carried out by the army, who could prevent its leader from perpetrating more? The Brumairians imagined that the conservative Senate would suffice to thwart him; on the contrary, it was the chief instrument of usurpation. But the people who were most disappointed were those who expected the eighteenth of Brumaire to lead to the abandonment of propaganda and even of that interpretation of the Constitution which, forbidding any cession of national territory, made a compromise peace impossible. In opposing the Garrau resolution, Porcher, in a little-known speech, had bluntly shown that he regarded as insane those who would not abandon some of their compatriots to the foreign yoke, in order to obtain peace; and the aforementioned article in the *Décade* blamed the Constitution for having, by declaring the frontiers sacrosanct, decreed perpetual war and "the annihilation of all the French people." These revisionists had no inkling of the invincible romanticism of the Napoleonic imagination!

But of all that that imagination dreamed or produced— a new dynasty, the partial restoration of the *ancien régime*, the European Empire—nothing has remained. What has endured is the predominance of the notables, the work they completed under his guidance, the final consolidation of

457

the Revolution which, by making a dictatorship useless in the future, made it possible to begin the liberal experiment again in 1814. This is the real significance of the eighteenth of Brumaire: initiated by a few bold bourgeois, it finally established the power of the bourgeoisie.

BIBLIOGRAPHICAL SUGGESTIONS

No comprehensive study of the Directorial period has been written since the appearance, between 1895 and 1897, of *Le Directoire*, by L. Sciout, 4 vols. in-8°, which represented an advance in documentation, but which had been conceived as an indictment. A. Aulard, *Histoire politique de la Révolution* (1901; 5th ed., 1921), deals only with internal political history; the same is true of A. Meynier, *Les coups d'état du Directoire; Le 18 fructidor an V* (1927); *Le 22 floréal an VI* (1928); *Le 18 brumaire et la fin de la République* (1929). A. Mathiez, *Le Directoire*, posthumously published by J. Godechot (1933), does not go beyond the eighteenth of Fructidor. L. Madelin deals with the history of the Directory only insofar as it concerns Bonaparte: *La jeunesse de Bonaparte* (1937); *L'ascension de Bonaparte* (1937). *Le Directoire et la paix de l'Europe* (1911) by R. Guyot is a classic work, but deals only with foreign policy.

As a basis for study, see the chapters devoted to the Directory by G. Pariset in Vol. II of *L'Histoire de France contemporaine*, published under the direction of E. Lavisse (1920); and by R. Guyot in Vol. XIII of *Peuples et civilisations*, the collection published under the direction of L. Halphen & Philippe Sagnac (1930; 2nd ed., 1938); the new version of this last vol-

459

ume by G. LEFEBVRE (1951; 2nd ed., enlarged, 1956); G. GODE-CHOT, *La Grande Nation*, 2 vols. in-8° (1956); M. REINHARD, *Le Grand Carnot*, 2 vols. in-8° (1950, 1952).

For internal history, see: J. GODECHOT, *Les institutions de la France sous la Révolution et l'Empire* (1951); important articles by J. SURATTEAU in the *Annales historiques de la Révolution française; Les élections de l'an IV* (1951, 1952, 1955) and *Les élections de l'an V* (1957); M. REINHARD, *Le département de la Sarthe sous le régime directorial* (1935); R. SCHNERB, *Les contributions directes à l'époque de la Révolution dans le département du Puy-de-Dôme* (1933); *La dépression économique sous le Directoire* (*Annales historiques de la Révolution*, 1934); THÉRÈSE AUBIN, *Le rôle politique de Carnot depuis les élections de germinal an V jusqu'au coup d'état du 18 fructidor* (*Annales historiques de la Révolution française*, 1932); G. CAUDRILLIER, *L'association royaliste de l'institut philanthropique à Bordeaux et la conspiration anglaise en France pendant la seconde coalition* (1908); J. STERN, *Le mari de Mlle Lange: Michel-Jean Simons* (1933); E. DELCAMBRE, *La période du Directoire dans la Haute-Loire* (1940); *Le coup d'état jacobin du 18 fructidor et ses répercussions dans la Haute-Loire* (1942); *La vie dans la Haute-Loire sous le Directoire* (1943); G. COIRAULT, *Les écoles centrales dans le Centre-Ouest* (1940); CHARLES H. VAN DUZER, *The Contribution of the Ideologues to French Revolutionary Thought* (Baltimore, 1935); GEORGIA ROBISON, *Revellière-Lepeaux, Citizen Director* (New York, 1938); J. BOURDON, *Le mécontentement public et les craintes des dirigeants sous le Directoire* (*Annales historiques de la Révolution française*, 1946); J. GODECHOT, *Le Directoire vu de Londres* (*ibid.*, 1949-50).

For military history and foreign policy, see: H. BOURDEAU, *Les armées du Rhin au début du Directoire* (1909); G. VALLÉE, *La conscription dans le département de la Charente* (1937); J. GODECHOT, *Les commissaires aux armées sous le Directoire* (1937); *Les insurrections militaires sous le Directoire* (*Annales historiques de la Révolution française*, 1933); J. DROZ, *La pensée politique et morale des Cisrhénans* (1940). For Bonaparte's early career, as well as the aforementioned works by L. MADELIN, see:

J. Colin, *L'éducation militaire de Napoléon* (1900); Spenser Wilkinson, *The Rise of General Bonaparte* (Oxford, 1930); G. MacClellan, *Venice and Bonaparte* (Princeton, 1931); G. Ferrero, *Aventure: Bonaparte en Italie* (1936); see also the articles in the review *La Révolution française*: P. Muret, G. Ferrero, *historien de Bonaparte* (1937); G. Ferrero, *Bonaparte et l'Italie*, and P. Muret, *Encore quelques remarques sur l'Aventure de Mr G. Ferrero* (1938); D. Bernard, *Documents et notes sur l'histoire religieuse du Finistère sous le Directoire.*

See also: G. Lefebvre, *Napoléon* (Vol. XIV of the collection *Peuples et civilisations*, 1935; 2nd ed., 1941). The present work is a condensation of a course of lectures given at the Sorbonne.

ABOUT THE AUTHOR

GEORGES LEFEBVRE was born in France in 1874. At the age of fifty, he began his extensive publication on the French Revolution with a dissertation submitted for the degree of *Docteur es lettres*. It consisted of four volumes on the rural sociology of the Departement du Nord before and during the Revolution and was perhaps the longest doctoral dissertation ever written. Until his death in 1959, M. Lefebvre was Professor Emeritus of the History of the French Revolution at the University of Paris. His *Coming of the French Revolution*, first published in English in 1947 and now available in the Vintage paperback series, has become one of the most distinguished contributions to history written in the twentieth century.